Reality TV

Reality TV

Remaking Television Culture

EDITED BY

Susan Murray and Laurie Ouellette

New York University Press

NEW YORK AND LONDON

NEW YORK UNIVERSITY PRESS
New York and London
www.nyupress.org

Library of Congress Cataloging-in-Publication Data
Reality TV : remaking television culture /
edited by Susan Murray and Laurie Ouellette.
    p. cm.
Includes bibliographical references.
ISBN 0–8147–5687–5 (cloth : alk. paper) —
ISBN 0–8147–5688–3 (pbk. : alk. paper)
1. Reality television programs—United States.
I. Murray, Susan, 1967–   II. Ouellette, Laurie.
PN1992.8.R43R45   2004
791.45'6—dc22   2003023814

Manufactured in the United States of America

c 10 9 8 7 6 5 4 3 2 1
p 10 9 8 7 6 5 4 3 2 1

Contents

Acknowledgments

The editors are indebted to the authors of this volume, and to Eric Zinner and Emily Park at New York University Press, who both guided the manuscript to fruition in an exceptionally professional and timely manner. Melissa Aronczyk provided superb research assistance. Susan Murray would also like to thank her colleagues in the Department of Culture and Communication at New York University for their encouragement and generosity. Laurie Ouellette wishes to thank her colleagues in the Department of Media Studies at Queens College, City University of New York. This work was supported (in part) by a grant from the City University of New York PSC–CUNY Research Award Program.

Grateful acknowledgment is made to the following for granting permission to reprint in this volume: Jennifer Maher and *Bitch*, for "What Do Women Want? Tuning in to the Compulsory Heterosexuality Channel," first published in 2001, volume 15, pages 52–57; and *Jump Cut*, for "The Political Economy of Reali-TV," by Chad Rafael, first published in 1997, volume 41, pages 102–109.

Introduction

Laurie Ouellette and Susan Murray

In fall 2002, the characters on *The Simpsons* appeared as contestants on a fictional reality TV program. Donning nineteenth-century clothing and giving up all modern conveniences, they agreed to be filmed around the clock by the Reality Channel while living in a nineteenth-century-style home complete with TV cameras and a video "confessional" room. When their show fails to generate high ratings, the producers move the house to a remote location in the Amazon, forcing the cartoon family to navigate the ravages of nature as well as the hardships of premodern life and the surreal process of living their lives in front of millions of TV viewers. When the Simpsons encounter a disillusioned "tribe" of North Americans assembled for another reality show, they join forces to overthrow the production team, escape the house, and return to the comforts of their suburban life, which—most important to the family—includes television viewing.

The episode pokes fun at the recombinant nature and ratings-driven sensationalism of much reality TV in scenes where producers copy the format of successful European shows and frenetically scan U.S. channels for ideas about attention-grabbing plot twists. Taking the conventions of programs like *Survivor, Big Brother,* and *1900 House* as a shared cultural reference point, it satirizes viewer fascination with the televisual display of "real" people, the agreed-on surveillance inherent to reality TV, and the commercial pressures that have coalesced to create simultaneously "authentic," dramatic, popular, and profitable nonfictional television programming. The parody suggests that reality TV is a pervasive and provocative phenomenon that is remaking television culture and our understandings of it. In that sense, it points to transformations that this book will address.

Reality TV has come to permeate the popular zeitgeist, occupying lucrative time slots across the globe and a prominent place in the cultural imaginary. Scholarly attention has struggled to keep pace with this rapid development as the need to come to terms with the industrial and theoretical challenges that reality TV poses becomes increasingly apparent. *Reality TV: Remaking Television Culture* brings together a wide range of recent scholarship in an attempt to examine the roots and implications of this "new" genre from a broadly defined cultural studies perspective. Although there are numerous approaches represented in this collection, the essays are united by an overarching desire to locate the meaning of reality TV in its historical, commercial, and cultural contexts. Some authors focus on political-economic contexts, while others look at reception, generic conventions, cultural politics, and representation. Consequently, this book is aligned with the goals of cultural studies as it seeks to understand how reality programming connects with economic structures as well as other cultural texts and social forces.

Situating Reality TV

What is reality TV? The classification of generic labels is always contextual and historical, as several essays in this volume demonstrate. While there are certain characteristics (such as minimal writing and the use of nonactors) that cut across many reality programs, we are ultimately more concerned with the cultural and "branding" discourses that have coalesced to differentiate a particular moment in television culture. We define reality TV as an unabashedly commercial genre united less by aesthetic rules or certainties than by the fusion of popular entertainment with a self-conscious claim to the discourse of the real. This coupling, we contend, is what has made reality TV an important generic forum for a range of institutional and cultural developments that include the merger of marketing and "real-life" entertainment, the convergence of new technologies with programs and their promotion, and an acknowledgment of the manufactured artifice that coexists with truth claims.

We have seen the rapid proliferation of television programming that promises to provide nonscripted access to "real" people in ordinary and extraordinary situations. This access to the real is presented in the name of dramatic uncertainty, voyeurism, and popular pleasure, and it is for this reason that reality TV is unlike news, documentaries, and other sanctioned information formats whose truth claims are explicitly tied to the residual goals and understandings of the classic public service tradition. Although the current wave of reality TV circulates ideologies, myths, and templates for living that might be called educational in nature, it eschews the twin expectations of unpopularity and unprofitability that have historically differentiated "serious" factual formats from popular entertainment. If the reality programming that we examine here celebrates the real as a selling point, it also distances itself from the deliberation of veracity and the ethical concerns over human subjects that characterize documentary programming in its idealized modernist form.

While the convergence of commercialism, popularity, and nonscripted television has clearly accelerated, much of what we call popular reality TV can be traced to existing formats and prior moments in U.S. television history. The quiz formats of the late 1950s represent an early incarnation of highly profitable TV programming that hinged on the popular appeal of real people placed in dramatic situations with unpredictable outcomes. Other precursors include the staged pranks pioneered by *Candid Camera,* celebrations of ordinary people in unusual or unusually contrived situations (examples include *Queen for a Day, It Could Happen to You, That's Incredible,* and *Real People*), and the amateur talent contest first brought to television by *Star Search.* The landmark cinema verité series *An American Family,* which is often cited as the first reality TV program, also provides an important reference point, as does low-budget, nonprofessionally produced television, from the activist and amateur programming shown on cable access stations to the everyday home video excerpted on *America's Funniest Home Videos.* Daytime talk shows, the favored reality format of the late 1980s and early 1990s, anticipated the confessional ethos and cultivation of everyday drama that permeate contemporary reality TV. Yet it wasn't until the premiere of *The Real World* on MTV in 1991 that we began to witness the emergence of many of the textual characteristics that would come to define the genre's current form. By casting young adults in a manner intended to ignite conflict and dramatic narrative development, placing the cast in a house filled with cameras and microphones, and employing rapid editing techniques in an overall serial structure, the producers created a text that would prefigure programs such as *Survivor* and *Big Brother.* It could also be argued that *The Real World* trained a generation of young viewers in the language of reality TV.

Today, reality TV encompasses a variety of specialized formats or subgenres, including most prominently the gamedoc (*Survivor, Big Brother,*

Fear Factor), the dating program (*Joe Millionaire, Mr. Personality, Blind Date*), the makeover/lifestyle program (*What Not to Wear, A Wedding Story, Extreme Makeover*), and the docusoap (*The Real World, High School Reunion, Sorority Life*). Other examples include the talent contest (*American Idol*), popular court programs (*Judge Judy, Court TV*), reality sitcoms (*The Osbournes, My Life as a Sitcom*), and celebrity variations that tap into many of the conventions for presenting "ordinary" people on television (*Celebrity Boxing*). What ties together all the various formats of the reality TV genre is their professed abilities to more fully provide viewers an unmediated, voyeuristic, yet often playful look into what might be called the "entertaining real." This fixation with "authentic" personalities, situations, and narratives is considered to be reality TV's primary distinction from fictional television and also its primary selling point.

Beyond the textual characteristics and appearance of new subgenres, what differentiates today's cultural moment is a heightened promotion of the entertaining real that cuts across prime time and daytime, network and cable programming. For a variety of complex reasons that the authors explore, reality TV has moved from the fringes of television culture to its lucrative core as networks adopt reality formats to recapture audiences and cable channels formulate their own versions of reality formats geared to niche audiences. Consequently, not since the quiz show craze of the 1950s have nonfictional entertainment programs so dominated the network prime-time schedule. Talk shows and game shows have historically been relegated to daytime or late-night hours, while networks have relied on dramas and sitcoms to secure their evening audience base. While cable stations were the first to begin airing reality programs during prime time, the success of CBS's *Survivor* eventually led the networks to follow suit. By early 2003, the staying power of the genre, along with the success of new shows like *American Idol, The Bachelorette,* and *Joe Millionaire,* convinced networks to make long-term plans for reality TV and its accompanying business strategies. In a front-page story on the topic in the *New York Times,* Leslie Moonves, president of CBS Television, proclaimed that "the world as we knew it is over."[1] The networks plan to stagger the release of new reality programs throughout the year instead of debuting them en masse in September. They also plan to jettison repeats of the programs altogether. These additional scheduling shifts will help networks compete more aggressively with cable channels and, they hope, retain reality TV's young, upscale audience base. By January 2003, one-seventh of all programming on ABC was reality based. ABC executives, along with NBC,

Fox, and CBS, promised to bring even more reality to their schedules in the coming season and cut back on scripted fictional drama series and sitcoms.[2] A few months later, the first "reality movie," *The Real Cancun,* was released in theaters just as development plans for Reality Central, an all-reality cable channel scheduled to debut in 2004, were announced. While some industry insiders remain skeptical about the long-term viability of the reality craze, the spread and success of the genre has already exceeded expectations.

Is Reality TV Real?

Reality TV's staying power renders an investigation of its relationship to truth and authenticity even more urgent. Many reality formats maintain noticeable connections to the documentary tradition. In particular, the use of handheld cameras and lack of narration found in many reality programs is reminiscent of observational documentaries, and carries with it an implicit reference to the form's original promise to provide direct access to the experience of the observed subject. This has the effect of bolstering some of reality TV's claims to the real. Scholarly discussions of documentaries have tended to turn on issues of the ethics of representation and the responsibilities associated with truth telling and mediation. In *New Documentary: A Critical Introduction,* Stella Bruzzi points out that at the root of these discussions is a naive utopian belief in a future in which "documentaries will be able to collapse reality and fiction" by "bypass[ing] its own representational tools" with the help of particular techniques such as those commonly associated with cinema verité.[3] The reception of reality TV programming evokes similar questions and concerns as critics (but not necessarily audiences) wring their hands over the impact that editing, reconstruction, producer mediation, and prefab settings have on the audience's access to the real. Despite such similarities in claims and critical concerns, however, reality TV also establishes new relationships between "reality" and its representation.

Although reality TV whets our desire for the authentic, much of our engagement with such texts paradoxically hinges on our awareness that what we are watching is constructed and contains "fictional" elements. In a highly provocative and influential article in the *Television and New Media* special issue on *Big Brother,* John Corner claims that the commingling of performance with naturalism is a defining element of what he calls television's "postdocumentary context."[4] In this contradictory cultural environment, critics like Corner contend that viewers, participants, and producers are less invested in absolute truth and representational ethics and more interested in the space that exists between reality and fiction. Reality TV promises its audience revelatory insight into the lives of others as it withholds and subverts full access to it. What results is an unstable text that encourages viewers to test out their own notions of the real, the ordinary, and the intimate against the representation before them. Far from being the mind-numbing, deceitful, and simplistic genre that some critics claim it to be, reality TV supplies a multilayered viewing experience that hinges on culturally and politically complex notions of what is real, and what is not.

Central to what is "true" and "real" for reality TV is its connection to the increase in governmental and private surveillance of "ordinary" individuals. In an era in which a "total information awareness" of all U.S. citizens has been made a top governmental priority, the recording and watching of others—and ourselves—has become a naturalized component of our everyday lives. Surveillance cameras are everywhere in the United States. In fact, the American Civil Liberties Union found in 1998 that in New York City alone, 2,397 cameras (both privately and governmentally operated) were fixed on public places such as parks, sidewalks, and stores.[5] By 2001, a company providing security services, CCS International, reported that the average New Yorker was recorded seventy-three to seventy-five times a day.[6] Since the events of 11 September 2001, even more cameras have been installed. Reality TV mitigates our resistance to such surveillance tactics. More and more programs rely on the willingness of "ordinary" people to live their lives in front of television cameras. We, as audience members, witness this openness to surveillance, normalize it, and in turn, open ourselves up to such a possibility. We are also encouraged to participate in self-surveillance. Part of what reality TV teaches us in the early years of the new millennium is that in order to be good citizens, we must allow ourselves to be watched as we watch those around us. Our promised reward for our compliance within and support of such a panoptic vision of society is protection from both outer and inner social threats. Surveillance is just one of the promises of "public service" that reality TV makes. Reality TV is cheap, common, and entertaining—the antithesis of public service television and a threat to the well-informed citizenry that it promises to cultivate, according to conventional wisdom. And yet, a closer look at reality TV forces us to rethink the meaning and cultural politics of public service, democracy, and citizenship in the age of neoliberalism, deregulation, conglomeration, and technological convergence.

The Commercialization of the Real

If reality TV raises cultural and ethical questions, it also points to the medium's changing industrial context. In the late 1980s, a shifting regulatory climate, network financial troubles, and labor unrest forced the television industry to reconsider its programming strategies. Finding reality formats cheap to produce, easy to sell abroad, and not dependent on the hiring of unionized acting and writing talent, the industry began to develop more programs like *Unsolved Mysteries, Rescue 911,* and *America's Most Wanted.* In Europe, public television stations also embraced reality programming, mainly as a financial survival mechanism. Faced with deregulatory policies and heightened pressures to compete with commercial channels that aired popular (and often U.S.-produced) programs, public stations in the United Kingdom, the Netherlands, and other European locales developed the reality genre.

The explosion of reality programming in the 1990s was also the product of a changing industrial environment—both in the United States and abroad. Feeling threatened by new recording devices such as TiVo and ReplayTV (which contained commercial-skipping features) and an ever increasing number of cable stations, U.S. television networks were open to the possibility of new production and financing models, including the purchasing and selling of formats rather than completed programs, the expansion of merchandising techniques, an increased emphasis on audience interactivity, and the insertion of commercial messages within programs. (This last strategy isn't entirely new, of course, but is a variation on the indirect-sponsorship model used in the 1950s and revived within the deregulated policy milieu of the 1990s.)

If reality TV is at the center of major shifts within the television industry, its proliferation has also corresponded with the rapid development of new media technologies. Much of reality TV in the late 1980s and early 1990s, such as *Cops* and *America's Funniest Home Videos,* depended on the availability and portability of handheld video cameras. The most recent wave of reality programs has relied on small microphones and hidden cameras to capture private moments such as those that occur on *Big Brother* and *The Real World.* Yet the marketing and distribution of reality

TV has also developed in particular ways in its use of the Internet, streaming video, cell phone technology, radio, and digital television. Viewers are no longer limited to just watching the completed text of a show, but can keep in touch through short message service (SMS) updates sent to their cell phones, by accessing live twenty-four-hour footage on websites, and by calling to cast their votes. New technologies have also facilitated new advertising strategies that enable sponsors to cut through the clutter of traditional television advertising.

One of the most compelling aspects of reality TV is the extent to which its use of real people or nonactors contributes to the diversification of television culture. *Survivor,* for example, has made it a point to use people from diverse age, racial, geographic, class, and sexual backgrounds. Reality TV opens up new possibilities and limitations for representational politics, as the authors in this volume demonstrate. The fifteen minutes of fame that is the principal material reward for participating on the programs limits the selection of "real people" to those who make good copy for newspaper and magazine articles as well as desirable guests on synergistic talk shows and news specials. Indeed, many of the participants on *Survivor* and other successful reality programs have gone on to star in Hollywood films, host television shows like MTV's *Spring Break,* and appear as contestants on new reality programs. While participation in reality TV doesn't seem to lead to an acting career, it does appear to provide a continuation of the observed life, as former participant/players' offscreen behaviors are tracked by the media even after their show airs. The celebrification of "average" folk further complicates the contours of television fame and the way that its star personas have been constructed as existing in a space between the ordinary and the extraordinary.

For some critics, reality TV's commercial orientation has co-opted its democratic potential. The dream of "the people" participating directly in television culture can be traced to the alternative video movements of the 1960s and 1970s, which sought to collapse the hierarchy between producers and receivers, and to empower everyone to participate in electronic image making. Influenced by the writings of Hans Magnus Enzensberger and Bertolt Brecht, video pioneers sought to "remake" television as a democratic endeavor, bypassing one-way transmission for a participatory model that allowed a full range of people to tell their stories and document their struggles, "unfiltered" by the demands of convention, stereotyping, and commercial sponsorship.[7] While this philosophy lives on in the alternative productions of Paper Tiger TV, Deep Dish TV, and Free Speech TV, it is now more commonly associated with the television industry itself, which emphasizes the democratic potential of reality TV by promising unscripted programs filled with (and sometimes made by) real people from all walks of life. Even advertisers have jumped on the trend, as the Gap uses real people to sell jeans and the Subway sandwich chain claims that a recent television commercial was "shot by real teenagers."

However opportunistic, the commercial embrace of popular reality programming does signal representational shifts, and with them, openings that warrant special consideration. The reality boom has spawned an opportunity to wrest control of television images and discourses away from the culture industries. This opportunity cannot be fully contained by producers—or can it? The authors in this book grapple with that question, and they ultimately demonstrate that "access" and "authenticity" are tenuous and contingent, created in an ongoing cultural struggle between producers, participants, and television viewers.

From historical precedents and political-economic impetuses to aesthetic issues and representational politics, the essays assembled here present a multilayered examination of reality TV in its various incarnations and forms. In addition to situating the reality TV phenomenon within contexts that highlight its economic, cultural, generic, representational, and reception dimensions, the chapters in this book indicate the need to update television scholarship. The theoretical assumptions and methodological principles on which we have come to depend are no longer sufficient tools to analyze an increasingly complex televisual environment. As these chapters demonstrate, television has become more sophisticated, not just in the presentation of reality programming that simultaneously claims authenticity yet rewards savvy viewers for recognizing constructed or fictional elements but in its reliance on interactive technologies, novel commercial strategies, and an intertextual environment in which real people slip in and out of the roles of celebrities, and vice versa. The global context in which reality programs are produced and shared is changing too: as media conglomerates become international entities, and as television formats are exchanged and revamped across national boundaries, we need to revise our political-economic frameworks and ways to understand how meaning can be both culturally specific and globally relevant.

Genre

The essays that make up the book's first section consider the question of genre from a variety of perspectives. In the first chapter, Anna McCarthy takes a historical approach, tracing the roots of reality TV to liberal cultural reformers, cold war social scientists, and *Candid Camera* producer Allen Funt. If reality TV is now dismissed as cheap and lowbrow, its "first wave" was championed by the prestigious Ford Foundation, highbrow TV critics, and behaviorist researchers, who all saw the representation of "real life" in Funt's work as both a respectable genre and a boon to liberal democracy. While reality TV's high cultural status has slipped, McCarthy shows that today's programs bear the traces of the affinity between reality TV producers and social scientists set into motion during the medium's early years.

Susan Murray compares the packaging of two genres, documentary and reality TV. Taking the HBO documentary series *America Undercover* and the canceled Fox program *American High,* which later appeared on public television, as twin case studies, Murray grapples with the question of what, exactly, reality TV is and how it differs discursively from traditional notions of documentary. In this way, Murray's essay demonstrates how cultural labels intersect with aesthetic hierarchies, brand images, and audience expectations and competencies as much as generic conventions.

Nick Couldry's essay moves us away from specific questions of form and conventions and focuses instead on how reality TV reformulates documentary reality claims. In performing a ritual analysis of a particular subgenre, Couldry shows how British gamedocs like *Big Brother, Castaway,* and *The Experiment* work as technologies of surveillance or governmentality, reproducing power relations and enlisting viewers to participate in the mobilization of societal myths. Although Couldry claims that every gamedoc has its own specific myth or way of representing the world, all gamedocs reinforce the idea that "mediated reality is somehow 'higher' or more significant than nonmediated reality."

Mary Beth Haralovich and Michael W. Trosset also look at the gamedoc, but they set their sights on what they consider to be its most distinctive characteristic—unscripted chance. The authors use Roland Barthes's analysis of the pleasure of the text along with mathematical theory to illuminate the importance of chance in *Survivor,* showing how the possibility of unpredictable outcomes differentiates this program from the closed narratives that govern fictional formats. While producers attempt to control the contestants and narrative every step of the way, they must leave room for unpredictable outcomes, for the pleasure of *Survivor* (and thus its popularity) depends on it.

Derek Kompare revisits the legacy of *An American Family* in the final essay in this section, comparing the documentary portrait of an upscale California family to *The Osbournes*. The creation and reception of both programs, he contends, hinges on their abilities to navigate the "normative" parameters of genre and family. *An American Family* sought to capture "fly on the wall" reality, but it was criticized for mediating the truth by monitoring (and exploiting) the liberal, upper-class Loud family. *The Osbournes*, on the other hand, has been praised for reworking the fictions and conventions of the TV family sitcom. Tracing the shifting meanings of reality over three decades, Kompare shows that these programs are simultaneously alike and unalike to the extent that the "real" family is produced as well as understood within shifting codes and conventions.

Industry

The second part of this book looks at the industrial and commercial contexts that spawned and spread the reality TV genre. Chad Raphael, in the first essay of this section, explores the economic origins of reality TV by revisiting the specific factors—union battles, deregulation, increasing competition from cable stations, and financial scarcity—that led networks in the 1980s to air more nonfictional programs such as *Cops* and *Unsolved Mysteries*. Raphael continues to trace such factors through the 1990s, and in doing so, he disputes the myth that audience demands are responsible for the growth of reality TV and demonstrates just how central political-economic forces have been in its development.

Ted Magder picks up where Raphael's essay leaves off, focusing on the wave of reality programs that first appeared in summer 2000. In looking at the industry during this period, Magder identifies three unique reality TV business strategies that have the potential to forever alter the logic of TV production: the increased use of product placement, a strategy that aims to insert commercial messages within the television program; the expansion of merchandising tie-ins, such as *Survivor* bug spray and Baskin-Robbins's *Fear Factor* gross-out sundae; and finally, the extension of the program outside the confines of the television set itself through the use of new interactive technologies. Magder also underscores the importance of European program suppliers who have filled the U.S. market with many of the most successful multiplatform reality formats.

Chuck Kleinhans and Rick Morris concentrate on the programming and business practices of one cable station—Court TV. Kleinhans and Morris track the inherent tension between Court TV's commercial and public interest goals, showing how the quest for profit has shaped the on-screen presentation of potentially "boring" trial coverage, and has also led to the station's success in an environment of increasing competition and declining prime-time ratings.

Cultural Politics

The third section of this book examines the cultural politics of reality TV programming. Jon Kraszewski's essay situates reality TV as a site of ideological maneuvers that because they are couched in the discourse of the real, can be difficult to discern. Focusing on the construction of racism in *The Real World,* Kraszewski contends that MTV's embrace of racial diversity is mediated and contained by an ideology of "enlightened racism." While the program invites racial controversy by casting politicized African Americans as housemates, the attempts of these characters to force awareness of structural inequalities are managed through editing and narrative conventions that emphasize personal friendships and confine the problem of racism to the ignorance of rural whites.

Jennifer Maher turns our attention to the politics of gender in her chapter on The Learning Channel's reality programs for women. Her analysis of the real-life weddings and births chronicled on *A Wedding Story* and *A Baby Story* demonstrates that reality TV programs can be just as invested in the construction of patriarchy as fictional ones. According to Maher, both programs construct a pleasing middle-class, heterosexual fantasy that mediates the contradictions of gender socialization. In contrast, TLC's *Maternity Ward* uses different conventions and techniques to construct unwed, lower-income mothers as deviants and "others."

Elayne Rapping situates the long-running program *Cops* within the rightward-drifting political climate of the 1990s to show how reality TV has been enlisted in the policing of people characterized as criminals, outsiders, and social misfits. According to Rapping, the portrayal of the impoverished suburban abyss patrolled by the officers on *Cops* represents a new televisual construction of criminality, characterized by a shift away from the prosecution of particular crimes to the totalizing "social control" of immigrants, people of color, and the underclass. In this sense, programs like *Cops* correspond with, and work to justify, repressive police tactics and the acceleration of imprisonment in the United States.

While Rapping focuses on official policing, Laurie Ouellette's essay analyzes reality TV as a technology of citizenship that governs indirectly, in sync with neoliberal discourses and policies. She argues that court programs like *Judge Judy* exemplify this trend by taking lower-income women caught in the drama of everyday life as the raw material from which to train television viewers to function, without direct state intervention, as self-disciplining and "self-enterprising" citizens. Linking reality TV to a neoliberal conception of public service, Ouellette argues that programs like *Judge Judy* do not subvert elusive democratic ideals as much as they construct templates for citizenship that complement the privatization of public life, the collapse of the welfare state, and the discourse of individual choice and personal responsibility.

Jeffrey Sconce scrutinizes reality TV's relationship to public service from a different angle. Sconce considers the "real life" spectacles found on *Celebrity Boxing*, where rival celebrities bring their bodies—and a history of intertextual meanings—to the boxing ring. Rejecting traditional distinctions between public service and commercial entertainment, Sconce contends that programs like *Celebrity Boxing* provide a popular version of public service to the extent that they work out political issues and articulate resentments toward the wealthy celebrity class. Critics who condemn this populist "theater of the absurd" as a sensationalist ploy overlook the pleasures of seeing symbolically charged celebrities duke it out in a media-saturated society, he argues.

Reception

The essays assembled in the final section are united by a concern with reception strategies and practices. Although written from different viewpoints, each essay takes the audience as the starting point from which to assess the meanings and implications of reality TV. Kathleen LeBesco focuses on fan responses to gay characters on *Survivor,* one of many reality programs on which viewers have come to expect to see gay characters. Her case study proposes that neither producers nor gay characters can control the final meaning of these representations. The progressive potential opened up by reality TV is grounded in the understanding of sexual orientation—and its historical representation on television—that viewers bring to their discussion of reality programming.

Justin Lewis addresses the broader question of how audiences understand the blend of realism and artifice that defines popular reality programming. Lewis unpacks the contradiction between television's drift toward a formal postmodernism and what he calls the "popular epistemology" of TV viewing. Drawing from a range of empirical audience studies, he shows that the pleasures and politics of watching real people on television remain rooted in a tenuous, but decidedly modernist distinction between realism and artifice. If reality TV encourages this contradiction with its ambiguous truth claims, it did not create it: our desire to recognize the real elements of a postmodern mediascape is symptomatic of the paradoxical ambiguity that contemporary television cultivates, he contends.

John Hartley explores the playful and performative possibilities of reality TV viewing in his chapter. Comparing the reception of the Australian *Big Brother* to that of William Shakespeare's *Taming of the Shrew,* he argues that the play between mediated and unmediated reality embraced by both texts requires a multiconscious engagement on the part of audiences. By pointing out similarities in the reception of these texts across time periods, Hartley also situates reality TV within a trajectory of active audiences. In examining this process, he shows that the "democratization of play" does not stem from canonized playwrights or corporate authors but is instead the result of audience-based performances and practices.

Pamela Wilson analyzes the new reception practices opened up by reality TV's use of digital feeds and Internet forums. Tracing the attempt of fans who watched the first U.S. season of *Big Brother* on-line to influence its outcome, she sees in reality TV the potential for a new form of audience-based "narrative activism." Wilson documents the attempt of culture jammers to subvert the intentions of *Big Brother*'s corporate producers with airplane banners and other unanticipated forms of contact with the program's confined houseguests. For Wilson, the ensuing struggle to determine who would produce the *Big Brother* program points to the space where the democratization of reality TV might occur.

Together, the essays that follow enhance our understanding of reality TV as a cultural form, an institutional and sociopolitical development, a representational practice, and a source of meaning and pleasure. Using various approaches, the authors in this book come to terms with these developments, deepening our understanding not just of reality TV but of the emergent television culture that it represents. If Leslie Moonves is correct and the television "world as we knew it is over," the scholarship represented here provides an initial foray into the roots and implications of this shift. In addition to helping students, scholars, and viewers understand the reality TV phenomenon, we hope that the collection will stimulate further attention to the remaking of television culture that it has brought about.

NOTES

1. Bill Carter, "Reality Shows Alters the Way TV Does Business," *New York Times*, 25 January 2003, A1.

2. Lynn Elber, "ABC Defends Increased Use of Reality TV," *Associated Press*, 15 January 2003.

3. Stella Bruzzi, *New Documentary: A Critical Introduction* (New York: Routledge, 2000), 255–59.

4. John Corner, "Performing the Real: Documentary Diversions," *Television and New Media* 3, no. 3 (August 2002): 255–69.

5. Dean E. Murphy, "As Security Cameras Sprout, Someone's Always Watching," *New York Times*, 29 September 2002, A1.

6. Ibid.

7. See Bertolt Brecht, *Brecht on Theatre*, ed./trans. John Willett (New York: Hill and Wang, 1964), and Hans Magnus Enzensberger, "Constituents of a Theory of the Media," in *Video Culture*, ed. John Hanhardt (New York: Visual Studies Workshop Press, 1986), 96–123. For an overview of the history and goals of alternative television, see Dee Dee Halleck, "Towards a Popular Electronic Sphere, or Options for Authentic Media Expression beyond *America's Funniest Home Videos*," in *A Tool, a Weapon, a Witness: The New Video News Crews*, ed. Mindy Faber (Chicago: Randolph Street Gallery, 1990), n.p.; Deirdre Boyle, "From Portapack to Camcorder: A Brief History of Guerilla Television," *Journal of Film and Video* 44, nos. 1–2 (1992): 67–79; William Boddy, "Alternative Television in the United States," *Screen* 31, no. 1 (1991): 91–101; and Laurie Ouellette, "Will the Revolution Be Television? Camcorders, Activism, and Alternative Television in the 1990s," in *Transmission: Toward a Post-Television Culture*, ed. Peter d'Agostino and David Tafler (Newbury Park, Calif.: Sage, 1995), 165–87.

Part I

Genre

"Stanley Milgram, Allen Funt, and Me"

Postwar Social Science and the "First Wave" of Reality TV

Anna McCarthy

I come more and more to think that TV's forte is as it
plays on life and that . . . the make-believe of drama
strains the psychological and physical dimensions of the
TV screen.   —Charles Siepmann[1]

Charles Siepmann, a professor of television studies at New York University, wrote the above note in response to a telecast of the Ford Foundation's prestigious arts and culture variety program *Omnibus* in 1954. One of several in-house critics hired by *Omnibus*'s producer, Robert Saudek, Siepmann wrote weekly reviews of the ninety-minute program for the entire 1954–1955 season. The representation of "life" that drew his praise was a short, humorous, hidden-camera film called *Children of the U.N.* The film was shot at an international school in New York, and featured interviews with and observational footage of children from around the world. One of several "candid films" made for the 1954–1955 season of *Omnibus,* it was produced by Allen Funt, creator of the comedic hidden-camera program *Candid Camera* (1959–1967). *Children of the U.N.* was a timely social document. Airing on United Nations Day, it offered viewers, as *Omnibus* host Alistair Cooke noted, a glimpse of "a miniature international society . . . without protocol, and without taboos, but with a pride all its own." Funt's ability to communicate this idea of a microcosm of international relations was what stirred Siepmann to state his preference for the aesthetics of actuality to those of drama on television.

This appreciative assessment is striking for several reasons. First, Siepmann seems at first to be an unlikely person to profess admiration for the work of Funt. Siepmann was a TV blue blood. A former program director at the BBC, he was a staunch advocate of public service broadcasting—in fact, he was the primary author of the Federal Communications Commission's (FCC) 1946 "Blue Book" outlining the public service responsibilities of U.S. broadcasters. In contrast, Funt is most often remembered as the lowbrow prankster of *Candid Camera* and its R-rated feature film spin-off, *What Do You Say to a Naked Lady*. Second, the very fact that Funt's films appeared on *Omnibus* is itself notable. *Omnibus* was a program designed to appeal to "minority taste groups" with edifying presentations of learning and artistic genius. Even without the jokey sound effects that would later characterize Funt's candid camerawork, hidden-camera films were a far cry from *Omnibus's* typically didactic documentary fare, which ranged from recycled United States Information Agency propaganda films to industrial films to short human interest stories about people with unusual occupations, like tugboat captains. Third, Siepmann's remarks on "TV's forte" are especially notable in light of the prevailing definitions of "good television" at that time. This was a period when aesthetic ideals for television rested on the medium's ability to reproduce the conditions of live theater (the so-called Golden Age). In 1954, prior to the quiz show scandals and the subsequent valuation of network documentary as the "oasis in the wasteland,"[2] it is striking to find a prominent advocate of high standards in television belittling make-believe in favor of actuality programming. Siepmann's praise suggests that the reality genre's "first wave" might occupy a quite different relationship to the medium's aesthetic hierarchies than its current manifestations. Indeed, it implies that Funt, often hailed as reality TV's creative ancestor, belongs in the postwar pantheon of liberal-minded, aesthetically ambitious television pioneers such as Reginald Rose, Worthington Minor, Edward R. Murrow, and Robert Saudek.

If the hidden camera's view of social life provided Siepmann with an opportunity to articulate a realist ideal of television, it also offers a way of thinking about the cultural value, and social uses, of what might be called reality TV prior to its (re)emergence in the 1990s. Reality TV today is a cheap, endlessly recyclable and licensable programming format, a product of the collapse of the three-network system and the rise of cable television and new networks like Fox.[3] But in the postwar period, Funt's covertly

Allen Funt (right) with Durwood Kirby on the set of *Candid Camera*.

filmed records of real people in unusual situations were an esteemed form of culture. Even as critics condemned his work as an invasion of privacy, many agreed with sociologist David Riesman's assessment of Funt as the "second most ingenious sociologist in America" (after Paul Lazarsfeld).[4] This assessment, widely cited in postwar studies of Funt's work, suggests that the television programs and films that he made were, at least for some observers, a valuable and educational visual record, capable of providing a critical analysis of modern society within mass culture.[5]

The value of the hidden camera's social record for postwar observers lay in the way it could supplement liberal projects of reform and advocacy. Indeed, Funt's method was frequently cited or duplicated as a way of inculcating responsible forms of citizenship both domestically and internationally. The hidden camera could document the world of institutions, from the judiciary system to the mental hospital.[6] It could, moreover, present an image of planetary unity for North Americans—an image that

resonated strongly with centrist liberals of all political stripes in a period
when U.S. foreign policy and international economic policy went global.
And it could do so in ways that combined the powers of apparent "objec-
tivity" with polemicism. Thus, writing on Funt's *Children of the U.N.*, another of Saudek's hired reviewers, Ruth Sayers, commented on the "nice
quiet vein of one-world propaganda running through it in an unobtrusive
way."[7] The New York magazine *P.M.* had a similar view of Funt as a sociological spokesperson for the liberal viewpoint, regularly reprinting transcripts from Funt's radio program *Candid Microphone* as illustrations of
broader problems in U.S. society.[8] And Funt's status as a privacy-busting
truth teller led University of Chicago professor Richard Stern to immor-
talize him in the 1960 novel *Golk,* in which a morally ambiguous Funt-like
figure uses his candid camera to expose corruption in the government. In
these moments of engagement with Funt's work, the representation of real
people through concealed observation on television is understood as
working in the service of socially liberal models of culture.[9]

In what follows, I situate this first wave of reality TV in the broader
context of popular and intellectual culture, examining the intersections
between the realist capacity of the hidden camera as a potent tool for the
production of social knowledge and the methods as well as techniques of
social science. The kinds of social dramas that liberal media producers like
Funt played for laughs throughout the 1950s and 1960s were simultaneously raising deep moral questions for experimental social scientists like
Yale University's Stanley Milgram, the instigator of the ethically compromised obedience experiments. Milgram, as we shall see, was only one of
several social psychologists who turned to the work of Funt as a template
for their experimental situations and a teaching tool in the classroom. In
fact, up to and including the broadcast of PBS's *An American Family,* a series Margaret Mead hailed as a social scientific breakthrough, reality TV
served as a place where popular culture and social science overlapped via a
realist ideal in which social norms, mechanisms of conformity, ritualized
scripts, and modes of interaction were put on display.

It might be tempting to construct a narrative of decline in which this
first wave of reality TV, understood as unequivocally good, instructive, and
socially progressive through its association with social science, is replaced
by the current wave of voyeuristic, theatrical, and exploitative formats and
modes of address. But social scientists continue to serve as consultants for
reality TV to this day, screening contestants for reality game shows like
Survivor and *Big Brother,* and helping to design situations and guidelines

for interaction. Similarly, reality TV producers then and now cross over into non-entertainment terrains of culture. Funt used his hidden-camera skills to make industrial and training films for corporations in the 1950s and 1960s; *Survivor* producer Mark Burnett has a second career as a management consultant, serving as a motivational speaker in workshops designed to help brand managers and executives develop team-building skills to compete effectively in the corporate "jungle." In short, the stark differences in status and prestige accorded to reality TV in the 1950s and today should not obscure the fact that in both moments, the genre occupies a privileged place in aesthetic discourses about the medium, and in each case, it is a place where TV and social and applied psychology come together.

A preferable interpretation is to see each stage of reality TV's vision of social life as an expression of broader ideologies of citizenship. If, as Laurie Ouellette persuasively argues, reality genres today often serve a neoliberal cultural agenda that outsources the state's social functions (for example, policing or social welfare) to popular media, it is worth asking how the hidden camera's production of knowledge about ordinary people might have expressed models of civic responsibility and moral behavior in an earlier period.[10] My reading of the close affinity between the first wave of reality TV and the scenarios played out in social psychology at that time proposes that both conform closely to a cold war elite understanding of the uses of visual culture. For Funt, Milgram, and others, covertly filmed behavior was a tool for teaching responsible citizenship on multiple scales, from the interpersonal to the institutional to the national. As will become evident, however, this thinking was beset by ongoing tensions between pedagogical presentation and sensational entertainment. As a visual document, the hidden camera's social scientific record seemed poised between fiction and reality; this equivocalism shaped popular and scholarly production, and reception, creating persistent dilemmas for those who would use it for the broader purposes of social critique and knowledge production.

The Sociological Realism of Allen Funt

The worst thing, and I see it over and over, is how easily people can be led by any kind of authority figure. . . . [W]e need to develop ways to teach our children to resist unjust or ridiculous authority.   —Allen Funt[11]

The emergence of deception and simulation as scientific tools—as means for exposing how real people really act—in both *Candid Camera* and the social psychology laboratory can be seen as part of two broader tendencies in art and science in the postwar decades. One was the development of realist aesthetic norms in postwar visual culture and their specific articulation in relation to television—a topic I will sketch in this section as a context for understanding the way that tensions between science and art manifested themselves in the cultural phenomenon of *Candid Camera*. The second tendency, which I will treat in the following section, is the rise of avant-garde thinking in the areas of the social and natural sciences dealing specifically with the unthinkable.[12] The latter concept, linked to horrific forms of state violence from the Holocaust to nuclear war, was the behavioral science preoccupation in which Milgram's experiments at Yale emerged.

The aesthetic values attached to Funt's work on *Omnibus* are fully in step with a broader discourse of television realism in the postwar period—one that was actually, despite Siepmann's separation of the two, quite compatible with the Golden Age ideal of live drama. Hinging on the idea that TV could represent "ordinary" people better than any other medium, this discourse of social realism manifested in multiple sites, formats, and modes. Whereas today, "real people" define the lowest of televisual forms, from the afternoon talk show to various reality genres, in the postwar period they defined what the medium could ideally accomplish. This is evident in the neorealism-inspired social dramas written by playwrights like Paddy Chayefsky and the method acting performance styles these dramas showcased. It is also an animating force in the work of Murrow, who despite his enthronement in the pantheon of TV history for the low-rated, though critically acclaimed *See It Now*, achieved most of his popular recognition in the early 1950s for the much more highly rated weekly program *Person to Person* (CBS). This show, which aired on Friday evenings, featured Murrow interviewing celebrities at home via live remote. Hailed for its ability to show the real person behind the celebrity, *Person to Person* can be thought of as the unacknowledged precursor of "celebrity-at-home" reality programs like *Cribs* (MTV) or *The Osbournes* (MTV). Thus, although he disparaged drama, Siepmann's comments on the hidden-camera film's ability to record social life, and by extension represent people as they actually *are*, should be interpreted as an expression of the postwar realist sensibility toward which all television—both fictional and nonfictional—should strive.

Underlying this realist sensibility is an aesthetic ideal in which the theatrical and everyday converge, although how that convergence might be accomplished was not always clear. The difficulty of balancing the two is evident in Siepmann's remarks on a second Funt film for *Omnibus, Jury Duty,* in which the hidden camera investigated the social world of the judiciary system. This film dwelled at length on the arguments ordinary people made in order to get out of jury duty, and it showed viewers the difficulties faced by judges and other legal workers trying to select jurors. Siepmann's comments were generally positive. He commended Funt's efforts at depicting reality and, in particular, exposing the hypocrisy of the judiciary system: "We mouth devotion to democracy and fairly run when called on to enact it."[13] Like Siepmann, Ruth Sayers also praised this film: "Allen Funt's ability to give us a look-in on the real thing was never more effectively used. This slice of Americana had its connection with every viewer—and a moral to boot—which added depth to the very considerable interest of the feature." Sayers's assessment of the film emphasized "the *honesty* of the piece—the obvious fact that it was not being done for television but that we were being allowed to spy on some actual occurrences."[14] For Siepmann, however, this honesty was insufficiently compelling, and he criticized the film's visual flaws and lack of editing: "The realism had interest but it lacked art." In the end, real people's appearances on television needed to be shepherded by the hand of the artist; Siepmann unfavorably compared Funt to Murrow, who managed to do a "skilled and remorseless job of refining out the dross."[15]

The difficulty that the candid film faced on television, in other words, was its tendency to lapse into an overly sociological, noninterventionist mode of representation. In fact, this was Funt's ideal for what *Candid Camera* could achieve. His own evaluation of his work tended to bemoan the necessity for deception and manipulation that made the program more suitable for prime-time TV. If left to his own devices, he would have spent his time producing an unadulterated record of the social—indeed, his aesthetic preferences leaned toward a nascent form of cinema verité. In his 1952 book, *Eavesdropper at Large,* Funt noted that "the reflection of life through a camera lens without interpretation, without individual expression, is something less than real art, say some critics." Countering with the idea that the selection of material itself constitutes a form of art, Funt proposed that "both sides of this argument can be applied to a comparison of creative drama and real-life drama. . . . [W]hether or not candid speech is artistic, I confess it has great appeal to me."[16] The appeal, for Funt, was the way that "real-life drama" revealed "the ever-changing scenery and natural resources of the human mind."[17] What he wanted to show the public was "'pure' situations, where the subjects are relatively unprovoked . . . or on 'mood spots' (a father telling his child a bedtime story, children playing with a kitten)."[18]

Funt thus saw himself as both an aesthetic pioneer in the realm of minimalist realism and a social scientist. In both capacities, he had lofty goals for the social impact of the hidden camera. Indeed, he thought of this impact in therapeutic terms. In a 1976 interview he told social psychologist Philip Zimbardo, "I wish I could use *Candid Camera*'s humanness and non-threatening approach to help parents, teachers, or salespeople reexamine what they are doing to learn from their mistakes."[19] This sense of the camera as a social tool led Funt into consulting work for psychologists in the 1950s, when *Candid Camera* was only sporadically on the air. Noting this sideline, a *New Yorker* profile went on to describe other projects that Funt hoped might have a social impact: "One of his proudest experiments was a hidden camera study of disturbed children under clinical observation. A cherished objective of his was, and still is, a full-length 'Candid' film depicting the working day of an average twentieth century American. . . . Another was somehow to employ his camera with the educational aim of breaking down harmful national stereotypes."[20] In these aspirations for his candid camerawork, Funt expressed an ideal of the hidden camera as a tool for advocacy social science; if it was art, it was art with a larger, liberal-reformist social purpose.

This advocacy orientation makes the uses of Funt's films on *Omnibus* seem less incongruous, for *Omnibus* was itself founded on an instrumental model of culture—one in which ideals of informed, responsible citizenship were fully active.[21] *Omnibus* viewers were understood to be interested in bettering themselves through exposure to U.S. and foreign forms of high culture, educational and didactic presentations of national and world history, and work being done on the frontiers of science. This construction of the audience and the programming decisions that emerged from it reflected the broader cultural mission of the Ford Foundation in the postwar period, when it expanded from its original role as a local philanthropic concern in Michigan to become the largest foundation in the world. In the first decade or so of its operations, the foundation obeyed the dictates of its 1949 mission document, the so-called *Gaither Report*, which specified a particular, highly instrumentalist understanding of the purpose of funding cultural programs. For example, a discussion of the need for liberal education to "train youth for better citizenship" includes among the tools for attaining "the balance necessary to live integrated and purposeful lives" the goal of assisting individuals "to acquire tastes for literature, music, and the arts."[22] *Omnibus* and the Television-Radio Workshop that produced it represented one such method of assistance. As the 1952 press materials for the program's inauguration explained, the workshop was established "as the first major implementation of a mandate of the [Ford Foundation] trustees that 'the Foundation will support activities directed toward the effective use of mass media for non-academic education and for better utilization of leisure time for all age groups.'"[23] Culture, from the perspective of the Ford Foundation, was all about producing a U.S. populace capable of stepping up to the challenge of citizenship in an internationalist United States.

Funt's use of the hidden camera to expose the mechanisms, behaviors, and rituals of everyday interaction was fully in tune with the ways in which *Omnibus* presented high culture to its imagined audience of aspirants. Both hinged on the mode of address Neil Harris calls "the operational aesthetic."[24] Like the displays of P. T. Barnum, in whose work Harris identifies the formation of the operational aesthetic's simultaneously didactic and sensationalist appeals to its viewer, *Candid Camera* and *Omnibus* sought to both educate and entertain. *Omnibus* translated classics of Western art, literature, and learning into a commercially sponsorable and popularly palatable form; Saudek worked hard to make the arcane accessible to a mass audience. Funt similarly endeavored to show how ordinary social situations work and (à la Barnum) how hoaxes are staged, without diminishing the powers of technological surveillance and deception in the process. The operational aesthetic was thus integral to the representation of social reality and promotion of citizenship ideals via artistic representation as well as a popular social science interested in norms of behavior and the extent to which individuals will work to maintain them.

If both *Omnibus* and the candid film were poised between theatricality and pedagogy as modes of address, the history of Funt's transition to prime time suggests that the wider circulation of his work required the subordination of the pedagogy to the theater. *Candid Camera* entered CBS's prime-time lineup in the 1960s, airing on Sunday evenings immediately before another sociological TV classic, *What's My Line*. But the network insisted that the show have a more "showbiz" host. It hired Arthur Godfrey as the front person communicating with the audience and relegated Funt to the role of onscreen prankster. Another significant theatricalization occurred when the show entered prime time. During the 1962–1963 season, Funt hired dramatist and *Omnibus* veteran William Saroyan, possibly at the instigation of *Candid Camera*'s producer, Bob Banner, who had worked as a director on *Omnibus*. Named "writer in residence," Saroyan was hired to create sketches for actors to perform; Funt would then try to duplicate the social situations Saroyan created in his interactions with people on the street. Saroyan's remarks on the show indicate the affinities between hidden camerawork and naturalistic television theater: "It shows people who don't know they're being watched. And that's the essence of drama, isn't it?" The point of using both modes of presentation, according to *Newsweek,* was "to compare fiction and reality."[25] The idea of comparing reality and fiction strengthened the show's reliance on the operational aesthetic. It engaged the spectator both on the level of *spectacle*—showing real people in unusual situations—and *pedagogy*—inviting viewers to contrast drama and real life, presumably as a way of understanding the extent to which codes of fiction depart from the social world they represent.

As a form of popular social science, blending educational and entertaining elements, *Candid Camera* quickly attracted the attention of social scientists themselves. The points of institutional, biographical, and intellectual contact between social scientists and Funt are numerous. James Maas of Cornell University's psychology department persuaded Funt, an alumnus, to donate film segments from *Candid Camera* to the university for distribution to psychology departments across the country. Maas was the first of several social scientists to publish essays on the value of *Candid Camera* as an educational tool for social psychology. Two other prominent—if ethically compromised—social scientists also expressed their admiration for Funt as an amateur experimentalist. In the 1970s, Milgram coauthored an essay on *Candid Camera* as a form of social science with one of his graduate students.[26] And Zimbardo, the psychologist who created a mock prison using Stanford University students as guards and prisoners, was particularly close to Funt, collaborating with him on a series of classroom films called *Discovering Psychology.* For Zimbardo, there was a concise patrilineal explanation for the intellectual affinity between *Candid Camera* and experimental social science. Noting that Funt was an undergraduate research assistant for social psychologist Kurt Lewin's famous experiments on mother and infant interactions, Zimbardo described Lewin as "the intellectual grandfather of Stanley Milgram, Allen Funt, [and] me."[27]

As the next section suggests, the continuities between Funt's social scientific vision and that of people like Milgram and Zimbardo go beyond their genealogical connection to Lewin. Rather, these men shared a sense of theatricality, simulation, and dissimulation as necessary tools for understanding the complex dimensions of human behavior in modern society. Each saw techniques of deception as components of empirical investigation, and each articulated a working model of realist representation as the foundation for such investigations. But what were the broader circumstances that made it possible for intellectuals engaged in politically motivated, if ethically unconscionable, empirical research to locate the imaginative horizons of their work in the world of popular entertainment? One suggestive coincidence offers a way into the answer to this question. Both Funt and Milgram received money from the Ford Foundation in 1955. Funt's check was payment for his *Omnibus* films; Milgram's was a stipend. Like many graduate students in psychology during this period, Milgram was the recipient of one of the fellowships created by the foundation to strengthen the behavioral sciences in the 1950s. He went to Harvard to study conformity with Solomon Asch. Under Asch's guidance, he instigated the first of the many experimental practical jokes through which he would investigate social norms: a comparative study of conformity mechanisms in the United States, Norway, and France. Milgram staged an experimental group situation in which he led unwitting subjects to agree with the statements of others in the group even though they were obviously incorrect.

This was the kind of situation that Funt would dramatize many times over in his candid camerawork. In the TV version, for example, he posed as a public opinion researcher and solicited emphatic opinions on a nonexistent TV program called *Space Doctor* from people on the street. In *What Do You Say to a Naked Lady,* his hidden camera filmed a roomful of men, all but one of them hired as plants, waiting for a job interview. When the plants started taking off their clothes, the "mark," bewildered yet resigned, removed his too. This was the kind of observational revelation that Milgram particularly admired. In the 1970s, when choosing *Candid Camera* films from the Cornell catalog in preparation for his article on the program's social scientific value, Milgram selected the *Space Doctor* segment for further analysis.[28]

Social scientists' infatuation with *Candid Camera* must be understood in the context of the behavioral sciences in the postwar period. These years saw the emergence of a liberal social science in which the predictability of human behavior was a matter of heavily funded research as well as popular ethical discourse. It was a moment in which role-playing and deception seemed utterly necessary as research techniques and methods. Alongside mainstream approaches to social psychological problems, like attitude change, the Ford Foundation was placing a great deal of money into the emerging field of "systems research" in the behavioral sciences. As a model of totality, systems research was thoroughly compatible with cold war scientific programs, especially those involved in the global threat posed by nuclear war. It was thus integral to the social and natural science projects funded by the Defense Department, as Sharon Ghamari-Tabrizi shows in her fascinating study of the culture of war gaming at the RAND Corporation during this period. As she notes, this was a moment in which civilian defense intellectuals like Herman Kahn, in many ways the "avant-garde" of the behavioral and physical sciences, began to use *simulation* as a problem-solving tool. Simulation, in the kinds of projects undertaken at the RAND Corporation, was not just a technique for modeling ideas but also a means for producing new knowledge. Anti-empirical skills like "intuition, insight, discretion, and artistry" were essential given that there was no empirical way of testing the validity of the "data" produced in simulated exercises concerning thermonuclear war.[29] Behavior prediction and control were important for this culture of civilian war modelers because of the need to be able to organize and depend on the actions of the citizenry if the bomb were to be dropped.

At the same time that people like Kahn were bringing games and simulations to the Defense Department, liberal intellectuals like Milgram set a different agenda for behavioral research through simulation. The legacy of the Holocaust coupled with McCarthyism's effects on political culture and the recent exposure of Stalinist atrocities created a need to understand how ordinary people could commit unconscionable and frequently horrific acts as part of the bureaucratized hierarchies of the state. Deceptive games were, for Milgram, a necessary tool for probing the dynamics of human behavior in situations of perceived social threat. As we have seen, ordinary people were crucial to Funt's work as they allowed him to position his films as a documentary corollary to the socially realist drama of the Golden Age and as part of the entertaining pedagogy of the operational aesthetic. For Milgram, similarly, the behaviors of what Funt called "the average man in a crisis" was central to his research program.[30] Only by using the most "ordinary" of subjects could he understand the social processes of obedience that enable the perpetration of large-scale atroci-

ties. It was the very ordinariness of Milgram's subjects that demonstrated
to the citizens of an era haunted by authoritarianism's effects that there is
no such thing as an authoritarian personality. Rather, in situations where
individuals believe they have no power, Milgram concluded, most people
are capable of committing acts that are unthinkable to them under ordinary circumstances. It was not possible to re-create the Holocaust in the
laboratory in order to study the social relations that allowed it to continue
and grow, but it was possible, through simulation, to re-create situations
in which these relations could be studied. As the next section proposes, the
methodology of *Candid Camera,* taken to an unethical extreme, helped
define the structure of Milgram's simulated interaction between the state
and its citizens.

Candid Compliance: Milgram's Experimental Film

Whether all this points to significant social science or merely good theater is
an open question.
—Stanley Milgram, notes on the *Obedience* experiments, 1962[31]

As the above quotation illustrates, the same tensions between pedagogy
and sensationalism that marked Funt's work were present in Milgram's,
too. Much as Funt found himself wondering whether *Candid Camera*
could really be considered art, Milgram pondered whether his experiments could legitimately be called science. These experiments, which are
considered some of the most notorious in the history of social psychology,
were devised to test how far people would go in obeying orders. They were
indeed highly theatrical. Using actors, props, a script, and an artificial laboratory setting, Milgram deceived human subjects into believing that they
were administering punitive electric shocks to other participants, ostensibly as part of a Yale University experiment on the role of pain in the learning process. But although he used the term "theater," the kind of deception
that Milgram carried out was more directly reminiscent of Funt's popular
sociology. Like *Candid Camera,* the deception rested on a misleading scenario. And like many segments of the highly popular program, it was
structured as a macabre practical joke. To create the impression that subjects were participating in an experiment on learning, Milgram hired an
actor to play the part of a scientist in a white coat. A second actor took on
the role of another subject, the "learner." The so-called naive participants

who came to Milgram's lab were asked to administer a memorization test to the learner. When the learner gave the wrong answer, they were instructed to correct the learner and reinforce the point by pressing a lever on a formidable-looking technical apparatus that would, they were told, deliver an electric shock. The shock levels increased as the experiment wore on, as did the frequency of wrong answers. The subjects eventually heard the learner register vocal protest and injury with every shock (the cries of pain were recorded on tape and played back to minimize the impact of performance variables on the experiment). At this point, thinking that they were causing harm, most subjects refused to participate further in the "experiment." But once the "experimenter" pressured them to continue, almost two-thirds of the subjects did so. Although it caused them obvious distress, they administered increasingly higher shocks as the learner's cries grew louder, and even after the learner fell completely silent.

The theatrical nature of this research situation fascinated Milgram. The experiments, he felt, derived their "drawing power" from their "artistic, non-scientific component."[32] Indeed, this sense of theatricality was so strong that he made a documentary about them, using hidden-camera footage. *Obedience* (1965), an audiovisual mainstay of the psychology classroom, was the first of six films Milgram would make before his death at the age of fifty-one. He took classes in film production in the 1970s, and eventually included the title "filmmaker" in his professional biography.[33] While conceiving of *Obedience*, Milgram must have recognized the ethical problems attendant on the visual experience of the experiments in action, which after all involved seeing people in obvious psychological distress complying unwillingly with orders to hurt another person. This may explain why his 1962 speculations on the art versus science question concluded with a musing that reflects both his anticipation of the experiment's notoriety and a sense of himself as a historical figure—a misunderstood genius. "It is possible that the kind of understanding of man I seek is an amalgam of science and art. It is sure to be rejected by the scientists as well as the artists, but for me it carries significance."[34] In making the film, Milgram sought to synthesize and manage the theatrical as well as pedagogical, the art as well as science, perhaps in order to cement his place in the pantheon of genius. In the end, he merely mapped the two tendencies on the sound track and image, respectively. He recorded an extensive voice-over commentary that outlined the experiments along with their social and moral significance for the viewer, but he also hired a Harvard graduate with strong aspirations in the area of narrative filmmaking to select and edit the footage. This assistant, Christopher Johnson, viewed all the raw footage and gave Milgram his handwritten notes on the performances of the various subjects. Essentially, he treated the hidden-camera film as a screen test and saw himself as "casting" the film. Johnson's notes focused exclusively on the theatricality of the interactions and performances on the screen. One man, for example, is characterized as "reeking of obedience . . . cringing look." Johnson mentioned details like a subject's "nervous smile" or the "learner's" gaffs ("he doesn't yell right").[35]

Watching the film, it is hard not to think of *Candid Camera* as its closest intertext. Although Milgram's personal papers, housed in Yale's Sterling Library, are voluminous and complete, they do not contain any direct evidence that Milgram modeled the experiment, and the film based on it, on Funt's work. They offer plenty of direct material, however, in which to read the points of commonality between the two men's projects. The overlap between the obedience experiments and *Candid Camera* extends beyond their structural similarity—the fact that both created situations in which unwitting individuals are observed responding to and performing within unusual or extreme social situations—and even their dependence on ordinary people. Perhaps the most obvious parallel is the fact that *Obedience* and *Candid Camera* both end with a moment of unmasking: a return to "normalcy" that Funt called "the reveal" and which he communicated to his subjects with the trademark phrase, "Smile, you're on *Candid Camera!*" Milgram integrated a similar, though obviously less jocular moment of revelation into the end of his experiment. Once the subject either refused to participate any further or, in the case of the majority, continued to administer electric shocks to the learner up to the highest level, Milgram would enter the room. Much like a bearded, academic-looking version of Funt, he informed the subject that the situation was contrived and that the electric shocks were simulated. A "debriefing" followed in which subjects discussed their responses to the situation with Milgram. Finally, to dispel any residual misunderstanding, McDonagh (the putative learner or "victim") joined Milgram and the subject to confirm that he was an actor and had not received any shocks. In the film, the reveal is not a moment of levity, although the film's subjects nevertheless uncannily replicate the reactions of the subjects recorded by Funt's camera. As Funt noted in his autobiography, "marks" tended to conceal their surprise when informed that they have been filmed. Milgram's on-camera participants adopted a similarly guarded nonchalance, merely nodding or saying "oh" when told of the real experiment in which they had participated. In the script of the film, Milgram asks one man, on camera, whether he objected to the hidden-camera film being shown to other psychologists and students. The man defers at first, and it seems likely that *Candid Camera* is on his mind when he asks whether "my face is nationwide or something." When reassured that this will not be the case, he agrees.[36]

The common structure of the reveal is an important element of the experiment's pedagogical program. As Funt pointed out, the reveal is itself a form of social pressure as it asks the victim to accept his or her deception and be a "good sport."[37] The reveal also exploits the conventions of the operational aesthetic; unmasking the hoax is a way of affirming the fact that it was mounted not out of cruelty or sadism but rather in the interest of knowledge. The similarities between Funt's reveal and the experimental debriefing were not lost on Milgram, although he seems to have been unable to reconcile himself to the parallel. A decade after he completed the film, Milgram coauthored an essay on *Candid Camera* with John Sabini, who had studied under Milgram at the City University of New York's Graduate Center and was then a professor at the University of Pennsylvania. In his hurriedly penned notes for this project, Sabini recorded extended observations on the social scientific function of Funt's reveal as "formally analogous to the experimental debriefing."[38] Despite the fact that Sabini spent some time articulating this point, though, it may have resonated a little too strongly with Milgram given the criticisms of his work's ethical implications in human subjects research. The point did not appear in the final essay.[39]

What would have made the comparison between *Obedience* and *Candid Camera* unwelcome for Milgram was the fact that it exposed the possibility that there was something entertaining in the horrifying image of coercion and cruelty that *Obedience* presented to its spectators. But in his notes on the experiment, Milgram spent as much time thinking about staging and dramatic effects as he did the broader moral and scientific implications. These notes show that Milgram clearly relished planning the mise-en-scène details of the situation he was setting up. This relish is apparent in the great attention he lavished on the design of the simulated shock generator, making at least four detailed drawings of it in the experimental setting. More disturbingly, Milgram's desire for verisimilitude meant that he spent significant time wondering how to produce a convincing audio impression of physical pain for the experiment. In April 1961, he wrote a note to himself considering the notion of contacting two other psychologists who were using real electric shocks in their work on "traumatic avoidance conditioning" to see if it would be possible to borrow "good recordings of a persons [*sic*] vocal response to high level electric shock."[40] And even more horrifyingly, he considered producing a test of the experiment using *actual* victims and real electric currents. His interest in doing so was expressed in purely clinical terms: "This might be quite interesting in seeing how persons actually react as victims."[41] This is another reason why Milgram might have avoided the comparison between his own work and Funt's in his 1979 essay coauthored with Sabini; it suggested that the experiments could easily be interpreted as a sick joke. Like a cruel prank, the experiments relied on Milgram's emotional distance from the struggles of his subjects in the laboratory. This sense of detachment was something Milgram noticed in himself and the others who viewed the experiment in action. In particular, he was curious about the ways that the experiment, when viewed, produced laughter—often hysteric laughter—among those who viewed it.[42] But although this would have been an obvious point to bring up in his essay on *Candid Camera,* the comparison between Funt's audience reactions and Milgram's is significantly absent from the piece.

Nevertheless, despite what seems to be a clear attempt to "de-sensationalize" *Obedience* by avoiding comparisons with *Candid Camera,* media producers were immediately drawn to the former's sensationalist representation of real people. After he completed *Obedience,* Milgram found himself negotiating repeatedly with TV corporations interested in broadcasting his film. In 1969, several producers from Canada contacted him for this purpose, citing its ethical relevance to the emerging evidence of U.S. military atrocities in Vietnam. Milgram at first denied these requests because showing them on English-language stations would have violated the privacy of his subjects. But as time went on, he was more and more liberal in granting rights to the film and in abetting the sensationalization of his work. He did not hesitate to grant permission to use the film to television producers in Italy and Germany in the 1960s, and according to Sabini, Milgram allowed *60 Minutes* to air the film in the 1970s. In this broadcast, apparently the first in the United States, Milgram insisted that only the compliant subject segments be shown. This was because those in which subjects defied the orders revealed how easy it would have been to disobey—a revelation that Milgram felt would have been psychologically damaging and socially stigmatizing for those subjects who complied.[43] But of course, these compliance segments are also the most suspenseful and sensationalist elements of the film. Milgram's evident willingness to exploit the theatricality of his work is evident in the fact that in the same period, he served as a consultant for the 1975 CBS TV movie based on the experiments. Called *The Tenth Level*, it starred William Shatner as Milgram and interspersed the story of Milgram's experiments with a romantic subplot. The week it aired, *TV Guide* featured an article by Milgram that explained his thinking and the broader ethical and moral implications of the work.[44]

The media afterlife of the obedience experiments in the 1970s suggests that Milgram should join Funt as an ancestral figure in the genealogy of reality TV. Indeed, Milgram's work seems closer to the contemporary hidden-camera genres than Funt's. In popularizing his experiments on TV, Milgram might have seen himself as a crusader, educating the populace about the microlevel operations of totalitarianism, but these broadcasts exhibited a cruel and exploitative disregard for those unwitting subjects he deceived and covertly filmed. Moreover, the extreme nature of the *Obedience* situation, quite different than the routine institutional worlds that Funt placed under the microscope in films like *Jury Duty*, make it far closer to contemporary reality programs than Funt's observational realism. But Milgram merely extended the theatrical and sensational tendencies that were present in Funt's work, too. Potentially, all observational footage of ordinary people can be appropriated within other genres and modes of address. The PBS program *An American Family*—surely the type of purely observational, nondeceptive documentary that Funt valued most—may have been conceived within the postwar liberal project of displaying the everyday lives of ordinary citizens, but this did not prevent critics from seeing it as a soap opera.

Social Scientific Theater Today

The shift toward the criminalizing and conservative visions of law and order that defined the rise of reality TV at the end of the 1990s is not so much the triumph of the sensational over the pedagogical as it is the transformation of the political imaginary underlying the depiction of ordinary citizens on television. Just as electoral politics and dramatic TV programming took a "right turn" during this period, so did the citizenly uses of the real-life dramas of the hidden camera. It is a testimony to the changing cultural role of experimental social psychology that Zimbardo, once regularly quoted as a prison reform consultant because of his notorious and ethically compromised Stanford prison experiment, is now far more likely to appear in print as a commentator on and even consultant to the new reality TV programs. An August 2000 *New York Times* article titled "Hey, What If Contestants Give Each Other Shocks?" compares social psychology to reality TV, although it stressed that unlike reality TV producers, Milgram, Zimbardo, and others "had noble aspirations."[45] This recognition of the obedience experiments as reality TV's ancestors would surely have pleased Milgram, who told a researcher in 1974 that he was blessed with something he called "prescient ability" and claimed that many of his randomly jotted, undeveloped ideas regularly showed up in the work of others decades later.[46] And indeed, his sick jokes live on among today's reality TV generation, where pranksters portray average citizens as mooks and buffoons, and critics bemoan the fact that people respond with homemade pratfall videotapes of their own. Tom Green, Johnny Knoxville, and the creators of *The Man Show,* who recently used a hidden camera to capture men's room visitors fishing a twenty dollar bill out of a loaded toilet, might want to add Milgram's name to the credits.

NOTES

I am grateful to Susan Murray, Laurie Ouellette, Sharon Ghamari-Tabrizi, Torey Liepa, Meghan Sutherland, and the staff of the Wesleyan Cinema Archives and Yale University's Sterling Memorial Library for their help with the research and writing of this essay.

1. Wesleyan Cinema Archives—Omnibus Collection (henceforth WCA–OC), series 4, box 18, folder 801.

2. This was the title of a *Commonweal* article (6 October 1961, 30) on *Walk in My Shoes,* Bell and Howell's 1961 ABC documentary on black life in the United States.

3. See the essay by Chad Raphael in this volume.

4. See, for example, J. M. Flagler, "Student of the Spontaneous," *New Yorker,* 10 December 1960, 59–72.

5. David Riesman with Nathan Glazer and Reuel Denney, *The Lonely Crowd: A Study of the Changing American Character* (New Haven, Conn.: Yale University Press, 1950).

6. The film about mental hospitals was *Out of Darkness,* a CBS documentary that aired 18 March 1956.

7. WCA–OC, series 4, box 18, folder 798.

8. Flagler, "Student," 84.

9. On the broader cultural implications of technological observation in relation to *Candid Camera*, see Andrew Ross, *No Respect: Intellectuals and Popular Culture* (New York: Routledge, 1989), 105–7.

10. See the essay by Ouellette in this volume.

11. Cited in Philip Zimbardo, "Laugh Where We Must, Be Candid Where We Can," *Psychology Today* 119 (June 1985): 47.

12. Sharon Ghamari-Tabrizi, "Simulating the Unthinkable," *Social Studies of Science* (April 2000): 163–223.

13. WCA–OC, series 4, box 18, folder 801.

14. Ibid., folder 798.

15. Ibid., folder 801.

16. Allen Funt, *Eavesdropper at Large* (New York: Vanguard Press, 1952), 128.

17. Flagler, "Student," 59–60.

18. Ibid., 64.

19. Cited in Zimbardo, "Laugh Where We Must," 47.

20. Flagler, "Student," 82.

21. See Robert Saudek notes, WCA–OC, series 1, box A.

22. Ford Foundation, *Report of the Study for the Ford Foundation on Policy and Programs* (Detroit, 1949), 40.

23. WCA–OC, series 1, box A.

24. Neil Harris, *Humbug: The Art of P. T. Barnum* (Boston: Little, Brown, 1973), chapter 3.

25. "Time of His Life," *Newsweek,* 10 September 1962, 94.

26. Stanley Milgram and John Sabini, "Candid Camera," *Society* 16 (1979): 72–75.

27. Philip G. Zimbardo, Christina Maslach, and Craig Haney, "Reflections on the Stanford Prison Experiment: Genesis, Transformations, Consequences," in *Obedience to Authority: Current Perspectives on the Milgram Paradigm,* ed. Thomas Blass (Mahwah, N.J.: Lawrence Erlbaum Associates, 2000), 197–98.

28. Cornell University catalog of *Candid Camera* films; Milgram's annotated copy is in the Stanley Milgram Papers, Sterling Memorial Library, Yale University (hereafter MP), box 66, folder 208.

29. Sharon Ghamari-Tabrizi, *The Intuitive Science of the Unthinkable: Herman Kahn, the RAND Corporation, and Thermonuclear War* (book manuscript).

30. Funt, *Eavesdropper,* 29.

31. MP, box 46, folder 164.

32. Ibid.

33. Thomas Blass, personal communication.

34. MP, box 46, folder 164.

35. MP, box 76, folder 440.

36. MP, box 76, folder 439.

37. Cited in Zimbardo, "Laugh Where We Must," 47.

38. MP, box 66, folder 209.

39. John Sabini, phone interview with the author, 29 October 2002.

40. MP, box 46, folder 165.

41. Ibid.

42. MP, box 46, folder 163. For a fascinating discussion of inappropriate humor in the postwar scientific avant-garde, see Sharon Ghamari-Tabrizi's work.

43. John Sabini, phone interview.

44. "Obedience to Authority," *TV Guide,* 21 August 1976, 24.

45. Erica Goode, "Hey, What If Contestants Give Each Other Shocks?" *New York Times,* 27 August 2000, 3.

46. Cited in Carol Tavris, "Man of a Thousand Ideas," *Psychology Today* 8 (June 1979): 74.

2

"I Think We Need a New Name for It"

The Meeting of Documentary and Reality TV

Susan Murray

Shooting with handheld cameras, a film crew follows the everyday happenings and interpersonal relationships of an upper-middle-class Californian family for seven months. Television viewers have a "fly-on-the-wall" perspective as the family engages in heated political debates at the dinner table, frequents neighborhood dinner parties, struggles with internal and external conflicts, takes vacations, works, and attends high school. Viewers are also privy to the breakdown of the parents' marriage and the details of one son's openly gay lifestyle in New York City. All of this is tied together through interweaving multiple plotlines, presented without voice-over narration or interviews and edited in serial form.

Based on this brief description of the premise and style, are we able to identify whether this nonfictional series was a documentary or reality TV program? Would it help us to know that it was funded by and shown on public television or that it was made by two well-respected, independent filmmakers and produced by someone whose past works had focused on the fine arts? What if we also discovered that it was simultaneously criticized for exploitation and sensationalism? Or that it was marketed in newspaper ads as a "starkly intimate portrait of one family struggling to survive a private civil war"?[1]

Producer Craig Gilbert called the above nonfictional program, *An American Family*, a "real-life soap opera" in regard to its narrative structure, but crafted it using many of the stylistic techniques of the direct cinema movement.[2] By the time it aired in 1972, the program's resulting generic hybridity and instability so befuddled critics that they ended up comparing it to everything from home movies to situation comedies.[3] Such confusion over how to place the series led anthropologist Margaret Mead to remark to *TV Guide,* "I do not think that *American Family* should be called a documentary. I think we need a new name for it, a name that would contrast it not only with fiction, but with what we have been exposed to up until now on TV."[4] Thirty years later, the program's generic status remains liminal as it is now alternately discussed as an observational documentary and an early form of reality TV. The struggle to define exactly what *An American Family* was bespeaks much of what is at stake in our current generic placement of texts into the categories of documentary and reality TV.

While some nonfictional television texts fit squarely within the generally agreed-on borders of either documentary or reality TV, many others seem to defy easy classification. In a recent essay on *Big Brother* and telereality, John Corner argues that the "extensive borrowing of the 'documentary look' by other kinds of programs, and extensive borrowing of nondocumentary kinds of looks by documentary, have complicated the rules for recognizing a documentary."[5] For this and other reasons, Corner wonders whether we are entering a postdocumentary cultural moment. In this chapter, I am not interested in redefining, reclaiming, or reasserting the documentary genre—or in predicting its demise. Instead, I want to explore how a network's brand image and its marketing and positioning of particular programs work in conjunction with our critical judgments, expectations, and knowledge of previous documentary and reality forms, to help us as viewers and/or critics decide what is "reality TV" and what is a "proper" documentary. In this way, I'm engaging in the type of analysis that Jason Mittell calls for, which at its base, conceives of television genres as discursive practices. As Mittell argues, "[The] goal in analyzing generic discourses is not to arrive at the 'proper' definition, interpretation, or evaluation of a genre, but to explore the material ways in which genres are culturally defined, interpreted, and evaluated."[6] Traditional analyses of the documentary form have focused on the textual elements that distinguish it from other forms of nonfictional film and video. While there is no doubt that such elements do work to define the genre, the goal here is to examine the ways in which certain extratextual factors can impel the viewer to see a nonfictional television text as either documentary or reality TV—sometimes even despite its textual characteristics. This type of discursive generic analysis helps us understand what reality TV is, since it reveals many of the assumptions that surround the generic category as well as the cultural role assigned to it, particularly in relation to that of documentary.

Genre, "Social Weight," and the Observational Mode

In order to begin a discussion of the reality TV genre, it's important to first recognize that there are many different formats—most of which are generic hybrids themselves—that fall within this category. Some of these formats are more readily differentiated from documentary than others. Gamedocs (such as *Survivor*), for example, embody only a few aesthetic or textual characteristics of the documentary and instead seem more closely aligned with game shows. The types of reality programs that share the most textual and aesthetic characteristics with documentaries tend to focus on the everyday lives of their subjects in somewhat "natural" settings without a game setup, use cinema verité techniques, and do not contain flagrantly commercial elements such as product placement or the promise of prizes. One such type is the docusoap, which Stella Bruzzi has identified as a legacy of direct cinema (also called observational or cinema verité).[7] She points out that British nonfictional programs such as *Vets in Practice* and *Driving School* (U.S. equivalents include *The Real World* (MTV) and *American High* [Fox/PBS]) combine many of the textual and aesthetic elements of direct cinema (handheld camerawork, synch sound, and a focus on everyday activities) with the overt structuring devices of soap operas (short narrative sequences, intercuts of multiple plotlines, mini cliff-hangers, the use of a musical sound track, and a focus on character personality).[8]

Yet there are programs that have been classified rather definitively by critics as documentaries that look—in terms of their aesthetics and narrative structure—quite similar to the docusoaps mentioned above. In the United States, the public television series *An American Love Story* (which chronicled a year in the life of an interracial family in Queens, New York) and *A Farmer's Wife* (which centered on a Midwest farming family's economic and domestic struggles), for instance, followed the *American Family* model quite closely, yet they were never considered to be reality TV. Therefore, there must be characteristics beyond narrative form and aesthetic qualities that help critics and viewers define such programs. Indeed, much of our evaluative process is based on the belief that documentaries should be educational or informative, authentic, ethical, socially engaged, independently produced, and serve the public interest, while reality TV programs are commercial, sensational, popular, entertaining, and potentially exploitative and/or manipulative.[9] These somewhat subjective assumptions work to construct a dialectical relationship between documentary and reality TV, even as they share many similar features. Documentary is seen as a valid and productive social as well as artistic endeavor, while reality TV is often vilified or dismissed. Consequently, generic placement becomes a way in which to gauge a program's cultural value and import through discursive means.

Documentary has traditionally been assumed to be rather highminded, and if not fully educational, then at least informative. Mobilizing a "discourse of sobriety," documentaries reference established traditions of ethical and political mandates for their own form.[10] Although observational documentaries tend to concentrate on the mundane, everyday, and personal—and as a result, can appear just as obsessed with the intimate as reality TV—they are seen by many viewers and critics as doing this for the greater good of the subject, viewer, and society at large.[11] Bruzzi contends that the most important distinction between observational projects and docusoaps is the "social weight" of their content—specifically, the latter's focus on entertainment rather than the exploration of cultural/political issues.[12] This is familiar logic, and it has been borne out throughout the history of TV as documentaries have often been produced and aired in order to compensate for the "sins" of commercial television. For instance, in response to the quiz show scandals in the late 1950s and growing criticism of the networks for their failure to serve the public, networks commissioned more documentaries as a way to recoup their public image, appease critics, and win back the trust of the viewing audience.[13] Largely because of this rhetorical/social positioning, documentary producers are often the recipients of governmental and private funding, and their resulting work is commonly shown on PBS—which maintains a mandate to provide its viewers "programs that the present system, by its incompleteness, denies [them]."[14] Documentaries are thus *believed* to play a central cultural role in representing minority viewpoints and having serious historical or social significance (although this has been troubled during different historical moments, such as the "culture wars" of the 1980s).

Yet "social weight" is an interesting and potentially contentious distinction here, since claims of social relevance are frequently made by the creators of docusoaps as well. As Jon Kraszewski's research has shown, *The Real World*, for example, often highlights the ways in which it consistently deals with issues of race and sexuality.[15] Social weight is not something that can be empirically measured, nor is it necessarily an inherent textual characteristic. Rather, it is a rhetorical stance that can be mobilized in an effort to endorse or authenticate a particular television text and attract an audience who cherishes liberal notions of social responsibility or public service. Even if it is possible to measure social import/impact in some way, it is still crucial to ask whether or not "entertainment" and "social weight" really exist as mutually exclusive terms, since as I will detail later in this chapter, programs such as *American High* and *America Undercover* are presented as both sensational and educational.

In order to court a particular type of audience identification and set of expectations, television networks can take a program that has somewhat liminal textual generic identifiers and sell it as either a documentary or reality program by packaging it in such a way as to appear either more educational/informative or more entertaining/sensational, or in some cases both. In this way, the networks are working with the audience's prior experience and expectations of each form, and then highlighting certain aspects of the text to ensure that it is read (and therefore classified) in a particular way. As Bill Nichols points out, "The distinguishing mark of documentary may be less intrinsic to the text than a function of the assumptions and expectations brought to the process of viewing the text."[16] Although Nichols is talking primarily about the ways in which an audience's experience with prior documentaries informs its encounters with future examples of the genre, I would also add that the site of exhibition (and the discourses that construct it) plays a vital role in the audience's process of generic classification and its assignment of social weight to a particular text.

In the following section, I will focus on two programs, *American High* (Fox/PBS) and *America Undercover* (HBO), that serve as productive examples of the ways in which the context of reception of a program can be manipulated so as to encourage a viewer to understand the meaning of the text through a specific generic lens. If a viewer reads the text through the lens of documentary, for instance, that viewer will be more likely to read it as socially engaged, informative, authentic, and artistic. In the examples below, I will explore the ways that Fox, the U.S. public television channel PBS, and the premier cable channel HBO mobilized their different brand images along with publicity and marketing tools to push viewers to see programs carrying signifiers of both documentary and reality TV as simply one or the other. In these cases, genre turns on the industrial management of extratextual discourses. Through these examples, however, we'll see that these strategies do not always work out as planned, since the tensions that exist in the bifurcation of the two generic categories can, at times, be difficult to contain.

American High *and* America Undercover: Packaging Documentary/Reality TV

American High was sold as a reality program on Fox and, a year later, a documentary series on PBS. Obviously, these two networks have disparate brand images, financing structures, and target audiences, and therefore had different interests to serve. Yet executives at both networks believed that they could alter the reception context of *American High* to suit their particular needs.

The production context of the series reveals direct links to documentary practice. Director R. J. Cutler, a renowned documentarian who received an Academy Award nomination for *The War Room* (1993), shot two thousand hours of film tracking the lives of fourteen seniors in a suburban, Chicago-area high school. He also arranged for the students involved in the show to take a video diary class, the results of which were edited together with the vérité-style footage to create the final product. Cutler claimed to use *An American Family* as his model, yet he also told reporters at the time of the program's premiere that he was influenced as well by the fictional teen drama *My So-Called Life,* thereby underscoring the hybrid nature of his series.[17] He appeared to avoid using the term documentary to describe the project in interviews and press conferences, but also refused to overtly align it with reality TV. In a chat room interview, Cutler told fans that shows like *Big Brother* and *Taxicab Confessions* "are not real the way our show is. . . . Our show is a drama series with real characters and real stories that continue over the course of a year."[18]

On the other hand, Fox was eager to label *American High* as a reality program as executives were hoping that it would be Fox's answer to CBS's recent success with *Survivor* and *Big Brother.* Aired on the network late in summer 2000, the show was scheduled against *Big Brother,* and it was expected to win over the youth demographic with its combination of reality and teen drama. At a press conference before the show's premiere, a cast member played up the program's competition with other reality series: "This is our real life. We're living in our real houses, and we get cameras where we get to talk about what we're really feeling. Compared with *Real World* and *Survivor*, I think we are the closest you can get to reality."[19] Gail Berman, Fox entertainment president, used the documentary heritage of the series to make a similar assertion: "This is the real *Real World*. No false settings, no contrived situations. This is a type of reality programming that can be enlightening as well as entertaining."[20] Despite such allusions to enlightenment, Fox hyped *American High* with its usual anti-establishment style, creating bumpers that declared (over a hard rock sound track), "What you're about to see will get you hooked! Real kids! Real families! Real life! . . . Find out what it's like to be young in America. The bold new summer series—*American High*!" Such promotions played up the series' sensational aspects and reality TV conventions in order to better suit the network's brand identity.

Since its inception, Fox has crafted itself as an anti-establishment provider of innovative and often controversial, youth-directed programming. As such, it was one of the first networks to experiment with prime-time reality formats in the mid-1990s. Under the leadership of Mike Darnell, Fox's alternative programming unit succeeded in attracting large numbers of young male viewers with reality specials such as *When Good Pets Go Bad, World's Scariest Police Chases,* and *Alien Autopsy,* which were derided by critics as "gross-out shockumentaries and socially unredeeming freak shows."[21] In February 2000, however, the network was forced to rein in Darnell's programming style as a result of the backlash from the airing of *Who Wants to Marry a Multimillionaire?* Although highly rated, the special—a bridal/beauty pageant culminating in an on-air wedding— was lambasted by the press, and it also scared off advertisers after the bridegroom's background and financial standing was put into question. Coming in the wake of that scandal, *American High* allowed Fox to retain its reputation for groundbreaking and risky programming while providing an opportunity to clean up its public image. It was a balancing act meant to redefine reality TV for Fox, while not straying too far from viewer expectations. Even though it did receive much critical acclaim at the time of its premiere, Fox dropped *American High* from its lineup after only four episodes. Although network heads simply cited low ratings as the reason for their rather hasty decision, it appears that this series' particular blend of formats and aesthetics did not ultimately square with the average Fox viewer's vision of what reality TV was supposed to provide. By the time *American High* aired on public television almost a year later, the series had been repackaged in a strikingly different manner.

Pat Mitchell, a former CNN producer, was hired in 2000 as president and chief executive officer of PBS after the channel's prime-time ratings hit a historic low and its average viewer age had reached a high at fifty-six.[22] As part of a larger effort to attract younger viewers, in 2001 Mitchell acquired *American High,* touting it as a hip, but ultimately educational documentary series from an acclaimed independent filmmaker. Just like the executives at Fox, Mitchell tried to use *American High* to renegotiate her organization's brand identity. Yet in contrast to Fox's marketing strategy, she downplayed the "boldness" of the program's more controversial elements—such as its use of explicit language, frank discussions of sex and sexuality, and intense family conflicts—and emphasized its "authentic" and informative representation of the adolescent experience. In other words, in an effort to temper the negative connotations that accompany the reality TV label, Mitchell worked strenuously to assert the program's ties to the values and traditions of both PBS and the documentary project. She was also aware that a program harboring similarities with network reality programs would help draw younger viewers, particularly when such a show centered on teen life. At this point, PBS had already experienced success with one reality program, *1900 House,* which placed a family in a demodernized London townhouse in order to experience middle-class life as it was in 1900. This series, however, was produced with the average PBS viewer in mind, and therefore eschewed commercialism, had historical reference, and represented an idyllic vision of family togetherness. *American High* did not contain any such features; nevertheless, it had the potential to resonate with the PBS audience through its references to documentary traditions.

By engaging in a two-pronged campaign, utilizing both conventional PBS marketing methods as well as overtly commercial strategies, it would seem that Mitchell hoped to appeal to new and old viewers alike. She convinced Coca-Cola to sponsor the series, and entered into promotional deals with MTV (which cosponsored a contest in which the winners would appear on *Total Request Live* with the *American High* cast) and *Teen People* to cohost dances at high schools wherein clips of the program would be shown on dance floor Jumbotrons.[23] In addition, ads for the series (shots of individual cast members in their bedrooms or school hallway accompanied by copy such as "No actors. No scripts. Just life") were placed on the teen websites alloy.com, launch.com, and bolt.com. In an attempt to balance the PBS mandate with her aggressive marketing, though, Mitchell also used the PBS.org *American High* website to situate the program as an educational and therapeutic documentary tool for families and teachers.

Besides the message boards, chat rooms, production stills, cast biographies, and streaming videos that make up most television program websites, the *American High* one contained a Teachers' Lounge and Parents' Guide. The Teachers' Lounge utilized the tools of media literacy to instruct teachers how to teach students to make their own videos of their high school experience as well as to explore "the legal and ethical aspects of reality TV." (It's interesting to note that the only time the term reality genre is discussed in this campaign is when it's directed toward the teens, and then only in regard to its ethical ramifications.) The downloadable twenty-five-page Parents' Guide, which consistently describes the series as a documentary, begins with a letter from Mitchell:

> [*American High*] is not just a remarkable window into the lives of teens, but also a frank, gripping and often poignant depiction of the teens' parents and the daunting challenges they're facing in raising teens. As a mother of a teenager now, and having raised another, I immediately felt a sense of gratitude for what I learned from watching *American High*. The father of one of the teens in the series told the press, "watching the series is like the anthropology of our family. It made us look at issues in a completely new light—one that probably saved our relationship with our son." We at PBS believe this series can be meaningful for you, as well. And, to deepen your viewing experience, we have created this *American High* Parents' Guide. With insights from parenting experts and psychologists, the Guide uses the real-life stories from *American High* as catalysts to help you better understand the world through your teenager's eyes. Plus, the Guide provides a wealth of ideas to support you in what is arguably the most difficult relationship on earth: parent and teen.[24]

For parents and teachers, the series was constructed as what Mitchell calls "an observational documentary in the tradition of PBS."[25] Or as the parent in the above quote describes it, it was formulated as an anthropological project to be viewed and processed within an institutional context—either school or family—so that the more sensational or explicit aspects of the program could be "properly" narrativized as socially relevant issues. The idea was to attract teens to PBS by making the series appear entertaining, while simultaneously appeasing PBS's core audience—mostly parents or grandparents—by wrapping it in the discourse of education.

The strategy failed on both fronts, however. Although the program did attract a significant number of young viewers, it was not as popular as PBS executives had initially hoped. And perhaps even more important, *American High* so offended and alienated the sensibilities of the network's older viewers with its frank themes and explicit language, Mitchell was forced to admit that by choosing to air the series, PBS had "built an audience and then let them down."[26] It would seem that a specific set of expectations for and understanding of the form and function of documentary was so developed in the minds of the core PBS audience, that Mitchell's attempt to refashion it through extratextual means did not take. It's also possible that PBS viewers may not only be sensitive to sensational and sexual content but may also reject programs that could be seen as too commercial in regard to content or marketing.

While PBS viewers may have a difficult time accepting strategies that work to redefine social relevance and public service outside the conventional liberal model, HBO viewers seem to be more willing to ascribe social weight to programs that are both sensational and commercial. This may have to do with the history of HBO's nonfictional programming division, which grew largely in response to PBS's content limitations. The early and mid-1990s saw a significant shift in the market for television documentaries since the culture wars over arts funding and increasing competition from cable outlets left PBS (the primary venue for television docs up until that point) in a state of crisis. Due to the close scrutiny the network was receiving, it became increasingly difficult for PBS to not only fund documentaries but also air work that was explicit and/or controversial. And it is exactly this type of content that HBO excelled at. The very nature of HBO's premium channel payment structure allows the network to escape the cultural vilification and calls for censorship that plague broadcast and some basic cable stations. Coupled with an audience who wishes to see itself as more capable, responsible, and mature than the average television viewer, this creates an ideal setting for the presentation of "tasteful," but possibly lurid nonfictional programming. Over the past decade, HBO has aggressively marketed itself as a quality network for the (paying) television connoisseur. Through its original programming, such as *The Sopranos, Six Feet Under,* and *Sex in the City,* the cable network has refashioned liberal notions of "quality" television to include "adult" content. Consequently, viewers come to programs such as the nonfictional anthology series *America Undercover* with the expectation that what they are about to see is above and beyond the usual network fare.

Shelia Nevins admits that early in her career as HBO's head of adult documentary and family programming, she saw documentaries primarily as cheap time-fillers, but now considers them an essential marker of prestige for the company. Certainly Nevins has deliberately cultivated this prestige, as she has spent years showcasing the work of renowned established talent, such as Albert Maysles, Jon Alpert, Barbara Kopple, Lee Grant, and Alan and Susan Raymond (*An American Family*), as well as supporting up-and-coming independent filmmakers. And the resulting critical praise and industry accolades that her programs have acquired over the years have helped HBO in its effort to brand itself as *the* quality cable network. Yet Nevins is also responsible for such series as *Real Sex, G-String Divas, Autopsy, Cathouse,* and *Taxicab Confessions,* which have all come under some scrutiny from critics for their sensational subject matter. These programs share a number of aesthetic characteristics with the networks' more serious fare, are often shot or directed by independent documentarians, and are packaged alongside more traditional documen-

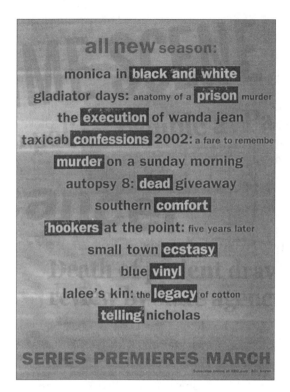

America Undercover's ad in a spring 2002 issue of the *New Yorker* reveals the way that HBO highlights the sensational in the series even as it tries to appeal to a so-called quality audience.

taries as part of HBO's "investigative" *America Undercover* series. Although Nevins packaged many of her documentary programs under the *America Undercover* heading for nineteen years, in 2002 the program was moved into one of HBO's prime program slots. Showing at 10:00 P.M. eastern standard time on Sundays in the spring and summer of that year, the program followed *Six Feet Under* and *The Sopranos,* which gave the show not only increased visibility but also a higher level of prestige. The network has invested more in its promotion of the show, even taking out two-page, full-color ads in highbrow venues such as the *New Yorker.*

America Undercover is marketed in such a way as to intentionally blur the boundaries between reality and documentary. Alternating between works that engage in the "discourse of sobriety"[27]—covering topics such as labor struggles, racial profiling, terrorism, and the death penalty—and the regular round of sex-based programming, *America Undercover* straddles traditional formats and viewing positions. As Nevins herself states, she and her staff "try to balance programs that nudge the world and programs

that are more titillating and fanciful" in order to temper or contain the reception of its risqué episodes and help sensationalize more staid subject
matter.[28] It's important to note, however, that the narration and editing of
Real Sex works to position the program as an investigative and somewhat
cerebral exploration of the sexual underground rather than straightforward pornography or erotica. In other words, it employs the discourse of
traditional documentary to mitigate or justify its more voyeuristic tendencies. It also enables the viewer to feel better about engaging with the text as
one can more easily read it as educational if one wishes. Outlining the way
in which she negotiates the often conflicting desires of her audience,
Nevins told the *Los Angeles Times* that "if you could see it on A&E, if an
advertiser would sponsor it, then I don't want to put it on HBO, because
people are paying to see something a little spicier. But if it's ugly like *Playboy*, if it's lowbrow sexuality, then it's not what I like to call 'erotic eros.' I
don't want it."[29] Nevins also has asserted that the unifying element of the
nonfictional programs that air on *America Undercover* is their ability to
fully represent "the real." As Nevins *RealScreen* in 1998,

> The concept of our unexpurgated [programs] began to mean a certain
> kind of license to push reality to where it would naturally go without any
> censorship. There was no need to curtail what was happening. That's
> when reality began to be as interesting to me as theater, because it meant
> people could realize their stories to their full extent and where they could
> take them, whether the stories were happy or sad or violent or tragic or
> sexual.[30]

Nevins is making a claim here for all her nonfictional programming
that equates the lack of mediation or censorship from higher authorities
with the ability of these programs not only to make truth claims but to
move beyond realism and into the area of unfiltered reality. In doing so,
she is touching on arguments that are made by both reality TV and documentary producers and marketers. Yet texts that are placed in the documentary genre tend to make an additional claim: that of social and historical relevance, or in the language of television, public service. In Nevins's
statement above, we can see that she is trying to shift the discourse to incorporate her presentation of sexual and other such controversial content
as a public service in itself.[31] Or at least she's alleging that sensational/sex-
ual and educational/informational content is not mutually exclusive. In
Nevins's explication of her tactics and reasoning, it becomes clear why the

documentary label is so important in this context. If her programming was classified as simply reality TV, it is possible that programs such as *Real Sex* would be evacuated of any sense of social weight. As it stands, *America Undercover* is able to mix content and form because it is wrapped in a re-defined discourse of public service or education. Viewers of the program consequently exist in a context of reception that tells them that documentary, as defined by HBO, can both educate and titillate.

With *America Undercover*, HBO was able to do what Fox and PBS could not: successfully incorporate popular pleasure into a discourse of quality. Nevins and her team reworked the discourse around their program not only to suit their network's brand image but also to redefine the terms on which it was understood and classified. Certainly *America Undercover*'s anthology format contributed to the success of their strategy, but it was also a result of an audience who, through its prior experience with HBO and conception of itself as a unique and select group, was willing to accept a dismantling of the bifurcations that separated traditional definitions of documentary and reality TV. Some of this willingness can be attributed to HBO's championing of the First Amendment, which Nevins says provided "[HBO] with a comfort zone. If you had a Richard Pryor special, you could do a show called *Eros America*; if you showed an [unedited] R-rated movie, you could push your exposure of a crack house to the full extent of what was going on inside. It was the mandate of the network, because that's what people were paying for."[32]

With *American High*, both PBS and Fox had difficulty balancing their audiences' notions of quality with mainstream tastes and pleasures. Fox has cultivated a core constituency of viewers for its nonfictional programming who have little interest in texts that profess social significance, and instead find delight in the outrageous, lowbrow, and sensational. The meanings that accompany the documentary are contrary to what they hope to get out of Fox's reality lineup. *American High*, while sold as reality TV, still bears many of the marks of documentary conventions and therefore held little interest for Fox viewers. In contrast, PBS has constituted an audience for documentaries who imagines itself as above the machinations of commercial or mass entertainment.[33] Their pleasure is contingent on a text's perceived social weight or historical relevance, and as a consequence, PBS viewers seem to prefer more conventional documentaries such as those produced by Ken Burns. They may resist nonfictional programming that is "tainted" by the popular or marked by a relationship to the commercial.

The generic instability of *American High* and *America Undercover* demonstrates just how difficult it is to define documentary and reality TV (or any television genre for that matter) outside of reception and industrial contexts. As I've shown, it is possible for networks to frame a generically unstable program as a documentary or reality program in order to activate the perceived values and implications that surround these categories. Yet the success of such rhetorical framing is contingent on an audience's preconceived ideas about the functions of that genre. A viewer may accept that a program is a documentary if a network proclaims it as such, yet that doesn't guarantee that the text will meet their needs and expectations. If a program is ultimately unable to provide them with the knowledge and pleasures they have come to expect from documentaries, they may simply choose to stop watching it. To put it another way, textual signifiers commingle with present and past extratextual generic discourses to generate spectator positioning.

American High and *America Undercover* also remind us that the often tenacious assumptions that structure our prior knowledge of nonfictional television genres not only inform our ability to classify a new program but also subjectively assign it a particular level of social value and artistic validity. This is because, as Mittell argues, genres are malleable, historically situated, cultural categories, and as such, "evolve out of the specific cultural practices of industries and audiences."[34] The distinctions we make between forms of nonfictional television are not based on empirical evidence but largely contained in the evaluative connotations that insist on separating information from entertainment, liberalism from sensationalism, and public service from commercialism. When it comes to reality-documentary hybrids, we may not, as Mead suggests, "need a new name for it." Instead, we might just need to look at why it's so important for us to label it at all.

NOTES

1. Jeffrey Ruoff, *An American Family: A Televised Life* (Minneapolis: University of Minnesota Press, 2002), 101.

2. Ibid., 23.

3. Ibid., 108.

4. Ibid., xxv.

5. John Corner, "Performing the Real: Documentary Diversions," *Television and New Media* 3, no. 3 (August 2002): 255–69.

6. Jason Mittell, "A Cultural Approach to Television Genre Theory," *Cinema Journal* 40, no. 3 (2001): 9.

7. Stella Bruzzi, *New Documentary: A Critical Introduction* (New York: Routledge, 2000), 89.

8. Programs such as *Cops* (syndicated) and *Maternity Ward* (TLC) are episodic in structure rather than serial, but they are otherwise stylistically related to the docusoap.

9. Some network executives fear the documentary label will turn off mainstream viewers because they don't tend to associate the genre with pleasure. When asked why networks shy away from the term documentary, ABC News Senior Vice President Phyllis McGrady answered: "When you think documentary, you think black-and-white, old, and boring. People are just afraid of the word. We did let it get a little fuddy-duddy" (cited in Gary Levin, "None Dare Call It a Documentary," *USA Today*, 18 June 2002, 3D).

10. The phrase "discourse of sobriety" comes from Bill Nichols, *Representing Reality: Issues and Concepts in Documentary* (Bloomington: Indiana University Press, 1991), 3–4.

11. Corner argues that the discourse of sobriety is no longer relevant in television's postdocumentary context as most documentaries are now infused with a "lightness of being" ("Performing the Real," 264).

12. Bruzzi, *New Documentary*, 78–79.

13. For more on this, see Michael Curtin, *Redeeming the Wasteland: Television Documentary and Cold War Politics* (New Brunswick, N.J.: Rutgers University Press, 1995).

14. Carnegie Commission on Educational Television, *Public Television: A Program for Action* (New York: Bantam, 1967).

15. See Kraszewski's chapter in this volume.

16. Nichols, *Representing Reality*, 24.

17. See Mark Jurkowitz, "'High' Time at PBS," *Boston Globe*, 4 April 2001, C10, and http://www.pbs.org/americanhigh/behind/index.html.

18. From the chat room transcript, http://www.pbs.org/americanhigh/behind/index.html.

19. Cited in David Zurawik, "This Is as Good as It Gets: School Series Really Is Reality TV," *Baltimore Sun*, 2 August 2000, 1E.

20. Cited in David Zurawik, "A Silver Lining in the Reality Cloud," *Baltimore Sun*, 23 July 2000, 5F.

21. Alex Kuczynski and Bill Carter, "Point Man for Perversity; 'World's Scariest Programmer,' Starring Mike Darnell as Himself," *New York Times*, 26 February 2000, C1.

22. By the end of 2001, PBS was being viewed by 1.7 percent of U.S. homes (see Elizabeth Jensen, "A Network's Mastery Has Gone to Pieces," *Los Angeles Times*, 12 May 2002, A1).

23. Kay McFadden, "Kid You Not: PBS Going After Adolescent Viewers," *Seattle Times,* 31 March 2001, C1.

24. Parents' Guide, www.pbs.org/americanhigh.

25. Cited in David Bauder, "Finding an Audience for a Worthy Documentary," *Associated Press,* 24 April 2001.

26. Cited in Elizabeth Jensen, "A Network's Mastery Has Gone to Pieces," *Los Angeles Times,* 12 May 2002, A1.

27. "'Undercover' Wins Spotlight," *Boston Globe,* 9 March 2001, C4.

28. Ibid.

29. Cited in Paul Lieberman, "Confessions of an HBO Original," *Los Angeles Times,* 28 May 2000, C3.

30. Cited in Ed Kirchdoerffer, "Flash, Cash, and the Ratings Dash: HBO's Shelia Nevins," *RealScreen,* 1 September 1998, 33.

31. It's important to note that Brian Winston decries this sort of thinking since he considers this willingness to investigate sexuality and nudity—which he calls "docu-glitz"—cable's "un-public service" contribution to the documentary form" (cited in Nichols, *Representing Reality,* 48).

32. Cited in Kirchdoerffer, "Flash, Cash, and the Ratings Dash," 33.

33. The history of the public television audience and how it has been constructed by PBS is a long and complicated one. It is described in detail in Laurie Ouellette, *Viewers like Us: How Public TV Failed the People* (New York: Columbia University Press, 2002).

34. Mittell, "A Cultural Approach," 10.

3

Teaching Us to Fake It
The Ritualized Norms of Television's "Reality" Games

Nick Couldry

Whatever its contribution to the overblown claims of semiotics as a general "science" of language, Roland Barthes's analysis of "myth" and its connection to ideology remains useful as a specific tool to understand particular types of media language such as advertising and also that most striking of recent phenomena, reality TV.[1] Myth itself, Ernesto Laclau has argued, is increasingly a requirement of contemporary societies whose divisions and dislocations multiply.[2] If so, reality TV's mythical claim to represent an increasingly complex social space—for example, in the largely entertainment mode of the gamedoc or reality game show—may have significance far beyond the analysis of the television genre. I will make this assertion more precise by considering reality TV's ritual dimensions and their link to certain media-centric norms of social behavior.

The idea underlying reality TV is hardly new. Here is the television anchor who commented on the 1969 Apollo moon touchdown speaking three decades ago: "[Television's] real value is to make people participants in ongoing experiences. Real life is vastly more exciting than synthetic life, and this is real-life drama with audience participation."[3] This notion—and the associated claim of television to present real life—does not disappear in the era of television "plenty," but rather comes under increasing pressure to take new forms.[4] The subgenre of gamedocs on which I will concentrate is a later adaptation to those pressures, succeeding an early wave of docusoaps and television verité in the mid-1990s, and a subsequent crisis of many docusoaps' documentary authority because of scandals about fake productions—for example, over Carlton TV's documentary

The Connection (1999), which supposedly uncovered an operation for smuggling drugs from Colombia, but was alleged by the *London Guardian* to have faked various scenes.[5] But if the gamedoc signifies a shift to a "postdocumentary" television culture, the result is not an abandonment of reality claims but their transformation.[6] As John Corner puts it in regard to the first British series of *Big Brother*, "*Big Brother* operates its claims to the real within a fully managed artificiality, in which almost everything that might be deemed to be true about what people do and say is necessarily and obviously predicated on the larger contrivance of them being there in front of the camera in the first place."[7]

My interest here is less in the gamedoc as generic form (excellently discussed by Corner), but in the wider social process that gamedocs constitute. At stake in these often much-hyped programs is a whole way of reformulating the media's (not just television's) deep-seated claim to present social reality, to be the "frame" through which we access the reality that matters to us as social beings.[8] In the gamedoc, this involves the promotion of specific norms of behavior to which those who court popularity by living in these shows' constructed spaces must conform.

To get analytic purchase on this complex process, the term "myth" by itself is too blunt. Instead, we need the more precise notions of "ritual" and "ritualization" that can link the television form to the wider issues of authority and governmentality.[9] Most contemporary self-performance can, as Gareth Palmer notes, be interpreted in light of Michel Foucault's theory of governmentality, whereby power is reproduced through norms not just of control but also of expression and self-definition. I want, however, to push further than Palmer does the implications of the fact that in gamedocs, "what develop[s is] not so much a self [as] a *media self*."[10]

What is this media self? What is its social status, and what are its social consequences? To link gamedocs to governmentality is not enough since all contemporary social space is in this sense governed by norms that regulate what is acceptable, meaningful, and pleasurable, and what is not. We need also to ask: Are gamedocs such as *Big Brother* spaces for reflecting on governmentality shared by performers and audiences alike, or spaces for audiences to reflect on governmentality by watching others (the performers) being governed, or finally, a process whereby both performers and audiences are in effect governed through the unreflexive naturalization of particular behavioral norms?[11]

The Ritual Space of the Reality Game Show

What might we mean by the ritual properties of television forms such as the gamedoc?[12]

Ritual Action and Media Form

First, it is important to emphasize that by ritual, I mean more than habitual actions. While much of gamedocs *does* consist of rituals in this commonsense use of the term (as people get up, eat, wash up, chat, and sleep for the cameras), this use adds nothing to the idea of habit. Instead, I am interested in the two more substantive anthropological senses of ritual: as formalized action; and as action (often, but not necessarily formalized) associated with certain transcendent values.

The first sense captures how certain action-patterns are not only repeated but organized in a form or shape that has a meaning over and above any meaning of the actions taken by themselves. So putting a ring on a finger in the context of a wedding signifies the act of marriage, and putting a wafer in a mouth, again in a specific context and not elsewhere, signifies the act of Holy Communion. The leading theorist of ritual, the late Roy Rappaport, defined ritual as "the performance of more or less invariant sequences of formal acts and utterances *not entirely encoded* by the performers"—ritual action, in other words, is always more than it seems.[13] In the second sense of the term, less emphasis is placed on the formality of actions and more on the kinds of values with which those actions are associated. In a line of argument that goes back to the great French sociologist Émile Durkheim's *Elementary Forms of Religious Life,* many have seen in ritual action an affirmation of the values underlying the social bond itself that's more important than its exact formal properties.[14]

When I talk of media rituals, I want to combine aspects of these two senses. From the formal analysis of ritual, I want to take the idea that rituals can reproduce the building blocks of belief without involving any explicit content that is believed. Far from every ritual expressing a hidden essence in which the performers explicitly believe, rituals by their repetitive form reproduce categories and patterns of thought in a way that *bypasses* explicit belief. On the contrary, if made explicit, many of the ideas apparently expressed by ritual might be rejected, or at least called into question; it is their *ritualized* form that enables them to be successfully reproduced without being exposed to questions about their "content." This is useful in understanding how ritual works in relation to media, where quite clearly, there is no explicit credo of shared beliefs about media to which everyone signs up. From the transcendent account of ritual, I want to take the idea that there is an essential link between ritual and certain social values, or at least certain large *claims* about the social. As I have argued elsewhere, there is a striking similarity between the socially oriented values (our sense of what binds us as members of a society) that underlie Durkheim's sociology of religion and the types of claims that media, even now, implicitly make about their power to represent "the social."[15]

Media rituals are actions that reproduce the myth that the media are our privileged access point to social reality, yet they work not through articulated beliefs but the boundaries and category distinctions around which media rituals are organized. Let us adopt the following working definition: media rituals are formalized actions organized around key media-related categories and boundaries whose performances suggest a connection with wider media-related values.[16]

What aspects of the gamedoc process would count as media rituals under this definition? One example would be the "ceremony" developed in the British version of *Big Brother* on each night when a housemate is evicted. Once the result of the week's popular vote has been announced to the inmates by live link from the *Big Brother* studio, the evictee is given one hour exactly to get their baggage ready. With one minute to go, the lead presenter, Davina McColl, walks live from the studio across the barrier to the house. The door to the house is opened and the evictee emerges, clutching belongings, usually to the cheers of supporters in the crowd outside. From the house door, McColl leads the evictee, as they take in the adulation of the crowd, back to the studio for a live interview, where the evictee is asked to reflect on their time in the house.

This weekly pattern has been repeated in each British *Big Brother* series until the series' final week, when the last inmate leaves the house as the winner. In its regularity, we have a clever simulation of other forms of television ceremonial. But it is not the formalization that I have most in mind in calling this a media ritual; rather, it is the way the whole sequence is based around a fundamental boundary between "ordinary person" and "media person"—in other words, around the media-value celebrity.[17] A basic point of *Big Brother* is to enact a transition for each housemate from ordinary person to media person; the eviction ceremony is designed to make that transition seem natural (natural as television event, that is). The

"celebrification process" in *Big Brother* is obvious to everyone, both performers and viewers, even though far from transparent in its details and
exclusions.[18] But its significance is greater, since underlying the idea that
the housemates become celebrities is another more basic media value: that
being in the *Big Brother* house is somehow more significant than being
outside the house. In short, mediated reality is somehow "higher" or more
significant than nonmediated reality—which as I have maintained elsewhere, is the value that underlies the legitimation of media institutions'
general concentration of symbolic power.[19] Kate Lawler, the winner of the
third series of *Big Brother* (hereafter BB3), in her reactions to her final
hour in the house, vividly enacted the boundary and hierarchy between
media and nonmedia "worlds." She cried and seemed overawed by the
transition from the apparently private, though of course intensely mediated world of the *Big Brother* house to the explicitly mediated world outside with its cheering crowds and press flashbulbs. When McColl came to
interview her *inside* the house (on the series' final night, the winner gets to
be interviewed inside the house, where only they have earned the right to
stay), Lawler had difficulty speaking. She acted starstruck in front of Mc-
Coll (who in Britain, is a minor celebrity in her own right because of *Big
Brother*). McColl gave Lawler the standard phrase used by fans on meeting
their idol: "No, it's me who can't believe I'm sitting here with *you*" (BB3, 26
July 2002).

At this point, I want to shift the focus to the related concept of ritualization. For it is in the dynamic relationship between the ritual high points
of, say, *Big Brother* and the wider process of ritualizing the often banal actions in the *Big Brother* house that we find the best entry-point to the social, not merely textual, process that gamedocs constitute.

Acting "Up" for the Cameras

Media rituals cannot, any more than rituals in general, be studied in isolation from the larger hinterland of ritualization: that is, the whole gamut of
patterns of action, thought, and speech that generate the categories and
boundaries on which media rituals are based. It is this hinterland of everyday action that makes the special case of media rituals possible.

As the anthropologist Catherine Bell contends in her study of religious
ritual, ritualization organizes our movements around space, helps us to
experience constructed features of the environment as real, and thereby
reproduces the symbolic authority at stake in the categorizations on which

ritual draws.[20] The background ritualizations that underlie media rituals work in a similar way, through the organization of all sorts of actions around key media-related categories ("media person/thing/place/world," "liveness," "reality").[21]

The term ritualization is our way of tracing how rituals connect to power; for media rituals, the link in question is to the increasing organization of social life around media centers. Drawing again on Bell, we must study how

> the orchestrated construction of power and authority in ritual . . . engage[s] the social body in the objectification of oppositions and the deployment of schemes that effectively reproduce the divisions of the social order. In this objectification lie the resonance of ritual and the consequences of compliance.[22]

In principle, this could lead us from the celebrification rituals of *Big Brother* to the mass of actions whereby all of us contribute to celebrity culture (buying celebrity magazines, for example). But with gamedocs, there is also a tighter link between ritual and ritualization: What are the nine weeks in the *Big Brother* house if not a space of ritualization, where inmates' banal, everyday routines are tested for their appropriateness to a mediated space?

If rituals are naturalized, stable forms for reproducing power relations, ritualization is the much wider process through which the categories underlying those power relations *become* naturalized in action, thought, and words. The raw material of ritualization is much more liable to be destabilized by doubt, reflexivity, and correction. The action in the BB3 house reflected similar instabilities, as various inmates thought about leaving the house voluntarily (see below). A particular focus in BB3 was inmates' mutual accusations of performing to the cameras and the anxious denials that resulted. It could be argued, of course, that all this was part of BB3's developing plot and entertainment value, but we see below how, on the contrary, this issue opened up conflicts among inmates, and between inmates and the show's producers, about the norms of behavior in the house— conflicts that could not be contained within BB3 as a "game."

Gamedocs and Real "Experience"

One of the words most frequently used by BB3 contestants was "experience": they wanted to make the most of the *Big Brother* experience, they were asked how their experience in the house had gone when they left, and so on. Although hardly a simple word to disentangle, experience connotes something both significant and real, and usually something *more* significant and real than the everyday run of things. But since the conditions of the *Big Brother* house made it exceptional from the start, there was always a tension: Was the *Big Brother* experience significant because it was exceptional, or was it significant because however exceptional it seemed, it showed something important about the underlying continuities of human nature? Such ambiguities are the very stuff of myth in Barthes's sense.[23]

Yet however ambiguous the claims of *Big Brother* and other gamedocs to represent reality, without *some* such claim their status—as shows that make celebrities out of real ordinary people—collapses. Every gamedoc has a specific myth about how it represents the social world. A number of British shows rely on the myth that in the face of extreme physical challenges, especially those requiring team collaboration (however artificially constructed), an important aspect of human reality is shown. This is the myth underpinning *Survivor* (Carlton TV, 2000), an international format less successful in Britain than *Big Brother*, perhaps because it is less obviously aimed at a stereotypical, "young" audience (having some middle-aged contestants, and much less emphasis on celebrity and sex), although arguably the almost comic exoticism of *Survivor*'s British version (with its tribal gatherings and the like) undermines its wider reality claim in any case.[24]

In *Castaway 2000*, a failed variant on the *Survivor* theme produced for the millennial year (BBC1, 2000), thirty-five people were put onto Taransay, a deserted island just off the coast of the Hebridean island of Harris, for one year to see how they would survive. Taransay is, in fact, in full view of one of the most beautiful beaches in Scotland (I know because I holiday on Harris myself), so its claim to present a controlled experiment in genuine isolation was strained from the outset. Still, the program's mythical intent was clear from its opening voice-over:

> *Castaway 2000* is a unique experiment to discover what happens when a group representative of British society today is stranded away from modern life. On the deserted Scottish island of Taransay, they'll have a year to decide

how to run the community, devise new ways of living together, and reflect
on what aspects of life are really important in the 21st century.[25]

Other recent experiments have sought to mine the old myth of "human
nature" even further. *The Experiment* (BBC2, 2002, with a subsequent U.S.
version) offered a reworking by two psychologists of the well-known U.S.
1970s "Prisoner" experiment, which had pitted two selected groups against
each other, one in the role of "guards" and the other in the role of "prisoners," in order to test how far the former exploited their artificial authority
over the latter. The television program relied both on the myth of objec-
tivity built into psychological experimentation and the additional myth
that cameras changed nothing significant about the so-called experiment.

The BBC has now produced a further variation on *Castaway* and *Survivor,* sending a group of selected teenagers to the Borneo jungle. *Serious
Jungle* has not been broadcast as of this writing, but from the producer's
comments, it is the youth (and supposed innocence?) of the contestants
that underwrites its claim to truth, refracted through the fictional model
of *Lord of the Flies*: "*Serious Jungle* has a serious point to it, and because it
is focused on children, the viewers will see very clear and honest reactions
to their experiences."[26] At the same time, the organizer of the teenagers'
trip showed a touching faith in the quality of the experiences they would
undergo, mixing the myth of television's superior reality with the older
one of the encounter with nature:

> For the first time these children will be forging relationships that are no
> longer about what music they like or what trainers they wear. They will
> change so much during these few weeks that going home to their old
> friends could be quite difficult for them.[27]

In spite of the implied distinction from the youth culture represented by
Big Brother here, nowhere is the underlying myth of gamedocs challenged:
that there is plausibility in reading human reality into what transpires in a
space made and monitored for television.

The particular success in Britain of *Big Brother* may derive, in part,
from its clever mix of mythical authorities: the suggestion of scientific experiment is there (with "top psychologists" even being given their own
show on each Sunday night of BB3), but also the validating myths of
celebrity and popular "interactivity." Popular participation is itself, of

course, a useful myth; viewers of *Big Brother,* after all, have no control over its format, the initial choice of participants, the instructions or rules given to participants, the principles of editing, or indeed how the "popular vote" is interpreted to contestants and audience.

None of these contradictions should surprise us. For it is precisely in the oscillation between contingent detail and some broader, mythical value that for the anthropologist Maurice Bloch, echoing Barthes, the power of ritual lies.[28] In Bloch's analysis of Madagascan rituals, the broader value is that of "ancient history" lost in the mists of time; in contemporary societies, no one believes in history in that sense, but the myths of human nature, science, and what Marc Augé has called "the ideology of the present" are powerful substitutes.[29]

The Norms of Reality Performance

There is another myth reproduced through the gamedoc form and its apparently innocent rituals of television celebrity. I say myth, but it is more like a half statement that works largely by *not* being articulated—hence its affinity to ritual. This is the idea that surveillance is a natural mode through which to observe the social world. Few, perhaps, would subscribe explicitly to the will to "omniperception" (as the leading sociologist of surveillance puts it) implied here.[30] Yet by constant media repetition, this notion risks rigidifying into a myth that is fully integrated into our everyday expectations of the social.

The Pleasures of Surveillance

What are we to make of the idea that to find out about an aspect of social reality, it is natural to set up an "experimental situation" (with or without the endorsement of qualified psychologists), watch what happens when people are either not yet aware of the presence of cameras or are presumed to have forgotten it, and treat the result as "reality"? You might think it hypocritical for a sociologist like myself, who regularly interviews and observes others, to protest so much. But there is an obvious difference between the gamedoc and the normal context for sociological or indeed psychological research: confidentiality. Remember that *The Experiment* was in part designed by two psychologists as a hybrid of the entertainment form and an experimental situation.[31] Never in the recent history of the social and psychological sciences have studies been conducted for a simultaneous *public* audience, unless we return to Jean-Martin Charcot's public demonstrations in the 1870s with hysterics at the Paris Salpêtrière, and also recall the long history of public operations on the living and dead that preceded Charcot. Yet even in that early modern history of public experiment, there is no parallel for experimental subjects being watched in permanently retrievable form by an audience of millions.

The emerging model of surveillance and governance, and the rejuvenated "experimental science" that is parasitic on them, is disturbing. Its implications are greater than the popular legitimation of everyday surveillance, important as that is.[32] For surveillance-entertainment (a cumbersome, but equally accurate name for the gamedoc) has implications for everyday social relations that surveillance focused on criminal activity does not. While the saturation of public space with closed-circuit television is, of course, a matter of concern, the issue is more its effects on the quality of everyone's experience of public space, rather than the effects on how people might perform in front of the visible and invisible cameras— which is precisely why the New York art campaigners the Surveillance Camera Players' *performances* in front of surveillance cameras are striking, as ways of denaturalizing a dimension of public life that we screen out of our consciousness entirely. But in surveillance-entertainment, the impacts on "performance" are surely the *key* issue since its underlying premise is that we can expect *any* everyday activity legitimately to be put under surveillance and monitored for a huge, unknown audience.

What is remarkable is how easy it is to hide this disturbing idea beneath the cloak of ritual. In a six-part series introduced by Britain's Channel Four in 2002 called *Make My Day*, the *Big Brother* format was turned adeptly into a pure entertainment package. The idea of the program was a simple, if alarming extension of the *Candid Camera* format: friends or family nominate someone to the producers to be put under secret surveillance for a day to test their reactions to five challenges; if all are passed, the unwitting contestant wins £5,000 and retrospectively the "benefit" of having "starred" for national television "in her very own game show" (as one episode put it). The "challenges" are simple tests of the subject's ability to act as a person with a "normal" sexual appetite and a "natural" interest in celebrity. Will this young woman let into her house a half-naked man (recruited to match her tastes in men) needing to make an urgent phone call? Yes!—move to stage two. Will the same young woman allow herself to be

The Surveillance Camera Players, New York art campaigners, perform in front of surveillance cameras—in this case, by holding up a sign. Photo courtesy of Bill Brown.

distracted from getting to work when a member of her favorite pop band approaches her in the street, pretending to be lost and needing help to find his way? Yes!—move to stage three, and so on.

This series attracted little attention, and the predictability of its challenges was surely a weakness. What is interesting, however, is how the unwitting contestants reacted at the end of that day, when its strange events were explained to them by the well-known British celebrity and show narrator Sara Cox.[33] What we saw on the program—and of course, we have no way of knowing how far this was rehearsed or edited—is the contestant delighted, even awestruck, at the revelation, clutching her face, crying out "oh, my God!" and the like. Any later reflections by the contestant on having in effect consented to being submitted to twelve hours of secret filming for national television (including an opening scene in their bedroom) were left to our speculation.

My point is not to moralize about this particular series but to offer it as an example of how easily consent to the process of surveillance before a national audience (even if quite counterintuitive) can be made to seem natural, given the right ritual context. Here are Cox's explanatory words to one contestant:

> Hello, it's Sara Cox here. You must be thinking you have had the strangest day of your life. Well it's all because of Channel 4's *Make My Day.* We have been secretly filming you using hidden cameras all day long and we reckon it's about time you got out from under your mother's feet so as a big thank you we would love to give you a deposit on your first flat. . . . I really hope we've made your day.

The program is useful because it is so artless. Here we see quite directly how two positive behavioral norms (one automatically positive—obtaining your own, independent place to live—and the other increasingly constructed as positive in contemporary British culture—showing an interest in celebrity) are combined to make the program's whole sequence of events seem natural and legitimate. (It must also have helped the producers that the "contestant" was living with her mother, who presumably gave legal consent to the presence of cameras in her daughter's bedroom.) Underwriting those norms here is the principle that "media experience" (discovering that the contestant's meetings with celebrities were not just accidental but real—that is, planned specifically by the media for her) automatically trumps "ordinary experience," including any questionable ethical dimensions it may have. This is a social "magic" (in Marcel Mauss's sense): a transformative "principle that eludes examination" that we must nonetheless try to unravel.[34]

The Real (Mediated) Me

BB3 differed from previous British series of *Big Brother* in its emerging divide between those inmates who were clearly unhappy with the expected norms for behavior in the house and those who broadly accepted them. Even among the latter were a number who were unhappy at times, including the eventual finalists ("[*Big Brother* voice:] How are you feeling, Alex? [Alex:] Um . . . institutionalized").[35] Of the former, two left voluntarily, and another (Sandy, who happened to be the only housemate without fashionable, young looks) remained quiet and isolated for a few weeks before being voted out (as the *Big Brother* voice-over noted on one occasion: "Sandy was the first to go to bed" (cut to Sandy reading a book in bed).[36]

An interesting case was Tim, the only obviously upper-class inmate, a later replacement in the house who never settled. He was not so much withdrawn, like Sandy, as openly complaining at the tasks given to the inmates and the way others played up to the cameras. His complaints (in the program's famous Diary Room) were portrayed by the producers through editing and commentary as those of a moaner, who conveniently, was also discovered to be physically vain when his black hair dye started to show and he was caught on camera shaving his chest in the apparent privacy of his bed.

There was no particular drama to his eviction (on 19 July 2002) since he had made it clear on camera that he was "desperate" to leave the house. The eviction was presented in a hostile manner by McColl before the vote result: "The whole house thinks Tim's going to be out and to be honest the whole of the nation thinks Tim's going to be out." Tim emerged from the house to boos and hisses from the waiting crowd. His live interview was more dramatic; criticized by McColl for "whinging" and his unwillingness to play the *Big Brother* game, Tim responded that he had thought the set tasks "could have been a bit more mature." He was challenged to defend his charge that other inmates were playing up to the cameras:

> *McColl*: On a number of occasions, you talked about performing, other people performing. What did you mean by that?
> *Tim*: The whole time I was in there I was very much myself. I don't think my whole personality came out because there wasn't much to stimulate a lot of it . . . but there were a lot of people in there who I'm convinced are not like that in their normal life . . .
> *McColl*: [*interrupting*] Like who?
> *Tim*: [*continuing over McColl*]: and when I spoke to them one-to-one and you found out more about them as a person, that's the side I really liked, but they never showed enough of that. As soon as a camera came in or they felt they were being watched, they were up and [*mimes clapping to music*] singing and dancing and sure the public obviously like it because they get really into it, but . . .
> *McColl*: [*interrupting again*] But it's not that it's that. I think that generally some of them are quite up, positive people. [*cheering in background from*

crowd to whom the conversation is being relayed outside on large screens] If you can't perform, physically you can't do it, not for seven or eight weeks, you can't do it.

Tim: No, there were times when they didn't and they dipped, and that's the times you saw them when they weren't acting.

McColl: OK, Tim . . . let's move onto something a bit more positive.[37]

There is an unresolvable conflict here between two norms of how to behave in the house: first, to give the public what they are assumed to want ("singing and dancing" [Tim], or being "up positive people" [McColl]), and second, the unobjectionable, but also vague norm of "being yourself." If as an inmate you find the second norm is incompatible with the first, what are you to do? Many inmates betrayed anxiety about whether they had been themselves—for example, Jonny (the eventual runner-up), who asked Jade why his housemates had put him up for eviction more than once and was told it was because "you've studied it, you know what the people on the outside would like."[38] He vehemently denied this, but in his eviction interview on the series' final night (26 July 2002), he failed to resolve the contradiction. When asked by McColl, "Who's the real you?" the melancholy loner smoking by the pool or the comic performer, he responded immediately:

> *Jonny*: The real me's the stupid, idiotic clown, but it takes a lot to get us down to the serious, quiet Jonny, but it worked in there.
> *McColl*: It stripped you down, did it?
> *Jonny*: Yes.

Yet he admitted at another point: "I don't care what anybody says, you're always aware of the cameras, and on the other end of them cameras is your family and your friends who you love." Or take Sophie, a late arrival who appeared unhappy during much of her time in the house, but who (like Jonny) was treated favorably in the show's comments on her performance. What follows is an exchange from her eviction interview (28 June 2002), where McColl asks a standard question, drawing on the idea of media experience being better (or bigger) than ordinary experience.[39] Sophie's answer is ambiguous, however:

> *McColl*: What's it like in that house? . . . I mean it's like a pressure cooker.
> *Sophie*: It is.

McColl:. . . everything's big, feelings are felt stronger, what was it like for you?
Sophie: Um, I felt. . . . It's very . . . false in a way. . . . I mean, everyone in the house, . . . they've not got a mask on, but . . .

Here, contemporary media's wide-ranging myth that cameras tell us more about underlying reality because they magnify feelings that are presumed already to exist is directly contradicted. These contradictions matter because they cannot, in principle, be resolved. They are contradictions within the myth that *Big Brother* produces to legitimate itself: on the one hand, it claims to show us the human reality that must come out when ordinary people live for a long time under the cameras; on the other hand, it polices any differences of interpretation about what that reality should be, ruling out any behavior excluded by the production choices it makes and ruling in the so-called positive selves that it presumes the public wants to see and contestants want to display. Once contestants start to doubt the latter reality, as in BB3, there is nowhere for the producers to turn but ritual: rituals of vilification turned on Tim, who posed the most direct threat to the show's norms, or rituals of incorporation, affirming the show's status by including successful inmates in the club of celebrity. Here are McColl's final words on the last night:

> Kate entered the house unknown and now she's taking her first innocent steps into a world of unseen wealth and privilege, . . . offers of casual sex, fame beyond her dreams, and general admiration. . . . I hope you've enjoyed this as much as I have. This has been *Big Brother* 2002. Thank you for watching. Good-bye.

The producers could afford some irony here, of course, in the show's final moments, but not, as we have seen, when the show's myth was directly challenged.[40]

Toward an Ethics of Reality TV

Where has this brief, skeptical tour of the British gamedoc brought us? Clearly, the gamedoc is a generic adaptation of considerable robustness (after all, it no longer carries the docusoap's hostage to fortune, the residual claim to documentary authority), and in the case of the British version of *Big Brother,* great resourcefulness and commercial promise: BB3 was widely reported as having "rescued" Channel Four in the 2002 season.[41]

This chapter's argument, however, has been that our analysis cannot rest with observations on the adaptability of television genres. For *Big Brother* and all gamedocs are *social* processes that take real individuals and submit them to surveillance, analysis, and selective display as means to entertainment and enhanced audience participation. It is this social process, not the program's textual properties, that should be our main focus, and I offered some concepts (myth, ritual, and ritualization) to help us grasp its real and ideological dimensions.

There is, of course, one further step to which the argument needs to be taken, and that is ethics. What are the ethics of surveillance-entertainment? Or perhaps as the first question, where should we stand to get an adequate perspective on the possible ethical dimensions of the social process that gamedocs constitute, both by themselves and in their interface with the rest of social life? Finding that perspective is not easy. Part of the fascination of that oxymoron "reality TV" is its ambiguity, which in the case of *Big Brother* rests on another: between the expressive, almost obsessively self-reflexive individualization that it displays for us ("saturated individualism," as Michel Maffesoli has called it) and the barely accountable "exemplary center" that underwrites (or seeks to underwrite) the plausibility and legitimacy of that display.[42] By exemplary center, I mean the mythical "social center" that media institutions, even as they face unprecedented pressures from the dispersal of media production and consumption, attempt to project: the apparently naturally existing social "world" to which television likes to claim it gives us access.[43] The point is not that we can do without media or that media are exactly the same as other unaccountable forms of governmental or corporate power but rather that we cannot avoid at some point turning to an ethical critique if we are to address how media are transforming, and being transformed by, the social space in which, like it or not, we have to live. This chapter, I hope, has provided some useful starting points for that wider debate.

NOTES

1. Roland Barthes, *Mythologies* (London: Paladin, 1972).

2. Ernesto Laclau, *New Reflections on the Revolution of Our Time* (London: Verso, 1990), 67.

3. Cited in Carolyn Marvin, *Blood Sacrifice and the Nation* (Cambridge: Cambridge University Press, 1999), 159.

4. On television "plenty," see John Ellis, *Seeing Things* (London: IB Tauris, 2000).

5. On the early wave of the mid-1900s, see Ib Bondebjerg, "Public Discourse/Private Fascination," *Media Culture and Society* 18 (1996): 27–45; Richard Kilborn, "'How Real Can You Get?' Recent Developments in 'Reality' Television," *European Journal of Communication* 13, no. 2 (1994): 201–18. On the subsequent crisis of many docusoaps, see Caroline Dover, "British Documentary Television Production: Tradition, Change, and 'Crisis' within a Practitioner Community" (Ph.D. diss., University of London, 2001).

6. See John Corner, "Performing the Real: Documentary Diversions," *Television and New Media* 3, no. 3 (August 2002): 255–69.

7. Ibid., 256.

8. Nick Couldry, *The Place of Media Power: Pilgrims and Witnesses of the Media Age* (London: Routledge, 2000); see also Roger Silverstone, "Television, Myth and Culture," in *Media, Myths and Narratives,* ed. James Carey (Newbury Park, Calif.: Sage, 1988).

9. See Nick Couldry, *Media Rituals: A Critical Approach* (London: Routledge, 2002); and Gareth Palmer, "*Big Brother*: An Experiment in Governance," *Television and New Media* 3, no. 3 (2002): 311–22.

10. Palmer, "*Big Brother,*" 305–6, emphasis added.

11. *Big Brother,* third series (May–July 2002), is my main example.

12. The term "ritual" is a difficult one, and there is no space here to explain in detail its history or my specific use of the term "media rituals" (but see Couldry, *Media Rituals*).

13. Roy Rappaport, *Ritual and Religion in the Making of Humanity* (Cambridge: Cambridge University Press, 1999), 24, emphasis added.

14. Émile Durkheim, *The Elementary Forms of Religious Life,* trans. Karen Fields (1912; reprint, Glencoe, Ill.: Free Press, 1995).

15. Couldry, *Media Rituals.*

16. For further background, see ibid., chapters 1–3.

17. See Nick Couldry, "Playing for Celebrity: *Big Brother* as Ritual Event," *Television and New Media* 3, no. 3 (2002): 289.

18. See ibid. For "celebrification process," see Chris Rojek, *Celebrity* (London: Reaktion Books, 2001), 186–87.

19. See Couldry, *The Place of Media Power,* chapter 3.

20. Catherine Bell, *Ritual Theory, Ritual Practice* (New York: Oxford University Press, 1992).

21. On these categories, see Couldry, *Media Rituals.*

22. Bell, *Ritual Theory,* 215.

23. Barthes, *Mythologies.*

24. Interestingly, the *Survivor* prize money is £1 million, compared to *Big Brother*'s £70,000—surprising until you realize that the more successful *Big Brother* contestants have in the past picked up promotional deals, hosted television shows, or issued pop singles.

25. *Castaway 2000*, 25 January 2000.

26. Marshall Corwin, cited in *Observer* 31 March 2002, 15. For more on *Serious Jungle*, see its website: www.bbc.co.uk/talent/jungle.

27. Alex Patterson, cited in *Observer*, 31 March 2002, 15.

28. Maurice Bloch, *Ritual, History, and Power* (London: Athlone Press, 1989), 130.

29. Marc Augé, "Le Stade de l'écran," *Le Monde Diplomatique*, June 2001, 24.

30. David Lyon, *Surveillance Society: Monitoring Everyday Life* (Milton Keynes, Buckingham [England]: Open University Press, 2001), 124–25.

31. Steve Reicher and Alex Haslam, cited in *Guardian*, 3 May 2002, 7.

32. See Mark Andrejevic, "Little Brother Is Watching: The Webcam Subculture and the Digital Enclosure," in *Media/Space*, ed. Nick Couldry and Anna McCarthy (London: Routledge, forthcoming); Couldry, *Media Rituals*, chapter 6; and Palmer, "*Big Brother*."

33. Cox is host DJ of Radio 1's high-profile early morning show.

34. Cited in Pierre Bourdieu, *The State Nobility* (Cambridge: Polity, 1996), 7.

35. BB3, 17 July 2002.

36. Ibid., 29 May 2002.

37. This and later passages are the author's transcription.

38. BB3, 28 June 2002.

39. See Couldry, *The Place of Media Power*, 113, cf. 47–48.

40. Such irony is often misinterpreted as skepticism or distance, when in fact its effect is just the opposite (Slavoj Žižek, *The Sublime Object of Ideology* [London: Verso, 1989], 32–33; see also Couldry, *The Place of Media Power*, 45).

41. See, for example, *Guardian*, 27 July 2002, 7.

42. Michel Maffesoli, *The Time of the Tribes* (London: Sage, 1996), 64. The phrase "exemplary center" is from Clifford Geertz, *Negara: The Theatre State in Nineteenth-Century Bali* (Princeton, N.J.: Princeton University Press, 1980), 13.

43. See Couldry, *Media Rituals*, chapter 3.

4

"Expect the Unexpected"
Narrative Pleasure and Uncertainty due to Chance in Survivor

Mary Beth Haralovich and Michael W. Trosset

In the wrap episode of *Survivor*'s fifth season (*Survivor 5: Thailand*), host Jeff Probst expressed wonder at the unpredictability of the program. Five people each managed to get through the game to be the sole survivor and win the million dollars, yet each winner was different from the others, in personality, background, and game strategy. Probst takes evident pleasure in the fact that even he cannot predict the outcomes of *Survivor,* as close to the action as he is. He advised viewers interested in improving their *Survivor* skills to become acquainted with mathematician John Nash's theory of games. Probst's evocation on national television of Nash's game theory invites both fans and critics to apply mathematics to playing and analyzing *Survivor.*[1]

This essay explores our understanding of the narrative pleasure of *Survivor* through mathematical modes of inquiry. Such an exploration assumes that there is something about *Survivor* that lends itself to mathematical analysis: the element of genuine, unscripted chance. It is the presence of chance and its almost irresistible invitation to try to predict outcomes that distinguishes the *Survivor* reality game hybrid. *In The Pleasure of the Text,* Roland Barthes examined how narrative whets our desire to know what happens next.[2] In *Survivor*'s reality game, the pleasure of "what happens next" is not based on the cleverness of scriptwriters or the narrowly evident skills of the players. Even though the pleasure of knowing and guessing the final outcome becomes more intense and feasible as the number of variables decreases, unscripted chance can still intervene.

The pleasure of the text of *Survivor* is based in an essential unpredictability that is woven into the *Survivor* reality show genre.

Survivor is a hybrid of game and adventure with drama. This blend results in what a statistician would consider "genuine" unpredictability in its outcomes, in what happens next. The program's hybrid design allows for, indeed requires, unscripted chance to play a significant role in each episode and across the series. The possibilities of chance contribute to suspense about what happens next that is akin to the pleasure of scripted fiction. Furthermore, chance extends into the production and reception of the show. Although castaways are carefully selected and diverse attributes are combined to generate drama, the producers cannot predict how the contestants will behave during the game. In *Survivor*'s first season, its unpredictability allowed castaways to challenge the production for control of the program's direction and mission. Although the production gave in to the castaways in some areas, the producers ultimately devised strategies that would allow them to regain and maintain control of the program. In the reception of *Survivor*, prediction is promoted and encouraged as fans and former castaways try to predict outcomes in magazines, on TV shows, and on the Internet. Part of the pleasure of imagining scenarios for what happens next on *Survivor* is the fact that the activity of prediction is inherently uncertain—"expect the unexpected."

The Survivor *Hybrid*

> You have no idea the number of people far more experienced than I who told me that I needed to choose whether I was making a drama or an adventure or a game show. That I couldn't have that combination—that it really wouldn't work.
> —Mark Burnett[3]

In its assessment of *Survivor*'s production values, *Variety* aligns the program with episodic drama rather than reality TV: "Burnett knew American viewers expect top-notch production values in prime-time programs, so he eschewed the cheap-is-better convention of most reality shows and gave *Survivor* a virtually cinematic look that made the show look as good as (if not better than) the typical network drama." Indeed, the logistics of production justify Burnett's description of *Survivor* as "epic." The opening of *Survivor 1: Borneo* used "seven hours of nonstop shooting coverage, one take, live, 23 crew members." *Survivor*'s reality superproduction is paired

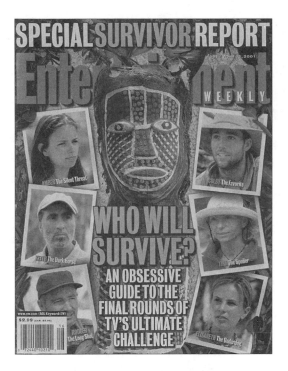

This magazine cover capitalizes on the pleasure of trying to predict the uncertain outcome of *Survivor*. *Entertainment Weekly*, 15 April 2001.

with a high-concept genre strategy. In *Survivor*'s recombination, each genre interacts with the others. Games and adventure, on their own, may not necessarily produce drama among the participants. *Survivor*'s unpredictability and pleasure come about as game collides with adventure and drama.[4]

Quoted in a *Variety* article on reality TV producers, NBC Entertainment President Garth Ancier observes, "In scripted programming, the horse that pulls the cart is the writer. But in reality, it's all about the producer." The *Survivor* hybrid of drama/adventure/game evolved from "method producer" Burnett's previous experiences with adventure television, nonfictional programs that foreground the impact of nature on people. In his advocacy of the *Survivor* hybrid, Burnett asserts that the popularity of adventure programming derives from basic human needs and contemporary lifestyle preferences. He imagines the audience to have "an innate desire to connect with the great outdoors" and "an innate desire to be adventurers." In preparing his pitch for the Emmy-nominated *Eco-Challenge: The Expedition Race* (1995–present), Burnett cited market research about the adventure lifestyle and its potential lure to the surrogate adventurer television viewer: "Family travel adventures . . . were becoming enormously popular even as hotel rooms in traditional destinations were going begging. This new trend was a lifestyle shift instead of a short-term travel phenomenon." Thus, the U.S. television market seemed primed for a program like *Survivor* in which North Americans seek adventure in exotic locations with global politics rendered invisible.[5]

Various production decisions on *Eco-Challenge* reveal how Burnett came to accentuate the dramatic potential of adventure situations in *Survivor.* In producing *Eco-Challenge,* Burnett found drama (conflict, emotion, suspense) in the relationships among Eco-Challenge team members. Burnett describes his self-discovery as a producer: "I didn't belong in a purely documentary world, I belonged in the dramatic world." He parted ways with the Discovery Channel, whose mission was more focused on nature documentary than the potential for interpersonal drama in the race, and took *Eco-Challenge* to USA Network. Unlike the Race Gauloises, in which Burnett raced and on which *Eco-Challenge* is based, *Eco-Challenge* insisted on mixed-gender teams ("In *Eco-Challenge,* the mountains, rivers, and forest are equal-opportunity punishers"). Similarly, "when MTV balked at airing another *Eco-Challenge* without a stipulation that all competitors be between 18 and 25," Burnett pitched the series to other networks. His experience with *Eco-Challenge* led to the casting dynamics of *Survivor,* whose diverse demographics of age, race, sexuality, and gender intensify the relationships between participants. The sixteen castaways are placed in wilderness conditions that figure prominently in the tension of the adventure—Burnett even asserts that "location is the seventeenth character on *Survivor.*"[6]

In *Survivor,* the castaways play layers of games. The Reward and Immunity Challenges severely limit the individual's scope of action through sets of highly specific rules, and are immediately recognizable as traditional games and sporting contests. Despite the critical importance of these games, when the castaways refer to "playing the game," they are not referring to the individual challenges but the overarching game of *Survivor* itself—whose objective is to "outwit, outplay, outlast" the other players. This larger game allows each individual enormous scope of action, but it too has its rules. The castaways are restricted to a remote location with a hostile environment; every three days, a tribe must submit to a Tribal Council and vote one of its members out of the game; one person has immunity and cannot be voted off; and so forth.

The rules of the *Survivor* game include unscripted chance. Subject to *Survivor*'s rules, its players enjoy the freedom to act as they see fit. The outcomes of the show are authentically unpredictable in the sense that no one is in a position to know what is going to happen. Although *Survivor*'s studied use of sporting phrases ("playing field," "game," "final four") is obviously self-conscious, it is also remarkably legitimate. *Survivor* has an essential need for faith in the game and the assumption that the program isn't fixed. In her 2001 lawsuit against CBS, *Survivor 1: Borneo* contestant and attorney Stacey Stillman claimed that she was voted out in the third Tribal Council because "Mr. Burnett 'breached my agreement' by deliberately manipulating the outcome of the tribal voting to banish her from the island." In covering the story, *Electronic Media* makes a crucial observation about the need for faith in the reality game show:

> What makes us watch these shows is the belief that what we are seeing, despite the forced situations and the tireless editing for dramatic impact, is real. Should Ms. Stillman's accusation turn out to be true, *Survivor* and others in the genre face a confidence crisis that could alienate viewers. The reality audience isn't the "Smackdown!" audience; if viewers get the impression the action is fake, they'll be voting themselves off the island in droves.

Indeed, the industrial and social trauma of the 1950s quiz show scandals convincingly demonstrates that the power and popularity of reality programming depends on the authenticity of the contrived reality. As Jeremy Butler remarks, some nonfictional programs "invite us to suspend our distrust of television's 'devious' ways. For their impact, these programs depend on our belief in the television producer's nonintervention." If the outcomes are found to be fixed, then a social and televisual contract with the audience will have been broken.[7]

Where the *Survivor* hybrid diverges from traditional game shows and sporting events is in the mutability of certain rules. In *Survivor 3: Africa*, the producers suddenly shuffled tribal membership, apparently to prevent the show from becoming too predictable. In one tribe, a faction was systematically eliminating their rival faction; the shuffle effectively stopped

that strategy. *Survivor*'s producers have attempted to rationalize this mutability as a sort of metarule ("expect the unexpected"), and they did a random shuffle of castaways in *Survivor 4: Marquesas.* As seasons go on, castaways demonstrate more awareness of "how to play the game," and *Survivor* reveals the hand of the producer refining and maintaining the
uncertainty of the playing field. While fiction hopes to provide the certainty of suspense and conflict between characters, *Survivor* is structured
to elicit and intensify drama without actually scripting it. *Survivor*'s reality
becomes dramatic through the careful casting of the contestants, circumstances and environment of the playing field, rules of the game, physical
and mental challenges, and (of course) Tribal Councils. On top of these
carefully engineered circumstances, "Tribal Chief" Probst asks questions
that spotlight the castaways' various fears, hopes, and machinations. The
Survivor production team has a word for all of this: "dramality"—"that
convergence of drama and reality" where drama is engendered by the real
events.[8]

In *Survivor* lore, a famous example of dramality occurred in *Survivor 1:
Borneo.* The producers pushed for melodrama by constructing a Reward
Challenge that allowed the castaways a small degree of contact with family
and loved ones. The castaways were told they would compete in an
archery contest for the prize of watching a videotape from home. Castaway Jenna, yearning for news of her two young daughters, was desperate
to win the challenge and practiced for it obsessively. At the Reward Challenge, each castaway was permitted to view only one minute of their
videotape. The winner of the archery contest would be allowed to view the
entire tape. Jenna was stunned and her spirit broken when she realized
there was no tape for her to watch. In the *Inside the Phenomenon* documentary, Probst recalls the value of this unscripted twist: "One of the most
poignant and most delicious moments was when Jenna's video didn't
show up. This was good television and I relished the chance to be the one
to deliver it, but how heartbreaking is this?"[9] Each subsequent *Survivor* series has included a similar Reward Challenge intended to tug at the hearts
of audiences, although never with such dramatic effect.

Survivor's "three-act structure" derives from the structure of the overall
game (tribe versus tribe; merger; final survivor), which seems calculated to
maximize emotional and interpersonal tensions. The first four seasons of
Survivor began by subjecting the castaways to a supremely disorienting introduction to their new reality, a race against time and a confrontation
with physical adversity.[10] In *Survivor 1: Borneo,* the castaways had just two

minutes to throw their possessions overboard, into the China Sea. Each tribe then maneuvered its raft of supplies to its respective beach—an effort that required hours of paddling and/or swimming. "Act One" goes on to pit tribe versus tribe in Reward and Immunity Challenges. Burnett relishes the drama: "By the end of Act One . . . life has been forged in the wilderness and stasis prevails."[11]

"Act Two" ruptures that stasis as the tribes merge, pitting the surviving castaways against each other in a free-for-all competition. Attributes that were valued in Act One (strength, athletic prowess) often become liabilities in Act Two because the castaway who possesses them is perceived as a strong competitor, a threat, someone to be eliminated. The words that Burnett uses to describe Act Two are compellingly dramatic: "friction . . . paranoia . . . power . . . intimidate the meek."[12] When stasis is ruptured on *Survivor,* the result is intense emotions and psychological states.

"Act Three" comprises the final week of *Survivor* and culminates in the last Tribal Council. This council may conclude the game by determining the ultimate winner of $1 million. But the jury members' sometimes-raw speeches about betrayal and integrity demonstrate that the final Tribal Council exacerbates the dramatic tensions that have been opened in the previous "acts." Some issues are put to rest in the "postgame" interview show, hosted by Bryant Gumbel for four seasons and by Probst for season five. *Survivor* does not attempt to reach narrative closure for each season, however. In the postgame show, *Survivor* reaffirms the reality and dramality of the game. The first castaway voted off is asked how it felt (some express bitterness, some relief, and some admit to not playing the game well). Key dramatic points in each season are kept alive, such as betrayal (Jerry's allegations about Kel eating beef jerky on *Survivor 2: Australian Outback*) and sexual tensions (Ted to Ghandia on *Survivor 5: Thailand*: "I never found you attractive.").

Some former castaways appear on television and in print commenting on the current *Survivor* game (as experts) or Emmy fashions (as ordinary people). Most recede from the spotlight. Unlike fiction, where writers can produce a happy ending for characters or an ambiguous open ending, the *Survivor* production maintains an aftermath for its castaways, thereby extending the popular life of each game and season.

Uncertainty due to Chance

You cannot predict how human beings will react in a strange, unfamiliar peer group situation plus unfamiliar harsh environment.

—Mark Burnett[13]

Unpredictability is fundamental to the series design and narrative pleasure of *Survivor*. Some aspects of the show are predictable: the sun will set and rise the next day; there will be hardships, challenges, and votes; Probst will referee Tribal Councils; and so on. Although the castaways' situation is contrived (that is, designed by the producers), one convention of the program is that castaway actions are unscripted and therefore not completely predictable. Unlike scripted entertainment, no one—neither producers nor crew, not even the castaways themselves—could know how the relationships within the game would evolve. With each episode of the series, one person is voted off. As the game goes on, the remaining relationships and castaway strategies become better known to the viewer. With this knowledge comes a presumed increase in ability to predict who will be voted off next, yet it never becomes certainty. No matter how much one knows, genuine chance is fundamental to *Survivor* and a source of its invitation to pleasure.

The role of chance in the *Survivor* hybrid is different from that in scripted productions. Some studies of film have explored how notions of chance and game may function in narrative and to produce audience pleasure. In Kristin Thompson's analysis of André Bazin's essay on the "illusion of chance" in *Bicycle Thieves,* she finds that "chance and peripheral events constitute a disproportionate amount of the film," but they are countered by "priming devices." That is, "the film provides a very clear-cut series of deadlines, appointments, and dialogue hooks that keep us oriented at all times, no matter how far the action digresses or how abruptly it shifts." In his study of Alfred Hitchcock's films, Thomas M. Leitch uses the concept of the two-person game played by Hitchcock with his audience as a metaphor for the process of watching a Hitchcock movie. Like Thompson, Leitch acknowledges the need for rules to contain chance, for "contractual limits to which the audience freely and knowingly subscribes" in an implied contract between the author of a fictional work and the audience. Both critics situate chance or game firmly within the containment structure of scripted narrative. Rather than producing uncertainty about outcomes, chance or game in fiction helps position the viewer more firmly within the narrative of the film.[14]

Rather than anchoring viewers, *Survivor* uses chance to place them in a space of uncertainty. In this regard, uncertainty is akin to the narrative concept of the gap between cause and effect. Narrative pleasure stems from the desire to know what will happen next, to have that gap opened and closed, again and again, until the resolution of the story. In scripted narrative, desire has particular and limited directions drawn from the story's characters and its conflict. In *Survivor,* unpredictability whets the desire to know what happens next, but how that gap will be closed is grounded in uncertainty due to chance. It isn't a scriptwriter who has already decided how the action will end but the players themselves and unscripted chance. This distinction between the pleasure of scripted entertainment and that of the *Survivor* hybrid can be seen as parallel to a familiar distinction in the discipline of statistics: the distinction between uncertainty due to chance and uncertainty due to ignorance.[15] The answer to what happens next in *Survivor* is based on uncertainty due to chance, while in fiction, the answer is based on uncertainty due to ignorance.

Uncertainty due to chance is associated with phenomena that are truly stochastic (that is, random). For statisticians, "chance" comprehends any phenomenon for which the outcome has some degree of uncertainty. Stochastic phenomena are not limited to situations that are completely random but include those that have some degree of predictability, in which some outcomes are more likely than others. For example, in the Belmont Stakes, we are uncertain about which horse will win, but we know that some horses are more likely to win than others. This uncertainty is quantified by the odds that each horse will win, and betting depends on such quantification. *Survivor* is like a horse race. Different castaways have different abilities (the odds are not equal), but only the competition itself will reveal what happens when these abilities collide (the outcome is uncertain). And of course, the outcome is also affected by unscripted chance events that cannot be foreseen: the favorite to win the 2002 Belmont Stakes stumbles as the horse leaves the gate; Michael falls into the fire in *Survivor 2: Australian Outback* and has to be airlifted out of the game.

In contrast, uncertainty due to ignorance describes a person's state of mind, the extent of knowledge, the strength of belief. For instance, suppose we ask Susan what will happen next in a Hitchcock film, *Vertigo,* after Scotty follows Madeleine up the tower. Susan could venture that Scotty will save Madeleine, that he would throw her off the tower, that she could fall. This is uncertainty due to ignorance, which Susan might attempt to quantify with a statement like, "I'm 80 percent certain Scotty will save her, but it's a Hitchcock film so she might fall." Susan might even make a friendly wager with J.J. that Scotty will save Madeleine, but no bookie will give her odds. The uncertainty is all in Susan's mind. The filmmakers already know how the film will end.

To put a finer point on this distinction, it is obvious that for the television audience watching the episodes each week, uncertainty about *Survivor's* outcome is uncertainty due to ignorance. The production team already knows what happens in each episode and how it will end. Yet chance played a crucial role in constructing the edited product that airs. Although this perspective is correct, it fails to describe the quality of the viewing experience. Viewers are asked to accept the *Survivor* time frame as if the events were occurring in the present and not in the past. In this regard, watching *Survivor* is like watching the Olympics or Emmy Awards in tape delay. Even for viewers who maintain a critical distance and awareness of production (that is, how editing may be directing suspicion toward the machinations of particular castaways), it is necessary to enter into the "present" of the episode to engage the pleasure of uncertainty due to chance. As Thompson and Leitch imply, scripted fiction can invite the viewer to suspend awareness that there are filmmakers and/or screenwriters working to produce the experience of the film. In the creation of *Survivor's* episodic experience, genuine chance is as powerful a force as the production team.

In its invitation to prediction, *Survivor* is more like a horse race than fiction. *Survivor* foregrounds the role of uncertainty due to chance in a way that fiction cannot. At the core of the program's narrative is the question of who will be voted out when. If we think of the outcome of the *Survivor* game as the order in which the 16 castaways are voted out, then the possible outcomes number 16!, pronounced "sixteen factorial" and defined by the formula,

$$16! = 16 \times 15 \times 14 \times \ldots \times 3 \times 2 \times 1 = 20{,}922{,}789{,}888{,}000, \text{ roughly 21 trillion.}[16]$$

The possibilities become more manageable when *Survivor* is analyzed in three-day cycles or "evolutions," each containing an Immunity Challenge and a Tribal Council. A simple example occurred in *Survivor 1: Borneo*. Initially, we know so little about the castaways that prediction is an exercise in futility. It would be ludicrous to attempt to predict which of 16!

possible outcomes will be realized. But suppose we pause as the first Tribal Council begins and try to predict its outcome. We know that the Tagi tribe must eliminate one of its eight members—a rather small number of possibilities to contemplate. Furthermore, we know that sixty-three-year-old Sonja fell in the Immunity Challenge, revealing her relative weakness in physical prowess. It's not difficult to predict that Sonja will be the first castaway voted off the island.

Trying to figure out what is going to happen is a source of *Survivor*'s pleasure. When there are too many possibilities, and no way of narrowing them down, so many outcomes can happen that prediction becomes overwhelming and ceases to be fun. With each episode, *Survivor* reduces the possible outcomes to a smaller and increasingly manageable number. The attributes and relationships of the remaining castaways become better known, allowing viewers to speculate about the castaways' actions and attempt predictions about what they will do next. This invitation to prediction runs through the books and ancillary products related to *Survivor*. Like major sporting events, *Survivor* has even spawned its own pregame show on MTV, on which panelists offer analyses such as the above.[17]

The official CBS website is heavily invested in prediction, devoting an entire section to viewer polls. The site maintains a "Who's Next Poll" (who will be voted off the island next week), a "Sole Survivor Poll" (who will be the sole survivor), and an archive that contains the results of each poll. The SurvivorAddicts.com site maintains numerous bulletin boards and chat rooms with threads such as "Critic's Corner," "Speculation," "Predictions," "Recaps," and "*Survivor* Gossip." The distinctions between prediction, speculation, and spoiling have to do with the extent to which one invests in the diegetic reality of *Survivor*. If one limits comments to information gleaned from the *Survivor* episodes, one engages in prediction. If one uses extradiegetic information (for example, analysis of promos for the upcoming episode of *Survivor*), one engages in speculation. If one uses information that is not generated by CBS's textual practices, such as a report that a castaway returned to the United States and had lost a lot of weight (thereby suggesting the castaway was in the game for a long time), one engages in spoiling (for instance, information from outside the diegetic world of the game can ruin the pleasure of prediction). Published before *Survivor 2: Australian Outback* aired, *Survivor II: The Field Guide* encouraged television audiences to engage in prediction. The book recounted the following anecdote about Richard Hatch, the legendary winner of *Survivor 1: Borneo*:

Eighteen days before [the Immunity Challenge involving Kelly, Rich, and Rudy], when the island still had half its original residents, that master schemer [Rich] had stood off-camera and told Probst exactly which individuals would be voted off all the way to the show's end—and in the proper order. He had not been wrong once.[18]

At that point in the game, there were 8 x 7 x 6 x 5 x 4 = 6,720 possible ways to progress from eight survivors to just three. Rich correctly predicted the one way that actually occurred. Had a crew member or viewer done so, it would have been uncanny. Rich's prediction may have been inspired. As a castaway, however, Rich had access to information, and as the maestro of the Tagi Alliance, he had the ability to influence events.

To help organize the viewer's predictions, the book includes a foldout "Play Along Pool" that allows up to seven players to chart their predictions for Tribal Councils one through fifteen. The instructions specify: "Before each Tribal Council, each player writes his/her guess for which castaway will be voted off in the space above. More than one player can vote for each castaway." The game awards points for correct guesses. The points are totaled to form a final score for each player. Interestingly, the number of points awarded varies with the difficulty of prediction. The first three Tribal Councils are each worth five points, the next three are each worth four points, and so on. As *Survivor* progresses, the number of points per Tribal Council decreases, suggesting that prediction will become easier (and therefore less valuable in terms of points) as the players accumulate information and the number of outcomes decreases.[19]

Even at season's end, though, when the outcomes should become most predictable, unscripted chance may intervene. The following analysis of the final Tribal Council of *Survivor 2: Australian Outback* is savvy about the winning strategy and would seem to be a plausible prediction:

> Colby, Keith, and Tina remain. There are six possible outcomes. Having won so many previous challenges, Colby seems like a good bet to win immunity. It appears that Tina is more popular than Keith, so Colby will eliminate Tina. It appears that Colby is more popular than Keith, so the jury will vote for Colby. Predicted order of elimination: Tina-Keith-Colby.

In fact, Colby did win immunity as predicted. The analysis assumes that Colby would pursue a strategy by which he would become the ultimate winner of the game. Thus, he would "play the game" and increase his chances of winning the million dollars by eliminating his friend, the popular Tina. In a choice between Colby and Keith, the savvy analyst predicts, Colby stands the better chance of winning. Yet that analysis is limited by the logic of the game, and does not allow for other and unpredictable values. Colby valued his alliance and friendship with Tina more than winning the game. In an unexpected move, Colby eliminated Keith, making the final choice between Tina and Colby. The jury of castaways selected Tina to win the $1 million prize. Observed order of elimination: Keith-Colby-Tina.

Compare the suspense of watching the finale unfold on *Survivor 2: Australian Outback* to that generated by a famous television event, the 1985 cliff-hanger of *Dynasty*. As Jane Feuer writes, "On the evening of the fall 1985 season premiere that would reveal the outcomes of the previous season's cliff-hanger (the Moldavian massacre), the lead story on the ABC-affiliate evening news in my local market concerned the way in which 'local citizens' had gathered to celebrate this event."[20] The outcome being celebrated was the revelation of the survivors of the Moldavian massacre. *Dynasty*'s producers and writers selected these survivors. Although the actors may have engaged in summer salary negotiations that could get their characters killed off, the characters did not "outwit, outplay, outlast" to determine which ones would return for the next season. Whether fiction or reality game, cliff-hanger outcomes are jealously guarded secrets that are absolutely critical to the pleasure of anticipation of what happens next. But in fiction, the pleasure of this suspense is a game with the producers based on uncertainty due to ignorance, not on uncertainty due to chance.

Survivor's invitation to participate in predicting who will be voted off next comes with a healthy skepticism about the authenticity of information in any episode. The edited version that becomes available to viewers is not an ethnographic attempt to document life in the tribes. There is an obvious need for editorial selection to meet the time constraints of episodic television, and the footage may provide false leads or cover up obvious leads to enhance the potential for viewer surprise at who is eliminated next. Thus, we can see that *Survivor* includes a degree of uncertainty due to ignorance. Yet the invitation of the program is not to outguess the editors and discover planted clues but to watch the remaining castaways manage through the game. To underscore the unscripted nature of *Survivor* and essential role of the castaways in creating the action, the show offers viewers a documentary device, a form of direct address.

As Jeremy Butler notes, "Most narrative television programs do not acknowledge the viewer . . . characters in narrative TV address one another. They are sealed within their narrative or diegetic worlds." *Survivor* opens its diegetic world to the viewer with a variation of the personal diary. These confessional videos of castaways function as the anecdote does in Barthes's description: "whatever furthers the solution of the riddle; the revelation of fate." *Survivor*'s personal diary anecdotes are like secret correspondence with the viewer, providing information about the game that the other castaways may not have. On the surface, the anecdotes offer viewers the delight of knowing something the other castaways don't (as when a castaway admits that they must betray another). The personal diaries, however, may not contain accurate clues for predicting outcomes. Burnett reports that as *Survivor 1: Borneo* progressed, the castaways began to dissemble, staging conversations about strategy that were intended to mislead the production crew.[21] Part of the game in the first season, unknown to the home viewer at the time, was the challenge the castaways gave the producers over control of the program.

Managing Uncertainty

The green [outwit flag] would stand for the production crew, desperately trying to stay one mental step ahead of the increasingly-brilliant castaways.
—Mark Burnett[22]

For better or worse, the tag line "expect the unexpected" describes the work environment of the production as well as the game played by the castaways. *Survivor*'s production team has to respond to uncertainty on the playing field (weather, storms, snakes, insects, jellyfish) and to castaways who, in *Survivor 1: Borneo,* challenged the production for control of the show. The host plays a crucial role in implementing strategies to contain uncertainty and make it productive for *Survivor*'s mission of dramality. Probst gives instructions to castaways and referees games. He manages castaways when their behavior threatens the mission of the program.

Survivor selects a cast of sixteen people with traits and attributes, but it cannot create characters to specification. The diverse demographics of the castaways suggest the producers try to select people who will lead to good drama. ("One reason Stacey had been selected for the show was her volatility.") In *Survivor II: The Ultimate Guide,* a chapter on casting *Sur-*

vivor 2: Australian Outback presents each castaway with a photo, first name, age, and occupation. That is followed by comments from the casting director and the *Survivor* psychologist (Dr. Richard Levak). Their remarks invite speculation on what the individual castaways will do when they play *Survivor,* on how they will potentially enter into dramatic relationships with other castaways ("Rodger is not used to deferring to anyone younger or female"; "Kimmi will manipulate the guys in order to advance"). After identifying the individual castaways of season two, the book goes on to present "Sixteen Strategies for Winning *Survivor,*" suggesting the sixteen castaways that form the complement of each season of the show. Each strategy is generated by a form of typage: the entertainer, leader, flirt, determined victim (aka, underdog), professor, zealot, mom, athlete, wild and crazy guy (or girl), quiet one, everybody's friend, feral child, introvert, redneck, slacker, or snake. Each character type has positive and negative strategic attributes reminiscent of personality charts in women's magazine articles or descriptions of astrological signs.[23]

The process of identifying the combination of personalities for *Survivor 2: Australian Outback* castaways began with 49,000 initial applicants. Casting director Lynn Spiegel Spillman, "one of just a handful of people in Hollywood who solely recruit regular people to play themselves on TV," winnowed the cohort down to 800 finalists, who were then screened by Burnett. Forty-eight were invited to Los Angeles for "an intensive two weeks of interviews" conducted by the *Survivor* production team and CBS network executives. Burnett relishes the scope and depth of the interviews: "Potential contestants were grilled relentlessly. No question—none!—was off limits: sex, drugs, you name it." In a separate process, the 48 were given psychological and medical testing by the *Survivor* medical team.[24]

Although the producers must know the final sixteen extremely well, even they cannot predict how the castaways will behave when thrust into the adventure game environment. In some ways, the castaways' situation is like that of game show contestants and talk show guests as described by Jeremy Butler: they "must come to . . . the space of a television reality" rather than being observed in their own reality. In entering the television reality, the castaways and contestants are "subjected immediately to the medium's rules and conventions." *Survivor*'s castaways, however, are not subjected to rules that "rigidly limit improvisation by situating the social actor within a tightly structured competition."[25] The castaways have greater scope of action than their game show counterparts.

Survivor 1: Borneo castaways challenged the constructs of the game. The production was faced with a variety of what Burnett and Probst depict as "mutiny" situations that required the producers to outwit, outplay, and outlast the castaways. Delays in setting up Immunity Challenges affected the budget and also the willing mood of the game players. Burnett recalls his concerns: "*Survivor*'s stars were standing in equatorial sun and rain. Making them wait not only angered them, it was rude. If they perceived us as [lacking respect for them], they could band together, mutiny, and become the puppeteers."[26] Clearly, unfettered castaways could pose a threat to the production. Yet the producers' awareness of the castaways and their negotiations with them can be considered a productive collaborative as well as creative relationship that is fundamental to the production of *Survivor*.

In *Survivor 1: Borneo,* Kelly's Malaysian cantina reward resulted from the production responding to castaway expectations for greater rewards. After Sean won a spectacular reward, a night on a yacht with his father flown in from the United States, the next reward was to be a single bottle of beer, the only one on the island. In the minutes leading up to that challenge, Burnett learned that castaways expected a new car for the reward. In *Survivor: Inside the Phenomenon,* a "making-of" documentary, Burnett and Probst good-naturedly relate the story:

> The rewards we provided to the castaways got continually bigger and bigger. . . . We made a mistake because we followed the yacht reward with a simple reward, which was a bottle of beer. While that's a great reward, it wasn't enough for them anymore. Sean had just been on a yacht and you'd better up the ante. We had heard that they were going to maybe mutiny and say, "You know what? We're not doin' it." I realized I had a problem. The one day the sponsors from the show, that make this show possible, are on the island, we have a potential mutiny.

What neither television audiences nor Kelly knew at the time was that the production made a last-minute decision to boost the reward to a night with Jeff at a local bar. This required the art department to transform the production compound into a Malaysian bar in the span of several hours.[27]

Reward Challenge adjustments can be seen as routine accommodations as *Survivor* establishes its production protocols during its first season. One of the castaways, however, presented a serious challenge to the mission of

Survivor and pushed the boundaries of the game. Greg's challenge illustrates the freedom of action enjoyed by unscripted castaways, the fundamental unpredictability of the show, and the strategic role played by the host in establishing and maintaining *Survivor*'s tone and level of drama.

Burnett recounts that Greg "was proving a master of mental manipulation. His goal was to control the pace of the island. To that end, he took to stalking camera crews when they trekked through the jungle. He delighted in leaping from bushes and scaring people . . . and recit[ing] rambling monologues." In Greg and other Gen-Xers in the Pagong tribe, Burnett and Probst perceived a threat that *Survivor* could devolve into parody. Obviously, the production had to play by the rules and could not intervene to influence the vote. They would have to wait for the castaways to vote Greg off the island. This was unlikely to happen any time soon because Greg had good relationships with other castaways.[28] *Survivor* used conversations at the Tribal Council as a means of controlling the castaways.

More than anywhere else, the Tribal Council brings together the elements of the *Survivor* hybrid. The Tribal Council is crucial to the dramality, the game, and the adventure. It is where Rudy found out Richard is gay; where a stunned cast and crew saw Gretchen voted off; where castaways answer Jeff's probing questions. Burnett reports that Greg "refus[ed] to accept the gravity of the Tribal Council. . . . Greg mocked it . . . [it] seemed absurd to him. . . . [His] nonstop schtick was designed to make him the center of attention instead of Jeff." Greg's disrespect for the Tribal Council threatened a key element of the show. *Survivor* host Probst had to minimize the challenge to the Tribal Council: "If Jeff didn't get it right the show might descend into parody, or worse, anarchy."[29]

The first Tribal Council of *Survivor 1: Borneo,* where Sonia was voted off, achieved the tense dramality Burnett sought. In contrast, the second Tribal Council (where B. B. was voted off) was irreverent and raucous, raising the possibility of viewer ridicule.[30]

The production team met to discuss how to regain control or "the final television show wouldn't resemble the reality of a deserted island so much as a peek into the lives of a dozen spoiled Americans." The producers called on the genres of game and adventure to help restore dramality and the *Survivor* hybrid. They decided to make the Immunity Challenges more difficult so that "the reality of *Survivor* would grow deeper and deeper, no matter how hard Greg tried to pretend it was absurd." Because "only time on the island . . . would curb Pagong's arrogance," they would "let the island do its work." The production team huddled on how to handle the third Tribal Council. Burnett decided to accentuate the drama as much as possible:

> I wanted Jeff to ask deeper, tougher questions of the castaways, not letting them dodge anything. I wanted to coordinate the logistics of the Council so that everything went off in a crisp, punctual fashion. I knew that keeping to a schedule would accentuate our control.

The production had a plan that relied on the *Survivor* host to pull it off in the improvisational question and answer of the Tribal Council.[31] Unscripted chance intervened. A violent tropical storm threatened to undermine the game plan for the crucial third Tribal Council.[32] Nevertheless, the production trumped both the castaways and the storm. Probst established his authority over discussions at the Tribal Council, and the crew filmed the Tribal Council in extreme weather conditions. One element of chance (the storm) became part of the dramality while the other (Greg's challenge) was diminished. Yet Greg's irreverence reemerged at the final Tribal Council, where his decision between Richard and Kelly was based on a classic game of chance—"guess a number from one to ten"—instead of the anticipated evaluations of a castaway's loyalty or betrayal and performance as a tribe member.

One of the key mechanisms used to control the castaways' challenge was the *Survivor* host. In important ways, the host acts to constrain the uncertainty and keep it within the limits prescribed by the series design. The role of the host is to maintain *Survivor*'s credibility, from the first episode when he receives the castaways in a handoff from Burnett (who remains off camera) through the Immunity Challenges and Tribal Councils. To a greater degree than a game show host or sportscaster, the *Survivor* host enters into the events that he is moderating.[33]

The *Survivor* host decides strategy at Tribal Councils to protect the dramality and suspense, and at the final Tribal Council, "to delineate the heroes and villains, the proud and regretful." As Burnett describes Probst's preparation for Tribal Councils,

> [Probst] spend[s] his spare hours studying tapes of their beach life . . . [preparing to ask] detailed questions about their relationships. He wanted to know who was vulnerable, who was strong, who was clueless about their fate. Of course, he already knew the answer. And each tribe member already

knew the answer. . . . *Survivor* was all about keeping secrets. Chief Jeff's job was to focus a laser beam on those secrets, bringing them into the light.

At Tribal Councils, the *Survivor* host is expected to tap into castaways' emotions, desires, and situations, working them for dramatic effect.[34]

The host must also exercise restraint to avoid intervening in the outcome of the game. The defining element of the way *Survivor 1: Borneo* unfolded was the secret Tagi Alliance, a group of tribal members who committed to support each other early in the game. The alliance membership was known to the production crew and viewers (through the personal diaries), but not to the other castaways. At one Tribal Council, alliance member Sue admitted the existence of the group and asserted her leadership. This opened the door for Jeff to ask for a response from Rich, the creator of the Tagi Alliance. But "Jeff didn't go to Rich. . . . Chief Jeff knew he [Rich] wouldn't be smug about Sue's admission. Something like that could crush the Alliance." Probst, in his ordinary capacity of Tribal Council host asking probing questions, could easily have revealed the composition of the alliance to the other tribe members, thereby substantially skewing the game's outcome.[35]

This chapter has explored the role that uncertainty due to chance plays in the design, production, and pleasure of the reality game series *Survivor*. In linking the viewer activities of outcome prediction and narrative desire, we find that mathematical as well as narrative processes are both involved in the experience of *Survivor*'s reality game hybrid. Mathematical methods have value for understanding the television experience, when unscripted chance is a fundamental component of the program. The *Survivor* mantra to "expect the unexpected" is more than an exploitation promo tag. It is from the unexpected that both outcome prediction and narrative pleasure are derived.

NOTES

1. John Nash became a familiar figure in popular culture through a best-seller and biopic, *A Beautiful Mind,* that concentrated on his schizophrenia. Nash is best known to mathematicians and economists for introducing the concept of what is now referred to as the Nash equilibrium, for which he shared the 1994 Nobel Prize in economics. In 1950, Nash showed that a game, in which the players behave according to certain "rational" rules, necessarily has a unique solution. Whether

these rules apply to *Survivor* and the actual behavior of castaways is a subject for future research.

2. Roland Barthes, *The Pleasure of the Text,* trans. Richard Miller (New York: Hill and Wang, 1975).

3. Cited in Jennie Phipps, "The Man behind *Survivor;* From Paratrooper to Nanny to Reality-TV Svengali, Burnett Is Hot in Hollywood," *Electronic Media,* 19 February 2001, 16.

4. Josef Adalian, "Producers Wield Power on TV's 'Real World,'" *Variety,* 25 September 2000, 1. About *Survivor 3: Africa,* Mark Burnett declares, "More than ever, I wanted my television show to look like a movie" (*Dare to Succeed: How to Survive and Thrive in the Game of Life* [New York: Hyperion, 2001], 206). "The way I planned to shoot *Survivor* bore more comparison, logistically, to a feature film than a television show," he also notes (Mark Burnett, *Survivor II: The Field Guide* [New York: TV Books, 2001], 151). Moreover, boasts Burnett, "My *Survivor* would be bigger, more dramatic, and more epic than any nonfiction television ever seen" (*Dare to Succeed,* 6). See also commentary by Mark Burnett, *Survivor: Inside the Phenomenon* (Season One DVD documentary, 2000).

Survivor received two 2001 Emmy Awards—for outstanding nonfiction program as well as outstanding sound mixing for nonfictional programming. It was nominated for four other 2001 Emmys in the categories of outstanding cinematography for nonfictional programming, outstanding main title theme music, outstanding picture editing for nonfictional programming, and outstanding technical direction, camerawork, video for a miniseries, movie, or special. The success of *Survivor* led directly to the production of Jerry Bruckheimer's *Amazing Race* for CBS. To create *Amazing Race* (described by Les Moonves as "*Survivor* on speed"), eleven camera crews follow teams around the world. See James Frutkin, "An Eye for Pop Culture," *MediaWeek,* 30 July 2001.

5. Adalian, "Producers Wield Power on TV's 'Real World,'" 1. Burnett's personal background includes adventurous pursuits (British paratrooper; the Race Gauloises). In his descriptions of producing television during raging weather or enduring terrifying turbulence in a small airplane with the castaways, Burnett refers to himself as a "method producer" (*Dare to Succeed,* 154). In-text Burnett cites are from *Dare to Succeed,* 184, 203–5, 87–88, and *Survivor II,* 145–46.

From ecochallenge.com: "Eco-Challenge is an expedition race. Each team of four, comprising men and women, races nonstop for 6 to 12 days, 24 hours a day, over a rugged 300 mile course using mountain biking, river rafting, horseback riding, mountaineering and fixed ropes, kayaking and navigation skills. The first team to cross the finish line together, in full complement, is the winner. If a team loses a member due to illness, fatigue, injury or a team disagreement, they are disqualified. Only teams that can work together as friends have any hope of reaching the finish line."

Documentary maker Beverly Seckinger has commented that the real survivors are the native peoples whose countries have been the subject of U.S. foreign policy and are now locations for adventure. Her experimental documentary video *Planet in My Pocket* (1995) is a satiric parody of First World adventurers exploring the world.

6. Burnett, *Dare to Succeed,* 127–28, 100, 106–7, 175.

7. "Suit against CBS: It's the Reality, Stupid," *Electronic Media,* 12 February 2001, 8. CBS countersued charging that Stillman violated a confidentiality agreement (see "CBS Sues *Survivor* Cast-Off," *Broadcasting and Cable,* 26 February 2001, 10; and "CBS Wins *Survivor* Round," *Los Angeles Business Journal,* 28 May 2001, 37). Jeremy Butler, *Television: Critical Methods and Applications,* 2d ed. (Mahwah, N.J.: Laurence Erlbaum Associates, 2002), 68.

8. Burnett, *Survivor II,* 25; see also Burnett, *Dare to Succeed,* 147.

9. Commentary by Jeff Probst, *Survivor: Inside the Phenomenon* (Season One DVD documentary, 2000). See also Mark Burnett, "Day Twenty-Three," in *Survivor: The Ultimate Game* (New York: TV Books, 2000), 139–45.

10. The fifth season had a different beginning. On the first day, the castaways gathered on a beach. The two oldest castaways took turns selecting members for their tribe.

11. Burnett, *Survivor II,* 152–54.

12. Ibid., 154.

13. Commentary by Mark Burnett, *Survivor: Inside the Phenomenon.*

14. Kristin Thompson, *Breaking the Glass Armor: Neoformalist Film Analysis* (Princeton, N.J.: Princeton University Press, 1988), 204, 208; and Thomas M. Leitch, *Find the Director and Other Hitchcock Games* (Athens: University of Georgia Press, 1991), 10.

15. Both types of uncertainty can be expressed in the language of probability: frequentist probability quantifies uncertainty due to chance, while subjective probability quantifies uncertainty due to ignorance. Frequentists usually confine themselves to the former, whereas Bayesians insist that all uncertainty should be quantified probabilistically. See William H. Kruskal and Judith M. Tanur, eds., *International Encyclopedia of Statistics,* vols. 1 and 2 (New York: Free Press, 1978).

16. The role that chance plays in *Survivor* resembles the role that chance plays in a sporting event. For example, the National Collegiate Athletic Association (NCAA) men's basketball tournament begins with sixty-four teams that will play a six-round elimination tournament. The tournament involves a total of sixty-three games (that is, a person attempting to predict the entire tournament would have to specify the winners of sixty-three games), so there are

$2^{63} = 2 \times 2 \times \ldots \times 2 \times 2 = 9,223,372,036,854,775,808$ possible tournament outcomes.

In neither NCAA basketball nor *Survivor* is the outcome scripted. Both involve uncertainty due to chance. Just as fans bet on which team will win/lose in the next round of the NCAA tournament after observing the results of the previous round, so might some persons bet on which castaway will be eliminated at the next Tribal Council. As both of these events progress, the number of unresolved possibilities decreases and becomes manageable. Both *Survivor* and the NCAA have a Final Four, the basketball variant admitting $2^3 = 8$ possible outcomes, and the *Survivor* variant admitting $4! = 24$ possible outcomes.

17. In the *Survivor* board game, players roll a die, draw cards, answer trivia questions, and solve puzzles. Curiously, the game does not involve negotiations between players, as in Monopoly. Both Monopoly and the *Survivor* show emphasize negotiating strategies, and both involve strategic concepts like immunity and alliances. Trading in immunity and forming partnerships are strategies suggested by Jay Walker and Jeff Lehman, *One Thousand Ways to Win Monopoly Games* (New York: Dell Publishing Company, 1975).

18. Burnett, *Survivor II*, 13.

19. "Play Along Pool" insert, in Burnett, *Survivor II*.

20. Jane Feuer, *Seeing through the Eighties: Television and Reaganism* (Durham, N.C.: Duke University Press, 1995), 136.

21. Butler, *Television*, 64; Barthes, *Pleasure of the Text*, 11; and Burnett, *Survivor: The Ultimate Game*, 204–5.

22. Burnett, *Survivor: The Ultimate Game*, 78.

23. Ibid., 45; and Burnett, *Survivor II*, 74–85, 120–30.

24. "A Listing of L.A.'s Biggest Players in Reality TV Game," *Los Angeles Business Journal*, 11 September 2000, 37; and Burnett, *Survivor II*, 28. For clips from the interviews, see the *Survivor* DVD.

25. Butler, *Television*, 83, 66.

26. Burnett, *Survivor: The Ultimate Game*, 183–84.

27. Commentary by Burnett and Probst, *Survivor: Inside the Phenomenon*. See also Burnett, "Day Thirty-Four," in *Survivor: The Ultimate Game*, 197–202. *Survivor* has seen an increasing commercialization of the rewards that undercuts the constructed reality of the show. The challenges were far more compelling (that is, the dramality was more intense) when the castaways competed for the pleasure of a piece of fruit than for branded vacations and SUVs.

28. Burnett, *Survivor: The Ultimate Game*, 109. For a description of Greg's relationship with other tribe members, see especially 50, 113.

29. Ibid., 50–51, 57.

30. Burnett, *Dare to Succeed*, 151.

31. Burnett, *Survivor: The Ultimate Game*, 53–54, 57, and *Dare to Succeed*, 152; and commentary by Probst, *Survivor: Inside the Phenomenon*.

32. Burnett, *Dare to Succeed*, 154–55.

33. Burnett, *Survivor: The Ultimate Game*, 14, *Dare to Succeed*, 185, and *Survivor: The Ultimate Game*, 54.

34. Burnett, *Survivor: The Ultimate Game*, 208, 79.

35. Ibid., 179.

5

Extraordinarily Ordinary

The Osbournes *as "An American Family"*

Derek Kompare

On 5 March 2002, on MTV, a voice-over invited us to "meet the perfect American family." A teenage girl is seen throwing a ball at her brother's crotch; their mother tells the camera that she's not Mother Theresa, and then tells the children to "shut the fuck up and go to bed." We see "the son" making annoying noises, and "the daughter" dismissing other people's opinions about her hair. Finally, we're introduced to "the dad," who screams "rock and roll!" at the camera, and is shown in a quick montage of onstage and offstage behavior: gyrating onstage, getting out of airplanes, watching TV, walking the dog. The opening sequence ends with a shirtless dad telling his family, "I love you all . . . I love you more than life itself . . . but you're all fucking mad!"

Welcome to the Osbourne family, the "perfect American family" of MTV's *The Osbournes*. Dad (Ozzy) is a veteran heavy metal rocker in rehabilitation from years of excess; Mom (Sharon) is his longtime wife/manager and the unyielding household authority; Son (Jack) is an "oddball" at school and plays with knives; Daughter (Kelly) throws fits, teases her colorful hair, and strategizes about staying out past curfew without getting caught. Even in an age of constant media hype, the enormous notoriety of *The Osbournes* in spring 2002 was surprising. By its fifth episode, it was MTV's all-time highest-rated regular series, capturing more than six million viewers weekly—numbers that the long-running reality pioneer *The Real World* had never attained. Moreover, the Osbournes' fame spread well beyond MTV as the series and family were the subjects of numerous articles, analyses, and interviews in the media throughout spring 2002.[1] While

The unconventional Osbourne family star in the first reality sitcom.

such coverage is not unprecedented for television families, it had been almost thirty years since a TV series centering on an *actual* family garnered this much attention in the mainstream media. The 1973 PBS documentary series *An American Family* featured the Loud family of Santa Barbara, California, who were subject to similar media and viewer interest as nearly a year of their lives unfolded in thirteen television episodes. Like the Osbournes, the Louds were featured on magazine covers and talk shows, quoted in reviews, and satirized in cartoons. As the title of their series indicated, they became an emblem for the "American family" of the early 1970s.

Both *An American Family* and *The Osbournes* were media phenomena. That is, they were idiosyncratic texts that commanded a sudden, high degree of attention during their initial runs, prompting discussions about family and television throughout the media and society. Although markedly "different" from regular television fare, however, both series still had to engage with established normative codes of genre and family in order to succeed. The operation of these normative codes reveals how much power they still hold, and how they are shrewdly used by newer techniques and approaches as a foundation of meanings from which to construct new texts. In tracing these familiar codes in these otherwise unique texts, we can understand how the categories of the "ordinary" and "extraordinary" are deployed in the pursuit of textual coherence and cultural significance.

While *An American Family* and *The Osbournes* are similar in many respects, they also have crucial differences. Foremost among these is the fact that the scandalous reaction to *An American Family* in 1973 did not materialize in regard to *The Osbournes* in 2002. In the early 1970s, *An American Family* was considered primarily as a manipulative sociological experiment in perpetual surveillance. The Louds themselves were generally seen by critics as either ciphers (i.e., symbols of the fallout of the 1960s), or, conversely, the victims of unscrupulous producers.[2] By contrast, in the media-saturated early 2000s, *The Osbournes* is hailed as a pinnacle of innovative television comedy, and the Osbourne family is celebrated for their hip parenting and let-it-all-hang-out media savvy.[3] The shifting mores of U.S. family life may explain part of this perception, but the changing parameters of media representation constitute a more decisive factor. That is, the question of how to represent a "real family" on television is answered quite differently in the 2000s than it was in the 1970s, as the normative boundaries of TV programming—particularly concerning the representation of "actualities": actual people and events—have changed considerably in the intervening years.

The very concept of a real television family points squarely to questions of "genre" and "family." Each category establishes limits within which programs, and depictions in general, must adhere to, or at least acknowledge, in order to succeed. Both *An American Family* and *The Osbournes* were conspicuously situated on the boundary between actuality and fiction, drawing established generic codes of reality from the former, and narrative and characterization from the latter. Each was widely touted as being the first of its particular hybrid genre: the "documentary soap opera" in the case of *An American Family,* and the "reality sitcom" for *The Osbournes.*[4] In both instances, a joint claim to reality and narration was made, promising an explicit as well as engrossing experience. Both series also purported to represent the family. The family has arguably been the primary normative concept governing human interaction since the beginning of recorded history, and its media representations have always been a matter of contention.[5] This has particularly been the case on television, perhaps the media form most suited to promoting and representing familial experience due to its domestic nature. Regardless of whether they are fictional or real, television families are sites of cultural anxieties, where the work of social cohesion is ritually enacted.[6] Despite differences between the series and in the families themselves, the Louds and Osbournes both performed the role of family on the national stage of television. It is important to note, however, that while the Louds achieved fame by becoming a TV family, the Osbournes had already gained some celebrity, via patriarch Ozzy's notorious career as a heavy metal performer.[7] Ozzy Osbourne is colloquially known as "the prince of darkness" for his theatrical performances—conveying standard heavy metal themes of gothic horror and, on occasion, biting the heads off of live animals—and lifestyle, which has included the requisite rock star litany of outrageous behavior and substance abuse. His famous physical and emotional excesses formed the basis for the representation of his family on television. Unlike the Louds, who were meant to represent an "every family" whose surface contentment hides emotional distance, the Osbournes were promoted as a specific "*anti*-family" whose visible eccentricities hid a reservoir of intimacy and affection. In keeping with turn-of-the-century reality TV codes, which center on the display of ignominious bodies, the Osbournes themselves literally embody this dichotomy of ordinary and extraordinary codes.

In this chapter, I will explore how normative discourses of television genre and family shaped both *An American Family* and *The Osbournes*. I will first trace how the terms "genre" and "family" are linked through television, and how each has been used to shape the medium's normative codes. Next, I will examine the representation of actuality on television and describe how codes of "documentary" have largely ceded to "reality" via a concentration on what I call "ignominious bodies." I will then focus more directly on *The Osbournes* itself, where these normative categories of genre and family are enacted largely through the Osbournes' bodies. In the end, the success of *The Osbournes* indicates how contemporary reality TV, no matter how innovative, relies on established normative discourses.

Genre and Family

Both *The Osbournes* and *An American Family* were premised on an awareness of the categories of genre and family. That is, their representations of "real" families were informed by established television and cinematic genres along with a self-conscious sense of normative family life. Genre and family are normative concepts that describe limited categories: a text or social grouping is only considered as an example of a particular genre or family if it meets certain expectations. While these expectations change over time and under various circumstances, the normative structure itself is constant. For instance, while there may be new or alternative conceptions of family (say, involving extended kinship, single parents, relationships of choice, and so forth), these are still separated from groupings that are somehow *not* family. Similarly, creators, users, and critics construct discursive boundaries between certain cultural artifacts organizing them into genres. While an artifact may represent multiple genres, it must also *not* represent others; otherwise the distinctions are meaningless.

Thus, the terms genre and family, while ultimately arbitrary, remain important across time, regardless of what they may describe in specific instances. Rick Altman refers to this temporal function of genre as "pseudo-memorial": "When trying to bring together spectators who actually share less and less, what better meeting place than the common past provided by genre itself?"[8] That is, genre itself functions largely as a space of continuity, where particular texts are placed in a common history. The category of family has functioned in a similar manner, persisting for millennia despite frequent social challenges. The two terms come together in media representations, where representations of family must adhere to particular generic codes. In turn, this genre of family circulates normative representations—that is, models—for real individuals and families to identify with and (ostensibly) emulate.

This process has been fundamental to television, where ideals of both genre and family have systematically organized representations, programs, and audiences for decades. Television genres delimit narrative and representational parameters, facilitating audience (including advertiser) expectations. Programs have adhered to these boundaries, with few exceptions, throughout the history of TV.[9] Similarly, an entrenched conception of the nuclear family continues to structure television's representational, generic, and financial economy: characters and situations are generally rendered in familial terms; channels, times, and programs are geared toward particular members of the family; and individuals and subgroups within the family are sought by advertisers as potential consumers. There are family channels, family programs, and family hours; soap opera families, sitcom families, and even TV news families. As Ella Taylor remarks in her introduction to *Prime-Time Families*, "[Television] is watched by a vast number of people in their homes; its advertising is geared to both the parts and the whole of the family unit; its images, in both news and entertainment, are stamped with the familial."[10]

Thus, genre and family are not mere descriptive concepts; they have a normative function, and are conceived of and applied as social ideals on television and in other forms of media. While the question of whether they actually function as social ideals remains one of intense scrutiny, the *presumption* that they do governs most of the expectations of the medium. Television representations have always had to hold close to these established parameters in order to maintain these expectations.

The normative parameters of genre and family affected the conception, production, promotion, and reception of both *An American Family* and *The Osbournes*. Although both series dealt with real families, they had to engage with the dominant conceptions of genre and family so as to make the broadcast schedule, let alone reach an audience. Yet there have been few available models for representing "real" families on television. Daytime talk shows and prime-time newsmagazines have regularly focused on the travails of families for almost two decades, but the families on these programs have functioned as ciphers for the voyeuristic and therapeutic purposes of these genres. The polarized thematic range of these shows, tending toward the "tragic" in prime time (for example, diseased or injured family members) and the "excessive" in daytime (such as cheating spouses), has exacerbated this anonymity. In addition, these are only "one-off" families, forgotten as soon as the program has ended.[11] In the twenty-nine years between *An American Family* and *The Osbournes,* only a handful of prime-time documentary series—most on PBS—have explored the idea of family on a more extended basis. Although these programs all examined multiple families, thus diluting the effect of following one family for a sustained period, they still broadened the repertoire of representational codes for the family genre on television, and certainly informed the style of *The Osbournes.*[12]

Regardless, in the dominant discourses of TV, fictional families like the Cleavers, Bradys, Huxtables, and Simpsons have defined the television family. The normative television family is thus a fully *scripted* set of generic expectations. While these expectations have shaped fictional representations, they have also had an effect on representations of actual families.[13] When the families in question are real, though, an additional set of normative expectations, based around the representation of actual people and events, also shapes the text and its reception.

Documentary and Reality

In *An American Family* and *The Osbournes,* discourses of genre and family are complicated by the fact that each series purports to capture not *normality*—the purview of fictional TV families—but *reality*—life as it "is." Over the past century, documentary has been the dominant cinematic genre of reality or, more accurately, "actuality": people, objects, and events from real life, not as it should be but, ostensibly, how it is.[14] As John Corner has recently argued, however, documentary is now "unhelpful" in accounting for the style and sociological impact of contemporary reality TV. "Documentary" carries "too many assumptions . . . and idealizations," according to Corner, and he suggests a return to an older concept: "documentation."[15] A broader practice, documentation entails the cataloging of documents—that is, productions of coded reality such as performances, writings, and recordings—and not necessarily an explicit rhetoric. While documentary has traditionally claimed to produce truth(s) about its subjects, documentation instead displays examples of actuality; the former functions explicitly as an *argument,* and the latter primarily as an *exhibition.*[16]

Documentation also allows for broader uses of cinematic actuality. Corner observes that whereas traditional documentary has followed the modernist truth-seeking functions of civic publicity, journalistic inquiry, and/or alternative exploration, it has historically not given much consideration for what he calls "diversion": the use of actuality for the production of entertainment rather than the pursuit of truth.[17] Yet as the familiar codes of actuality from documentary film and television are now not only normative but clichéd—"reality should look and sound like *this*"—they are now regularly enlisted in support of entertainment, rather than for the more austere practices of edification that the word documentary typically conjures up. Accordingly, "documentary," in quotation marks, has become another style to emulate, rather than only a set of practices between producer and subject. Actualities are now regularly used in the "realist" genres of comedy, drama, and melodrama; have been used to bolster more "fantastic" genres like science fiction and horror; and are essential to pornography. A new term is therefore needed to distinguish both the documentaries of the past and the broader uses of actualities today. The contemporary term, appropriately enough, is reality. As a major weapon in the pursuit of audience share, the current explosion of reality TV *depicts*, rather than *explains*, placing a premium on diversion over education. It dwells on the spectacle of the world for its own sake or in the service of narrative, rather than as proof of an extracinematic truth. Still, this does not necessarily negate the value of any particular reality text, nor of the endeavor of documentary in the traditional sense; I do not wish to revive the hoary argument that pits entertainment against education, as if the terms are mutually exclusive. Instead, I agree with Corner, who suggests that "documentary will need strategically to redevelop itself within the new economic and cultural contexts for engaging the popular audience, with an acknowledgment of the pattern of tastes that are newly established."[18]

Although Corner is concerned with this transformation in television (from "documentary" to "reality"), which commenced in the late 1980s in conjunction with the shifting economics and technologies of media, the same generic issue also applied to *An American Family*, produced years earlier. As Jeffrey Ruoff contends in his retrospective on the series, the narrative structure, cinematic style, and promotional strategy of *An American Family* indicate how the documentary ideals of the filmmakers—and to an extent, even of the Louds themselves—were adjusted throughout the project to more closely adhere to the generic standards of television *drama*, and more specifically soap opera, rather than documentary.[19] For example, the opening sequence of the series ended with the title literally exploding, suggesting at the very beginning that the titular family was going to go through traumatic, maybe even fatal events during the series.[20]

Fictional and nonfictional codes were blurred in both *An American Family* and *The Osbournes* because of similar concerns about genre and audience expectations. Both series contained as many generic elements from classical Hollywood as from classical documentary: the construction of real people as identifiable characters; the sequencing of events into clear, causal narratives; and the use of visual and aural "stings" to punctuate actions and dialogue. They each had a narrow range of codes to draw from as expectations were limited, on the one side, by fictional television families, and on the other, by the established genres of documentary and reality, respectively. While *An American Family* initially signaled a defiance of these limits, striking out against conventional fictional depictions of family life, it ultimately foundered, imploding under the weight of expectations (and even accusations) and achieving a kind of infamy in television history. Conversely, *The Osbournes* has thus far (at least as of this writing) succeeded in an environment in which "reality entertainment" thrives. The primary reason for its success is its embrace of the normative expectations of genre and family—the opposite of the strategy attempted by *An American Family*—and the primary vehicles for its expression are the bodies of the Osbournes themselves.

The Display of Ignominious Bodies

With an explicit goal of diversion, the reality TV of the 1990s and 2000s has utilized actualities differently than the documentary television of the 1960s and 1970s. Whereas *An American Family* proceeded from a concern with the "hidden truth" of its subjects, and attempted to reveal the "extraordinary" tensions beneath a veneer of "ordinariness," *The Osbournes* playfully depicts the very ordinariness of its otherwise extraordinary subjects. *An American Family* juxtaposes an archetypal family (for example, the middle-class dream of a comfortable southern California lifestyle) with representations of "deviant" behavior (son Lance's homosexuality, say, or the divorce) in pursuit of melodrama; *The Osbournes* contrasts a backdrop of "deviant" behavior (cursing or ostentation, to cite two) with displays of archetypal familial bonding (for instance, Ozzy's surprise birthday party) in the service of comedy.

As Ruoff describes it, the point of *An American Family* was to peek behind the screen of conformity, to get at "the truth" of the typical U.S. family.[21] Producer Craig Gilbert wanted to examine how family life had changed in the 1960s. His background in news production and observational documentary technique, particularly the style of Drew Associates, furnished a sociological dimension to the project that led to its financing and distribution by PBS.[22] Despite the ostensible pursuit of the truth, however, the producers stacked the deck in their choice of the Loud family of Santa Barbara, California, as "an American family." According to Ruoff, Gilbert deliberately sought a family that resembled the normative ideal as presented in 1950s and 1960s sitcoms like *Father Knows Best* and *The Donna Reed Show*.[23] Similarly, the chosen family's class status, southern California location, and simmering discontent were all inspired from preconceived ideals drawn largely from fiction.[24] Thus, to a great degree, the Louds were mere players in a preconceived scenario. Despite the project's documentary pedigree, the calculated casting and use of the Louds is similar to current practices in reality TV. The major difference today is that with a premium placed on entertainment, the reality genre has shifted even more toward self-conscious performance (that is, exhibition) rather than the revelation of "natural behavior."

The prevailing purpose of reality TV today, particularly on MTV, is to revel in public displays of ignominy, where actualities are used precisely for their violations of generic norms. Ignominy entails public shame or humiliation, and though this applies to the subjects of these programs, I believe it applies more directly to the genre and its viewers. That is, viewers should perceive these generic violations; a reaction of "you can't do that on television" is the goal of producers and participants.[25] Participants on these programs are regularly shown in various states of ignominy: exhausted, enraged, depressed, careless, undressed, asleep, inebriated, and sick. Indeed, MTV series like *The Real World*, *Road Rules*, and *Jackass* are premised on directly placing their subjects in potentially humiliating or even physically dangerous situations.[26] Reality in each series is conveyed as a series of explicit encounters between people, or between people and circumstances, generating an engrossing spectacle of actions and reactions. Importantly, while the people and events on these programs need to be demonstrably real—not acting—to satisfy generic requirements, they are cast and planned as carefully as in any fiction: the effect of the actualities is amplified if the subjects are more "telegenic"—closer to normative codes of televisual appearance and behavior.[27] Both the casting and limited scope of events allow for what might be called "maximum control of conditions of spontaneity": narrowing the likely range of actions to those with the greatest visual and/or narrative impact.

At the time of its original broadcast, the "invasion" of the private realm of the Loud family home in *An American Family* was perceived as scandalous. Indeed, the presumed manipulation of the family by the producers became the most contentious issue of public discussion, even more than the depicted actions of the family members themselves. By the time *The Osbournes* was produced, there was little left of the private realm that had not been made public, in a wide variety of media forms. The thrill and ignominy of reality TV is based around the notion that while privacy is still the norm, it can pleasurably be violated by voyeurism and exhibitionism, as people clamor to see and show "it all." This is a major shift in the representation of reality from the era of *An American Family*. While the Louds' typicality—though not their onscreen behavior—was to a significant extent a setup, it was at least *presented* as a genuine encounter with a real family. Conversely, no 2000s reality program makes a similar claim, as they are premised more on what Joel Black calls "reality effects" rather than an exploration of a "deeper" truth.[28] Media representation per se has become the so-called truth of contemporary genres of actuality, and ignominy is the most efficient means to attain it. It is crucial to note that while the observational technique of *An American Family* was the subject of scorn and ridicule throughout the 1970s, it has since become a standard style of reality TV and, in the form of Internet webcams and titillating videos like the *Backyard Wrestling* and *Girls Gone Wild* series, throughout society.[29]

Accordingly, just as the crew of *An American Family* was largely drawn from and shaped by the cutting-edge documentaries of its time, *The Osbournes*' production team has worked on the most prominent reality TV programs of the late 1990s and early 2000s, including *Big Brother, Survivor,* and *The Chris Rock Show*. Their professional experiences include not only the production of reality TV—and the now-codified ignominious bodies—but also the more specific use of the codes of reality for comedy.[30]

"The First Reality Sitcom"

The normative range of television content has expanded in recent years, as long-standing broadcast taboos against coarse language, nudity, violence, and bodily functions have been eroded in the pursuit of young, affluent audiences. This process has been accelerated by the enormous critical and popular successes of pay-cable programs like HBO's *Sex and the City* and *The Sopranos,* which have flouted old content limits.[31] While this trend has fueled the creation of new genres (such as reality TV itself), it has more profoundly affected established genres, which have had to adjust their traditional content with these broader limits in mind. Over the past decade, "old" genres have adapted to these demands and have shifted the level of their content while maintaining their basic generic codes. Given this, *The Osbournes,* in all its excessive glory, is more a *generic* product of its times than *An American Family* was of its era. *The Osbournes* was conceived of with these new limits in mind, coupled with MTV's simultaneous necessity for innovation. MTV has gone from strength to strength since the late 1990s by keeping its series fresh, overplaying an idea in the short term rather than extending it into the future. The network requires programming that appeals to the current exhibitionist sensibility, but also takes a new approach, or in the case of its most successful programs, provides a new take on an old approach. Accordingly, a "real" situation comedy about an aging rocker and his unruly family seemed a likely fit for their needs.

The Osbournes first appeared on a popular 2000 segment of *Cribs,* a series that features celebrities showing off their homes. The segment augured the potential of an extended visit to the Osbourne mansion, which the family was willing to accommodate in exchange for the publicity they might accrue if the series were successful. As recorded in late 2001, audio and video material culled from over a dozen cameras and microphones merged the now-familiar "roving" observational technique pioneered on *An American Family* with a bank of stationary surveillance equipment located throughout the house.[32] With a wide selection of material at their disposal and a relatively lengthy postproduction period (by reality TV standards), the producers were able to structure the episodes using familiar generic codes: problems are introduced, conflicts play out, and the end of the episode reaches a mild resolution. As such, MTV explicitly promoted *The Osbournes* as a sitcom. Brian Graden, the programming chief, appeared on *CNN Live Today* on the date of the premiere and claimed the series to be "the world's first reality sitcom because, like a sitcom, you have outrageous characters, very, very funny moments, and . . . the love between the cast members nonetheless."[33] Thus, both genre and family—via the sitcom—were identified up front as the key attributes of the new series.

The hook of *The Osbournes* is the fact that despite their apparent excesses of wealth and behavior, the family somehow still functions as a normative, loving unit. The primary generic marker of both excess and normativity on *The Osbournes* is the family's conspicuous, unrepentant physicality. As explicitly documented in the series, the Osbournes—including their many pets—hug, kiss, wrestle, eat, drink, scratch, fart, burp, piss, and shit. They ruminate about vaginas, scrotums, and breasts, and deal with dog turds left on the carpet. They reveal their bodies in various states of dress and decorum. They yell at their neighbors, shout at each other, and most famously, say "fuck" more often than Tony Soprano. Theirs is a world of explicit bodily sights, sounds, smells, and sensations.

Though we are shown the Osbournes in this explicit, "real" detail, however, the series still functions predominantly as a family sitcom, drawing heavily from well-worn generic codes. The Osbournes are self-consciously represented in the vein of the Cleavers of *Leave It to Beaver,* the Bradys of *The Brady Bunch,* and the Nelsons of *The Adventures of Ozzie and Harriet.*[34] Their house is a divided space of public and private areas, presented as in any family sitcom. The problems encountered—difficult neighbors, unruly pets, physical ailments, and an unwanted house guest—are clichéd sitcom staples and are conveyed in the standard stasis-disruption-resolution-stasis structure of TV narrative. Goofy musical bumpers even bridge scenes, as in any sitcom.

The series' opening sequence reproduces the archetypal family sitcom opening, as seen in the series listed above. An establishing shot of the family's Beverly Hills mansion leads to a series of tracking shots throughout the house, revealing the Osbourne mansion to be both ostentatious and comfortably domestic as recognizable domestic spaces (kitchen, living room, bedroom, backyard) open up to the camera. A series of framed family photos slides past, indicating a family history and reiterating normative expectations of the genre. Similarly, each family member is introduced in turn with an animated freeze-frame and their name in a "space age" font reminiscent of 1950s advertising. The poses of the family members in this sequence establish their personas as both typical *and* unique, engaged in quirky, yet recognizably "normal" behavior: mom Sharon is shown seated with her hands to her head, as if exasperated yet again; son Jack wears combat fatigues, a helmet, and a knife, suggesting the weird brother; daughter Kelly pokes her head out of a closet door and sticks out her tongue, all teenage sass; and finally, Ozzy himself is introduced (as "The Dad") while taunting one of the family's many dogs with a "barking dog" toy, every bit the supposed madman of his heavy metal persona. The sequence ends with a quick dolly up to the family posed on their front step and looking into the camera, as the title *The Osbournes* slides in. The theme song that runs under this sequence—a swing version of Ozzy's signature hit, "Crazy Train" (1980), sung by former 1950s pop star and Osbourne neighbor Pat Boone—underscores this mix of the clichéd codes of family sitcom and heavy metal chaos.

Despite these conspicuous sitcom trappings, the Osbournes of 2002 are not quite the Nelsons of 1959; this gap is precisely the point of the series. Although prior sitcoms have played with the idea of family normality, the relaxing content limits and ascendancy of reality TV have enabled further exploration (and exploitation) of aesthetic and social norms.[35] As conveyed through the bodies and behaviors of its principals, *The Osbournes* stretches the familiar sitcom representational codes to their limits while still remaining within recognizable normative constructions of dad, mom, son, and daughter.

In this case, dad is a veteran rock star notorious for his long hair, theatrical persona, and substance abuse. Ozzy's fifty-something body displays the legacy of his excessive life, as he shuffles around the house shirtless, bearing a tattooed, middle-aged paunch and an uncontrollable tremor in his hands.[36] Jack is overweight, wears trendy black-frame glasses, and sports several piercings and a modified Mohawk haircut. Kelly wears an explosive mix of thrift-store and haute couture, regularly changes the color of her unruly hair, and periodically unleashes her rage on her brother. Sharon appears to be a normative suburban mom, with short, stylish hair, sweats, and running shoes. Her behavior, though, reveals that she is the de facto ringleader of the household, taking charge of most situations, her sharp, profanity-laced voice cutting through the noise. She is also arguably the most ignominious member of the family, as she burps, farts, handles her breasts, and in one of the series' most infamous moments, apparently urinates in a houseguest's illicit bottle of whiskey.[37] The fact that the mom is in many ways the most excessive member of a family full of excessive characters indicates how shrewdly the series (and family) exploits normative expectations.

Ozzy's already-established celebrity as a heavy metal legend formed the rationale for the show and certainly ensured media attention. Yet the point of *The Osbournes* is to distinguish the "real" Ozzy (and his family) from that already-established celebrity. Accordingly, the series pushes Ozzy's star persona to the background. While he is frequently seen in typical tour settings (buses, hotel rooms, dressing rooms, and the like) as well as at home, his actual performances are only glimpsed. Instead, we are constantly shown a "backstage" Ozzy, one closer to the established codes of sitcom representation: a wealthy, somewhat addled, middle-aged dad who just happens to be a rock star. As the series' biggest star and least-normative body, Ozzy is most often the subject of comic sequences as he struggles with new technology (a state-of-the-art home theater system), animals (the unruly Osbourne pets), and the rest of the family (trying to restore order during an argument), all the while mumbling and stuttering in a near-incomprehensible Birmingham brogue, and enduring the bodily tremors associated with his rehabilitation treatments.

Significantly, unlike every other member of the family, Ozzy's body is not just on display (as it has been for nearly thirty years); it is quite literally out of control, bearing the visible signs of a lifetime of substance abuse. While Ozzy's body, the very medium of his notoriety and the family fortune, is frequently the subject of easy laughs, it is also a symbol of decay, a rather helpless condition of ignominy as opposed to the exuberant exhibitionism of younger reality show subjects. These scenes are among the most ambivalent of the series, pushing the codes of the so-called reality sitcom near the outer limits of the representation of ignominious bodies. Ozzy's body, however, still remains just inside the generic sitcom requirements that dictate that dad must be somewhat eccentric and befuddled.[38] Those limits, and perhaps the entire *Osbournes* endeavor, promise to be tested even more in the second season, which is in production as of this writing, as Sharon, who was diagnosed with colon cancer in July 2002 (and had several inches of her colon surgically removed), undergoes cancer treatments.[39]

"We Argue, but at the End of the Day, We Love Each Other"[40]

The Louds' and Osbournes' family lives were further reproduced through press articles and interviews, appearances on radio and television talk shows, and particularly in the case of the Osbournes, merchandising.[41] While space does not permit a more detailed investigation into each series' reception, it is clear that in expanding beyond their series, both families solidified their iconic status as archetypal U.S. families for their respective eras.

Even though the genre is reality, and the actions of the subjects are real, the production and promotion of reality TV programs ensure that its subjects function in the end as *characters*: attractive constructions of personality. In the current environment, such normative expectations have hit the Osbournes to a degree the Louds never had to endure. The family has had to deal with constant crowds outside its Beverly Hills home, and insatiable public curiosity about (among other things) Ozzy's past substance abuse and violence toward Sharon, Jack's dangerous dive off a Santa Monica pier, and Kelly's weight.[42] In addition, the protracted and secretive negotiations with MTV for the second season of the series indicated how this family's reality was now big business: the Osbournes are reportedly collecting $20 million for the second season, plus licensing fees and outright ownership of the series and concept.

Significantly, the television version of the Osbournes is one member smaller than the actual family, as Ozzy and Sharon's eldest daughter, Aimee, declined to participate, citing a desire to maintain her privacy. While this action may reveal a rift within the actual family, it also indicates how the normative codes of genre and family can still be considered too restrictive.[43] Her decision to forego appearing on a reality TV series is certainly uncharacteristic of our times. The genre continues to expand and has no lack of potential ignominious bodies. The success of *The Osbournes* has even inspired the development of other "celebrity reality" series as similar projects featuring celebrities like P. Diddy, Liza Minnelli, and Anna Nicole Smith are produced or at least considered.[44]

While *An American Family* and *The Osbournes* are certainly unique television series, they both had to function under particular normative categories of genre and family in order to be comprehensible, let alone successful. The fact that they functioned in radically different ways indicates how the content of these terms—and in particular, the effective meaning of television reality—has shifted considerably over three decades. Thus, the key question for reality TV, now and for the foreseeable future, is not *whether* its reality is produced but *how* it is articulated with existing codes and expectations.

NOTES

1. In the space of one month alone, they were on the covers of *Entertainment Weekly, Interview, Rolling Stone,* and *Time.*

2. The relative novelty and reputation of PBS, the network that aired *An American Family,* also contributed to these reactions, as the new service was created (and perceived) in part to be a challenging alternative to the commercial imperatives of the established networks and stations.

3. See, for example, Michael J. Bradley, "Put 'em on the Couch," *Rolling Stone* 895, 9 May 2002, 36; Paul Farhi, "Make Room for Ozzy; *The Osbournes* Recalls TV's Uncomplicated, Unpierced Past," *Washington Post,* 16 April 2002, C1; and Melanie McFarland, "Ozzy Knows Best?" *Seattle Times,* 22 April 2002, E1.

4. See Jeffrey Ruoff, *An American Family: A Televised Life* (Minneapolis: University of Minnesota Press, 2002), 23, 102; and Brian Graden, interview by Leon Harris, *CNN Live Today,* CNN, 5 March 2002. Alessandra Stanley of the *New York Times* also referred to *The Osbournes* as the first "docu-sitcom" ("No Rest for Family Values on Black Sabbath," *New York Times,* 2 April 2002, E1).

5. See Stephanie Coontz, *The Way We Never Were* (New York: Basic Books, 1992); and Ella Taylor, *Prime-Time Families* (Berkeley: University of California Press, 1989).

6. Whether the family is or even should be the fundamental unit of social cohesion is certainly a debatable point. I argue that the important point is not whether it is or not but rather that it is *treated as such* in virtually every society on the planet. Government policies, temporal and spatial organization, and commercial imperatives all center on conceptions of the family. The media's role in this is

to circulate representations of families—most normative, some (that is, "dysfunctional" ones) not—in order to facilitate this system.

7. Osbourne was the lead singer of heavy metal pioneers Black Sabbath in the 1970s, and became a superstar with a string of best-selling solo recordings in the early 1980s. During the 1990s, he parlayed his earlier successes into the annual Ozzfest tour, which linked his celebrity to younger, similar artists.

8. Rick Altman, *Film/Genre* (London: British Film Institute, 1999), 190.

9. As John Thornton Caldwell points out, despite periodic innovations in content, the situation comedy is, stylistically, arguably the most stable genre on U.S. television, remaining largely the same across several decades (*Televisuality: Style and Crisis in American Television* [New Brunswick, N.J.: Rutgers University Press, 1995], 5).

10. Taylor, *Prime-Time Families,* 1.

11. On occasion, some of these programs have had "where-are-they-now" segments that update the stories of particular families who have been presented on the show, but these are most often as brief and functional as the earlier segment.

12. A significant variation on this approach has been the *Survivor*-like genre of isolation and survival, in which groups (including nuclear families) are followed as they adapt to an uncomfortable environment without the luxuries of twenty-first-century life, as in series like *Frontier House, 1900 House,* and the British *Castaway.* While these series have a more earnest educational purpose than most reality series (for instance, in their display of long-outmoded homemaking skills), they also explore family relationships across the period of the show, which generally lasts for months or even, in the case of *Castaway,* an entire year. In the case of *Frontier House,* one married couple even endured a Loud-like emotional and eventually legal separation by the end of the series.

13. Indeed, as Stephanie Coontz observes in *The Way We Never Were,* representations of the archetypal "1950s" television family have even informed U.S. social policies, despite their disconnection from actual, lived family life (even in the 1950s).

14. Documentary's generic opposite is ostensibly fiction; hence the use of the broad term "nonfiction" as a synonym.

15. John Corner, "Documentary Values," in *Realism and "Reality" in Film and Media,* ed. Anne Jerslev (Copenhagen: Museum Tusculanum Press, 2002), 145–46.

16. Granted, the lines between documentary and documentation are blurry. Joseph Wiseman's often ambiguous films certainly *feel* more like an exhibition than an argument. Yet Wiseman's methodical technique and choice of subjects suggest an activist engagement with his material that exceeds the requirements of documentation.

17. Corner, "Documentary Values," 147–49.

18. Ibid., 153.

19. Ruoff, *An American Family,* 53–68, 109–11.

20. Ibid., 48–49.

21. Ibid., 11–15.

22. Gilbert's main collaborators, Alan and Susan Raymond, were also enthusiastic practitioners of the observational style and shot the entirety of the footage. A team of experienced news documentary editors, led by David Hanser, edited the series.

23. Ruoff, *An American Family,* 17.

24. Gilbert was particularly inspired by the detective fiction of Ross MacDonald, which portrayed the materially comfortable and morally bankrupt lives of the Santa Barbara upper crust. MacDonald was even personally consulted to help locate a suitable family in the area. See Ruoff, *An American Family,* 17–18.

25. For example, the *Naked News* website and television series feature attractive male and female newscasters who strip while they're reading the news, thus violating the boundary between professional TV journalism and pornography, producing the shock of ignominy. An early, long-running Nickelodeon series was actually titled *You Can't Do That on Television;* its trademark action was to "slime" its subjects with a load of green goo dropped from above, thereby humiliating them. Interestingly, yesterday's Nickelodeon viewers (born between the mid-1970s and 1980s) are precisely today's reality TV target audience.

26. Other prominent reality series, such as *Survivor, The Amazing Race, Fear Factor, Dog Eat Dog,* and *American Idol,* function in a similar manner.

27. A list of telegenic qualities would include physical attractiveness, gregariousness, intelligibility, and physical activity; in other words, attributes that translate most easily to the medium's visual vocabulary, time limits, and perceived audiences.

28. Joel Black, *The Reality Effect: Film Culture and the Graphic Imperative* (New York: Routledge, 2002), 15–20.

29. The entire endeavor of producing a film about a "real family" was mercilessly satirized in Albert Brooks's 1979 film *Real Life* and in a 1980 episode of the situation comedy *WKRP in Cincinnati* titled "Real Families."

30. *The Osbournes'* crew members worked widely on programs such as *Survivor: Africa* (Sound Supervisor Jenny Green), *Big Brother 2* (Editor Matthew Gossin), and *Bands on the Run* (Director Brendon Carter), and also in the "comedy reality" subgenre: Executive Producer Jeff Stilson was a producer for both *The Chris Rock Show* and *The Daily Show,* and a writer for Michael Moore's *TV Nation.*

31. Cable programming is not subject to the same legal content restrictions over-the-air broadcasters must abide by. Language barriers in particular are falling in basic cable and have increasingly been broken on broadcast television in recent years. For example, the FX original series *The Shield* regularly features once-taboo expletives; the Comedy Central series *South Park* had its animated characters say "shit" over 130 times in one episode; and a May 2002 episode of NBC's high-rated medical drama *ER* had the dying Mark Greene yell the familiar expletive.

32. Only the master bedroom and bathrooms were declared "off-limits" to surveillance. In addition, the now-standard use of video, rather than film, ensures that virtually everything that occurs in the house *will* be recorded and thus made available to structure episodes.

33. Brian Graden interview, *CNN Live Today.* Note that the Osbournes are referred to here as "cast members" rather than "family members."

34. Ozzie Nelson and Ozzy Osbourne obviously share first names, but that is only the most superficial comparison. Both families were actual families, their real personas sharing the same names and personalities as their TV counterparts. Both families were actively engaged in show business. While both families also had ultimate control over their television representations, the Nelsons' series was carefully scripted and produced; *The Adventures of Ozzie and Harriet* (1952–1966) is perhaps the only series in television history in which the entire regular cast play themselves as scripted characters.

35. The "fantastic" family sitcoms of the mid-1960s such as *The Addams Family, Bewitched,* and *The Munsters* are indirect influences on *The Osbournes.* Indeed, in an *Entertainment Weekly* article covering the success of his series, Ozzy implicitly compared his family to the fictional TV monster family: "My one regret is that we used our real house. I mean, the Munsters didn't use their real house!" (cited in Nancy Miller, "American Goth," *Entertainment Weekly,* 19 April 2002, 22). For an examination of these 1960s sitcoms in their original context, see Lynn Spigel, *Welcome to the Dreamhouse: Popular Media and Postwar Suburbs* (Durham, N.C.: Duke University Press, 2001), 107–40.

36. For the sake of clarity, I will refer to the Osbourne family members by their first names only for the remainder of the chapter.

37. A scene in which Sharon stuck her hand down her pants, rubbed her vagina, and chased Kelly around the room was cut from an episode, though the two are shown talking about the incident immediately afterward; Kelly is disgusted, while Sharon is amused.

38. Ozzy's befuddlement is reminiscent in particular of earlier sitcom dads Tim Taylor (*Home Improvement*), Cliff Huxtable (*The Cosby Show*), Howard Cunningham (*Happy Days*), George Jetson (*The Jetsons*), and Danny Williams (*Make Room for Daddy*).

39. Still, even this frontier is not unheard-of for MTV as the network covered gross-out comedian Tom Green's surgery and recovery from testicular cancer in 1999.

40. Sharon Osbourne, cited in David Bauder, "Ozzie and Harriet It Isn't," *Associated Press,* 5 March 2002.

41. While a few books were published by and about the Louds in the early 1970s, the Osbournes have been featured on a wider array of products, including a CD sound track of the series, a DVD set of the first season, and even a collection of back-to-school supplies.

42. Although she has become a new icon of independent-minded teenage girl-dom, Kelly has had to deal with public comments about her body. While her body is healthy and normal for her age and height, it does not meet the current stick-thin ideal as presented in most mainstream media. As is usually the case, real women are forced to bear the brunt of normative media codes. See Miller, "American Goth."

43. Given her famous father and industry connections, it is just as likely that she wishes to pursue other normative codes of celebrity than would be available were she to become a television Osbourne.

44. The series' success has also spawned the development of several series that place the focus back on noncelebrity ignominy. CBS is planning an updated *Beverly Hillbillies* as a reality series, this time with a real Appalachian family brought to live in luxury. Similarly, ABC Family is seeking real families for *My Life Is a Sitcom,* in which a real family plays itself in a four-camera, studio-shot situation comedy: a real, latter-day *Ozzie and Harriet.*

Part II

Industry

6

The Political Economic Origins of Reali-TV

Chad Raphael

From the sea change in U.S. television in the 1980s emerged a programming trend variously described as "infotainment," "reality-based television," "tabloid TV," "crime-time television," "trash TV," and "on-scene shows." The welter of terms created by television critics to depict these new programs masked their underlying connection as a response to economic restructuring within the industry. This essay offers a rough categorization of these programs, sketches the industrial context from which they emerged, and points to the economic problems they were meant to solve. I concentrate mostly on the distinctive conditions of prime-time series, putting aside made-for-TV docudramas and entire cable channels (such as Court TV) that may share similar production practices and genres. Although my focus here is on political economy rather than textual or audience issues, I do not want to imply that these programs' cultural significance can be reduced to their relations of production and distribution. Yet without understanding the political-economic forces that drove the spread of this genre, textual and audience studies may risk reifying it as an expression of audience demand, or of their creators, or of a cultural, discursive, or ontological shift unrelated to the needs of those who run the television industry. If this genre exhibits a kind of textual excess, its emergence reflects a relative scarcity of resources for television production.

Among the swirl of neologisms, my preferred term for these programs will be "Reali-TV," which points to the inseparability of the television industry's economic needs and how this genre represents reality.[1] This term stresses television's particular reasons for embracing reality shows as opposed to claims about the spread of infotainment across the media. At the same time, this designation illuminates the connections between seemingly different programs (such as crime-time television, tabloid TV, and on-scene shows) and avoids the high-cultural bias implicit in the notion of trash TV. The term indicates not only how these programs make distinctive claims to represent the real but also their common impact on the realities of power and economic relations in the industry. Reali-TV, then, is an umbrella term for a number of programming trends that have rapidly expanded since the late 1980s across all hours of network schedules, first-run syndication, and cable.

Production practices common to most of these programs include the extensive use of "actuality" footage of their subjects, whether these are police staking out a drug den or mom and dad yukking it up in front of the camcorder; reenactments of events, performed by professional actors, the people who experienced them, or a mix of both; a tendency to avoid the studio in favor of on-scene shooting, sometimes at the same place where the events they represent occurred; mixing footage shot by unpaid amateur videographers with that of professionals; appealing to the conventions of "liveness" and "immediacy" through on-location interviews, subjective camerawork, and synchronized sound; and appropriating traditional conventions of news coverage, such as the use of anchors or hosts, remote reporting, and the pretense to spontaneity. Studio-centered formats, principally game shows and confessional talk programming, are the obvious exceptions to these common practices.

These production techniques are combined differently in numerous Reali-TV formats, which can be distinguished according to how much each relies on nontraditional labor (for story development, writing, performing, and camerawork) and production inputs (such as sets, props, and costumes). Some formats continue to depend mainly on professional labor and traditional inputs. The network newsmagazines—whose ranks have swelled in the past few years with the introduction of *48 Hours* and *Street Stories* (CBS), *Primetime Live* (ABC), *Dateline NBC*, and others—are still entirely professionally produced, and employ the same mix of studio and location footage as the evening news. The same is true of tabloid TV shows (such as the syndicated *A Current Affair* or *Entertainment Tonight*), despite their unique representational strategies.

Several other Reali-TV formats use hybrid production techniques, however. Hidden-video programs (such as *Totally Hidden Video*), which enjoyed a minor resurgence in the early 1990s, rely on professional camera crews and actors maneuvering nonprofessional performers into embarrassing or humorous situations. So do experiment-based programs that place and observe nonactors in contrived living arrangements (*The Real World*), and increasingly add the element of competition for money and prizes (as in *Survivor* or *Fear Factor*). Crime-time and emergency response programs (*Rescue 911, America's Most Wanted, Unsolved Mysteries,* and the many imitators these shows have spawned on cable and first-run syndication) are shot and edited by professionals and introduced by a regular host. Yet they also may employ some amateur footage of disasters and nonprofessional performers enacting their own rescues or crime experiences. These programs also take advantage of props, sets, and costumes provided by law enforcement authorities, corrections institutions, parole boards, and emergency medical crews. Clip shows (such as *The World's Wildest Police Videos* and other "world's best/worst/most" programs) similarly mix amateur and professional video. Finally, home video programs (like *America's Funniest Home Videos*) rely entirely on amateur footage that is professionally edited. This format depends most heavily on nontraditional inputs and labor, not only for "scripting," performing, and shooting the high jinks, but also to do the work of studio audiences (who vote for the funniest video, for example). Before discussing how these techniques have lowered production costs, we need to examine the larger economic picture from whence they sprang.

Decline of the Networks: Webs Wane as Competition Climbs

As a fiscal strategy, Reali-TV emerged in the late 1980s in response to the economic restructuring of U.S. television. Much of the restructuring story has been told by scholars and in the trade press: how the number of video distribution channels expanded rapidly with the growth of cable, VCRs, the Fox network, and local independent stations; how the television audience was increasingly fragmented; how advertising revenues now had to be spread among a larger pool of distributors; and how this dilution of advertising spending created pressure on broadcasters and cablecasters to cut per-program production costs.[2] Less cited causes for production budget cuts included the high levels of corporate debt incurred by the big-three networks after each was sold in the mid-1980s and advertiser-driven changes in audience measurement techniques designed to identify specific market segments (the most notorious of these was the People-Meter, which yielded dramatically lower ratings for the networks).[3]

By the late 1980s, then, the economic picture of U.S. television had become decidedly more crowded. If the networks remained in the foreground as the major economic force in the industry, the purveyors of cable, VCRs, and first-run syndication winked and beckoned viewers in the background. Advertisers and audience measurement services busily tried to record who was watching what, how much attention they paid to the commercial breaks, and whether they were buying any of it. In order to understand how Reali-TV emerged as a cost-cutting solution in this new economic environment of the late 1980s, however, we need to examine how increased competition in the distribution of television programming affected the sphere of production.

The Squeeze on Production: Ouch! Webs and Suppliers Feel the Pinch

As television distributors fought over smaller advertising shares and shouldered more debt, program producers (network production arms, major Hollywood studios, and the few small, independent production companies) all faced rapidly rising costs in the 1980s. For prime-time producers, the average cost of an hour-long drama soared to over $1 million per episode by the end of the decade, and costs were increasing by roughly 8 to 10 percent a year.[4] Prices were driven up primarily by "above-the-line" costs such as talent, direction, scriptwriting, music composition, computer animation, and location costs.[5] The star system for above-the-line labor became especially pronounced as network programmers, agent-packagers, and production companies responded to the greater risks of capital involved in the creation of new shows by increasingly demanding names associated with a prior record of success. The greater demand for stars created an artificial labor shortage and inflated salaries for the lucky few.

These rising costs were accompanied by smaller per-show revenues, thereby squeezing production companies' earnings on both sides of the ledger. Producers now had to accept smaller license fees for their programs than they had commanded from the networks before the new era of competition. The threatened networks were scaling back outlays, and cable network distributors and syndicators also lacked deep pockets for program purchases. In addition, changes in federal tax laws eliminated producers' investment tax credits, which often meant the difference between earning a profit and taking a loss on a show. Prior to the 1986 restructuring of federal tax laws, producers were able to deduct 6.7 percent of the cost of their productions from their federal tax bills. By mid-decade, caught between rising costs and lower network license fees, most producers could no longer make back their investments in first-run network showings. By 1986, producers were losing up to $100,000 per episode for half-hour shows and $200,000 to $300,000 for hour-long dramas.[6] Producers now were forced to deficit finance their programs and cross their fingers in hopes the show would survive three network seasons, providing enough episodes for domestic and foreign syndication as well as a chance to recoup their initial investments.

Producers to Labor: Drop Dead

Feeling the pinch on profits, production companies and the networks initiated a series of cost-cutting strategies that translated into an attack on labor, mainly on below-the-line workers such as technicians, engineers, and extras.[7] The first move was a wave of staff cutbacks at studios and in network news departments. In the mid-1980s, Fox cut 20 percent of its studio staff, Capital Cities/ABC 10 percent of its staff, and CBS 30 percent of its administrative staff along with 10 percent of its news division. NBC resisted a seventeen-week strike by the National Association of Broadcast Employees and Technicians (NABET) in 1987, shedding two hundred union jobs. By 1992, NBC had eliminated 30 percent of its news division through layoffs and bureau closings. Even network standards and practices departments, the much-derided self-censors of the broadcasting industry, faced the budget-cutting ax.

The second part of the cost-cutting strategy involved bypassing union labor, spurring an unprecedented wave of strikes by above and below-line labor unions and craft guilds. In the 1980s and early 1990s, the NABET, Directors Guild, American Federation of Musicians, Screen Extras Guild (SEG), and American Federation of Radio and Television Artists all struck, while the Screen Actors Guild (SAG) struck twice, and the Writers Guild three times. Above-the-line workers especially sought more residuals for the use of programs on new media and overseas. Lower-paid labor, such as members of SEG, took a more defensive stand commensurate with their weaker bargaining power. The SEG strike ended with union members accepting a 25 percent wage cut, changes in overtime schedules, and the producers' prerogative to hire more nonunion labor (the extras' bargaining position was hurt by SAG's refusal to merge with the less powerful union or even to support its position in contract negotiations). This increase in labor unrest was both a response to and motivating force in attempts to break the power of the unions. As a result, producers exacerbated the long-term split in the Hollywood labor market between core workers (such as the successful SAG members who enjoy higher pay, more job security, and share in management tasks and interests) and periphery workers (such as SEG members, who have little job security, work part-time schedules, and endure far lower wages).[8] Producers also responded to union demands by using nonunion Hollywood labor and shifting production to regions where cheaper labor was available, such as Canada and the "right-to-work" states of the U.S. South. These tactics cut across entertainment and news program production. Disney and MCA led the industry shift toward building studio complexes in Florida. The loss of the investment tax credit, which was only applicable to programs produced in the United States, helped spur a shift of production to Canada, where lower costs and more pliable unions could save $200,000 to $300,000 an episode for dramatic series.[9] In news programming, CNN and Fox led the way in producing with lower-paid, nonunion labor and by breaking down job classifications. Their "success" was increasingly imitated by the traditional networks. One former CBS executive noted that the lesson of CNN was "Break the unions!"[10] NBC appears to have learned the lesson quickest, developing a twenty-four-hour-per-day affiliate news service based in Charlotte, North Carolina, staffed with nonunion labor. Some Fox affiliates experimented with subcontracting their entire evening newscasts.

Survivor Economics: Reali-TV Fits the Bill

Reali-TV shows gained currency in this environment of relative financial scarcity and labor unrest of the late 1980s. Economically, the genre fit the needs of producers and distributors alike for cheaper programming. These programs largely did away with higher-priced stars and union talent. In the early days, the only "name" actors on these shows were briefly seen as hosts. More recently, a subgenre has developed that trots out minor celebrities and has-beens who come cheap to endure humiliating tests of their mettle, fighting each other in *Celebrity Boxing* or plunging themselves into vermin in *Celebrity Fear Factor*. In the crime-time/emergency shows, roles in reenactments of crimes and rescues have been filled by unknown actors and, sometimes, the people on whom the stories were based. In programs such as *Cops,* segments followed law enforcement officials in the course of their work, eschewing reenactments and the need for actors entirely. The home video and hidden-video programs likewise avoided professional union talent, as have more recent experiment-based shows. In bypassing more expensive performers, program producers also escaped the grips of the Hollywood agents, who had come to occupy the role of program developers and packagers in the early 1980s, and who exacted considerable fees for their services.[11]

Producers of Reali-TV, particularly of the crime-time/emergency shows as well as home video and hidden-video programs, led a wider industry move toward using nonunion, freelance production crews. The Arthur Company offers a good example. In 1987, it lost the rights to produce the network prime-time drama *Airwolf* after battling with the Writers Guild over cable royalties, and then turned to producing low-budget, nonunion programs for syndication and basic cable. In 1991, the Arthur Company re-turned to prime time with *FBI: The Untold Stories,* a Reali-TV reprise of the bureau's long-running romance with the tube. Similarly, Fox's *America's Most Wanted,* one of the trendsetters of Reali-TV when it premiered in 1987, used different freelance crews for each segment. Even some news-magazines, such as *CBS Street Stories,* turned to freelance camera crews and news producers. The home video programs relied on amateur cam-corder enthusiasts and freelance professionals. Reali-TV producers also partook of the move to cheaper labor regions. Grosso-Jacobson Entertain-ment, a prolific creator of crime-time shows (including *Top Cops, True Blue,* and *Secret Service*), shot its patriotic paeans to U.S. law enforcers in Toronto.[12]

The genre has been an integral part of network strategies to control labor unrest as well. The 1988 writers' strike, a twenty-two-week affair that delayed the opening of the fall season, proved crucial to the rise of Reali-TV. Existing Reali-TV shows were largely unaffected by the strike as they already relied very little on writers. In addition, the delay of the season gave producers and programmers the impetus to develop future shows that did not depend on writing talent. Tabloid TV pioneer Peter Brennan (of *Hard Copy*), when asked whether he was concerned about a potential SAG strike in 1992, shrugged off the threat: "Remember the Writers Guild strike in '88? . . . [T]hat was the year that gave rise to reality TV."[13] The sec-ond wave of Reali-TV programming, ushered in by the ratings success of the game show *Who Wants to Be a Millionaire?* in 1999 and *Survivor* in

2000, came amid threatened walkouts by writers and actors. The networks ordered more Reali-TV series in part to prepare for potential strikes and not simply because they could be produced without union employees. Reality series can be developed more quickly than fictional programs partly because they do not rely on lining up talent and writers. Newsmagazines can be expanded relatively easily to fill additional hours on the network schedule because news workers are typically affiliated with different unions than other television talent. "There is a quick turnaround time with reality," noted CBS president Leslie Moonves in detailing his network's plans for a possible writers' strike in 2001.[14]

Reali-TV programs also cut costs by wholeheartedly embracing low-end production values. Direct cinema techniques such as handheld cameras and the use of available lighting made shows without reenactments (such as *Cops* and the network newsmagazines) particularly cheap. Programs that employed reenacted material (like *Rescue 911* and *Unsolved*

TABLE 6.1
Prime-Time Reali-TV Programs at the Start of the 1991–1992 Season

Program	Network	Minutes	Producers	Deficit	License Fee per Episode
America's Funniest Home Videos	ABC	30	ABC/Vin di Bona	$0	$375,000
America's Funniest People	ABC	30	ABC/Vin di Bona	$0	$300,000
American Detective	ABC	30	ABC/Orion TV/ Paul Stojanovich	$0	$450,000
FBI: The Untold Stories	ABC	30	The Arthur Company	$25,000	$450,000
Primetime Live	ABC	60	ABC News	$0	$500,000
20/20	ABC	60	ABC News	$0	$500,000
48 Hours	CBS	60	CBS News	$0	$500,000
Rescue 911	CBS	30	CBS/Arnold Shapiro	$0	$650,000
60 Minutes	CBS	60	CBS News	$0	$600,000
Top Cops	CBS	60	CBS News	$0	$650,000
Exposé	NBC	30	NBC News	$0	$300,000
Real Life with Jane Pauley	NBC	30	NBC News	$0	$300,000
Unsolved Mysteries	NBC	60	Cosgrove-Meurer	$0	$800,000
America's Most Wanted	Fox	60	STF Productions	$0	$500,000
Cops	Fox	30	Barbour-Langley/ Fox TV Stations	$0	$325,000
Cops II	Fox	30	Barbour-Langley/ Fox TV Stations	$0	$325,000
Totally New Totally Hidden Video	Fox	30	STF Productions	$0	$500,000

Source: Variety, 26 August 1991, 48–54.

Mysteries) often avoided traditionally painstaking lighting and makeup to approximate the "real" look of direct cinema footage and its relatively low production costs. Although reenactments required some expenses for on-location shooting, going on-scene was often less costly than renting studio space. In addition, crime-time and emergency shows minimized the cost of sets, props, and costumes by convincing the agencies they profile to donate police cars, equipment, and even uniforms for the production crew so they could pass for police at crime scenes.[15] Finally, research and logistical costs for most categories of Reali-TV shows are tempered by the information subsidies traditionally extended to the news and entertainment media by public relations operatives hoping to plant favorable stories about their corporate and government clients.[16]

As a result of their shoestring production budgets, prime-time Reali-TV shows cut production costs dramatically and recouped their makers' investments from network license fees alone. With rare exceptions, Reali-TV was the only category of prime-time programming that was not deficit financed in the early 1990s (see table 6.1, which lists production costs for a representative season). In the same year, hour-long dramas and thirty-minute sitcoms often lost $100,000 to $300,000 an episode. At a time when dramas routinely cost over $1 million per episode and half-hour sitcoms cost $500,000 to $600,000 apiece, Reali-TV programs offered considerable savings in production costs, sometimes over 50 percent compared to fictional programming.[17] Reali-TV also enjoyed success in the low-fee, first-run syndication and made-for-cable fields.

Deregulation: Reali-TV Right for Finsyn, Public Service Fights

A changing regulatory climate also contributed to the economic advantages of Reali-TV. In 1970, amid concerns about network power over production companies, the FCC barred the networks from owning a financial interest in and retaining syndication rights to most prime-time entertainment programming (daytime shows, sports, and news were not affected). The financial and syndication, or "finsyn," rules also limited the number of hours of prime-time shows the network could produce. A 1980 consent decree in an antitrust case further limited network prime-time entertainment production to 2.5 hours per week for several years. When the FCC enacted the finsyn rules, its stated goals were to encourage local programming and small independent producers. The FCC hoped that if network production were reined in, other producers might create more innovative, diverse programming. But the small independents did not flourish because the large capital investments and risks required of program producers meant that Hollywood studios with substantial financing still controlled the field. As with the small independents in the film industry, television's smaller production houses depended on winning network contracts for their programming before they could secure bank financing to make it.[18] Independents did not exercise much financial or creative power over the development of new programming, especially when compared with the major studios or top agent-packagers. In many ways, the same relations held in first-run syndication and the made-for-cable markets. Here, the small independents were often financed by large multisystem operators (such as AOL-Time Warner) and the dominant distribution companies (including those run by major studios) in exchange for syndication rights.

Throughout the 1980s, the networks challenged the finsyn rules, arguing that they were no longer in a position to dominate program distribution as they had been before the spread of cable and VCRs, and that they needed to be allowed to compete internationally in the global television market. In April 1991, the FCC allowed the networks to finance and syndicate their own in-house or coproduced programs, and to negotiate for the rights to some outside-produced shows. Hollywood studios and independent producers exhausted a long series of appeals, and the finsyn rules were repealed in 1995.

Although Fox was exempt from the finsyn rules and always produced the bulk of its programming in-house, the three major networks may well have anticipated the repeal of these restrictions and positioned themselves to syndicate Reali-TV programming domestically as well as abroad.[19] From the start, one of the striking characteristics of prime-time Reali-TV programs was that so many of them were network productions or coproductions (see table 6.1). This was true not only of the network newsmagazines, which are produced by their news divisions, but also of crime-time/emergency response and the home video shows. As producers and coproducers of the shows, networks could retain the rights to distribute them under the new rules.

Reali-TV has played a role in the redefinition of public service programming, too. In the Reagan–Bush Sr. climate of lax regulation, programmers did not need to fear FCC scrutiny of the violence and sexual content of Reali-TV, thereby avoiding the costs of in-house standards and practices departments' close screening of these programs, and the potential legal costs of defending them before the FCC. In addition, many Reali-TV producers recast broadcasters' "public service" and "educational" responsibilities to champion the civic value of their programs. Producers ignored traditional definitions of serving the public interest, which focused more on the discussion of public affairs, coverage of local issues, and developing children's intellectual or emotional abilities. Instead, the creators of crime-time programs in particular touted their public contribution as prompting citizens to help law enforcement officers track down their quarry. The executive producer of *America's Most Wanted* opined to *The FBI Law Enforcement Bulletin*: "I believe we are witnessing the birth of a new era in citizen involvement. *America's Most Wanted* has organized some 22 million viewers into the first nationwide neighborhood watch association."[20] In this vision of public service, surveillance and voyeurism replace debate over public affairs, an oxymoronic "nationwide neighborhood watch association" offers a false sense of localism, and education is reduced to instructing viewers about how to avoid becoming a crime victim.

The more recent crop of Reali-TV game shows and survival contests make far less pretense to public service, except for the network newsmagazines. These programs still purport to offer investigative reporting even as they abandon the kinds of subjects most in need of journalistic scrutiny. A recent study of four network newsmagazines found that over half of all stories focused on lifestyle, human interest, and celebrity news. Just 8 percent of reports were about politics, economics, social welfare, and education.[21] As the newsmagazines began to compete with fictional and tabloid television programs such as *Entertainment Tonight* or *Inside Edition*, all increasingly focused on the same topics. By 1997, there was little difference in story selection between the tabloid programs and network newsmagazines, according to one TV monitoring company. The runaway story of the year for both was Princess Diana's death.[22]

International Distribution: The Other Real World

Producers and network investors have also been attracted to Reali-TV because of its ability to sell abroad. Because prime-time Reali-TV earns back its production costs with the first U.S. network showing, any further syndication represents pure profit. U.S. Reali-TV has been sold overseas using two methods. Some shows are licensed outright to foreign broadcasters, the way most U.S. programming traditionally has been marketed. Episodes of top-rated network crime-time/emergency programs *Unsolved Mysteries* and *Rescue 911* have been sold abroad in this manner. One international program distributor claims that "the easiest and most profitable thing for a distributor to do with reality shows is to license them as they are. Prices can even approach what distributors get for action-adventure hours in some territories."[23] By 1991, *Rescue 911* could be seen in Germany, Denmark, and Sweden, and *Unsolved Mysteries* was available in Canada, Spain, France, and Japan.

Many more shows have been formatted because of their topical or local nature, however. This method involves selling or licensing the program's concept for local production with local subjects. U.S. program footage may be sold as well to supplement the local version. "In syndication," notes one executive producer, "shows tend to be more topical and current ... but they have to be more timeless for that backend revenue."[24] As Asu Aksoy and Kevin Robins observe, the challenge for contemporary media distributors "is to transcend vestigial national difference and to create standardized global markets, whilst remaining sensitive to the peculiarities of local markets and differentiated consumer segments."[25] Reali-TV has participated in this "glocalization" strategy. Fremantle, a distributor of game shows and *Candid Camera*, provides a good example of how formatting works. Fremantle's chief executive officer maintains that the company "operates in foreign markets like McDonald's does. . . . There are Fremantle subsidiaries in some countries; in others there are franchise-holders who produce their own local versions of the original product."[26] Home video and hidden-video shows tend to be formatted rather than licensed, allowing foreign broadcasters to insert their own clips into the programs. Crime-time shows have also been formatted. The Swedes developed a version of *Cops,* and *America's Most Wanted* was transformed into the short-lived *Australia's Most Wanted.* Tabloid TV programs and newsmagazines are especially likely to be formatted or customized because the appeal of their stories and journalists tends to be culturally specific. Newsmagazines such as *60 Minutes* often export stories after stripping them of their original graphics, voice-overs, journalists, and hosts so that local journalists can tailor the stories and insert themselves into them.[27]

Reali-TV's growth abroad, especially in Europe, was aided by the widespread movement to privatize and deregulate broadcasting. As one distributor put it in the early 1990s,

With some exceptions, public service broadcasters have always kept a tight lid on the definition of reality. . . . The taste [for Reali-TV] has been stimulated abroad by increased commercialism, but reality shows haven't yet taken hold *en masse.* . . . But because foreign broadcasters are tight for money, the attraction of reality will no doubt be considerable.[28]

Although both private and public broadcasters have purchased Reali-TV, the genre's growth was especially symptomatic of the need for European public broadcasters to operate according to the logic of private channels as competition for audiences and funding mounted.[29] Moreover, the explosion of distribution channels in the 1980s was not only a U.S. phenomenon but a global one. Thus, some of the same cost pressures encountered by U.S. producers were being felt abroad. To better adapt to an unevenly globalizing television market, some Reali-TV has been conceived for international audiences first. Time-Warner/HBO's *World Entertainment Report,* for example, was prelicensed across Europe, Australia, and Japan. The program had a modular format that broadcasters could recompose to fit their needs, inserting local entertainment coverage if desired.

The international spread of Reali-TV cannot be explained as the result of U.S. product innovation because many European and Japanese programs predated their U.S. counterparts. The top-rated U.S. tabloid in the late 1980s and early 1990s, *A Current Affair,* was developed in Australia. *Crimewatch UK,* which reconstructs crimes and asks for viewers' assistance, preceded *America's Most Wanted* and *Unsolved Mysteries,* as did a similar Dutch program. These transborder flows suggest that programs that appear to be products of rapid U.S. innovation when glimpsed from the national perspective were actually the result of an increased international circulation and recirculation of products through globalized media markets. For instance, the widely formatted *America's Funniest Home Videos* was itself inspired by segments of the Japanese variety show *Fun Television with Kato-chan and Ken-chan,* which broadcast humorous videos sent in by viewers. King World's early 1990s revival of *Candid Camera* for foreign and domestic syndication, an attempt to capitalize on the success of *America's Funniest Home Videos,* similarly indicated that there was as much recycling of program formats as rapid innovation at work in the growth of Reali-TV. Mark Burnett, a former parachutist for the British army and creator of *Survivor,* based his program on Swedish and Dutch models.[30] If U.S. television has always mixed the shock of the new with the familiarity of the formulaic, Reali-TV's rise suggested that U.S. producers looked further abroad for "new" ideas, then repackaged them for domestic and international audiences. To the extent that the spread of the genre represented a "victory" for U.S.-based media producers, it was largely a triumph of packaging and marketing.

What Price Reality?

U.S. television underwent a dramatic restructuring in the 1980s, largely precipitated by changing patterns of distribution with the spread of cable and VCRs. Audiences fragmented as these new forces challenged the networks' oligopolistic control over the distribution of television programming. Producers faced smaller license and syndication fees from an expanded customer base, which now included not only the networks but local independent stations, cable networks and superstations, and first-run distributors. Confronted with rapidly rising above-the-line production costs, producers took it out on below-the-line labor and sought cheaper forms of programming. Reali-TV fit the bill. In the early years, networks stepped in to produce examples of this programming that were permissible according to the FCC (newsmagazines for the big three; all forms for Fox), and coproduced kinds they were not allowed to own and syndicate under the finsyn rules until the rules were repealed. Reali-TV made a splash in Europe and Japan in the late 1980s and early 1990s as well, but many U.S. programs of this kind that were licensed and formatted abroad drew on foreign models in the first place. This suggests that if U.S. television turned to Reali-TV to solve its particular economic crisis, the industry both borrowed and exported abroad to do so, touching off a recirculation of products among global media corporations.

Reali-TV has not always solved the economic problems it was meant to address, however. The genre declined for several years in the mid-1990s for several reasons. First, Reali-TV was not always successful in off-network syndication markets as the genre's topicality and timeliness made it less attractive to audiences the second time around. *Unsolved Mysteries,* a top-ratings winner in prime time, was one of the first such programs to be offered for syndication. Although it was sold to broadcast stations in reedited and often updated episodes, it was a financial disappointment to its producers before it found a home on the Lifetime channel, a cable network that could settle for smaller audiences. Similarly, reruns of the first season of *Survivor* did not attract strong viewership. "Reality shows have a short shelf life," one programmer noted. "They just don't seem to sell well in syndication."[31] Under the old finsyn rules, when the networks could not take an ownership interest in most prime-time programs, executives did not have to worry about whether shows were attractive for syndication. Today, the networks produce and own most of their prime-time schedules, sharing the rewards but also the risks of investing in new shows. Thus far, the rewards have been few as no network has produced a hit series that has sold well in syndication, although that is likely to change soon as the current crop of hit programs reaches maturity.

Second, the genre's excesses drove away some advertisers who do not want to be associated with its tawdry image and generally lower-income audiences.[32] There have been public embarrassments, most notoriously Fox's *Who Wants to Marry a Multimillionaire?* in which a man picked his bride from the fifty women who auditioned on television for the job. Fox had to cancel the rebroadcast after news reports aired allegations of abuse by the groom's former girlfriend, raised questions about whether he was indeed a multimillionaire, and exposed the bride's claims to be a Persian Gulf War veteran as misleading. The on-air wedding was quickly annulled. Even more scandalous from advertisers' point of view, much Reali-TV has failed to attract affluent eighteen to thirty-five year olds, appealing more to preteens, seniors, and low-income viewers. This is especially true of the tabloid, crime-time, and emergency programs. There are exceptions that draw more upscale viewers, such as *Survivor,* or young consumers, such as *The Real World,* but the genre's demographics have sometimes forced the networks to sell advertising time on Reali-TV shows at a discount compared with other programs with similar ratings and shares.[33]

Finally, a small legal backlash raised costs to some producers and limited their access to some of the most sensational types of footage.[34] Programs that rely on producers' ability to ride along with police or emergency workers and follow them into homes and ambulances have provoked a rash of suits for invasion of privacy. In 1999, the Supreme Court ruled that it was a violation of Fourth Amendment protections against unreasonable searches for media personnel to enter a home on the authorities' coattails unless aiding in executing a warrant. This is unlikely to curb ride-alongs, but should discourage media entries into suspects' homes without permission. Some producers may be affected by the antipaparazzi laws that sprang up in the wake of Princess Diana's death in a high-speed car accident while fleeing photographers. California's law, for example, criminalizes the use of visually or aurally enhancing technology to capture sound and video in private places that would otherwise be inaccessible. The newsmagazines, indeed any show that relies on personnel going undercover or using deception to get information, must take stock of the unsettled state of law in this area. Many journalists were chilled by a 1997 jury award of $5.5 million to supermarket giant Food Lion in its lawsuit against an ABC *Primetime Live* undercover report that portrayed unsafe food handling and labor conditions at the chain. An appeals court later reduced the damages to $2, but upheld the convictions against ABC on two counts. The networks' journalists, who got jobs at several Food Lion stores so they could gather hidden-camera footage behind the scenes, were found guilty of trespass and breach of loyalty (the latter charge was for gathering hidden-camera footage for the network while being paid by Food Lion as its employees). The case is one of several that have cast doubt on some uses of deception and hidden cameras.

Nonetheless, Reali-TV is still with us and is not likely to go away. Television broadcasters now must compete with cable channels by airing new series all year round. The two biggest Reali-TV hits of late, *Who Wants to Be a Millionaire?* and *Survivor,* both debuted in summer. Their ratings success and the return of labor-management strife in Hollywood sparked a resurgence of the genre in 1999–2000. As long as the networks desperately need to fill the hours around expensive dramas and sitcoms with cheaper programming, offer new fare throughout the year, sell their products on international markets, and control labor, they will provide us with their peculiar brand of reality.

NOTES

1. The earliest use of this term I have encountered is in Ed Siegel, "It's Not Fiction, It's Not News. It's *Not* Reality. It's Reali-TV," *Boston Globe,* 26 May 1991, A1.

2. See, for example, Ken Auletta, *Three Blind Mice: How the TV Networks Lost Their Way* (New York: Random House, 1991).

3. See John Downing, "The Political Economy of U.S. Television," *Monthly Review* 42 (1990): 30–41.

4. See Harold L. Vogel, *Entertainment Industry Economics: A Guide for Financial Analysis,* 2d ed. (Cambridge: Cambridge University Press, 1990), 171.

5. See Patricia Bauer, "Production Scene: Hollywood's New Low-End Market," *Channels* 6 (1986): 14.

6. Ibid., 14.

7. The discussion of staff cutbacks and strikes at the networks draws on

Downing, "Political Economy of U.S. Television," 37–38; and J. Max Robins, "Hired Guns Take over Local News," *Variety*, 24 September 1990, 21.

8. On core and periphery labor forces in the Hollywood entertainment industry, see Susan Christopherson and Michael Storper, "The Effects of Flexible Specialization on Industrial Politics and the Labor Market: The Motion Picture Industry," *Industrial and Labor Relations Review* 42 (1989): 331–47.

9. See Bauer, "Production Scene," 14.

10. Cited in Downing, "Political Economy of U.S. Television," 39.

11. On the role of agent-packagers, see Todd Gitlin, *Inside Prime Time* (New York: Pantheon, 1983), 143–57.

12. On the Arthur Company, see Bauer, "Production Scene," 14. On *America's Most Wanted*, see Daniel R. White, "America's Most Wanted," *American Bar Association Journal* (October 1989): 94. On *Street Stories*, see J. Max Robins, "Producers for Hire," *Variety*, 24 February 1992, 81.

13. Cited in Robins, "Producers for Hire," 81.

14. Cited in Paula Bernstein, "CBS Set for Strikes with News, Reality," *Variety*, 16 March 2001, 1; see also Josef Adalian and Michael Schneider, "Fox Strike Protection: Reality," *Variety*, 11 August 2000, 5.

15. See Scott A. Nelson, "Crime-Time Television," *FBI Law Enforcement Bulletin*, August 1989, 5.

16. On the role of information subsidies in news selection, see Oscar H. Gandy Jr., "Information in Health: Subsidized News," *Media, Culture, and Society* 2 (1980): 103–15.

17. Economic data in this paragraph are from "1991–1992 Primetime at a Glance," *Variety*, 26 August 1991, 48–54.

18. On the constraints faced by "independent" film producers, see Asu Aksoy and Kevin Robins, "Hollywood for the Twenty-first Century: Global Competition for Critical Mass in Image Markets," *Cambridge Journal of Economics* 16 (1992): 1–22. On the similar financial dependence of small television producers, see Vogel, *Entertainment Industry Economics*, 117; and Gitlin, *Inside Prime Time*, 136.

19. The finsyn rules were not applied to Fox as the FCC did not define Fox as a network because it distributed less than fifteen hours a week of programming.

20. Cited in Nelson, "Crime-Time Television," 8.

21. Committee of Concerned Journalists, *Changing Definitions of News*, April 1998, http://www.journalism.org/ccj/resources/chdefonews.html. See also Bill Kovach and Tom Rosenstiel, "Are Watchdogs an Endangered Species?" *Columbia Journalism Review*, May–June 2001, http://www.cjr.org/year/01/3/rosenstiel.asp.

22. See Aaron Barnhart, "Lawrence Company Has Its Finger on the Pulse of TV Topics," *Kansas City Star*, 10 January 1998, E4.

23. Cited in Elizabeth Guider, "Yanks Deal for Real," *Variety*, 3 June 1991, 35.

24. Cited in James McBride, "'On-Scene' Shows Flood Airwaves," *Variety*, 3 June 1991, 32.

25. Aksoy and Robins, "Hollywood for the Twenty-first Century," 18.

26. Cited in Guider, "Yanks Deal for Real," 1.

27. See Clay Calvert, *Voyeur Nation: Media, Privacy, and Peering in Modern Culture* (Boulder, Colo.: Westview Press, 2000), 102.

28. Cited in Guider, "Yanks Deal for Real," 75.

29. See Graham Murdock, "Television and Citizenship: In Defense of Public Broadcasting," in *Consumption, Identity, and Style,* ed. Alan Tomlinson (New York: Routledge, 1990), 77–101; and Paddy Scannell, "Public Service Broadcasting: The History of a Concept," in *Understanding* Television, ed. Andrew Goodwin and Gary Whannel (New York: Routledge, 1990), 11–29.

30. See Edward D. Miller, "Fantasies of Reality: Surviving Reality-Based Programming," *Social Policy* 31 (2000): 10.

31. Cited in John Dempsey, "Hot Genre Gluts TV Market," *Variety,* 3 June 1991, 32.

32. See Michael Schneider, "True Believers: Nets Reap Ratings from Reality Shows," *Variety,* 12 November 1999, 1.

33. See Steve Coe, "Reality 1994: The Reality Is That [Some Network] Reality Bites," *Broadcasting and Cable,* 9 May 1994, 30.

34. The discussion in this paragraph is based on Calvert, *Voyeur Nation,* 133–206.

7

The End of TV 101

*Reality Programs, Formats, and the
New Business of Television*

Ted Magder

In the corridors of network TV, the summer television season has always been an afterthought—a time for reruns, old movies, cheap alternative programs, some pilots, and an out-of-favor, made-for-TV movie. But summer 2000 was the summer of reality TV, *Survivor,* and to a lesser extent, *Big Brother.* CBS, in a desperate attempt to boost its ratings, especially among younger viewers, tried its luck with two formats showing great promise in Europe. *Survivor* blew the lid off. Its ratings climbed each week, its viewers were skewed to a younger demographic, and by the time of its finale, it had become every programmer's dream—a "watercooler" must-see-at-least-once kind of show. Fifty-one million people tuned in for the final episode.

Casual observers and critics alike were prone to dismiss shows such as *Survivor, Big Brother,* and similar entries as a passing fad. Until summer 2000, shows like these fell into the "alternative programming" category, a hodgepodge of down-market entries like Fox's *Who Wants to Marry a Multimillionaire?* or *When Good Pets Go Bad,* and cable shows targeting younger viewers like MTV's *The Real World* (the longest-running reality TV series on U.S. television), the slime-covered game show *Double Dare* on Nickelodeon, and *Bug Juice,* a reality show about kids at camp, on the Disney channel. But the fad has not passed. To the contrary, reality TV—or unscripted drama, as it is sometimes called—has become an accepted program genre for prime-time network TV. For the 2002 season, the major networks devoted at least eight hours a week of their prime-time schedule to reality TV and challenge game shows—up from three hours in 2001. And a solid core of the new shows—*Fear Factor* (NBC), *American Idol* (Fox), and *The Bachelor* (ABC)—earned high marks, especially among younger viewers. They will all be back for the 2003 season, along with the old stalwarts, *Survivor* and *Big Brother.*

The choices TV programmers make about what gets made reflect more than their attempt to please audiences and tap the cultural zeitgeist. Behind the creative task of bringing programs to audiences, TV is a business. That matters because the way TV conducts its business has a direct impact on the process by which programs are selected, financed, and produced. Reality TV may have captured the attention of audiences, but it also looks good on the books and balance sheets of those whose business is television. As *Survivor* built to a crescendo that summer of 2000, network TV took notice. The old axioms of prime-time television production were wearing thin. A new model was in the works.

Thursday Night and the Tipping Point

"I never thought I would see the day," was how Leslie Moonves, president of CBS, reacted to the sudden change of fortune at the network after *Survivor*'s stunning first run.[1] Moonves is one of a handful of individuals who gets to decide what Americans will watch in their living rooms. Given the prominence of television in people's lives—only work, school, and sleep take up more time in a given week—the choices made by network executives may play a substantial role in shaping the texture of the cultural terrain.

Moonves decided to capitalize on *Survivor*'s summer success by scheduling its second installment at 8:00 P.M. on Thursdays, starting January 2001. It was a bold move. Thursday evening is the biggest night for network TV: advertisers looking to boost weekend sales, such as car dealers and Hollywood studios, are willing to pay a premium for spots on Thursday night. According to *Advertising Age,* of the five most expensive thirty-second commercial slots during the 2000–2001 season, four were on Thursday evening. And all four shows were on NBC: *ER* at $620,000, *Friends* at $540,000, *Will and Grace* at $480,000, and *Just Shoot Me* at $465,000.[2] NBC's dominance of Thursday night dates back to the mid-1980s, when *The Cosby Show* first carried it to the top of the network heap. It has been there ever since, becoming the most profitable network primarily on the revenue generated by Thursday night, which NBC has branded "Must-See TV." The phrase meant as much to the other networks as it did to viewers; it had become commonplace to program around Thursday night, the reasoning being that good shows on other networks could never become breakout hits against NBC's formidable lineup and track record. Moonves's gamble worked. By the end of the 2001 season, with *Survivor* in its Thursday night slot, CBS doubled its viewership that evening, from 10 to 20.5 million.[3] Among eighteen to forty-nine year olds, CBS's ratings went from 2.4 in 2000 to 8.2 in 2001 (each rating point is worth approximately 1.25 million viewers). NBC threw everything it could at the *Survivor* challenge: it ran extralong episodes of *Friends* until 8:40 P.M.; it ran highlight reels from *Saturday Night Live.* But by the end of the season, NBC's ratings among eighteen to forty-nine year olds dropped from 9.7 in 2000 to 8.9 in 2001. The two networks were now nip and tuck in a battle for Thursday evening supremacy.

Audience figures tell only half the tale, however. To understand the impact of *Survivor* (and reality TV more generally), one has to look at both sides of an accountant's ledger. Audience figures reveal a lot (though not everything) about the revenue side, but they reveal nothing about costs. NBC's dominance on Thursday night carries a high price tag. *Friends,* NBC's 8:00 P.M. anchor comedy, cost $5.5 million per episode in 2001, making it the most expensive half hour of network television; at 10:00 P.M., NBC shelled out $13 million for *ER* in 2001, the most expensive hour-long drama on television.

The lofty price tag for *Friends* and *ER* is a function of the business model that has driven network TV since the 1960s. NBC doesn't own either show; instead, it licenses the right to air both programs from the company that produces them, Warner Bros. Television.[4] Generally, a license deal permits the buyer to air the show twice over the course of a season and capture as much advertising revenue as it can. If the buyer likes the show, the contract calls for renewal at roughly the same price per episode over a set number of years—typically four. When hit shows outlive their original contracts, the price of renewal often goes up. Take *Friends,* for example. In 1994, the six principal actors agreed to five-year contracts at $22,500 per episode. At each renewal of the contract, the *Friends* cast negotiated as a group, with threats to move on and pursue less exhausting film careers. In 1999, they were paid $125,000 an episode, and the following two seasons, $750,000 an episode. For the 2002 season—the final year for the show—each cast member earned $1 million an episode, with each episode budgeted at $7.5 million.[5] What happened with *Friends* (and *ER*) is not unique. Traditional scripted drama on TV is expensive (or becomes expensive over the life of a series) in large measure because of the high costs of getting and keeping the above-the-line talent (actors, writers, and directors).

Survivor represents an entirely different business model. After making *Eco-Challenge* for MTV, Mark Burnett, *Survivor*'s producer, spent almost four years going network to network pitching the show. CBS agreed to a summer trial, but only if the basic terms of the business model could be changed. Instead of handing Burnett a license fee to deliver the show, CBS agreed to share *Survivor*'s advertising revenue with Burnett and asked him to presell the sponsorship.[6] Burnett secured eight sponsors before the first day of principal photography, selling not only thirty-second spots but also sponsorship space in the show itself. Eight advertisers in all, including Anheuser-Busch, General Motors, Visa, Frito-Lay, Reebok, and Target, paid roughly $4 million each for ad time, product placement in the show, and a website link.[7] For subsequent runs of *Survivor*, advertisers have shelled out close to $12 million. Put another way, CBS doesn't pay to have the show made; the sponsors do. And even though *Survivor* is probably the most expensive reality show to date, with production costs rising from $1 million

TABLE 7.1

Sample Production Costs of Programs on U.S. TV, 2001–2002 Season

One-Hour Dramas	
24 (Fox/FX)	$2 million
The Practice (ABC)	$1.2 million
ER (NBC)	$13 million
Half-Hour Sitcoms	
King of Queens (CBS)	$.6 million
The Drew Carey Show (ABC)	$3 million
Friends (NBC)	$7 million
Entertainment Magazines	
E.T. (Entertainment Tonight; E!)	$.2 million
Reality TV	
Survivor (CBS)	$1.4 million
American Idol (Fox)	$1 million
Big Brother (CBS)	$.6 million
America's Most Wanted (Fox)	$.5 million
Spy TV (NBC)	$.4 million
The Real World (MTV)	$.3 million
Trading Places (TLC)	$.09 million
Prime-Time Game Shows	
Who Wants to Be a Millionaire? (ABC)	$.65 million

an episode for the original *Survivor* to $1.5 million an episode for subsequent editions, the margins are good. With presold sponsorships covering the costs of production and thirty-second spots running just ahead of *ER* (*Survivor: Africa* topped *ER* with the most expensive thirty-second spot during the 2001–2002 season, at $445,000 to *ER*'s $425,000), *Survivor* is a golden calf.[8]

Everyone noticed, and *Survivor* became the tipping point not only for its content and the genre it represents but for the business model it offered. Scott Sassa, the West Coast president of NBC—the network that prides itself on premium, "high-quality," scripted entertainment; the network that owned Thursday night; the network that makes more money than any other—uttered the magic words: "Reality programming is not just a fad, it's a trend . . . and it is a genre that is going to be around for a while."[9] Sassa and Jeff Zucker, president of NBC Entertainment, were already hard at work striking deals to air *Fear Factor, Spy TV,* and *The Weakest Link.* They had also come to terms with Burnett for a show called *Destination Mir,* an astronaut-training competition with the winner taking a (real) trip aboard a Soyuz rocket to the Mir space station. General Electric—the owner of NBC and a major aerospace contractor—agreed to provide $40 million to fund the project. And as CBS had done with *Survivor,* NBC agreed to split the ad revenue fifty-fifty with Burnett. *Destination Mir* never happened. The space station fell out of orbit. But in this case it was the deal, not the show, that mattered. "This is just shocking, that NBC would do this," said one TV executive. "It's the cardinal rule. It's TV 101. We finance the 90 percent of shows that are failures with the ten percent that are hits. You can't share ad revenues."[10]

The End of TV 101 in the United States

The business of television begins with a simple observation: people like to watch. Since the late 1960s, on any given day (or night), the amount of time people spend with TV has been a stable, predictable number: television takes up almost 50 percent of the time North Americans spend with media products and cultural events; on average, each U.S. household watches just over 1,600 hours of TV a year.[11] Americans aren't fickle when it comes to watching television, but they can be fickle when it comes to watching particular programs. The challenge for television executives and programmers is getting the audiences' attention and keeping it once the TV has been turned on.

The attention of audiences is sold to advertisers—that's the most common way over-the-air U.S. television stations and networks make their money. Until the mid-1980s, one could have said that the unique feature of the U.S. TV market was its commercial or advertiser-funded orientation; publicly funded TV was and still is a marginal entity in the U.S. system. For much of the rest of the world, the opposite was true: publicly funded TV dominated most systems, even in cases where revenue from advertising was permitted on a limited basis. Now, TV almost everywhere relies heavily on advertising dollars. Even so, the U.S. TV system stands out— not any longer because it is commercial but because of the scale of the money in the system. In 1996, total TV advertising dollars spent per household in the United States amounted to $443. In the United Kingdom that same year, the comparable figure was $239, and in Germany it was $153. With almost 100 million households, U.S. TV advertising expenditures in 1996 amounted to $42.5 billion. For the following twelve countries combined—Australia, Canada, France, Germany, Italy, Japan, Mexico, the Netherlands, Spain, Sweden, Switzerland, and the United Kingdom—with more than 200 million households, total advertising expenditures amounted to $45 billion in 1996.[12] The U.S. TV market is awash with advertising revenue, and it goes a long way to explaining how the system— both in the United States and elsewhere—works.[13]

It is sometimes said that TV, as a business, does what any business tries to do: give customer what they want or need at a price they're willing to pay, and if possible, establish a relationship of trust and reliability to ensure a long and fruitful commercial relationship. But the customers are, for the most part, the advertisers, not the viewers. What TV in the United States does—and does rather well on the face of it—is triangulate between the wants and needs of advertisers and the wants and needs of viewers. Advertisers pay for the attention of viewers, but what they seek in particular are viewers who have money (or credit) to spend or those who are at the stage of their life where they may develop long-term brand loyalty. Not every viewer is valued equally; generally speaking, advertisers pay more for younger (adult) viewers—typically defined as eighteen to forty-nine year olds. Few people in the industry fully trust the validity and reliability of the underlying mathematics of television advertising, but this lack of faith matters less than one might think. The blunt language of age demographics, ratings, and shares (which at best tell you what channel a TV is tuned to, but nothing about the attention or interest of viewers) is the currency of the television business.[14] It is simple and easy to follow. Those who pay the bills seem willing to accept its imperfections.

Given these fundamentals on the revenue side, it is wrong to say that TV in the United States gives people what they most want to watch, or that it responds to the demands, interests, and needs of viewers. Instead, given the interests of advertisers and the habits of TV viewing, television executives try to produce or schedule shows that are only marginally better than the other offerings available at the same time. The goal of U.S. television is to give people programming that they are willing to watch or, at the very least, programming from which they will not turn away. From time to time hits emerge and programs can become events with loyal followings. But the day-to-day business of TV doesn't run on hits. It runs on habit.

The effects on TV programming and scheduling that flow from a dependence on advertising have to be considered in relation to the costs of producing television programming. Like the other creative industries, the economics of making content for television is risky and expensive. Grant Tinker, who piloted both NBC and MTM studios some years ago, once said: "Television would be wonderful if it were only on Wednesday nights."[15] Tinker was referring to the problem of creativity. There are only so many good writers, actors, and other talented people to go around, and the medium of TV requires hundreds—even thousands—of hours of new programs each year. The talent problem is real enough; it becomes an even more serious problem because of the peculiar economics of television production—a problem that characterizes the creative industries as a whole. In the making of television programs, as in the making of movies or books, close to 100 percent of the costs are incurred making the first copy. Once a program is finished, the cost of duplicating that show, or making extra copies, is virtually nil. In the case of TV, where most programming is serial, first-copy costs are incurred for a number of episodes in advance (the creativity deficit would be that much greater if television consisted mostly of one-time programs). The real problem comes next: until the show airs, it is almost impossible to predict its success. Pretesting programs is routine, but the history of U.S. TV is riddled with so many examples of hits that tested poorly (like *All in the Family* in the 1970s) as well as duds that tested well that the tests are rarely regarded as definitive by TV veterans.[16] Richard Caves refers to this problem as the "nobody knows" principle.[17] U.S. television runs on it.

To deal with the nobody knows principle, network TV has developed some programming axioms. First, deliver audiences to advertisers in a "buying mood." Viewers need to be tuned in, but not unduly upset or disturbed by the content. Next, stick to established program genres and avoid challenging the genre expectations of viewers. Third, recycle and copy successful shows. Imitation is the sincerest form of flattery on TV. Hit shows beget spin-offs, sequels, or siblings; the *Law and Order* franchise, which includes the original show as well as *Law and Order: Special Victims Unit* and *Law and Order: Criminal Intent,* is one example; ABC's development of *The Bachelorette* after the success of *The Bachelor* is another. Hit shows also beget copycats, shows that attempt to replicate the successful formula with slight modifications. The success of ABC's *Who Wants to be Millionaire?* instantly spawned the return of game shows to prime-time television with Fox's *Greed* and NBC's *Twenty-One.*[18] In each case, the goal is the same: to reduce creative uncertainty by using a template that has proven successful. The last axiom is the most important: every programming trend runs its course, and thus programmers must constantly scan the horizon for the next sure thing.

As program production costs escalated in the 1990s, by as much as 30 percent over the course of the decade, TV programmers developed other techniques to cut costs and raise revenues. On the revenue side, the average number of prime-time ads jumped from six minutes an hour in 1986 to nearly eleven minutes an hour by the mid-1990s.[19] To avoid the renegotiations that drove up the price of *ER* and *Friends,* standard contracts for dramatic shows have been lengthened to six or more years. At the same time, networks have turned to cheaper "alternative" programming during prime time and reduced the number of hours they commit to original dramas. Newsmagazines, such as NBC's *Dateline* and CBS's *48 Hours,* take advantage of overheads already committed to news divisions to produce an hour of television at less than 50 percent of the cost of fictional programming. Repeats have also become a more conscious cost-cutting strategy. Fox, for example, airs the drama *24* twice a week during its first run; it has also introduced a night of repeat comedies into its prime-time lineup. The newest strategy to reduce program costs goes by the names repurposing or multiplexing. *Law and Order: Special Victims Unit* and *Law and Order: Criminal Intent* are shown first on NBC and later the same week on the cable channel USA Network (the show is produced by Studios USA Television). Fox employs a similar strategy with *24.* The cable channel FX airs the show twice on weekends after its network run. The

Fox network pays a license fee of roughly $1.65 million per episode, while FX kicks in another $150,000. Both channels are owned by the News Corporation, which also owns the show's production company, Twentieth Century Fox Television. As is typical, the license fees don't cover the total cost of the program—roughly $2 million an episode. But keeping things in-house has its advantages: international sales of *24* are expected to generate more than $1 million an episode.[20] In the effort to find new strategies to reduce costs and increase revenues, no one is standing pat: "If we don't change the economic model of all of these things," NBC's Zucker recently remarked, "we are going to collapse under the weight of the overhead. The economic models are going to have to keep on evolving and changing."[21]

All Roads Lead to Aalsmeer: Endemol, Big Brother, and the Miracle of Formats

The emergence of reality TV is yet another strategy in the general effort to reduce costs and uncertainty. But it is also more than that. Reality TV represents three significant changes to the production side of TV: the increasing use of formats as the basis for program production; the increasing tendency to use TV programs as the basis for a multimedia exploitation of the creative property; and the increasing strength of European program suppliers in the U.S. market (See Table 7.2).

No company better illustrates the changes to the production side of television than Endemol.[22] The company's name itself reflects the merger in 1994 of two firms headed by men with long histories in Dutch television production: John de Mol and Joop van den Ende. In the 1980s, as the privatization of European television gathered momentum, de Mol and van den Ende pursued similar growth strategies, incorporating game shows and serial dramas based on formats both purchased abroad and devised in-house. Both companies became regular suppliers to RTL4 in the Netherlands (the first private commercial broadcaster in that country), and through RTL, major suppliers of programs in the German market. Endemol now claims corporate holdings and affiliates in over twenty countries, including France, the United Kingdom, Germany, Portugal, the United States, Brazil, Mexico, South Africa, and Australia. Capitalizing on its success, Endemol's founders sold the company to Telefonica, the Spanish telecommunications giant, for €5 billion in 2000. Since then, Endemol

TABLE 7.2
Sample of Reality TV and Format Shows on U.S. Broadcast Networks,
and Originating Production Company, 2000–2002

NBC	
Fear Factor	Endemol USA (Netherlands)
Spy TV	Endemol (Netherlands)
Dog Eat Dog	BBC Worldwide (U.K.)
The Weakest Link	BBC Worldwide (U.K.)
CBS	
Big Brother	Endemol (Netherlands)
Survivor	Castaway (U.K.)
Amazing Race	Touchstone/Bruckheimer (U.S.)
Fox	
American Idol	FremantleMedia (U.K.)
Boot Camp	LMNO Productions (U.S.)/Granada (U.K.)
Temptation Island	Rocket Science (U.S.)
ABC	
Who Wants to Be a Millionaire?	Celador (U.K.)
The Mole	T.T.T.I. (Belgium)
The Bachelor	Telepictures–Warner Bros. (U.S.)
UPN	
Chains of Love	Endemol (Netherlands)
Under One Roof	Endemol USA (Netherlands)

Sources: *Hollywood Reporter, Broadcasting and Cable, Variety, Electronic Media,* and the *New York Times* (various dates).

has continued to flourish. In 2001, Endemol's revenues topped €914 million, a 63 percent jump over the previous year. It is easily the most prolific pan-European producer of television programming.

Endemol has risen to prominence on the strength of its formats. By 2001, the company claimed to have over five hundred formats in its library, with a heavy emphasis on game shows and reality TV programs. At any one time, it has as many as three hundred formats in production around the world, including such titles as *Fear Factor, Big Diet, Star Academy, All You Need Is Love, Love Letters, $100,000 Show, Will They or Won't They, Domino Day, Blind Faith,* and *1 vs. 100.* No format better illustrates its success than *Big Brother,* which had been sold in seventeen different countries by 2002. In the United States, CBS bought the rights to *Big Brother* for $20 million, and though the first version of the program did not grab U.S. audiences the way it did overseas, the show is a classic example of the Endemol strategy as well as the value of reality TV to broadcasters and program distributors.

A good format—like *Big Brother*—is a template providing detailed production and marketing guidelines that can be tailored to each locale.[23] Peter Bazalgette, creative director of Endemol UK and a founding producer of *Big Brother*, has noted that "formats are simply concentrated ideas with rules. The key to most of these things is to have the kind of idea that works for everyone."[24] Everyone, in this case, means different audiences in different markets. Formats are designed for international sale; more precisely, they are designed to be adapted locally. Brian Briggs, an international line producer at Endemol, put it this way: "The reason why Endemol is so successful is that we take a format that works in one country, strip everything cultural off of it, export it to a new country and then, over time, add cultural aspects of that country to it."[25] The fundamentals differ little from market to market. Endemol supplies a "playbook" (or bible) and "coach" (or producer) who consults with the local producer on the adaptation of the show's basic elements. In the case of *Big Brother*, those fundamental elements include the closed set, length of time the show lasts, number of contestants, weekly competitions, weekly elimination of a contestant, and round-the-clock use of cameras that reduces to nil the contestants' privacy.[26] If things work well, a format becomes an international brand with distinctive and carefully modulated local variations—the formula is tweaked, like the sugar content in Coca-Cola.

For broadcasters who purchase format rights the advantages are considerable. Using a format greatly reduces the risks associated with first-copy costs and the nobody knows principle. Endemol has already assumed the creative challenge and expense of a generic first copy, and it has considerable experience honing a format's elements to meet varying audience and broadcaster expectations in different markets. Recalling an old industry axiom that four out of five original programs fail, Ben Silverman, who brokered the deals for *Big Brother*, *The Weakest Link*, and *Dog Eat Dog*, notes that three out of four shows based on a proven format succeed, or at least are renewed.[27] Not surprisingly, formats have been used more frequently outside the United States, where in general, commercial broadcasters cannot afford the trial-and-error approach that has been the hallmark of developing hit shows in the United States.[28] A further advantage accrues to broadcasters in countries with quotas and content regulations tied to domestic content: local adaptations of formats typically qualify as locally produced programming. Format shows, in other words, can satisfy regulatory as well as economic considerations.

Follow the Money: Before and Beyond the Box

Reality shows demonstrate the viability of three business strategies that together may fundamentally alter the logic of TV production (see figure on facing page.). First, almost every show in the genre demonstrates the enormous potential for product placement and the willingness of advertisers to invest in a show's production. Money from sponsors for TV production was common in the early days of U.S. television: as the names suggest, shows like *Texaco Star Theatre, The Colgate Comedy Hour,* and The *Goodyear Television Playhouse* were under the sponsor's thumb; *I Love Lucy,* initially sponsored by Philip Morris, featured Lucille Ball and Desi Arnaz puffing away.[29] But U.S. TV moved away from this model of funding in the 1960s. Advertisers bought time from the networks, but no longer played a direct role in the production phase of programming. Even as Hollywood discovered the advantages of product placement as a way of offsetting rising movie costs in the 1990s, TV generally steered clear of product placement.[30] *Survivor*'s $12 million placement deals opened the gates. So too did the success of *Who Wants to Be a Millionaire?* with its almost invisible product placement when its host, Regis Philbin, would call on AT&T to help reach a phone-a-friend lifeline. The examples proliferate: Fox's *Murder in Small Town X* featured placements by Taco Bell, Jeep, and Nokia; Ford and ad agency J. Walter Thompson sponsored *No Boundaries* on the WB network. Procter and Gamble, the company that might be said to have started sponsored programs with the soap opera *Guiding Light,* has renewed its interest in program production; it currently maintains a stake in *Sabrina, the Teenage Witch, Becker,* and *The King of Queens.*[31] It also produces its own show on G4, the new cable "gaming" channel; the show *Cheat! Pringles Gamers Guide* is named after Procter and Gamble's famous line of corrugated potato chips.[32]

Product placement, or product integration as some now call it, is more than just a good way to cover production costs. The arrival in 1998 of the Digital Video Recorder (DVR) only heightened the advertising industry's ongoing concern that the traditional TV spot is losing its hold on viewers.[33] Machines like TiVo and ReplayTV raise the stakes considerably because they can be designed to skip traditional ad breaks. If DVRs became popular (sales have been sluggish to date), ad-skipping models would strike at the heart of the traditional program supplier-network-advertiser relationship. The industry response to the DVR has been scattered. In the

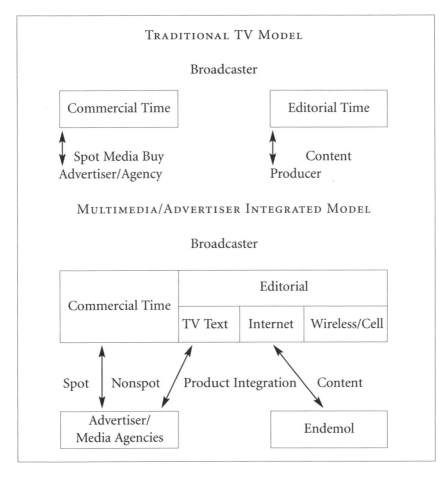

A New Model for Content Delivery and Financing. Adapted from a presentation by Michiel Dieperink, executive director for advertising-funded programming, Endemol International, June 2002, Aalsmeer.

development phase, Disney (ABC) and General Electric (NBC), among others, invested in DVRs to ensure they were on the inside of such a potentially revolutionary device. But in 2001, the networks filed a lawsuit against ReplayTV's parent company, claiming in part that the technology violates copyright by altering the content of their programming—namely, the ad breaks.[34] Leaving aside the legal questions, the TV industry now finds itself desperately searching for new revenue streams—something that may be a matter of survival.

Product placement and direct sponsorship represent one strategy in the search for new money. A second strategy is the expansion of merchandise tie-ins.[35] Merchandise tie-ins have been around since the beginning of television—*Hopalong Cassidy* gun-and-holster sets and the music of *The Monkees* are two classic examples—but the phenomenon has picked up steam, especially in connection with reality shows and their affiliated websites. There are now over 150 *Survivor*-themed products available in the United States, including everything from CDs and bug spray, to board games and bandanas. Fans can also play a *Survivor* trivia challenge online.[36] In Australia, Energizer Max batteries were sold with a sticker carrying a code that when entered into the *Big Brother* website, allowed viewers to watch up to ten audition videos.[37] In the United States, Baskin-Robbins ice cream has signed a cobranding deal with NBC to feature a "gross-out" sundae consumed on *Fear Factor* as well as *Will and Grace*'s Rocky Road of Romance and other frozen delights.[38]

The third business strategy is easily the most revolutionary in terms of its possibilities: it extends the "program" beyond the confines of the box in the living room and encourages audiences to pay to participate in the show's dramatic arc, or to use other media to stay in touch with the program. *Big Brother* has led the way. The Real Network/CBS webcast of *Big Brother 2* in summer 2001 drew 56,026 consumers who paid monthly subscription fees of between $9.95 and $19.95 to receive round-the-clock video feeds of the program. With $15 as an average purchase, the webcasts generated around $850,000. Said David Katz, vice president for strategic planning and interactive ventures at CBS: "Through this experiment we've seen there clearly is value in using our content on a subscription basis. It will allow us to diversify our revenue streams. This is just the beginning."[39] In the United Kingdom, where *Big Brother* captured up to 35 percent of the television audience in summer 2002, 3.5 million viewers (a little more than 50 percent of the average audience) voted on the eviction of Adele Roberts.[40] They paid twenty-five pence each to do so, which translates into £875,000, more than the cost of producing the episode and more than the roughly £40,000 paid for a thirty-second slot during eviction night. In Australia, some 250,000 people paid fifty cents to vote on the weekly eviction; the $125,000 compares favorably with the $50,000 paid for thirty-second spots during the show's finale (a princely sum on Australian TV).[41] In the United Kingdom, *Big Brother* devotees had access to SMS text news updates, logos, and ring-tones. They could vote by text message as well. Comments and suggestions could also be sent to the production team, and some of those ideas would run alongside the interactive version of the TV broadcast, which supplied four different video views of the house. In Sweden, the summer 2002 version of *Big Brother* featured live streaming to mobile phones.[42] As the head of interactive media at Endemol UK puts it, "We're creating this virtuous circle that excites the interactive audience about what's going on in the house, drives them toward the TV program, the TV program will drive them to the Internet, the Internet to the other ways they can get information, and the other ways back to the TV."[43]

In early 2002, Endemol unveiled a new corporate strategy to capitalize on these trends, declaring that it was now in the business of producing interactive multimedia content. John de Mol estimates that by 2005, close to 40 percent of the company's business will be "multiplatform."[44] In this model, the TV program functions as the driving force behind an array of alternative revenue-generating schemes using both the Internet and mobile phones. Endemol believes that audiences will pay for enhanced content (like video feeds not available via TV) as well as content delivered to cell phones and other wireless devices. For John van der Putten, director of Endemol Interactive International, TV programs may also serve as the gateway to an array of services that go beyond the program and its cast of characters. He explains:

> The most popular content will be cross-platform content. . . . For example, our Big Diet platform is comprised of a TV program also called *Big Diet* and "Diet Magazine" and an interactive website platform. In addition to watching the show's participants lose weight, viewers who also want to lose weight can register to become a member of the platform. They receive advice about losing weight and interact with "buddies," members like themselves who provide support. People pay €11 to become platform members.[45]

Is This It?

Television is a fickle business. Is it possible that reality TV is merely a passing fad? The evidence suggests not. The genre has proven reliable and cost effective. There is every reason to believe it will become one of the staples of TV. But the emergence of reality TV signals more important trends. First, the success of Endemol and U.K. producers highlights the growing internationalization of television production. To be sure, U.S. producers still control the lion's share of the international trade in TV products (raking in close to $5 billion in exports, or almost ten times the amount taken in by the next largest exporter, the United Kingdom), but they increasingly work with foreign partners, and even more significant, must respond to programming trends and revenue models developed elsewhere.[46] Yet what reality TV and formats reveal most of all is that the traditional revenue model used to produce commercial television is becoming anachronistic. We are entering a new era of product placement and integration, merchandising, pay-per-view, and multiplatform content. The emerging business models will change what we see and how we see it.

NOTES

1. Bill Carter, "Thanks to *Survivor*, CBS Gains on Thursdays," *New York Times*, 3 May 2001, C1.

2. See Stuart Elliott, "TV Networks Wonder How Much Lower Prices for Commercial Time Could Go," *New York Times*, 25 September 2001, C1, 16 (chart). CBS's *Everybody Loves Raymond*, on Monday nights, generated the fifth-highest return on thirty-second slots, taking in $460,000.

3. See Carter, "Thanks to *Survivor*, CBS Gains on Thursdays" and "Successes of Reality TV Put Networks in *Survivor* Mode," *New York Times*, 3 February 2001, C1.

4. See Michael Freeman, "TV in Transition: Forging a Model for Profitability; Repurposing the First Step toward Fiscal Viability," *Electronic Media*, 28 January 2002, 1. See also Harold Vogel, *Entertainment Industry Economics: A Guide for Financial Analysis*, 5th ed. (Cambridge: Cambridge University Press, 2001), chapter 4.

5. See Joe Flint, "NBC Finalizes Deal to Keep *Friends* for Final Season: Cast Will Get Raise," *Wall Street Journal Online*, 28 February 2002. Warner Bros. made twenty-two episodes for the 2002 season and received about $6 million in license fees from NBC. License fees typically cover about 80 percent of a show's production costs, and the producer picks up the rest of the tab. Because it owns the show, Warner Bros. reaps all the income from international sales and the market for reruns in the United States. It has been estimated that over its shelf life, *Friends* may generate more than $1 billion in revenue for Warner Bros. (The "friends" are not the highest-paid sitcom actors on TV. Kelsey Grammer makes $1.6 million an episode for his work on *Frasier*.) See also Bill Carter, "*Friends* Deal Will Pay Each of Its Six Stars $22 Million," *New York Times*, 12 February 2002, C1.

6. The story of Burnett and his negotiations with CBS is told at length in Bill Carter, "Survival of the Pushiest," *New York Times Magazine*, 28 January 2001, 66. The precise terms of the revenue-sharing deal between CBS and Burnett are a source of widespread speculation.

7. See Michael McCarthy, "Sponsors Line Up for *Survivor* Sequel," *USA Today*,

9 October 2000, 1B. See also Michael McCarthy, "Ads Are Here, There, Everywhere: Agencies Seek Creative Ways to Expand Product Placement," *USA Today*, 19 June 2001, 1B; and Stephen McClellan, "Surviving Sponsors," *Broadcasting and Cable*, 9 September 2002, www.tvinsite.com.

8. The show continues to do well. *Survivor: Marquesas* and *Survivor: Africa* were the sixth and seventh top-rated shows, respectively, during the 2001–2002 TV season. See Standard and Poor's, *Movies and Home Entertainment: Industry Series*, 9 May 2002. See also Warren Cohen, "Once a Cheap Date, Reality TV Bites into Network Budgets," *Inside*, 6 August 2001, http://wjcohen.home.mindspring.com /insideclips/reality.htm.

9. Cited in Cynthia Littleton, "Sassa: NBC to Get in Touch with Reality," *Hollywood Reporter*, 19 July 2000. NBC smartly passed on *Chains of Love*, the one Endemol reality format that did not do well in the United States.

10. Cited in Carter. "Survival of the Pushiest." See also Mary Motta, "Sign-up Begins to Be Cosmonaut on *Destination Mir.*" www.space.com/businesstechnology/business/realityTV_signup_000928.html.

11. CBS Office of Economic Analysis, cited in Vogel, *Entertainment Industry Economics*, table 1.2, 9.

12. McCann-Erickson and Zenith Media, industry estimates, cited in Vogel, *Entertainment Industry Economics*, table 6.3, 183. Total spending on advertising in all media mirrors this trend. At roughly $210 billion in 1999, total advertising expenditures in the United States were approximately 50 percent of the world total.

13. With the advent of cable, two new revenue streams emerged: cable TV channels, such as the Discovery Channel or MTV, are paid a fee by cable companies, such as Time Warner Cable or Comcast, to be part of the package of channels offered to cable subscribers; other channels, such as HBO, derive the lion's share of their income from monthly subscription fees paid directly by viewers. HBO does not interrupt the flow of its programs with advertising, but most cable channels derive considerable revenue from the sale of audiences to advertisers.

14. See Erik Larson, "Watching Americans Watch TV," *Atlantic Monthly*, March 1992, 66.

15. Cited in Todd Gitlin, *Inside Prime Time* (New York: Pantheon, 1983), 82.

16. See ibid., chapter 2. See also Joyce Nelson, *The Perfect-Machine: TV in the Nuclear Age* (Toronto: Between the Lines, 1987), especially chapter 6.

17. Richard Caves, *Creative Industries: Contracts between Art and Commerce* (Cambridge: Harvard University Press, 2000), especially chapter 1. For an excellent overview of the financial and economic dimensions of the media industry, see Vogel, *Entertainment Industry Economics*. For a superb recent assessment of scholarship in this area, see David Hesmondhalgh, *The Cultural Industries* (London: Sage, 2002).

18. See Bernard Weinraub, "Sudden Explosion of Game Shows Threatens the Old TV Staples," *New York Times*, 9 February 2000, E1.

19. Standard and Poor's, *Broadcasting and Cable: Industry Survey,* 24 January 2002, 14.

20. *24* reveals another relatively new feature of the TV business in the United States. Since the repeal of the financial interest and syndication rules in 1995, networks increasingly air shows that they own and produce or those produced by corporate affiliates. The repeal of finsyn made it possible for broadcast networks and Hollywood studios to merge since the studios were typically the "independents" from which the networks bought programming. See Freeman, "TV in Transition"; and Diane Mermigas, "Finsyn Repeal Has Yet to Pay Off," *Electronic Media,* 3 June 2002, 30.

21. Cited in Freeman, "TV in Transition."

22. The author has benefited from visits to Endemol's studio in Aalsmeer, Netherlands, in June 2001 and June 2002. See also Albert Moran, *Copycat TV: Globalisation, Program Formats, and Cultural Identity* (Luton, U.K.: University of Luton Press, 1998), 33–37; and "The Reality after the Show," *Economist,* 14 September 2002, 65. For a time, Endemol was also in the business of producing theatrical events (like *Les Miserables*) and live events (like *Holiday on Ice*)—the legacy of Joop van den Ende Productions. The theatrical and live-event wing of the company was sold back to van den Ende in 1999.

23. See Moran, *Copycat Television,* especially chapter 2. Good formats are also cost effective. John de Mol's original concept, called *The Golden Cage,* was to enclose participants in a dome for a year. Concluding that the idea was too expensive and risky, he shortened the duration to eighty days, changed the dome to a prefabricated house, and added a competitive element—each week a contestant is removed from the house. See Peter Thal Larsen, "Father of Big Brother," *Financial Times,* 12 August 2000, 9.

24. Cited in Michael Collins, "Who Owns Our Lives? Copyrights and Wrongs: In the Global TV Market, Great Ideas Are the Key," *Observer,* 22 April 2001, 17.

25. Brian Briggs, interview by author, Endemol, Aalsmeer, Netherlands, 19 June 2001.

26. In the case of *Who Wants to Be a Millionaire?* U.K.-based Celador Productions requires that the lighting, set, and sound be identical around the world. See Charles Goldsmith, "American Agent Strikes Gold with British TV Programs," *Wall Street Journal,* 18 May 2001, B1.

27. Silverman's remarks are borne out: of the first five Endemol formats introduced into the U.S. market, only one, *Chains of Love,* did not get renewed. The show also tanked in Australia. A North American, Silverman joined the William Morris Agency's London office in 1996. He is now the head of Reveille, a U.S.-based television production company that is part of Vivendi Universal Entertainment. See Goldsmith, "American Agent Strikes Gold"; and Michael Wolff, "The Missing Link," *New York Magazine,* 4 June 2001, www.newyorkmag.com/page.cfm ?page_id=4774&position=1.

28. Format TV did not begin with reality TV. In the international TV market, the most common format genre is the game show. The two most successful companies in this area are FremantleMedia and King World.

29. See, for example, Erik Barnouw, *The Sponsor: Notes on a Modern Potentate* (Oxford: Oxford University Press, 1978).

30. On product placement in Hollywood, see Mark Crispin Miller, "Hollywood: The Ad," *Atlantic Monthly,* April 1990, 41; and Janet Wasko, *Hollywood in the Information Age: Beyond the Silver Screen* (Austin: University of Texas Press, 1994), chapter 8.

31. See Paula Bernstein and Michael Schneider, "Sponsors Paying to Play," *Variety,* 18 September 2000, 21.

32. See Stephanie Thompson and David Goetzl, "P&G Melds Product into Entertainment," *AdAge.com,* 8 July 2002, www.adage.com/news.cms?newsId=35332.

33. See Michael Lewis, "Boom Box," *New York Times Magazine,* 13 August 2000, 36.

34. The ReplayTV 4000 series also makes it possible to send recorded programs to other units in the home or to other ReplayTV owners on the Web. See Fred von Lohmann, "Get Ready for the Next Big Copyright Battle," *California Lawyer,* June 2002, 29; and Doug Isenberg, "ReplayTV Lawsuit: Napster Redux?" *Cnet.News.com,* 12 November 2001, http://news.com.com/2010-1079-281601 .htm.

35. See Bob Tedeschi, "Television Networks Sell Tie-Ins on the Web," *New York Times,* 7 June 1999, C4.

36. See Michael McCarthy, "Major Marketing Deals for *Survivor* Win CBS' Vote," *USA Today,* 21 February 2001, 1B; Bill Carter, "New Reality Show to Place Ads between the Ads," *New York Times,* 30 April 2001, A1; and Michael McCarthy, "Ads Show Up in Unexpected Places: Line between Reality, Marketing Gets Fuzzy," *USA Today,* 23 March 2001, 1B.

37. See Orietta Guerrera, "How a Series Was Sold to Saturation," *Sunday Age* (Melbourne), 21 April 2002, 7.

38. See Paige Albiniak, "The Selling of Prime Time," *Broadcasting and Cable,* 16 September 2002, www.tvinsite.com.

39. Cited in Josef Adalian, "Webcasting of *Big Bro 2* Shows Net Can Be Profitable," *Variety,* 27 September 2001, 5.

40. See Leo Hickman, "*Big Brother,* Where Art Thou?" *Guardian,* 10 July 2002, 4; and Raymond Snoddy, "*Big Brother* Means Big Bucks for Channel 4," *Times* (London), 15 June 2002.

41. See "Four Corners: Reality Check," transcript of program broadcast on the Australian Broadcast Corporation, 30 July 2001, www.abc.net.au/4corners/stories/s335957.htm.

42. See Jeremy Head, "Technical Advances Are Turning *Big Brother* into a Big Money Spinner," *Irish Times,* 24 May 2002, 59; and Jason Deans, "A Date with

Davina: As *Big Brother* Fever Gripped the Nation, Viewers Flocked to Its Website," *Guardian,* 21 May 2001, 60.

43. Chris Short, cited in Head, "Technical Advances Are Turning *Big Brother* into a Big Money Spinner," 59.

44. Cited in Marlene Edmunds, "Endemol Rings the Changes: Producer Bets on More Phones, Internet Content," *Variety,* 21–27 January 2002, 29.

45. Interview with John van der Putten, "Endemol Wants Interactive Enhancements That Make Its Websites Live On without a TV Show," *Backstream,* 11 January 2002, www.europemedia.net/shownwws.asp?Article ID=7571.

46. See Chris Pursell, "To Import or to Format: That Is the Question," *Electronic Media,* 15 January 2001, 64; and European Audiovisual Observatory, *Yearbook 2002: Film, Television, Video, and Multimedia in Europe* (Strasbourg, 2002). On the internationalization of TV and film production, see Ted Magder and Jonathan Burston, "Whose Hollywood? Changing Forms and Relations inside the North American Entertainment Economy," in *Continental Order? Integrating North America for Cybercapitalism,* ed. Vincent Mosco and Dan Schiller (Oxford: Rowan and Littlefield, 2001); and Toby Miller, Nitin Govil, John McMurria, and Richard Maxwell, *Global Hollywood* (London: British Film Institute, 2001).

8

Court TV

The Evolution of a Reality Format

Chuck Kleinhans and Rick Morris

Court TV, which began broadcasting in 1991, is a twenty-four-hour-a-day, U.S. cable channel featuring live coverage of trials during the daytime along with syndicated court and police dramas, news features, and related legally themed programming during prime time. The channel began, however, as a relatively simple and low-cost "public service" content provider. In negotiating initial cable contracts with local governments, cable providers proposed that CNN, the Weather Channel, and other basic package channels provided a unique and educational benefit, and Court TV claimed to fill this educational and informational niche as well. The earliest programming presented a "window-on-the-world" depiction of courtroom reality, but since then the channel has evolved. Today, Court TV's trial coverage is marked by dense visualizations and constant commentary, while its prime-time programming, which once focused on re-playing trial highlights, follows the trends established by the major networks. The shift is the product of the bottom line. While adversarial legal dramas in the Western tradition go back to the Old Testament and Greek tragedy, and offer familiar narrative forms, Court TV faced many challenges in combining its ostensible public service function with enough entertainment to entice a sufficient and predictable audience in order to attract advertisers. In this chapter, we argue that the transformation of Court TV presents a model case for studying reality TV's evolution in a new era of declining ratings and growing competition.

Bankrolled by Time Warner, Court TV was founded by an iconoclast entrepreneur, Steven Brill, with an idea for a cable channel that would show judicial proceedings. An aggressive personality who founded the controversial *American Lawyer* magazine, Brill had a mission of opening courts to television cameras, informing the public, and making money. After a bumpy start-up, the channel hit its stride with the O. J. Simpson trial (1994), but then faced a decline in audience and revenues. This goal has been overlaid with the problems of uneven courtroom access, the nature of breaking news, time shifts across the country, and the need for expert commentary that contextualizes and explains legal fine points. Subsequently, the channel began to offer mainstream forms of talk and reality daytime programming, prompting spin-off and copycat derivatives. These formats filled the same demand for low-cost content in Court TV's prime time that fueled the expansion of reality TV.[1]

Early ratings were barely visible, but the ratings have risen over time. Even though the network started broadcasting in 1990, the ratings growth was slow. It was not until 1999 that the cable network could claim an average monthly prime-time rating of even 0.4.[2] Yet the growth after 1999 has been consistent; by 2002, the network was boasting a prime-time rating of 0.8 and fifty-one consecutive months of increased viewership.[3] In 2002, Court TV had seventy million viewers.[4] To accomplish this growth, it launched a rebranding campaign that reinforced a move to continuous sensationalism, positioning itself as the "home of investigative programming."[5] The channel's vision is to involve people in "puzzle solving and suspense" as well as the "process of investigation." Admittedly seeking to capitalize on the success of other reality programming, the network tried a show called *Confessions* that featured video-taped confessions of murderers and rapists.[6] In late summer 2002, Court TV sold episodes of its documentary show *Forensic Files* to NBC for prime-time broadcast.

We found six crucial factors that explain Court TV's success. First, its producers developed sophisticated televisual presentational forms, and second, the channel synthesized a hybrid narrative form, which maintains interest during daytime trials. Third and fourth, Court TV hooked viewers by using celebrity trials (and making some trial figures into celebrities), and by focusing on trials that raise hot issues such as physical, sexual, and emotional abuse, child abduction and murder, and physician-assisted suicide. Fifth, in contrast to the current commonplace that television has increasingly shortened people's attention span by using quick-cutting and collage forms, significant parts of the audience have not been conditioned to an MTV pace, and some of television remains "illustrated radio" or based on interviews and "talking heads." Finally, we live in a society in which the public is more aware of legal issues and more likely to find them interesting.

The Reality Effect: Boredom

Court TV presents interesting questions for thinking about "docutainment" in its most commercial, mass media form—that is, on television. These matters were raised to the level of national public discussion on the channel's third birthday, when the Simpson pretrial hearing began in 1994, and continued at a high pitch throughout the subsequent criminal trial, which put the fledgling network on the map of U.S. consciousness. As sensational as the trial was, however, the attention and ratings didn't hold, and Court TV faced a subsequent viewership and financial drought before reinventing itself beginning in 1999.

Court TV's central programming strategy is to air court trials, but this creates major challenges. Regardless of how interesting a trial might be, the rules and procedures of the U.S. justice system raise fundamental problems for the practice of broadcasting. To put it bluntly, most of the time most people find the courtroom process by its very nature slow moving and boring. The artistic techniques of re-created drama or docudrama—such as the various network presentations on Amy Fisher, or the dramatic trial scenes found on *Law and Order* or *The Practice*—are not present in actual courtrooms.[7] Unlike such fictional narratives, genuine trials contain unexpected delays, recesses, and unscheduled changes. Trial law strategies and tactics, taught in law school and refined by lived experience, call for the painstakingly slow, step-by-step, deliberate building of a prosecution case, and the equally methodical and systematic deconstruction of the prosecution's case by the defense. Even the most colorful criminal defense attorneys spend most of their time in the courtroom quietly sitting and listening.

Further complicating the situation, the use of television cameras in courtrooms is severely restricted. Thus, ingenuity is necessary for televisual presentation. For example, in most states the camera cannot show the jury. Coverage almost always takes place with a single camera in a fixed, usually remote-controlled position that must be placed in a relatively inconspicuous place in the courtroom. As a result, crosscutting is impossible, and the use of zoom and pan/tilt is the only option for variety.

In the early 1990s, limited camera position and captioning presented a spare view of the trial process. Here, a stony-faced complainant presents a simply mute and unexpressive demeanor during the events.

Since the camera operator often works from a remote location, what the camera observes at any one moment is further restricted. The operator may not know about a significant gesture or expression taking place in the courtroom but beyond the camera frame. While camera movement does take place, it is usually directed by the voices heard. Thus, if a witness testifies that they saw the defendant at the scene, the camera will typically move from the witness to the accused at this moment. In some cases, the view is restricted by law (for example, the alleged victim's face in the William Kennedy Smith acquaintance rape trial was obscured by a blue dot), editorial decision (when large police or coroner photos of murder and assault victims are introduced in court, typically the Court TV camera views them only in wide angle and quickly pans away), or environmental factors such as uneven lighting or court personnel in the line of sight.[8] In other situations, camera position may greatly restrict the view, as in the first Menendez brothers' murder trial where the camera was high above and behind the defense tables so that often only the backs of the defendants' heads could be seen or a rear-side view of them when they turned to speak with their lawyers.[9] (Their own testimony in their defense was head-on, however, providing maximum effect to their often tearful story.) Further complications ensue from restrictive microphone placements that sometimes drop audio levels when speakers turn or change position. In addition, audio privacy must be respected during consultation discussions among the defense and prosecution, the judge's bench conferences and asides, and communications among courtroom administrative and service staff. From the point of view of TV's creative personnel, it would be hard to imagine a more constrictive format for covering a slow-moving, methodical, and procedural courtroom process.[10]

Developing Court TV

Court TV had to find space on cable systems. In the relatively early days of cable, channel allocations were scarce due to a lack of technological capacity. Therefore, a new programming service had to justify why it was more compelling or important than other start-ups in order to gain access to an audience. One method used to get the attention of cable system operators was to be an essential public service. In the beginning, the channel proudly announced its public service aspects in self-promotional materials. One premise of its rhetoric was that the U.S. public would become better educated about and would participate more in their justice system.[11] The lure of a public service cable channel was that it helped cable operators gain franchise agreements with local city boards by promising programming that sounded important and that was not available on the commercial networks. Court TV used these public interest arguments not just for the public, to obtain vital access to the courts, and to gain acceptance and channel space within the cable industry but also for lawyers themselves—Court TV carried continuing education for lawyers in the early weekend mornings.

But as mainstream media's promises of public education have given way to general entertainment and sensationalism, so has Court TV moved toward appealing to the amusement interests of the audience. During the channel's early years, much of its schedule was devoted to actual trials during the day while prime-time trials were edited down to a "recap" show—one that would cover only the highlights of the day's trial. The prime-time version was more interesting because the pacing was enhanced through the time compression of selective editing, and commercial breaks were logically built into the format. The network featured other original programming including a prison documentary called *Lock and Key*, and municipal night court and small-claims court shows. The latter two eschewed sensation for unpredictable human interest drama. In one eviction case, for example, the tenant dramatically trumped the landlord's claims by bringing forward snapshots of unrepaired rat holes and even photos of rats on the kitchen counter and kitchen table near her children to bolster her assertion that she withheld paying rent because the owner did not take action on the vermin problem. The judge, after inspecting the pictures, found for the defendant and fined the landlord. For the most part, while watching Court TV in its early phase, one had a feeling of insider voyeurism: really observing the justice system. But such pleasures, even though the evening and weekend shows were edited down, were ones that rewarded the viewer with a taste for quotidian reality who found it interesting to view ordinary people rather than celebrities, routine cases such as "drunk and disorderly," or quarreling neighbors rather than high-profile murders. After a decade, the network has changed.

Court TV publicly states its trial selection criteria as follows: newsworthy; trials that contain important social issues (for instance, date rape or spousal abuse); and watchable (apparently a code word for "entertainment").[12] Nevertheless, it has been resoundingly criticized as pandering to the sensational. Although Court TV executives deny that they seek sensation and cover spectacles, they signed deals with Time-Life to release some of their more important trials on video. And their first choices to be released? The William Kennedy Smith date rape trial and "'Til Death Do Us Part," a case involving a New Hampshire school administrator charged with using her teenage lover to murder her husband.[13] The two John Wayne and Lorena Bobbit trials provided sensational topics, as have the several Dr. Jack Kevorkian assisted-suicide trials. The Jenny Jones civil trial managed to combine the TV talk show host's own celebrity with replays of the episode of the original Jones program on which a gay man confessed his "secret crush" on a heterosexual man. A few days later, the straight man murdered the enamored fellow; Jones was liable for setting up the initial ambush. Bodily violence, murder, sexual tension, and celebrity are recurring themes in the trials selected.

Celebrity and Sensation

As mentioned earlier, the Simpson trial created the decisive moment for Court TV's growth and change. It had all the elements of a media event: a sports star turned actor and corporate spokesperson charged with murder, a glamorous female victim, superstar defense attorneys, a cop caught lying on the stand, a media-saturated city, racial conflict, circumstantial evidence, the use of new high-tech science with DNA evidence, and an inept prosecution. The four national broadcast networks decided to cover the trial live daily, as did cable news networks. But it was quickly noted by most critics that Court TV offered the best minute-by-minute coverage and nightly recap. Its ratings received a big boost, and subsequently more cable providers signed up Court TV. In its first three years Court TV had perfected the formula, sharpened its skills at covering breaking news, and had on-air anchors and reporters with experience and expertise, while the major networks had reporters without legal experience, and thus hired Court TV staff. The trial, particularly in its aftermath, embodied social controversy in the public mind: male rage, spouse assault, African American versus white perceptions, and the "not guilty" verdict. In retrospect, Court TV was the remembered mode of the trial-as-event.

Critics of Court TV have often pointed to the network's celebrity trials and offered the charge of sensationalism.[14] As a matter of legal importance, the Smith trial was inconsequential except to the victim and the accused, and obviously "newsworthy" only because of the Kennedy family connection. Further, covering the victim's face with an electronic blue dot gave some formal level of privacy (a matter of journalistic ethics, not law, since the justice system only protects minors from disclosure), but signaled something that needed to be hidden and thus dramatized the situation.[15] Similarly, broadcasting a Charles Manson parole hearing had no significant legal or news purpose since it was a foregone conclusion that the event was a formality, but it made for "good television." The mass murderer began in a rational, controlled, and restrained manner, yet became increasingly wild-eyed and bizarre as the proceedings continued, producing a documentary Jeckyll-and-Hyde transformation.

Throughout U.S. history, certain celebrity trials and government proceedings have been the focal point for important public discussions. They provide a national framework for awareness and dialogue, and televised proceedings have amplified that effect. In the 1950s, for example, the televised Army-McCarthy hearings exposed the Wisconsin senator as a demagogue; in the 1990s, the Anita Hill testimony during the Clarence Thomas Supreme Court nomination hearings produced heated public discussion of sexual harassment issues, and the Bill Clinton impeachment process generated enormous controversy. Before television, the press dramatized trials that were turning points for public discussion such as the Scopes "monkey" trial for the issue of evolution, and later trials had the same effect, such as the insanity defense in the John W. Hinckley trial for shooting President Reagan, and murder-for-profit in the Claus von Bulow trials. The image of media interference with the process of justice was highlighted by the Lindbergh kidnapping case in the 1930s, which led to extensive reform and restriction on press activity during trials. But the emergence of televised trials demonstrated that an opening of public sphere discourse followed from the new technology. For instance, a classic sensational tabloid journalism case, the New York City murder of a child by her extremely abused mother, raised questions about the moral and legal status of abuse victims who in turn abuse, as well as child protection and feminist politics. It is extremely doubtful that public discussion would have been so informed if left to the tabloid reports.[16] Real-time Court TV trial coverage provides more information than headline news summaries.

Court TV's Televisual Form

What is Court TV's audience appeal? Certainly there is a segment of the audience who are law junkies, who for personal or professional interest like following legal proceedings along with the reportage and discussion of them. But Court TV has been proactive in making its product interesting.

For example, in a convergence of technology and textuality, Court TV was a leader in screen captioning.[17] From an ancillary device used to provide live-video explanations as in sports and election returns, Court TV developed it into the major source of information during the trial. The captioning takes up the lower third of the screen, and at times even more data are introduced. Typically during daytime programs, the very bottom of the screen contains a horizontally scrolling text of legal news headlines. Above that sit two ribbons that identify the trial being covered and identity of the speaker. This identity can contain the attorney's name, educational background, past trial record, and so on, or if it is a called witness, who they are and their relation to the events. In addition, a label may clar-

VAN DAM KILLER FACES DEATH

VAN DAM KILLER FACES DEATH
Fibers linked to the dead girl were also
found in Westerfield's R.V. and in his home
www.courttv.com or AOL Keyword: Court TV

Van Dam child abduction and murder case. Court TV's captioning has developed into a sophisticated means of communication unto itself. Here, "perp-walk" footage of the defendant from months earlier is used to liven up a stretch when the jury is in deliberation.

ify the technical part of the trial (direct examination, cross-examination, and so forth). Similar information appears about the other participants, including the judge and the parties.[18] Here, the captioning makes the complex legal proceedings accessible to those not trained in the law. Other shows have picked up this practice. At times, the text clutter can almost overwhelm the courtroom scene. For example, figure 8.3 shows a recap moment during a time when the live event was jury deliberation. We are watching a flashback to an earlier moment in the trial when the court was listening to an audiotape of a police interrogation of a neighbor, David Westerfield (who was eventually charged with kidnapping and murder). The audiotape was made when a child was simply reported missing. Open captioning is added to the upper part of the screen since the audio was not perfectly clear, and the left side of the screen adds a further explanation. The Court TV logo and a "jury watch" clock are on the right side of the screen. The courtroom camera, a small part of the screen real estate, shows

At one point during the Van Dam case, even more data are introduced on the screen.

the judge and some others present quietly listening to the recording. Nothing is happening, nothing is moving, except the captioning, headline scroll, and jury clock.

Thus we can see that Court TV often involves many layers of presentation. The complexity of visible language onscreen combines with live action to signify the multiple temporal layers of the trial itself. In this case, the official name of the court event (*California v. Westerfield*) is labeled the Danielle Van Dam murder trial, after the seven-year-old child who was abducted from her parents' house in a suburb of San Diego in early February 2002. She was missing for days during a media frenzy to find her. Her mother appeared on a national morning news show appealing to the kidnapper to return her daughter; the body was finally discovered and a suspect neighbor charged with the crime when the girl's blood was found in his RV and on his clothing. Hence, the victim was the initial headline celebrity. The case went forward with astonishing speed. The trial began on 1 June 2002, and jury deliberations started in mid-August. After Westerfield was found guilty, additional presentence hearings were held and jury deliberation on the penalty phase went into early September. While the case was most newsworthy in southern California (with a block-long set of tents, media vans, and trailers servicing the media present), it provided a national draw in the traditionally slow summer season because the defense sought to discredit the girl's parents. Lurid details of their swinging sexual lifestyle raised the possibilities of other "perverts" having access to the house when the child was abducted.

Despite the drawn-out nature of trials, Court TV offers familiar viewing pleasures. It can be fairly called a hybrid of two of the most successful TV genres: soap opera and sports. Court TV is a functional equivalent for soap operas. The real-world stories covered on Court TV are sometimes more bizarre and therefore fascinating than most fantasies that soap screenwriters could invent. Where else can you find a woman who cut off her husband's penis as revenge for forcing sex with her? The intangibles of soaps are also present. There are some quite likable "characters" in the proceedings. Some rooted for Leslie Abrahamson, the hard-fighting lawyer in the Menendez case, and some were attracted to the Menendez boys themselves. Fan T-shirts and bumper stickers appeared saying "I believe Lyle and Erik." Common within a lawyer's education is a theme that if they are litigators (that is, appear before juries), much consideration must be given to the affective areas such as acting, demeanor, and conduct before the jury, the psychology of the jury, the physical appearances of the lawyers and their clients, and most of all, the ability to tell a story—the story that the lawyer wants the jury to believe. A good lawyer is one who is a good "scriptwriter" in that their story is the most passionate, believable, and consistent/airtight. Technically, the lawyer's education and training involves extensive preparation in developing "the theory of the case." This is basically the story that the lawyer will tell about the client/accused; and this story must unfold in a logical and meaningful way. Much the same as a good script must provide for character development, the lawyer must attempt to introduce their "characters" in the light (hero, villain) that is most crucial to their script. They continue to unfold their story, within the rigors and structure imposed by the legal system, until they get to the final scene, the summation, where they reveal the importance of each vignette in the "big picture" and try to convince the jury that their script was the best. This all proceeds in the legal system's search for justice, and it is all guided by the lawyer's professionalism.

Yet these are also the same subjects as daytime soap operas. Like the soaps, a trial has a fixed number of characters with well-defined roles (judge, prosecutor, defendant, police, witness for the prosecution, and so on) and distinct personalities (aggressive/passive, colorful/conservative, and the like). Depending on the case, we often see strong female leads. Trials and soaps present strong, emotional situations: sex and violence are a main interest, but they are also of limited duration. Their narrative relies heavily for narrative on the past (testimony is like a flashback). The expression of emotion is controlled by the externals (the courtroom), but it is also essential (tearful testimony, say). There are long stretches in which little happens. You can often miss a day or two, and still come back and easily follow what is going on.

Court TV is also like sports programming, however. There are two sides locked in a dramatic combat with the thrill of an uncertain outcome.[19] The judge is like a referee, and the jury the spectators. There is an offense (direct examination) and a defense (cross-examination). The event is restricted to a specific place and time. Time is dramatically arranged (during recesses, jury deliberations, and so forth, highlights are replayed). Replays of significant plays (testimony) are common, and during waiting periods there may be cutaways to other contests. Coverage is set by an anchor who is joined by one or more color commentators. The set for anchors and experts is much like that of a sports show, and the commentary is based around evaluations of performance and strategy for the future.

There is no guarantee of the outcome; it is a live contest. A trial is a test of tactics, and Court TV provides a constant stream of commentary analyzing these tactics. The commentators are lawyers of some repute or experience in the area. Court TV commentary is run much like network sports shows, where ex-coaches and players along with other athletes gather to comment on the action on the playing field, offering their opinions on the skills of the participants and the probable motives for their strategies. The spectacle created by this imitation of sports programming creates "excitement" that keeps the audience entertained and tuned in. It feeds the audiences' familiar pleasures developed from mainstream programming such as soap operas and sports.

Court TV's Success

It wasn't until the last quarter of 1993 that Court TV was monitored by the Nielsen Company. Until that time, the channel's audience was a speculative matter. Broadcasters were unsure of who they were addressing, and advertisers were unsure of what they were buying. But once available, the data showed that the network had strong demographics. In a 1994 telephone interview, Court TV's director of public relations stated that not only did the network's viewing demographics skew decidedly female but also that its highest viewing is during the day, particularly in the 1:00 to 5:00 P.M. period, when the trials are live.[20] This makes some sense in terms of the daytime television audience. And with slow-moving repetition, verbally driven narrative and exposition, and anchor/guest expert discussions, the format fits general expectations for the kind of daytime television you can leave on for hours while doing other things at home.

Indeed, the choice of trials often seems skewed to a female audience. Many trials chosen have a contemporary social interest for women as well as the promise, at least, of interesting drama. The Maglica palimony case showed a de facto female spouse and business partner suing for half of a large fortune she helped create. The Bobbit case showed a woman acting against marital rape, retaliating under duress with a sensational action—actually cutting off her husband's penis. The Nielsen ratings also showed that viewers tend to watch in more sustained stretches than other channels and more per week. Only the Cartoon Network, perhaps a baby-sitting choice, had better statistics. Thus the truth of Court TV's mid-1990s self-promotional blurb, "If watching Court TV were any more addictive, it would be illegal."

While its viewing universe of fourteen million homes in 1994 was only about 15 percent of the total U.S. TV households and 25 percent of the homes reached by cable, its cultural impact rapidly outreached its marketplace penetration. For example, most of the major three television networks used their techniques (and video) in their own coverage of trials, most notably copycatting during the Simpson trial. At the same time, Court TV invaded regular television with a syndicated version of the "network's most high-profile cases" with *Court TV: Inside America's Courts*, and had found ninety-six stations representing 92 percent of the country to carry it.[21] Also, as parody is certainly a mark of impact, early on Court TV was mocked on *Saturday Night Live* (a Menendez brothers skit).

Today, among the current cable networks, Court TV can be considered a success. It has been on the air for over a decade and continues to garner strong ratings. Another, more salient measure of success is that of commercial advertising rates—in summer 2002, the network's "up-front" commercial sales were showing a 5 percent increase in the "cost per thousand," a measure of the price of commercials.[22] This was during a downturn in the economy, and while larger cable channels such as CNN, A&E, and USA were all showing negative numbers in the same measure. By both ratings and rate cards—two traditional measures of media success—Court TV has made it.

But to achieve that, Court TV has moved from its roots of televised justice in its raw and gritty form to more "legal-tainment" programming—from reruns of Fox's *Cops* to a refurbished evening lineup including *NYPD Blue, Profiler,* and *Homicide.* The changes were not incidental; one industry publication observed that in 1998, the network was on "death row" and in danger of being sold to the Discovery Channel until its owners (Time Warner, now AOL Time Warner and Liberty Media) put cash into the network to buy programming like *Crime Stories* and *Homicide.*[23] They brought in an executive who had previously run Studios USA, where he oversaw the production of the Jerry Springer and Maury Povich shows.[24]

Court TV claims it is investing $160 million for new programming over the next two years, including three hundred hours for the 2002–2003 season.[25] In this programming change there are four new documentary series. These include the highly successful *Forensic Files,* a show that highlights crime scene investigations and medical forensics, and *The System,* which reexamines notable crimes and trials. Furthermore, Court TV has moved into the field of made-for-television movies, with its second such movie aired in 2002, as well as airing theatrical release films including thrillers/action movies such as *The Panic Room* and *Training Day.*[26] The channel has moved far from its so-called public service origins to legal-themed mainstream programming. Gone are the days of early morning and weekend professional education shows aimed at working lawyers. Now the network produces series that imitate other broadcasts on other channels: *Hollywood at Large,* a rehash of *Entertainment Tonight*–style press release items; *Hollywood and Crime,* replaying old celebrities in court stories; *Mugshots,* biographies of famous criminals; and crime among the wealthy elite with Dominick Dunne's *Power, Privilege, and Justice* series.

Court TV's Industry Impact

TV network broadcasting's move to low-cost reality TV content is evident in changes to traditional network news division programs. Court TV material has been imitated and directly reproduced in shows such as *Dateline NBC.* Relatively unknown past trials are repackaged in a one-hour format with additional interviews (in the present) with key actors in the drama (victim and accused, if both are alive; often prosecution and defense lawyers; sometimes the jurors, but seldom the judge). The conclusion/verdict is withheld until the last segment. The trials deal with highly dramatic personal events rather than socially or politically significant cases such as corporate pollution or political corruption. For example, a summer 2002 episode of CBS's *48 Hours* covered a spouse murder investigation and trial. *48 Hours* began as an investigative news show covering institutions and events such as two days in the life of a high school or police station, or two-day events such as behind the scenes at a sports competition. Now called *48 Hours: Monday Night Mystery*, it features simple coverage of a trial. In a typical case aired 12 August 2002, "The Mystery on Slide Mountain," a husband murders his wife. He drives their SUV off a mountain cliff, claiming that his brakes failed, he lost control, and then he fell out before the vehicle went down the mountainside. The show centers on courtroom coverage (single camera) and lots of interviews (the accused, the defense and prosecution lawyers, the cop who suspected it was murder, members of the wife's family, and so forth). The narrative sequence proceeds through the event, investigation, and trial process. An on-scene "investigative," stand-up reporter (Susan Spencer) visits the accident site. The show returns to this location numerous times—there's news footage of the Emergency Medical Service, a talk with the highway patrol investigator, another visit with the victim's family, and during the trial the jury visits the scene.

Classic techniques of dramatic suspense are employed by use of withheld information to make plot points before each commercial break. For example, with no foreshadowing, at about thirty-five minutes into the show, we find that while his wife was away on business trips, the husband flirted with other women. During the show, viewers are invited to "vote" on his innocence or guilt by phone or the Internet, and the pro and con running tally is announced several times. In contrast to the traditional journalistic "pyramid" structure in which every key element is quickly reported at the start, followed by elaboration, explanation, and expansion, this organization makes a well-known (locally) public event into a "mystery" for the national audience. Without explanation, we suddenly discover at about forty-eight minutes into the show that there was a hung jury in the first trial, and in the second one (barely covered) the defendant was found guilty.[27] The entire show is bookended with Dan Rather being especially pontifical, and badly and hastily reading from a teleprompter in a "courtroom" setting that doesn't in any way match the actual courtroom. Thus *48 Hours* goes from being a CBS news division standard-bearer into tailing after the *Dateline NBC* format.[28]

Following the same pattern of decline, in summer 2002 NBC rolled out a new series under the *Law and Order* franchise, *Law and Order: Crime and Punishment.* In a significant innovation, the trial is shot in a multi-camera San Diego courtroom that allows crosscutting in the edit. The trial is supplemented by additional out-of-the-courtroom footage of the deputy district attorneys. In one show, the deputy district attorney is a fortyish female, visibly pregnant, who is shown talking to cops and prepping them for the courtroom testimony as well as speaking with the victim and her family along with a potential defense witness. She is shown at lunch with other deputy district attorneys (all women), and at dinner with her husband and kids. No serious analysis of the trial or its process is provided in these asides; rather, they serve to humanize the prosecutor and discuss her emotional state: worried about the case, concerned about a child victim testifying and facing the defendant who was accused of assaulting the child. The entire show is rather remarkably one-sided—and thus drives directly to a guilty verdict. The case was a sixty-five-year-old man allegedly luring and tying up a twelve-year-old girl in the same apartment complex. There was some room for "reasonable doubt"—the accused had an alibi (an elderly woman who testifies he was visiting her during the events), and the guy had a new male roommate with a record of violating a minor, which the defense tries to introduce as perhaps mistaken identity as to the culprit. But the accused is found guilty. And without any explanation of the discrepancy, the sentencing judge is a different person than the trial judge. There is no behind the scenes with the defense attorney, or even a formal interview with him or the defendant, no postmortem with the jurors, and no expert commentary.

From Window on the World to Data Screen

The metamorphosis of Court TV over the past decade shows the change from a fairly simple production technique and standard visuals to a more highly articulated form. The original appeal of Court TV relied on a stripped-down, simple presentation of trials in real time. The current articulation presents a dense screen real estate, which combined with an extensive commentary and website tracking of specific trials, encourages information gathering and updating on an continual basis. At the same time, the remarkable variety and diversity of the initial days has continuously given way to "mainstreaming" and attempts to copycat trends in other industry sectors. Court TV has thus evolved from a C-SPAN type of public service programming to a glitzy, mainstream-influenced, dramatic, sensational, and celebrity-based concept. It has had to make these changes for the sake of its own survival in a multichannel universe populated by more and more competitors.

Although Court TV has moved toward the traditional entertainment network model, the mainstream networks have incorporated some of the successes of Court TV. From *Dateline NBC*'s direct use of Court TV packages, *Survivor*'s jurylike Tribal Council, or *48 Hours*' "Monday Night Mystery," Court TV's influence can be seen across popular reality programming. While Court TV has moved more aggressively to "crimes of the rich and famous" and entertainment business squabbles that end up in litigation, in turn, a channel like Animal Planet searches for success with its new show *Animal Court* (conducted by the well-known Judge Wapner) with trials that involve pet owners.

NOTES

The authors are equal coauthors. We first presented parts of this work as "Juridical Visual Forms: The Evolution of Court TV and the O. J. Simpson Pretrial Hearing," at the Visible Evidence conference, University of Southern California, 1994. Court TV staff provided valuable background information in 1994 phone and in-person interviews.

1. See Chad Raphael's foundational discussion of the economics of reality programming, "The Political Economy of Reali-TV," *Jump Cut* 41 (1997): 102–9, and the version in this volume.

2. See http://www.courttv.com/press/rtngsaug.html.

3. See "Court TV Has Highest Quarterly Ratings in Network's History," *Business Wire,* 2 April 2002; and "Court TV to Spend Record $160 Million on Programming over the Next Two Years," *Business Wire,* 24 April 2002.

4. See "Court TV Has Highest Quarterly Ratings in Network's History."

5. "Court TV Launches Multimillion Dollar Rebranding Campaign for Seventy-Million Viewer Network," *Business Wire,* 5 March 2002.

6. See Jim Rutenberg, "Reality Television Strikes a Stark Note in a New Show," *New York Times,* 21 August 2000, C1.

7. Teenager Amy Fisher was charged with shooting the wife of her lover, Joey

Buttafuoco. The notorious event and the personalities involved made the incident a running joke on late-night TV, and in the aftermath, three different network dramatic re-creations appeared: "Amy Fisher: My Story," NBC, 28 December 1992; "Casualties of Love," CBS, 3 January 1993; and "The Amy Fisher Story," ABC, 3 January 1993.

8. Smith's uncle, Senator Edward Kennedy, was called in defense of the accused. The trial was one of the first major celebrity trials that put Court TV on the map of public consciousness.

9. Southern California twenty-somethings Erik and Lyle Menendez were tried for the shotgun execution of their wealthy parents. The defense in their first trial centered on presenting them as victims of parental abuse who were thus justified in their murder. After a hung jury in the first trial, in a second one they were convicted.

10. Perhaps the only more restricted format in cable television is CSPAN, which was mandated to cover congressional proceedings with a continuous, fixed camera after senators and representatives complained that providing reverse shots of the often empty chamber gave a technically true, yet misleading (and more to the point, embarrassing) depiction of official speeches and congressional activity.

11. Court TV appealed to images of a well-functioning Jeffersonian democracy, one in which a more informed public is more active.

12. Lloyd Trufelman, director of public relations at Court TV, telephone interview, 9 February 1994.

13. See David Tobenkin, "Court TV Takes Case to Video," *Hollywood Reporter*, 2 December 1993.

14. See Alan M. Dershowitz, "At Issue: Court TV," *American Bar Association Journal* (May 1994): 46. Of course, Dershowitz is himself one of the country's top celebrity lawyers.

15. The dot and blur have become signifiers of "authenticity" and documentary truth. Subsequently, the blue dot and digital pixilation blur became joke elements in parody skits on *Saturday Night Live* and *Mad TV*.

16. An extended discussion of the Steinberg/Nussbaum trial based on interviews forms the core of Paul Thaler, *The Watchful Eye: American Justice in the Age of the Television Trial* (Westport, Conn.: Praeger, 1994). Left liberal academic George Gerbner has argued against TV trial coverage, asserting that "reporters" should be the appropriate experts to interpret judicial events for the public—a view that seems naive about the nature of the press, and derogatory to democratic ideals and the jury system itself (Gerbner on *Morning Edition*, National Public Radio, 12 July 1994).

17. While this makes intrinsic sense to those who are not involved in the media, it is significant to the industry, and the ramifications are great. The characters that appear across the bottom of the television screen, most often to identify the person speaking, are made by a device called a "character generator." This de-

vice made more instantaneous the communication of identity and changing data information (sports scores and election returns), but these functions were conceptually limited while live video was available. Within the industry, the device, the use of it, and the results of its use were denoted by the various parts of speech formable by the words "character generator," "CG," "title," and the brand name of the equipment (Chyron, Dubner, and so on).

18. Captioning has also been a "term of art" in the media industry, referring principally to closed or open captioning for the hearing impaired. In this case, the authors are speaking about the graphics as captioning or labeling the action and providing external information that the producers have determined might be of interest to the viewer.

19. The media-as-sports metaphor has also been applied to news. Allison Romano, a media news executive, "prefers what some have called play-by-play news, which covers the stock market more like sports" ("CNBC's Cohen Declares Split," *Broadcasting and Cable,* 12 August 2002, 14).

20. Trufelman, telephone interview.

21. Mike Freeman, "New Line Courts Success," *Broadcasting,* 13 December 1993, 28.

22. See *Broadcasting and Cable,* 8 July 2002, 4. The "cost per thousand" viewers is a common metric in the television industry to show the relative pricing of different channels.

23. See Valerie Block, "A Reprieve for Court TV," *Crain's New York Business,* 3 January 2000, 1.

24. *Ibid.*

25. See "Court TV to Spend Record $160 Million on Programming over the Next Two Years," *Business Wire,* 24 April 2002.

26. *Ibid.*

27. "Mystery on Slide Mountain," 13 August 2002, CBSNews.com, http://www.cbsnews.com/stories/2002/03/08/48hours/printable503311.shtml.

28. Internal evidence reveals the show was put together in terms of an extremely economical production process, and was probably rough cut before the second trial began and quickly finished off days after the verdict.

Part III

Cultural Politics

9

Country Hicks and Urban Cliques
Mediating Race, Reality, and Liberalism on MTV's The Real World

Jon Kraszewski

Within the very first minutes of its premiere, MTV's *The Real World* announced that race would be one of the show's most prominent cultural concerns. As its premise, the first season brought together seven strangers between the ages of nineteen and twenty-six in a luxurious New York City loft for thirteen weeks.[1] The series seemed to capture a real-life portrayal of young adults living in the wake of the Rodney King trial and Los Angeles riots, both of which occurred just a few months before *The Real World*'s May 1992 debut. As the roommates sat down for their first dinner, conflict erupted between three housemates: Heather, Kevin, and Julie. Heather and Kevin were two African Americans already living in New York City; Heather was working as a professional rapper, and Kevin was a professional writer. Julie, still in a bit of culture shock, had just moved to the city from Alabama. As Heather's beeper went off during dinner, Julie asked, "Do you sell drugs? Why do you have a beeper?"

Although the very title *The Real World* propounds that the show simply *presents* reality, we should interrogate such face-value claims and explore how this opening scene *mediates* race and reality itself. *The Real World* does not simply locate the reality of a racist statement and neutrally deliver it to an audience. Although not scripted, the show actively constructs what reality and racism are for its audience through a variety of production practices. For instance, the reality encountered on the show was partially created through the casting decisions of the producers, Mary-Ellis Bunim and Jonathan Murray, who chose these three individuals who

The friendship between Julie and Heather was constructed as a solution to the problem of rural white racism on *The Real World* (season one).

might have potential conflicts over race. The reality was also shaped by the decisions made about where to film and what to film. The producers chose to set the show in New York City, which automatically put Julie in the position of outsider, and the directors chose to film the dinner in the first place. Thus, the producers selected potential elements of racial conflict and misunderstanding, setting up possible versions of reality for the show. Editing also shaped the reality of the issue. The show produces millions of hours of footage that the producers, in the case of the New York season, cut into thirteen twenty-two-minute episodes. Numerous events took place when the roommates first moved into the loft, and the producers could have focused on any of them to start the show. Odds are that some of them raised different issues of racism. For example, what if the show fixated on a racist statement from one of the white, liberal, and urban roommates? The very idea of racism and where it is located would be diff-

erent. Finally, the narrative structure of the series placed the event as a catalyst that brought Julie and Heather together, where they would eventually
overcome this incident and become best friends. Hence, the show narra-
tively constructs this opening event less as a quintessential moment of U.S.
racism, and more as a lesson of how people can overcome and discard
their own racisms. Rather than assuming that this incident involving Julie,
Heather, and Kevin displayed the reality of racism and race relations in the
United States, it's better to ask why *The Real World* would use this event to
mediate racism and reality to its audience.

In exploring this issue, it helps to conceive of a show like *The Real
World* as, on some level, a media event. John Fiske defines this term as

> an indication that in a postmodern world we can no longer rely on a stable
> relationship or clear distinction between a "real" event and its mediated rep-
> resentation. Consequently, we can no longer work with the ideas that the
> "real" is more important, significant, or even "true" than the representation.
> A media event, then, is not a mere representation of what happened, but it
> has its own reality.[2]

In other words, media that attempts to document reality actually shapes it,
filtering it through a variety of discourses and unequal fields of social
power. But in using Fiske's concept of the media event, we should pay
careful attention to key differences between Fiske's project and my own.
One is the nature of the event itself. Fiske analyzes events that happen
once: the beating of Rodney King, the Los Angeles riots, or the O. J. Simpson trial. Part of Fiske's goal is to examine how these taped events are re-
peatable when various agents replay and alter them in legal and media institutions, recasting the tapes in new discourses and different fields of social power. *The Real World,* on the contrary, uses a different concept of
time. A new episode airs during each week of a new season, and the producers create one or two new seasons each year, with a season lasting between three and six months. This brings with it different strategies for mediating reality, most notably the casting of roommates, the editing of the
show, production decisions of what to film, and the organization of events
into a serial narrative. We need to consider how these production decisions specific to a reality TV show construct cultural representations of
racism. Another difference between Fiske's project and mine is that Fiske
draws on a large number of media outlets, ranging from the courtroom
and court coverage to CNN and televised debates to amateur video. I am

more concerned with how mediations on *The Real World* fit so well into MTV's identity as a cable channel. In other words, whereas Fiske studies how different social players use different discourses to mediate reality, I analyze how *The Real World* discursively constructs racism for a specific demographic: the MTV audience.

Fiske can therefore help us see how the recording of reality on a show like *The Real World* is never neutral; its mediations draw on distinct discourses caught up in fields of social power. Yet we need to adjust Fiske's theory to suit the production practices, network goals, and textual strategies that go into a show like *The Real World* to understand its cultural resonance in a cable environment like MTV, aimed at the identity of a youthful, liberal demographic.

Given this, what's most striking about this opening incident on *The Real World* is not that Julie associated Heather's blackness with drug use and criminality. What's most interesting is why *The Real World* would use this controversial incident with conservative views to start their series on a channel that prides itself on having a liberal viewership. With this in mind, just as important as Julie's claim is the way her background as a rural southerner gets associated with her statement. Throughout its twelve-season run, *The Real World* has mediated race and reality through discursive tensions between urban and rural America as well as liberal and conservative politics. Within these tensions, white rural figures such as Julie, and later Julie from season nine and Mike from season ten, cover significant discursive terrain in the way the show addresses racism. Through mediations of casting, filming practices, editing, and narrative strategies, *The Real World* suggests that racism is a phenomenon located within rural conservatives, not liberals with an urban feel. And here I use the phrase urban feel to call attention to the way the channel promotes a certain type of image so that rural viewers in the Midwest can feel urban if they buy the right clothes and have the right attitudes. Because of this, the show constructs a reality that frees the audience of any implications in racism by blaming rural conservatives for the problem. And yet, these rural figures contain a certain hip quality, both in their appearance and manners, that in some ways suggests they are urban and liberal. The rural characters discursively experience a dual existence on the program, living partly as members of a liberal urban clique and partly as conservative racist outsiders. The show then constructs serial narratives to expel racism from these characters in order to make them full-fledged, city-dwelling liberals. Yet by using discourses about the rural United States and conservatism to construct racism as a problem of individual opinions, the show as well as channel overlook the systemic nature of racism and the way it operates in liberal urban environments.

Mediating Racism as a Rural Conservative Phenomenon

From its inception, MTV has promoted itself as a hip liberal channel with a predilection for youth. One of its earliest slogans was "MTV, some people just don't get it," a declaration implicitly naming teenagers and young adults as its target audience. Yet in these defining years, MTV faced a crisis that implicated its liberal identity in the perpetuation of racism in the United States. As Sut Jhally and Justin Lewis argue, racism "is now embedded in a iniquitous capitalist system, where economic rather than racial laws ensure widespread racial segregation and disadvantage."[3] White liberalism, however, often envisions racism as a problem of individual opinions, not economic structures. This, as Jhally and Lewis contend, places a tremendous amount of blame on African Americans, who are disadvantaged by their own actions, not an unfair class system.[4] In their early years, MTV hardly had the luxury of masking its own structural racism and relegating discrimination to the level of personal belief. The channel refused to air black music videos, claiming its white, middle-class target audience lacked interest in black artists. This is a prime example of the way racism works in the U.S. economy, here disempowering a group of black artists by denying them a major market for record sales. Many black artists protested this policy, most notably Michael Jackson, whose record company threatened to pull all of its videos from MTV if the channel failed to air Jackson's *Thriller, Billie Jean,* and *Beat It* videos. Through a combination of artist, audience, and record company protests, MTV eventually decided to air black videos, fearing that their refusal to do so would hurt the channel's economic well-being.

Certainly it is a good thing that MTV lifted its black artist ban. By doing so, the channel offered African American musicians access to a wider economic market while allowing audiences to experience the pleasures and politics of black music. As Andrew Goodwin notes, to counter its implication in explicit and systemic racism, MTV created black music programs like *Yo!, MTV Raps*; aired cutting-edge, politically controversial music videos such as Public Enemy's "By the Time I Get to Arizona," where the band assassinates white officials in Arizona, a state that fails to celebrate Martin Luther King Jr. Day; and supported a Free James Brown campaign when the singer was jailed on drug charges.[5] At the same time, by starting a voter registration drive, campaigning for the ethical treatment of animals, and counterbalancing anti-Soviet propaganda in the 1980s, the channel increasingly looked to support liberal causes in general. According to Goodwin, these liberal specials helped MTV regiment a standardized schedule and redefine itself less as an around-the-clock video jukebox. Even music videos were organized into half-hour- or hour-long shows.[6]

The Real World is part of MTV's explicit efforts to create a routine schedule, promote liberal values, and amend its previous charges of racism. It offers the channel a thirty-minute weekly show for viewers to watch regularly. Yet as much as the show wants to take cutting-edge stances on race and racism, it mediates racism through discourses of ruralness and conservatism, masking the racism of liberals, propounding that racism is a matter of personal belief, and failing to address the systemic nature of racism. This construction begins during the casting process of the program. As stated earlier, The Real World is not scripted, so the producers do not order the roommates to talk explicitly about racism in the United States. Nevertheless, throughout the seasons Bunim and Murray have consistently cast innocent, sheltered, and young white rural Americans in houses with two African Americans from urban areas. Certainly the seeds of a specific type of racial conflict and misunderstanding are in the house. In focusing on the culture shock these rural Americans face, the show suggests that racism is primarily a problem of misinformed individuals. For instance, early in an episode from the New Orleans season, Melissa, who is biracial, asks Julie, a white Mormon from Wisconsin, to pass her a paper towel. Julie responds by saying, "What color do I look?" shocking Melissa with such an offensive statement and the fact that Julie originally thinks she has done nothing wrong. The show resolves this problem with Julie claiming that her parents brought her up to say things like that, and Melissa then helps Julie try to overcome her naive and racist upbringing. As awful and hurtful as this statement is, it is fairly easy for viewers to digest, primarily because the liberal viewership of MTV is not implicated in such a racism discursively filtered through Julie's conservative upbringing in rural Wisconsin.

But the casting process is more complex than simply picking rural conservatives to mediate racism, and it speaks to the complex ways that whiteness operates in society. Richard Dyer approaches whiteness as a phenomenon of color, claiming it functions both as a visible system of privilege and an invisible regime of power.[7] Whiteness demands visibility in order to mark its subjects as empowered. Yet Dyer devotes more time to exploring how whiteness is invisible. White people tend to see themselves as unmarked or unspecified. As such, whiteness largely remains unseen, operating as a position from which a dominant social group can survey and control other races.[8] The very power of whiteness, according to Dyer, stems from its apparent neutrality and ordinariness.

Not stopping his analysis there, though, Dyer also makes several important claims about the battle over whiteness itself. Because whiteness offers power and privilege, its borders remain highly contested. The Jews, Irish, and Italians are grouped as white sometimes, but not other times, when situated in fields of social power.[9] But even within its borders, whiteness orders various levels of itself, some more acceptable than others. In these cases, certain regimes of social power graft themselves onto the skin. For example, working-class whites often come across as an inferior version of the race. Their lack of economic power shows up in their tainted hue, darkened because of numerous hours spent performing manual labor outside. Their whiteness is visible, and hence inferior, because their skin stands out. In this system of economic discrimination and disempowerment, middle-class and upper-class whites offer a more genuine version of the race because their labor does not tarnish the color of their skin.[10] The casting process of *The Real World* picks specific types of rural Americans, ones whose whiteness is perched between hipness and inferiority. Rural America has stereotypically been associated with the working class due to all of the farming there. The many hours in the sun because of manual labor taints the white hue of these workers. As Dyer rightly notes, this social group faces discrimination since their connection to labor somehow makes them less white. In all of the seasons with these rural characters, the show always dedicates an episode to their parents' visits. The parents are more strictly defined rural Americans, with their accents, skin color, and clothing. But the actual rural American cast members are much more urban than their family. In fact, their bodies aren't marked as an inferior version of whiteness, as Dyer would claim; rather, their mannerisms are. As college students or aspiring entertainers, their skin has not been tainted by labor, and they dress rather hip. Mike looks like a J. Crew model, and Julie is the quintessential skater girl. That said, their connection to their inferior whiteness has more to do with their relationship to their parents and their views, not their own bodies. Since

MTV has always been antiparents, marking this social unit as the center of racist beliefs makes it easy for viewers to distance themselves from this social ill. By casting such people, the show says that one can shed this inferior version of whiteness attached to racism simply by changing one's views.

Beyond casting, filming practices also contribute to this specific mediation of racism and reality. The decision to film in major cities automatically positions these rural characters as outsiders. What is particularly fascinating, though, is the fact that these supposed rural conservatives all hail from urban areas in the South or Midwest—Julie from Birmingham, the other Julie from a Milwaukee suburb, and Mike from a Cleveland suburb. Thus, the filming locale does not so much automatically or naturally function as a strange land for these characters; rather, the show discursively constructs these characters as rural Americans, positioning the city locale as another world that can cleanse their racism. But more important than where to film is what to film. In an interview for a book on *The Real World: Chicago*, Bunim talks about the show's production practices:

> Well, it begins with the producers and directors and crew in the field as they are documenting each day in the lives of these cast members. They are watching to see if the events are more than mundane, if they have significance. So, the directors—and we have five of them who lead the crews—are focusing the cameras on any situations that are meaningful. So, it begins with the directors in the field deciding where to put the cameras because we only have one camera, maybe two, on per shift.[11]

Coproducer Murray responds to this by saying, "We have seven cast members, so if Chris and Tonya are going to the gym and Theo and some girls are going on a date, we'll go with Theo and the date, thinking that's the better story."[12] Given this, much of the focus on the discursive conflicts between rural whites and urban African Americans is a result of the filming process, in which directors decide that shooting these roommates might eventually produce usable footage. In the case of Julie's argument with Kevin and Heather on the first season, it was logical to shoot the dinner because all seven roommates were there. Nothing else was happening. In the case of Julie and Melissa's conversation about the napkin on the New Orleans season, however, there were only a few people in the room. This desire to document rural conservatives with urban liberals is even more apparent on the tenth season of *The Real World*, again set in New

York. In the first episode, Mike, billed as the rural American from Ohio, goes out to breakfast with Coral and Malik, two African Americans from California's Bay Area. While there, the cameras capture Mike saying that his uncle, who owns a business, will not hire black people as they are slower than whites due to their lack of education. Coral and Malik challenge Mike's racist statement, pointing out that it illuminates his uncle's own racism more than our education system's. This mixture of the rural white and urban blacks is something to which the show always pays close attention in order to document it as much as possible.

Of course, this documented event gains significance through the editing, which positions rural conservatives as enactors of racism and urban liberals as decoders of it. While the statements made by the two Julies and Mike might seem naive and blunt, they are actually more complex than they first appear. For instance, none of them explicitly state racism or demand the economic oppression of African Americans. Instead, their racisms cloak themselves in other discourses. Julie from New York addresses blacks through the discourse of criminality while the other Julie as well as Mike claim their statements stemmed from their family. This is ultimately what Stuart Hall calls inferential racism, and what Fiske refers to as nonracist racism. For Hall, overt and inferential racism operate as two different modalities, the former entailing intentional statements explicitly declaring hatred against racial others, and the latter functioning more dangerously because speakers do not necessarily intend their racism. In fact, people often express antiracist intent in nonracist racism, perpetuating racism in less visible and less overt ways.[13] As Fiske notes, this tactic reframes a statement about race in other discourses such as family, education, economy, or law.[14] For example, Fiske analyzes Dan Quayle's reference to the 1992 Los Angeles riots as a crisis of family values. By reframing a race problem in terms of the family, Quayle sidesteps placing blame on white hegemony in the insurgency and locates all fault within black families, who are unfairly accused of being a center of immorality.[15] Part of what lends credence to the hipness of the liberal characters on *The Real World* is that the editing calls attention to the way they can unpack the inferential racism of the rural conservatives. After Julie's comment on Heather's beeper, the show cuts in a series of personal interviews with the cast members. Both Kevin and Heather, the two African American roommates, remark that Julie's casting of Heather as a criminal is trenched in racism. Moreover, Andre, a white roommate pursuing a music career in New York City, also mentions the potentially offensive nature of the comment. On season ten, after Mike says that his uncle won't hire black people because they are poorly educated, *Real World* editors piece together footage of Malik, Coral, and Kevin, a white roommate from the University of Texas, each separately in the confessional discussing how Mike's statement was indeed racist.

In the process of putting together the episode, the editing uses footage that foregrounds these rural conservatives as the locus of racism in the United States, but editing choices also include clips that highlight racism as a problem of individual intentions. While there is footage of white liberal roommates decoding Julie's and Mike's inferential racism, the editors also add clips of those same roommates questioning whether or not Julie and Mike intended the statement to be racist. According to this logic, the statement is not as racist as it seems since that might not have been the intention of those individuals. Racism can be easily solved if roommates can make the rural conservatives aware of their statements and have them consciously change their opinions. The same issues coalesce around Julie in New Orleans when many of the roommates believe that her opinions about race stem from her parents being conservative Mormons, not from Julie's own intentions.

If the editing plants the seeds that racism can be solved through individual attitudes, then *The Real World*'s narrative grows this idea to its fullest potential. In all of the seasons mentioned so far, the show foregrounds the friendships between a white rural conservative and a black urban liberal. While these friendships occurred through genuine interpersonal communication, they nevertheless were not the only ones to develop in the house that season. The producers gave these interracial, politically opposed friendships priority when piecing together the narrative. Bunim's background in soap operas is extremely useful in illuminating the way that narrative operates on *The Real World*. Soap operas resolve narrative conflicts through serial narratives. As Jeremy Butler argues, the serial provides connections between episodes as the problem/solution dilemma expands over several episodes or seasons; characters have a history as they learn from issues featured on previous episodes.[16] Given this, we can see repeated narrative constructions in the way each of *The Real World* seasons develops friendships between white conservatives and black liberals. The seasons deal with these initial events of racism by having an urban black teach the rural white about black culture over the course of several episodes. For instance, Malik educates Mike about a new figure in black history each day. After hearing Julie's remark about the beeper, Heather takes Julie to a recording session for her upcoming album, allowing Julie to see African Americans working professionally, not selling drugs. Melissa teaches the other Julie that many of Julie's own beliefs about African Americans are stereotypes.

The serial narrative always follows how the pedagogical nature of these relationships turns into friendships, in the process amending the rural American's personal views on racism. Most of the episodes in season one dedicate time to showing Julie and Heather going out and having fun together. On the very last episode, both Julie and Heather discuss how they have become best friends. During the New Orleans season, the last episode devotes time to Julie and Melissa planning to move to Los Angeles together. Mike becomes extremely close to Malik and eventually Coral. But *The Real World* extends its narrative issues beyond the run of the season itself by finding ways to reunite casts. On the first reunion show, which brought together the casts from the first four seasons, Julie and Heather arrived together and spoke about how they talk on the phone every day. The producers also hold athletic challenges between the casts of *The Real World* and *Road Rules,* another reality TV show on MTV where contestants between the ages of eighteen and twenty-four travel in a Winnebago and perform extreme stunts across the country. On the latest *Battle of the Seasons,* Mike and Coral represented season ten, and many of the cast members from other seasons talked about how Mike and Coral acted like a husband and wife even though they were not married or even dating. Their friendship was that strong. By stretching these events throughout the seasons and beyond, the show foregrounds how racism can be solved by changing your opinions.

Masking Liberal Racism: Mediating Blackness through the City

In many ways, the mediations that coalesce around Julie on the first season of *The Real World* functioned as a blueprint for how later seasons would filter race and reality through rural conservative characters. The casting, filming, editing, and narratives of the ninth and tenth seasons all remain similar to the original New York show. Yet the mediations of race on the first season through Kevin, an African American character, represent an important moment for *The Real World.* In casting an African American with a background in political science and a career in polemical writing, the producers of *The Real World* promised to deliver a reality about race that hardly accepted the liberal wish-wash of racism simply being a matter of personal belief. Kevin added a different spin, insisting that racism operates through complex systems of power and economic suppression, and for a while, it seemed as if the show was going to mediate race partly through these discourses. Kevin would write proclamations about U.S. racial orders and place them next to the entrance to the loft. In one instance, the editors show Andre, a white liberal, telling Kevin that no one in the house is racist, while Kevin claims racism exists in more complex ways than personal beliefs. Another moment where Kevin calls attention to the racism of white liberals comes in an episode where Becky, another white liberal, states that the United States is a great country and everyone has the opportunity for success; Kevin insists that the economic system denies African Americans the same opportunities as whites. The show then cuts to a poetry reading of Kevin's where he recites the line, "All I want is the opportunity to have an opportunity," punctuating Kevin's point.

These moments, however, were all too unique for the show. Never again would the show cast someone who so explicitly critiques economic systems of racism in the United States, and/or devote so much narrative time to having a character like this express his views. In fact, a character's ability to critique racism in the United States and not be represented through stereotypes would even become problematic by the end of the first season of *The Real World,* and this speaks directly to the contradictory way that the show uses discourses of urbanity to mediate race and reality to its viewers. While the city functions as a liberal location that cleanses racism from rural Americans, it also constructs African American male characters as potentially violent, hence relegating them into complex systems of stereotypes. The second-to-last episode of the first season is particularly telling about this transition. The episode opens with Julie crying, her tears brought on by a fight she had with Kevin. According to Julie, she picked up the phone, was angered that Kevin was on it, and then hung up. This led Kevin to come downstairs, say "Fuck you" and "Suck my dick," and then throw a candleholder at her. Kevin's version of the story differs, as he explains how he was on the phone with a future employer, trying to get a job, since his stay on *The Real World* and teaching gig at New York University were coming to an end. While Kevin agrees that he yelled at Julie, he insists he never said "Suck my dick" and never threw a candleholder at her. One of the most fascinating aspects of the episode is that it never shows the fight between Julie and Kevin. Instead, it pits Julie's story against Kevin's. In the process, the episode balances Julie's turn to the other roommates for emotional support with footage of Kevin visiting the neighborhood where he grew up. Oddly, the episode before this one is dedicated to a "homecoming" theme. Julie's family visits New York City, and so does Andre's mom. Additionally, the episode includes footage of the housemates finding a lost dog and eventually returning it to its owners. Certainly the editors could have put Kevin's story about returning home to Jersey City in the previous episode and have it fit more thematically. Moreover, there is no direct time correlation linking Kevin's going home to Julie's talking to the other roommates, and *The Real World* manipulates the timing of events to connect different stories in the same episode thematically. Why crosscut between scenes where Julie relies on the housemates for emotional support and Kevin returns home to Jersey City?

Linking Kevin's supposed threat of violence against Julie to Kevin's upbringing in a lower-class, black, urban neighborhood discursively constructs Kevin's blackness in stereotypical, yet complex ways. There is a long historical trajectory connecting black sexuality to violence in the United States. According to Donald Bogle, the buck is violently sexual and ultimately a threat to white woman.[17] As Robyn Weigman argues, the buck stereotype emerged in the United States of the nineteenth century after the freeing of slaves had given white and black men supposedly equal claims to citizenship. Numerous, and most often false, tales of black men raping white women circulated in order to brand African Americans as criminals and deny them citizenship. Because the buck represents a threat to white authority through his own sexuality, he needs to be disciplined, frequently through castration.[18] Of course, the legacy of socially positioning black males as sexually violent is discursively complex. While whites can mobilize these fears to disempower blacks, blacks can also seize such stereotypes as sources of empowerment. As Weigman notes, the Black Panthers promoted the image of the black buck to suggest potential ways to overthrow white power.[19] Certainly urban gangs and gangsta rappers offer another instance of African Americans appropriating fears of black sexuality to represent themselves as subverting a white social system that disempowers them economically. Ice-T's song *Cop Killer* was a fitting response to the Rodney King ruling and unfair police brutality in the early 1990s. Other gangsta rappers of that period, such as N.W.A., Snoop Dog, and Dr. Dre, connected gang life to an ultrasexuality in music videos that focused on violence and/or sexual exploits. And yet, white institutions use these same images to dismiss African American claims and position them as socially abject.

When Kevin visits Jersey City, *The Real World* places him in this long line of stereotypically violent black men. As Kevin walks through his neighborhood, the show's editors play nondiegetic gangsta rap beats and cut back to Julie expressing her fear of Kevin. Kevin walks his current girl-friend through the neighborhood and points out all of its potential dangers, from violence to drug dealing. Although this discourse is available for dominant and subaltern groups to seize, this clearly is the case of the dominant using this discourse to dismiss and disempower the subaltern. Having Kevin walk through his dangerous old neighborhood cut with Julie, who claims Kevin is dangerous to her, directly goes against Kevin's own argument about the fight, where he insists he never threatened Julie and was only looking out for his economic well-being. Even more fascinating, the show ends with Julie stating that her fight with Kevin had nothing to do with race or racism; it was only an interpersonal conflict. What the show does, then, is position Kevin, an articulate social critic of the way race operates in the United States, as a stereotypical, violent black male, and then deny that these issues have anything to do with race, placing them within a liberal discourse of individualism.

As a pivotal moment in the history of *The Real World*, this incident set an important precedent for the ways black males would be represented through stereotypical sexuality. It also represented, as mentioned earlier, the last moment where *The Real World* would allow black characters to have screen time to explicitly critique the social system. Although the city functions in *The Real World* as a place that cleanses racism from rural conservatives, it also operates as a space where dangerous black sexuality lurks. In season two, set in Los Angeles, David, a young black male, pulls the bedsheets off of Tammy, another African American, and is accused of attempted rape. In Seattle, Stephen, a black male, is coded as gay throughout most of the season, and yet he is staunchly homophobic. Midway through the season, a white liberal roommate, Irene, has to leave the show because of a relapse of her Lyme Disease. Although she had joked with Stephen throughout the season that they should get married, on her way out, Irene tells Stephen that a marriage between them would never work since he is a homosexual. Stephen, enraged, fakes masturbating to prove Irene wrong and then hits her in the face. Here, Stephen's body is discursively positioned as sexually out of control. He has desires for men, himself, and women. The editing of both the scene with David and Stephen emphasizes how violent black sexuality can be. The editors constantly return to these events in flashbacks, often excluding the events that lead up to the violent act and just focusing on how violent these black characters are.

But if these incidents mediate race through urbanity and a historical trajectory of stereotypes, other seasons use editing to erase history and historical trauma as a source of racism. Take an episode from season eleven, set in Chicago. After season four, the show had its cast work together on a specific job throughout the season. In Chicago, midway through the season, the cast had to script and then perform a Halloween play for the Chicago City Parks District. Keri, a white female, suggests a play where a woman becomes pregnant out of wedlock and kills the father. A jury sentences the woman to death by hanging, but postpones her execution until she gives birth to her child. At that point, Theo, an African American on the show, requests that the play not involve a hanging because many of his ancestors were lynched. While Theo is willing to perform the play as long as they change the style of execution, all the white roommates who discuss the issue insist that his pleas are petty and that Keri in no way intended the story to be racist. After splicing together interview clips of Theo talking about the historical trauma of hanging and white roommates maintaining that Keri's story in no way relates to the history of slavery, the episode ends with an interview with Kyle, a white liberal, who frames the conflict not as a battle to define U.S. racism but as the possible outcome of a conflict on the job.

As such, *The Real World* never interrogates the inferential racism of white liberal characters on the show. Kyle's cloaking of the racism present in this scene through discourses of work goes unchecked. In fact, by giving Kyle the last word on the fight, the episode punctuates the conflict with Kyle's perspective. In this way, the rural conservatives on *The Real World* are not the only house members to express nonracist racism. It is just that the editing and narrative structure on the show both fixate on the rural conservatives as the source of these social ills and ignore how the liberal house members are implicated in them as well. In fact, dwelling on the racisms of the rural conservatives deflects the show's own racism. No doubt, part of the reason why the program has remained so popular for so long on the channel is that it encourages the audience to position themselves as liberals against racism without reflecting on how this strategy for viewing race perpetuates racism itself. While it's certainly noble that MTV's audience usually does not participate in, and is in fact appalled by, explicit racism, they have certainly found rather blunt and misguided tools for combating racial oppression on *The Real World.*

Conclusion

Many of the production strategies for mediating reality that I've discussed in relationship to *The Real World* also take place on other reality TV shows. *Survivor* and *The Amazing Race* hold extensive casting calls and pointedly choose specific types of people to represent reality on their shows, and they structure interpersonal conflicts and friendships through serial narratives. Shows like these, as well as reality dating shows such as *Dismissed* and *Elimidate,* edit in such a way that characters comment on the actions of other characters. And with any reality TV show, too much happens during the filming process to capture everything that every character does. Directors have to decide to film some actions and not others. What I've tried to argue is not so much that these production practices on *The Real World* are unique but that they have played a specific role in the way the show mediates race, racism, and liberal identity for a particular cable channel.

Recently, Bunim and Murray's production company came to Indiana University in Bloomington, where I teach, and held an open casting call for the upcoming thirteenth season of *The Real World,* set in Paris. Before class one day, I was talking with my students about this open call and asked if anyone planned to audition. One student, a huge fan of MTV, admitted wanting to try out but not knowing what to say. Another student quickly chimed in with, "Just say you're a racist from a small-town in Indiana and you want to expand your mind. They'll pick you." To which the first student responded, "But I'm not a racist. I don't have a racist bone in my body." And the other student replied, "That's okay. By the end of the show they'll portray you as a nonracist. They always do." This incident speaks to the complex cultural operations and mediations of race on MTV. The show airs on a self-purported liberal cable channel. My one student was an astute observer of how the mediation of race on MTV starts during the casting process, where the show surveys the country to look for a rural American to represent racism and plans to expunge racism from this person through the serial narrative. All of my students, black and white, laughed at the comment, perhaps because MTV makes us feel like we're not implicated in the perpetuation of racism at all—as my one student thought. Racism in this liberal cable environment discursively exists only through rural conservatives. It's no surprise that in other classroom discussions about race, both formal and informal, students often feel more uncomfortable and less willing to laugh. Understanding racism as systemic, subconscious, and inferential is less fun, yet ultimately necessary. Perhaps to lead to a more critical understanding and mediation of race and racism in the United States, MTV should make us feel a little less comfortable.

NOTES

I would like to thank Susan Murray and Laurie Ouellette for their insightful revision suggestions. I have received feedback on many of the ideas in this article in a C190: Introduction to Media class that I taught during the spring 2002 semester at Indiana University. I am especially grateful to Liz, Carrie, Tory, Claire, Martha, Jen, Bria, Courtney, Christine, Kathryn, and Ali for their comments. Finally, to my wife, Sue, who commented on this article and watched more episodes of *The Real World* than she probably would have liked, I owe special thanks.

1. Seasons now usually film for five or six months and can also take place in a house or, in the case of the Las Vegas season, a hotel suite. Current seasons cast people between the ages of eighteen and twenty-four.

2. John Fiske, *Media Matters: Race and Gender in U.S. Politics* (New York: Routledge, 1992), 2.

3. Sut Jhally and Justin Lewis, *Enlightened Racism: The Cosby Show, Audiences, and the Myth of the American Dream* (San Francisco: Westview Press, 1992), 97.

4. Ibid.

5. Andrew Goodwin, "Fatal Distractions: MTV Meets Postmodern Theory," in *Sound and Vision: The Music Video Reader,* ed. Simon Frith, Andrew Goodwin, and Lawrence Grossberg (New York: Routledge, 1992), 62–63.

6. Ibid., 53.

7. Richard Dyer, *White* (New York: Routledge, 1997), 44.

8. Ibid., 45–46.

9. Ibid., 51–53.

10. Ibid., 57.

11. Cited in Alison Pollet, *The Real World: Chicago* (New York: Pocket Books, 2002), 1–2.

12. Ibid., 2.

13. Stuart Hall, "The Whites of Their Eyes: Racist Ideologies and the Media," in *The Media Reader,* ed. Manuel Alvarado and John Thompson (London: British Film Institute, 1990), 8–23.

14. Fiske, *Media Matters,* 37–39.

15. Ibid., 38.

16. Jeremy Butler, *Television: Critical Methods and Applications* (Belmont, Calif.: Wadsworth Publishing Company, 1994), 30–33. Butler also discusses the narrative structure of a series, whose episodes are self-contained narratives. For a more detailed look at the difference between a series and serial, see ibid., 25–33.

17. Donald Bogle, *Toms, Coons, Mulattoes, Mammies, and Bucks: An Interpretive History of Blacks in American Films,* expanded ed. (New York: Continuum Press, 1989), 10.

18. Robyn Weigman, *American Anatomies: Theorizing Race and Gender* (Durham, N.C.: Duke University Press, 1995), 90–95.

19. Ibid., 107.

10

What Do Women Watch?

Tuning In to the Compulsory Heterosexuality Channel

Jennifer Maher

I should be a big fan of Personal TLC, The Learning Channel's block of daytime reality programming, and its crown jewels, *A Baby Story* and *A Wedding Story*. After all, I am securely within their stated demographic (eighteen to thirty-four and female), and I enjoy popular documentary television like *Forensic Files, City Confidential,* and VH1 specials about Stevie Nicks. I have baby fever, modified as it is by writer's fever (I want a book contract before a baby shower). I read fashion magazines on occasion, abuse hair dye, and sometimes shop in the juniors department. I have been known to listen to mindless pop music. By TLC standards, I live a relatively normal life. But during one week when, in the interest of research, I watched Personal TLC for days (with breaks for eating, answering the phone, and taking naps), I discovered that demographics notwithstanding, just a few hours of these shows leaves me restless and anxious. I set about trying to figure out why.[1]

For those who are unfamiliar with Personal TLC, here's a brief introduction. Besides *A Baby Story* and *A Wedding Story,* the daytime TLC lineup includes *A Dating Story* and *A Makeover Story.* Both are juicy fodder for analysis (*Dating* is delightfully masochistic to watch and chock-full of the worst clichés of gender indoctrination you can imagine), but they are beyond the scope of this essay. The same goes for TLC's latest addition to its daytime ratings coup, *A Personal Story,* which in one recent episode presented plastic surgery as a life-enhancing treat.[2] During my viewing period (spring 2001), the Personal TLC shows ran solidly, in paired half-hour episodes, from 9:00 A.M. to 4:00 P.M. The schedule ran as follows:

9:00–10:00, *A Baby Story*; 10:00–11:00, *A Dating Story*; 11:00–12:00, *A Wedding Story*; 12:00–1:00, *A Makeover Story*; 1:00–2:00, *Dating*; 2:00–3:00, *Baby*; and 3:00–4:00, *Wedding*. While there are currently no ethnographic studies of TLC's daytime audiences, I tend to think that many viewers of these shows watch continuously (if distractedly) throughout the day, much as they do soap operas. As Tania Modleski writes, "The formal properties of daytime television . . . accord with the rhythms of work in the home . . . tend[ing] to make repetition, interruption, and distraction pleasurable."[3] I would also argue that TLC's reality programs (like soaps) are particularly well suited to a college student's life. While a student may work as well as go to school, there are periods during the day when they can perform school or work chores with the television on. An informal poll of my own students suggests that many viewers also tape daytime programs they might otherwise miss while they are in class. A recent article in the *Los Angeles Times* agrees, stating that "some college women are abandoning their beloved soaps to watch the [*Baby Story*] births."[4] Thanks in no small part to the power of this demographic, these shows are a ratings gold mine for TLC—they're the channel's most watched programs. As daytime programming chief Chuck Gingold told the *Washington Post*, "The ratings are phenomenal, especially for young women."[5] According to the same article, ratings more than doubled with the early introduction of *A Baby Story* and the concomitant expansion of TLC, though (and perhaps most important) "scarcely any men are watching."[6]

Despite my affinity for the kind of programming that men don't watch, my discomfort with *A Wedding Story* and *A Baby Story* lies first in how their near-endless parade of white dresses, blow-dried hair, and bassinets exemplify Adrienne Rich's famous criticism in "Compulsory Heterosexuality and Lesbian Existence," that "heterosexual romance has been represented as *the* great female adventure, duty, and fulfillment."[7] But rather than just label the viewers of these programs as unthinking conformists to compulsory heterosexuality (though believe me, watching as much as I did might easily lead one to that conclusion), I'd like to examine the shows' seeming appeal to women more closely. In other words, the pleasures experienced by seven hours a day of TLC must provide some kind of recompense for its viewers, something that goes beyond simple indoctrination; after all, that's what the commercials are for. (As might be expected, TLC's afternoon includes quite a few advertisements for diaper rash ointment, scented body washes, hair care products, baby formula, and the like, or all you need for each phase—dating, marriage, baby, makeover—of the femininity life cycle.) Something important—though not necessarily good—is going on when so many women watch the same thing for so many hours a day, and when they apparently feel such a strong need to watch. Indeed, as I will discuss later, TLC's website is home to message boards full of testimony to this need, with female fans who consistently use the words "addicted" and "obsessed" to describe their relationship to the shows.

In fact, the work being done by *Wedding* and *Baby* is duplicitous and complex. On the one hand, these programs are indoctrinating women into traditional gender roles, confirming the dominant cultural beliefs regarding love and romance that Rich and other feminist theorists have critiqued. On the other hand, we can also view *Wedding* and *Baby* as revealing the unhappiness that occurs when you have bought the romance-as-ultimate-fulfillment idea hook, line, and sinker. Unless you are a celebrity mom like Catherine Zeta-Jones, real life inevitably pales in comparison to popular culture's representation of both true love and male-female bonds. That women indulge in "documentary" romance narratives in such quantity—seven hours a day, five days a week, not to mention sporadic marathons (like the recent Baby Story one on, you guessed it, Labor Day)—might just let us in on a dirty little secret. As Janice Radway argues of the romance novel in *Reading the Romance: Women, Patriarchy, and Popular Literature,* real-life conventional heterosexuality can be a bit of a drag, one that is sometimes alleviated and displaced via an immersion in romance texts: Harlequin, soap operas, and now The Learning Channel.[8]

So while *A Wedding Story* and *A Baby Story* simply reinforce this nothing-without-a-man ethos, the fact that so many women feel such a need to watch these shows also indicates that something in heterosexual "real life" is sorely lacking. Though it is all too easy for (mostly male) critics to patronizingly dismiss all women's shows as "escapist," this idea has some credence. They *are* escapist, but what viewers are escaping is dissatisfaction with compulsory heterosexuality—even though the shows themselves are advertisements for the very concept. In short, women are escaping the "reality" of the romance fantasy that women have been promised since they got their first baby dolls, made their Barbies fight over bump-mounded Ken, or greedily watched older sisters prepare for the prom. By now, the falsities and fallacies of the heterosexual propaganda girls are taught from a very young age—some day your prince will come; your wedding will be the happiest day of your life; having a baby is every woman's desire and will only strengthen your relationship to your husband—are themselves feminist truisms. But there are still plenty of women for whom the original version is more familiar than the feminist revision, and when heterosexual romance is supposed to be the ultimate fulfillment of your femininity and the highlight of your life, imagine the surprise when reality sets in. He resembles neither a pirate nor prince, he has nose hair, and he doesn't pay that much attention to foreplay anymore. And of course, the pirate/prince might never come at all. How do you get out of feeling let down? For many women, as Radway also suggests, you don't challenge the compulsory heterosexual system or marriage as state-sponsored monogamy, you find ways to soothe yourself within the system. You pop in *Pretty Woman,* read *The Thorn Birds,* or now, turn on TLC.

As mentioned earlier, you can watch TLC's relationship documentaries from 9:00 in the morning until 4:00 in the afternoon, longer, I suspect, than Cindy Crawford spends in the gym each day. That's a lot of compulsory heterosexuality. And it's compulsory heterosexuality at its most uniform. While there is some race and class variation among the *Wedding*'s and *Baby*'s real-life couples, they are, like the vast majority of characters used to present the "average" person on TV, mostly white and seemingly middle class, and most relationships are monoracial. The occasional interracial pair does pop up, but it's worth noting that these couples are few and far between, and I've only seen white men with Asian women. And even though some couples on *A Baby Story* have grand pianos and restored Victorians while others live in cinder block apartment complexes, class differences are so smoothed over (everything is clean; the furniture always looks newish) that class is reduced to decorating preferences with no basis in financial disparity. On *A Wedding Story,* one couple rents an expensive ballroom, another a meeting hall, but these differences are presented as being of as little consequence as one bride choosing lavender bridesmaid's dresses while another chooses teal. There are no single parents and no gay wedding or commitment stories, despite TLC's website claim that the shows "spotlight the wonderful diversity expressed by modern couples."[9]

From the outset it's clear that *A Wedding Story* is creating romance fantasies as much as it is reflecting them. The series actively constructs but does not invent a gendered narrative that is made most visible in the wedding ceremony itself. In the opening credits, editing, and formulaic nature of the narrative of the show itself, the participants and producers are working together to create and mirror the romance for/through its participants, and by extension, female viewers at large. The beginning of each episode shows a wedding photo album with gold cursive writing on the cover (spelling out *A Wedding Story,* of course). The album then floats open via an unseen hand—much like children's fairy-tale books in film and television "open up" onto the visual story itself—while rose petals drift down from above. "Inside" the album are video montages from previous shows meant to look like wedding photographs come to life. The individual "stories," lasting thirty minutes each, follow the same narrative trajectory.

First, the future groom and bride are shown separately, telling the story of their relationship: how they met, what happened when one of them had to move, career choices, and so on. The editing between the male and female talking heads makes the story flow seamlessly; it appears as if they almost complete each other's sentences, and there's none of that "he said/she said" comic relief so present on talk shows and sitcoms. Sometimes there's a prewedding dinner, with toasts by best men or matrons of honor, where the bride usually thanks her mother or older sister for what she is today. We are next treated to the preparations for the wedding itself. How much the show arranges this, I'm not sure, but more often than not on the morning of, the members of the groom's party go off to play golf or go running or engage in some other active "masculine" behavior. In the bride's party they mostly sit—getting their nails, hair, and makeup done at a salon or at home. The penultimate moment occurs when the bride's tiara/wedding veil is placed, hands shaking like in a game of Jenga, as disrupting her hair-sprayed updo might require a late arrival at the altar. The men get into their tuxes rather quickly, punching each other in the arm, and even hugging, but not shedding a tear. When the bride is twisted into her dress by at least three other women, the tears flow immediately.

In perhaps the clearest example of producer/director machination, the last three minutes of each episode show the bride and groom in a medium shot, by themselves in varied spaces, outdoors or on a carriage ride, for instance. While they seem entirely comfortable with the more obvious performance of the wedding and reception itself, when the camera zooms in for a close-up, they turn to each other to congratulate or reaffirm their love in what appears to be the most scripted of ways. Though what they say in these moments is modified with specific details from each couple's relationship history, the lines are delivered woodenly and sometimes the white grooms even blush. Facing each other, then, in what should be the most "authentic" moment of the whole process—looking into each other's eyes and discussing their love for each other—comes across as an embarrassing afterthought. It's as if the producers of the show want to ward off the fetishization of the wedding itself, but when the lovebirds are alone, it looks suspiciously like this is exactly what the wedding's about: not a declaration of commitment but a presentation of a spectacle.

The most consistent element of *A Wedding Story* (and only slightly less so, of all the Personal TLC shows) is the universal commitment the participants and producers have to cultural clichés regarding what men and women should act like, look like, and expect from each other. This is, after all, The Learning Channel, and what's being taught or at least reinforced are traditional gender roles. While the featured wedding might occasionally include an out-of-the-ordinary venue or dress style (for instance, the Halloweenish wedding of a Goth couple), the narrative constants mentioned above clearly demonstrate the program's role in affirming, naturalizing, and showcasing only the most traditionally gendered of weddings. Usually the groom gets his "breath taken away" by the sight of "the love of his life" walking down the aisle in a dress that looks like a big, three-tiered cake; the bridesmaids wear matching uniforms in smooth fabrics and pale colors; and friends wave their inevitably French-tipped nails as they take their places to catch the bridal bouquet. The groom's eyes well up at just the right time. With the addition (sometimes) of carriage rides and weeping parents, flattering lighting, and an expert editing out of mistakes, these young people seem more than assured that their life together will fall into place as gracefully as a hand-beaded wedding train. Not a single episode I saw had the bride and groom announced to their assembled guests as anything but "Mr. and Mrs. Insert Male First and Last Name Here." References to fairy tales abound. According to the participants themselves, it appears that women want to look like "princesses" and they do indeed continually refer to their betrothed as a "Prince Charming." One featured wedding actually took place at Sleeping Beauty's Castle in Disneyworld, a horrific idea that is becoming increasingly popular, thanks in no small part, I assume, to TLC's televising it.

The union of Candy and Tom exemplifies this genre of ultimate fantasy wedding. They met on their gym's Life-Cycles and decided to meld their two life cycles into one as soon as he finished up his schooling. They got married in the Biltmore's Crystal Ballroom in Los Angeles (lots of money here, on both the bride's and groom's side). Speaking into the camera, with the ostensible question of why they chose to get married there edited out, Candy explains her choice of the building with "I'm into the old history. . . . It's very romantic." Cut to Tom, who can only commend his bride's depth of historical understanding by exclaiming, "Candy is the epitome of femininity. . . . She's so happy."

Thus the show reinforces the notion that romantic love ("she's so happy") is the pinnacle of a woman's existence (she's the "epitome of femininity"). That blissful moment when two become one (more specifically, when she becomes him) epitomizes the romantic promise of a coupling so clear that even your own family can't produce any fissure in the fantasy: they are no longer part of your identity; you are your husband's. After you've unpacked the gifts, framed the photos, and gotten used to your new name, that spectacular moment in the Crystal Ballroom/Sleeping Beauty's Castle/the chapel of a Georgia plantation becomes more a fading memory than a frisson of pleasure. This produces a desire to relive the ceremonial moment; you can eradicate your discontent via nostalgia stoked by watching others go through their vows again and again and again. This, of course, only serves to reinvigorate the fantasy, priming you to wake up the next morning and watch it all over again.

Like *A Wedding Story*, *A Baby Story* also promises a perfect life through a perfect coupling—with an addition or two. *Baby*'s opening credits feature tinkly piano music as a pregnant white woman's belly comes into view over a light blue background (signifying the hoped-for boy child?), while a white male hand, wearing a wedding ring, comes around and protectively circles the enormous stomach containing his future heir. The essence of *Baby* is that just this kind of happy and secure life lies in wait for every child the viewers will watch being born. In fact, the show takes pains to ensure that this is true in every way. *Baby*'s producers have assured reporters that "negative outcomes . . . are not televised."[10] Part of the editing/selecting process as I saw it similarly excluded couples who fight, divorce, or are in any way ambivalent about or less than fully committed to parenthood. At the beginning of each segment, the couple faces the camera to discuss their relationship and the progress of the pregnancy. Only one episode that I know of featured an unmarried couple. No mention was made of this fact in the episode itself, and I was surprised to see their "impending nuptials" noted on *Baby*'s website, where viewers can go to catch up on the lives of the new families through paragraph-long "updates" usually written by the mother. No "negative outcomes" get introduced here either—I imagine those in charge of the site leave out divorcing couples. After the program's introduction, viewers are often shown a real-life baby shower. The party typically involves assorted friends and family members who surreptitiously glance at the camera as they are forced to play ritualized games and contests like guessing the size of the mother-to-be's belly with a piece of string, or tasting and identifying baby food while blindfolded.

At the birth, the father usually stands or kneels at his laboring wife's side, brushing away her sweaty hair as she grunts and insists that she cannot go on. But of course, she does go on, and from between her paper-covered knees comes a little person—crusty, bluish pink, and covered in what looks like rubber cement. The camera is consistently positioned in a medium shot of the whole scene: bed, hospital room, and various assorted guests and observers, with cutaways to the faces of the mother and father. At no time does the camera actually zoom in between mom's legs to record her vagina dislodging a head or shoulders; such a private space, even in the context of a show that invades countless other intimate moments, is preserved.

This is not the case on TLC's *Maternity Ward* (*MW*) the flip side of the cuddly babydom that is *A Baby Story*. Though *MW* (shown at 10:00 P.M.) does not show genitalia either, the vastly different demographic of its participants allows for far more invasive and voyeuristic shots of its subjects' bodies. The mothers-to-be and fathers-to-be in *MW* are more or less incidental to the proceedings at hand. Poor, drug-addicted, and nonwhite, the structuring of the show presents them more as generic bodies than the subjects of *A Baby Story*, whose direct addresses to the camera about themselves and their partners invest them with a subjectivity (if a clichéd one) that is lacking in the vignettes of *MW*. Unlike *A Baby Story*, *MW* also televises difficult and life-threatening births, replete with voyeuristic close-ups of cesareans, infant spinal surgery, and newborn death. There's no tinkly piano music on *MW* to set the mood for a story of two healthy, middle-class, committed people in love waiting to meet the object that they have purchased all those clothes and accessories for. Some mothers who appear on *MW* are as young as fourteen, and even more are drug addicted, lower income, and single. One episode featured a thirteen-year-old girl—under the protective custody of her older sister and brother-in-law—who leaves the hospital promising to finish junior high in order to make a better life for the newborn child she seems ill equipped to raise. Before she goes into labor dressed in a child-sized nightgown, she listens distractedly as her eighty-year-old father offers advice about staying away from boys. Such dysfunction fuels *MW*, and seems almost as important as the traditional emergency room reality show narrative of urgency and blood. Cameras focus on close-ups of chipped-green-nail-polished hands grabbing the homemade-tattooed wrists of fathers-to-be who aren't old enough to drink. A wrenchingly drug-addicted mother names her son (in an incubator, but generally OK) Brian after her court-appointed lawyer, one of the few people who she has ever been able to count on. That the race and (presupposed) class demographics are exactly the opposite of those on *A Baby Story* gives the impression that simply being nonwhite and poor ups your chances for Down's syndrome, conjoined twins, congenital deformities of the limbs, spina bifada, and stillbirth.

With such at-risk pregnancies served up for the middle-class TLC audience, the producers have to be careful to moderate how much heartache and cathartic weepiness will keep viewers tuned in long enough. If the viewers were introduced as in-depth to the parents of *MW* as they are to the parents on *A Baby Story*, they'd learn some very uncomfortable things. They'd be forced to swallow the story of how a thirteen year old met the father of her child, what growing up in a series of foster homes means, or what an apartment available to someone working minimum wage with no health benefits looks like. Such visions might make the viewer switch the channel as quickly as when Sally Struthers appears in an African village during the commercial break. So our information about the participants of *MW* is kept at an emotional distance while their immediate medical circumstance produces enough sadness, worry, and tension to keep the viewer engaged: close enough for tsk-tsking, but far enough removed that no one gets too attached to folks who are, in one way or another, victims of a society gone haywire. Such distancing works by eliminating all but the most skeletal context of, say, two extremely young Hispanic parents whose daughter, referred to throughout as "Baby Chavez," is diagnosed with Down's syndrome.

As recompense, perhaps, we are treated to drawn-out scenes of the families of the physicians themselves, whose full names, personal histories, education, and reasons for choosing medicine are given at the beginning of each segment, and are referred to throughout the episode. Their spouses (most often wives, but with an occasional husband of a female doctor) and broods traipse down the hospital runway, rapturous at seeing mom or dad saving the babies of all the poor people. Shoot to talking heads of the featured doctor or doctors, who face the camera, like the couples profiled on *A Baby Story*, to talk about their own family bonds and how their surgical skill has everything to do with their innate maternal or paternal feelings. The patients, however, are de-contextualized enough to allow the viewer to focus on the gore. On a typical episode of *MW*, you might see a deep cut to a woman's abdomen along with the layers of intestines and fat that are necessary for the doctor to dip into in order to perform a cesarean section. A cesarean section on *A Baby Story*, in contrast, entails a little sigh of exhaustion from the mother and a shot of the baby being lifted out from the sheets. The subjectivity of what Emily Martin calls "the woman in the body," is, in other words, constructed much differently on *MW*.[11] In surgery, the recognizability of the human subject on the table is covered up with the blue sheet of the operating room—a sheet covering all but the section to be operated on. There are all kinds of reasons for this, I imagine, from a medical perspective, not the least of which would involve allowing the doctors to focus more closely on the tissue at hand. But the show itself enacts a kind of narrative "blue sheet" over the women it films, too, effacing their subjectivity so that graphic footage can be anted up.

A *Baby Story*, in contrast, doesn't even show the afterbirth, instead replacing bloody body shots with lots of tears as the baby is held up like a trophy in the evolutionary Olympics. Each episode then ends with a quick posthospital wrap-up, usually with the newly expanded family in a park or getting ready for a "family" activity. The baby has always "changed their lives in ways they couldn't even imagine," "truly made them a family," and "brought their love even closer." Births like those televised on *MW*, then, are excluded from *A Baby Story* because they fail to fulfill the romance fantasy of the show, itself a continuation of the romance fantasy of *A Wedding Story*. Since these women are often poor and husbandless, they can't be shown either strolling with their babies in a well-manicured park or snuggling with supportive partners on overstuffed couches.

But what really sets the TLC romance narrative trajectory apart from traditional romance narratives (most romance novels, for instance, *end* with a wedding) is the way that *Baby* reconciles the irreconcilable—romance and real life—through what would appear to be (but really isn't) a refiguring of gender roles. As Joan Foster, the romance-novel-writing protagonist of Margaret Atwood's *Lady Oracle*, explains, women need romance fiction precisely because they can't get what they want from the actual men in their lives. Of her readers, she muses:

> They wanted their men to be strong, lustful, passionate and exciting, with hard rapacious mouths, but also tender and worshipful. They wanted men . . . who would rescue them from balconies but they also wanted in-depth

relationships and total openness. . . . They wanted multiple orgasms, they wanted the earth to move, but they also wanted help with the dishes.[12]

It's precisely the man who makes the earth move and helps with the baby bottle who embodies masculinity as shot and packaged on *A Baby Story*. These men are represented as highly concerned with the very minutiae of this traditionally feminine process. All of them attend the birth, whether held at home with a midwife or in a hospital. They are completely supportive, holding hands, cheering "good job," accompanying the wife on the ubiquitous shopping trip to buy new baby stuff. Here the couples are led, looking rather stunned, across the maze of products necessary for bringing the squab home. No waiting on a bench outside the store reading the sports page for these guys (as stereotype would have us believe their own fathers did); they are too busy trying out the baby monitors and listening carefully as the store assistant explains the newest research into crib mobiles. The couples fold baby clothes together, assemble a crib, or arrange stuffed animals against teeny pillows. Near-Aristotelian decisions are hammered out over the advantages and disadvantages of a car seat that stays permanently in the automobile or one that can be taken out and used as a baby carrier. The fathers ask intelligent questions about breast pumps and receive well-planned corporate answers from the trained staff of whatever baby-supply chain they happen to be in.

Thus, the fathers as filmed in these half-hour vignettes become avatars of masculinity: we know their hard rapacious mouths (or some version thereof) had to have been involved to get the little seedling in the uterus, but guess what? They are happy as clams to do the proverbial dishes. So while there is a slight transgression of the traditional gender roles—he shops, he nurtures—the importance of the heterosexual family is upheld consistently at the same time. And rigid gender roles are held up too in the shopping, as parents browse for clothes for their girl babies that will make them look like "little ballerinas" and proud fathers-to-be search long and hard for teeny baby sports accessories for their "little sluggers." Nevertheless, there are no ambivalent parents here, just loving heterosexual couples with supportive families, money to spend on child-rearing accessories aplenty, and the apparent psychological preparedness to have their lives change with the new arrival.

Certainly, *A Baby Story* has its pleasures. Despite how boring its featured couples can be, when the squishy, uncooked-chicken-looking thing that is their newborn comes out, it's, well, moving. *Salon* TV critic Joyce

Millman, writing in the *New York Times* of her own puzzling obsession with *A Baby Story*, discusses its appeal. She claims childbirth is a pride-inducing female experience, a pleasure that goes hand in hand with the physical desire for babies themselves:

> We'd sell our own grandmothers to hold an infant and get a fix of that intoxicating scent known as "new baby's head." Childbirth is a test of a woman's stamina, proof of her body's power. It's an unbelievably heady feeling giving birth, probably akin to winning a marathon (but how many of us ever win a marathon?)

Millman goes on to describe *A Baby Story* as "childbirth porn," with its "undeniable voyeuristic tingle," and names the baby's exit from the womb as "the mommy shot."[13]

With exceptions for the adamantly child-free, the near-universal appeal of babies cuts across all kinds of imposed differences; it's hard not to get emotional, no matter how alienated you feel from the couple or the show's very premise. Furthermore, since we are so used to seeing women's bodies valued only for how they look, it's refreshing to watch a woman for what her body can do.

After viewing so many episodes of *A Wedding Story*, however, it's clear how *A Baby Story* completes the traditional female life narrative, no matter what order the shows are broadcast in. The loving husband's filmed involvement stands as proof that such narratives "work": if you pay attention and take your vows in his name, you can have your romance cake and have him wash the plate you eat it off of, too. Interestingly, we don't see a continuation of the same couples moving from wedding to babyhood. But maybe we wouldn't want to—seeing "perfect," "feminine," "beautiful" Candy with a big belly and support hose might ruin the fantasy, turning the whole affair into a continuous "real-life" narrative that would no longer serve its purpose. Instead, the message is: follow the rules dictated by your feminine role as starry-eyed princess and fine specimen of male-exchanged property, and you can get a perfect parent in the bargain. When so many fathers are bailing out of even their commitment to support their children financially, the fantasy of the ideal man/dad of every *Baby* episode is the perfect antidote.

But *Baby*, especially when watched in tandem with the other TLC Lifestyle Stories, confirms that in order to obtain the perfect heterosexual fantasy, you have to go along with a lot of gender clichés to make it all run smoothly. From door opening to white dress wearing, these shows give with one freedom-of-choice hand—it's all up to you, ladies, to pick the right guy and reception hall—and take away with the other sexist one.

And though most viewers might not describe it in feminist terms, their responses to *A Wedding Story* and *A Baby Story* are solidly grounded in dissatisfaction with this state of affairs. While their primarily female demographic and the shows themselves provide clues to viewers' dissatisfaction, it's their feedback on the Web that confirms and illuminates it. Of course, some viewers may have alternative or subversive readings of these shows. We can view the wedding with pleasure for its demonstration of how, in Gloria Steinem's words, at the onset of puberty one learns to become a "female impersonator."[14] It's easy to picture glorious drag reenactments of the solemnity with which dishes, cakes, and shoes are given as much or more weight as love. But The Learning Channel both maintains and monitors its fan sites for its most popular shows, so if alternative or subversive reactions were to be expressed there, it's not certain they would remain. What does remain on the bulletin boards for both *Wedding* and *Baby* are entire threads about an "addiction" to and "obsession" with the programs themselves. Such self-professed addiction (however casually the term is used) indicates that the gap between real-life relationships and compulsory-heterosexuality romance fantasies is indeed wide, demanding precisely the sort of fantasy provided by TLC to shore it up.

On *A Wedding Story*'s official Internet forum, TLC proposes that its audience view the show as an educational opportunity, a place to get ideas for cakes and bridesmaid's dresses for one's own upcoming wedding. (Interestingly, Radway notes that many readers of historical romances consider the genre educational as well.)[15] But there's more to it than the simple gathering of reception ideas. The intense interest in other people's weddings is utterly normalized. As one devoted viewer, a production assistant, states, "Of course girls love it because of the fact that it's many girls' biggest dream and the most important day of their lives."[16]

Perhaps most significant, a majority of the fan-site participants are already married. Their posts are full of speculation about the personal lives of the featured couples and rhapsodic comments about the televised setting, the adorable flower girl. This is certainly not an educational viewing practice; any ideas gathered would have to be for their next wedding (and it goes without saying that in the happily-ever-after framework of *Wedding*, the dissolution of an existing marriage is just not contemplated). As further proof of how real-life men don't pay up on their romance-fantasy end of the bargain, these fans mention that their real-life husbands do not understand their wives' investment in these documentary romance narratives, and are even hostile to it. In *Reading the Romance,* Radway documents the same male hostility to their wives' reading of romance novels; husbands complain that time spent reading takes away from their wives' time caring for them and the rest of the family.[17] These concerns are echoed by the *Wedding Story* fans themselves, as motivated by husbandly reproof, they ask for reassurance from other fans as to whether they are OK for having such a close relationship with the show, even though their own weddings are in the past. But while my argument is that the fact that they are already married is what causes so much repeated viewing, the fans support each other with straightforward feminine solidarity, connected through mild male (husband) bashing.

As "newlywed_june2000" writes: "My husband asked me yesterday, 'Why do you still watch *A Wedding Story*?' He thinks that since our wedding is over (24 June 2000) that I shouldn't watch the show anymore. What do you think? Am I weird? I can't stop watching it. I love to see the people as happy as we are, plus I love to see the dresses, cakes, and the rings."[18] A plethora of recently married women soon respond, and there is a general agreement that once again, husbands just don't understand. Correspondents offer support to writers like "newlywed" by admitting their own addiction to the show and letting others know that they shouldn't worry, as it's only "natural femininity" that causes them to watch so much TV. As "joshanddawn" (her e-mail address includes not just her first name but her husband's as well) states (with her own wedding date in the first line of her post), "We love love and this show is all about it and why not watch it and share in someone's big day?"[19] A high school student (gulp) adds:

> I've been addicted to the show for about three years now. I watch it faithfully and can't bear to miss an episode! I'm quite infatuated(sp?) with weddings and have been since my sister and I first started purchasing bridal magazines at the young age of thirteen. . . . I think I love weddings because of the excitement and joy they bring to people! It's usually one of the happiest days of someone's life, apart from the birth of a child. . . . I'm planning my wedding right now, though I have yet to find my soulmate! It's many girls' dreams to live out that Cinderella fantasy! Watching it gets people like me sooo excited about my future, even though I'm only just starting in col-

lege. The show is an excellent way to keep your hopes up, and get some great ideas for weddings!

Hope that helps,

Lacey[20]

And another viewer rather wittily advises "newlywed" to "Ask [her husband] if he wants you to start watching the baby story instead—he'll quit asking."[21] Though such investment in these shows seems ripe for feminist analysis, none of the viewers appears to relate her dissatisfaction to her need for televised assuagement. No bulletin board writer ever considers abandoning the ship of compulsory heterosexuality by questioning her devotion to the perfect life it promises.

The postings of *Baby Story* fans are similar. Current mothers have e-mail names identifying them as such, like "lovebeingamommy," "mommaof3," and "littlemommaof2angels." Viewers typically talk about their favorite episodes, "celebrity" sightings ("littlemommaof2angels" ran into the Hirsh couple at the Atlanta airport recently), and how, again, their husbands hate their watching of the show and don't understand why they do it. One woman (screen name: "mrsgillmore") writes, "I have to say I am a baby story junkie also. My husband and I have only [been] married 3 months and I am so ready to have a baby. He always sighs [when] she he [*sic*] walks into the room and sees *Baby Story* on TV. I used to watch *Wedding Story* before I was married . . . but have moved up to *Baby Story*."[22]

What's most interesting about these posts is the almost hysterical devotion to an institution—heterosexual romance generally and marriage specifically—that leaves so many women unsatisfied, especially its most devoted participants (the ones who use their husband's names and wedding dates in their postings), whose actual husbands don't understand them at all. This dissatisfaction is made evident not only in the nature of the Web posts themselves but in the necessity for repeated viewing of more and more TV weddings in order to feel better. Women watch these shows because they televise, over and over, the Holy Grail of heterosexuality, engraved with "Tom and Candy, 18 June 1999." As Radway asserts of the Harlequin romance readers she studied, "This need to see the [romantic] story and the emotions aroused by it are so intense that . . . [these] women worked out an ingenious strategy to insure a regular and predictable arrival at the anticipated narrative conclusion."[23] As she discovers that her real romantic life is not as exciting as the televised narrative, the viewer soothes the pain of the dissimilarity between experience and fantasy by watching another episode that evokes the same romance-fantasy emotions, which of course, serves to sustain the fantasy. And the cycle begins anew.

What such postings reveal about TLC's reality programming is the complicated nature of female longing for love, dissatisfaction with that love, and a need to be reassured that such love is still possible. This viewership is more complicated and potentially deconstructive than it at first appears. Perhaps Sigmund Freud's perpetually unanswered question, "What do women want?" can be partially answered by what women watch. Paradoxically, *A Wedding Story* and *A Baby Story* reveal the discontent of perfect love as we've been coached to feel and live it as well as the repetition compulsion such dissatisfaction engenders. If feminists could politicize this dissatisfaction, we might go far in breaking the hold that compulsory heterosexuality has over our culture. Watching TV isn't the revolution, certainly; it pacifies more than it incites. But watching ourselves watching it might rouse us from the complacency couch, if only to challenge the channel(ing) of our desire.

NOTES

1. My analysis of Personal TLC is based on episodes aired during a ten-day span, in the second and third weeks of April 2001.

2. Jennifer Maher, "A C-Cup Is a Versatile Breast," *Bitch: A Feminist Response to Popular Culture* 16 (spring 2002): 27–28, 87.

3. Tania Modleski, *Loving with a Vengeance: Mass-Produced Fantasies for Women* (New York: Methuen, 1982), 102.

4. Patricia Ward Biederman, "When It Comes to Babies, This Show Delivers," *Los Angeles Times,* 12 February 1999, 1.

5. Cited in Paula Span, "Reality TV Goes Feminine with Hugs Instead of Thugs," *Washington Post,* 16 March 1999, A1.

6. Ibid.

7. Adrienne Rich, *Blood, Bread, and Poetry: Selected Prose, 1979–1985* (New York: W. W. Norton, 1986), 648.

8. Janice Radway, *Reading the Romance: Women, Patriarchy, and Popular Literature* (Chapel Hill: University of North Carolina Press, 1984).

9. Cited on tlc.discovery.com/fansites/babystory/babystory.html, 14 December 2000.

10. Gail Pennington, "Some Moms May Disagree, but TV Sees Entertainment Value in Childbirth," *St. Louis Dispatch,* 12 May 2000, E1.

11. Emily Martin, *The Woman in the Body* (Boston: Beacon Press, 1987).

12. Margaret Atwood, *Lady Oracle* (New York: Simon and Schuster, 1976), 241.

13. Joyce Millman, "The Addictive Spectacle of Maternal Reality," *New York Times,* 13 August 2000, A25.

14. Cited on www.motherjones.com/mother_jones/ND95/gorney.html.

15. Radway, *Reading the Romance,* 61, 106–12, 113, 116, 192.

16. Cited on tlc.discovery.com/fansites/weddingstory/weddingstory.html.

17. Radway, *Reading the Romance,* 90–93, 100–102, 103–4, 111–12.

18. Cited on tlc.discovery.com/fansites/weddingstory/weddingstory.html, 12 December 2000.

19. Ibid., 22 December 2000.

20. Ibid., 18 December 2000.

21. Ibid.

22. Cited on tlc.discovery.com/fansites/babystory/babstory.html, 14 December 2000.

23. Radway, *Reading the Romance,* 19.

11

Aliens, Nomads, Mad Dogs, and Road Warriors

The Changing Face of Criminal Violence on TV

Elayne Rapping

"It is no longer possible to discuss crime without talking about the media, and vice versa," say the editors of an anthology on *Crime and the Media: The Postmodern Spectacle.*[1] At a time when criminal trials have become major media events, and nightly newscasts devote "42 percent of their airtime to crime, violence, terrorism and disaster," the argument seems indisputable.[2] Crime is one of the major public issues of our day. As Stuart Hall demonstrated in his landmark *Policing the Crisis: Mugging, the State, and Law and Order,* in a highly complex and fragmented social environment, "events and issues only become *public* in the full sense when the means exist whereby the separate worlds of professional and layperson, of controller and controlled, are brought into relation with one another and appear, for a time at least, to occupy the same space."[3] And it is the mass media of course—and especially television, which is on, and so in some sense consumed, an estimated seven and three-quarters hours per day in the average U.S. home—that provides the communicative means by which this common public space is constructed.

To understand this process is to understand the crucial role of the crime drama in maintaining social stability and the authority of the state. For it is through these symbolic narratives of wrongdoing and retribution that we internalize the shifting rules as well as norms by which we distinguish between right and wrong, between which acts of violence are authorized, even valorized, and which are forbidden. But the role of television is even more complex than this. For when major shifts in the processes and policies that drive law enforcement systems occur, it is invariably television—in both news and entertainment divisions—that plays the most powerful role in "informing" the public of these shifts, and helping it to adjust, culturally and psychologically, to their implications. Thus, in times of paradigmatic cultural, social, and political change, it is the media that must perform the difficult work of "redefining the cultural context within which the criminal justice system operates," and indeed, redefining "the very concepts, of crime, justice and retribution," to fit the needs and norms of the changing social order.[4] The 1990s were such a time. With the Clinton presidency, we saw what can only be viewed by future historians as a radical shift in the very meaning of the terms "liberal" and "conservative." A new consensus emerged in which Democrats joined Republicans in a middle ground far to the right of the traditional political center, and which has escalated with the coming of the Bush presidency.

In no area was this rightward drift more dramatic than criminal justice. By 1997, prison construction and management had become the greatest growth industry in the nation. And the imposition of more harsh and punitive measures defined an increasingly repressive society in which those in power grew more fearful and hostile toward those they worked to control.[5] Nonetheless, for all the hype about rising crime rates justifying these policies, the actual rate of violent crime fell dramatically in those years. Yet new inmates arrived in droves to fill the newly constructed prisons for longer and longer terms. Who were these dangerous criminals? They were, for the most part, people convicted of nonviolent offenses involving drugs, prostitution, and other activities associated less with human aggression or greed than sheer survival—both psychological as well as material—in an increasingly harsh and hopeless world. Not surprisingly, most were members of minority and underclass populations. Indeed, studies showed that by 1994, "one out of every three African American men between the ages of 20 and 29 in the entire country—including suburban and rural areas—was under some form of criminal justice supervision."[6] Members of immigrant populations were also increasingly visible among the prison population. And the fastest growing of all segments of the chronically incarcerated in the 1990s was women, previously a negligible problem for law enforcement officials, but whose numbers, across racial and ethnic lines, rose dramatically.[7]

It is clear that the role of law enforcement has shifted decisively to a terrain on which social control of an increasingly large population of the disaffected, disinherited, and dysfunctional has replaced the traditional concern with seeking out and punishing serious crimes against persons and property. The newly imprisoned are not for the most part armed robbers, murderers, or even—media hype to the contrary notwithstanding—serial killers or child molesters. They are nonviolent drug users along with other cultural and social outsiders and misfits; they are the people who have increasingly fallen through the system's cracks or have never been allowed to enter its gates. And they pose a serious problem for the state not so much because they are viciously aggressive by nature or motive but because they do not easily fit lawfully into the newly restrictive and intolerant version of U.S. democracy.

It is in the context of this social transformation that the changing nature of television crime drama—of the very representation of what criminal violence looks like, as well as how, why, and where it functions—must be analyzed. For as we move into a new century, there is arguably an increasing shift in the hegemonic norms by which criminal violence and law enforcement are portrayed on television—one that is very much in keeping with the actual shifts in social policy cited above. This shift is most evident in the new reality crime series. For it is often in the "lower," less established genres that cultural innovations and shifts first tend to emerge. And when one turns to these newly minted forms, one sees an image of "crime" and "criminality" markedly different from earlier genres, but eerily suited to the current political climate, in which paranoia, intolerance of difference, and a laissez-faire attitude toward repressive police tactics seem the order of the day.

The Politics of Crime Drama Convention

There are two ways in which crime drama fulfills the symbolic function of constructing, within the mediated public sphere, the major mind-sets within which we come to understand and accept the values and norms of the dominant social order. The first has to do with setting. The crime drama delineates the symbolic geography within which social order must be maintained; it outlines the political imaginary within which the endless rituals of social disruption, and the return to harmony and peace, are performed. The second is characterological. The crime drama sketches out the human (or subhuman) contours by which we distinguish "deviance" from "normality," the "outlaw" from the good citizen who lives "within the boundaries of the law."

In the reality series I am analyzing here, *Cops*, criminals are different from what crime series viewers have come to expect. They are incorrigibly "other" and "alien," incapable of internalizing or abiding by the norms and values of a liberal democracy, for they are far too irrational, uncontrollable, and inscrutable for such measures to be effective. They are part of a newly constructed image of "crime" and "criminal violence" in which more harsh and repressive measures are suddenly necessary to maintain social order, because those who threaten that order are—or have become—inhuman brutes and freaks.

There have been many examples and varieties of reality crime TV—from the *Hard Copy/Inside Edition* "Shocks, horrors, and sensations of the day" version, to the *America's Most Wanted/Unsolved Mysteries* "They're still out there" version, to the *American Detective/Top Cops* "Let's ride along with Officer Jones" one—that have come and gone, most rather quickly, since the genre first emerged in the 1990s. But all share a more than prurient interest in the more irrational forms of criminal behavior, both minor and extreme, as either the major or sole subject matter. They also share a low-budget, "video verité" style based on documentary interviews, tapes of actual police work, and in some cases, dramatic reenactments of past, but not yet solved crimes. Of all of these, *Cops*—the longest running series of its kind—is the one that most strikingly reveals the contours of what is a newly emerging construction of criminal violence. *Cops*, for one thing, focuses exclusively on crime and crime control, with no diversionary detours to other sensational matters, a staple of other reality shows, which include a variety of themes and formats. But more important, it is the series that most thoroughly jettisons the traditional paraphernalia of crime drama to present a radically new vision of the landscape and nature of crime, criminality, and law enforcement. And it is a vision so expressionistically marked as to allow a clear glimpse of the key assumptions and implications of current political trends.

From the City to the Borders

In traditional crime drama, the landscape of crime has been the city—the urban centers of industrial, Western society. According to Hall, "The city is a concrete embodiment of the achievements of industrial society" that "embodies our civilization and the degree to which we are successful in maintaining that achievement."[8] Hence, the city's fall into disorder or violence represents a grave threat to our common survival and well-being.

On television, the crime genre begins in the 1950s with *Dragnet,* a series about a straight-arrow cop as baffled by the iniquity he saw evolving on the city streets as his audiences. The genre has been updated recently to fit a time when even TV audiences (perhaps especially TV audiences) are cynically savvy enough to know that good and evil are not so easily distinguishable. And so, in series like *Law and Order* or *Homicide,* crime and criminality are no longer portrayed as wholly different from the more "normal" characteristics and actions of the law abiding among us, but rather as exaggerated versions of what are normal flaws common to most people in modern societies.

This is also close to the landscape within which Michel Foucault—whose writings on crime and punishment in modern times have arguably been the most influential of the twentieth century—developed his analysis of how the assumptions, institutions, and practices of judgment and punishment have evolved within liberal democracies. Foucault assumed that society was a "biopolitical" whole within which individual subjects were integral units, both understandable and manageable through the technologies of power/knowledge. "This deviation, this potential danger, this illness" was how Foucault described criminality as it had been constructed within modern discourses. And because the criminal was a "pathologized subject," he was transformed from a figure of essential evil to a subject of study for the new science of criminology, in which a "gentler way of punishment" for "docile bodies"—disciplined from birth to internalize and conform to the norms of society or feel guilt for the failure to do so—could be managed.[9]

On traditional TV series, this is very much the way criminals are portrayed. Murderers, muggers, even inner-city gang members are much like us, only they have given into their most dangerous and antisocial impulses. Who dunnit? is answered with sociological, psychological, and moral analyses that make sense, as "motives" in a criminal trial must make sense. When we turn to reality series like *Cops,* we know we are *not* in Foucault country. No longer do we see the savvy New York cops, lawyers, and experts who work and live within a coherent, if darkened and flawed version of the political imaginary. *Cops* is set in a metaphoric border territory—literally "out where the buses don't run." This is a landscape of highways, strip malls, trailer parks, and convenience stores. And while it may resemble places we have all seen and visited, it seems—despite the

Officer Ty Dickinson

On *Cops*, cameras follow a police officer on his rounds. This man is being arrested for soliciting a prostitute.

echt-verité quality of the representation—somehow more "foreign" than any U.S. landscape we may have entered.

Cops each week follows a police officer, in some area of the United States not typically seen on TV, as he (for the cop is usually a "he") makes his nightly rounds, patrolling the highways and answering calls about neighborhood and domestic disturbances. The program begins each week—and this is how the viewer is introduced to the city or town being visited—with a collage of random shots of local denizens, each more strange, menacing, or simply pathetic than the last. Against a sound track playing an upbeat version of the reggae song "Bad Boys" ("Bad boys, bad boys, whatcha gonna do?/Whatcha gonna do when they come for you?"), we see a barrage of fast cuts of, perhaps, a drunk about to strike out or simply wobbling on the point of collapse; a black, dreadlocked rollerblader dressed only in a scant bikini; an armed "offender" of some kind being violently apprehended and cuffed as he puts up a wild, but hapless struggle; a cop comforting or even diapering a wailing, unkempt baby as the child's parent is dragged away—all intercut with road markers identifying the city and county in question.

There is no narrator or voice-over giving direction to the series. The cop who is featured each week—always clean-cut in appearance, and articulate and civilized in manner as well as speech—speaks directly to the audience, eschewing all traditional televisual apparatus by which viewers know they are on familiar media terrain. Here we are confronted directly with "real life," it is implied, with no Dan Rather or Barbara Walters to spin it to us. In this way, the series signals the viewer that it will forgo the artificial constructions by which traditional TV smoothes the edges of reality and sugarcoats the horrors of what *real* cops, in the *real* world, are up against. And yet, the distortions of media convention, only of a less familiar variety, are as salient here as anywhere on television.

The cop begins by introducing himself. He explains a bit about his own background, his motives in becoming a cop, the gratifications and frustrations he receives from the work, and so on. "I wanted to be a priest," says one officer, typically, "but I began to think I could serve better in law enforcement." The cops—who always know, even if the audience is lulled into forgetting, that the camera is running—present themselves in the most cleaned-up, wholesome of terms. They are constructed as the image of the traditional, U.S. male heroism that audiences want so much to believe in. And because they are so pure and angelic, the contrast between them and those they police is dramatic.

The half-hour segment takes the viewer from site to site (usually, six or seven "cases" are covered in the twenty-two-minute period) as the cop answers calls on his car radio; chases down and stops suspicious-seeming cars on the streets and highways he patrols; and apprehends suspicious individuals who happen to be walking along the generally unpopulated roads or highways. Intoxicated, drugged-out drivers; domestic and street brawls; out-of-control or suspicious-looking loiterers—these are the "crimes" the officers on *Cops* are most likely to attend to week after week, as they drive their police cars through the rough-and-tumble roadways and trailer park settlements they endlessly police. The structure of the series thus follows a serial format rather than the narrative arc—crime, investigation, capture, and punishment—of traditional crime drama. And crime itself, as we have been taught to understand it by the media, is therefore radically reconstructed. No more do criminals plot and scheme toward nefarious goals; no more do they act out of jealous rage, greed, or anger, and then hide out, dissemble, and attempt to cover their tracks as in traditional narratives. Now we have characters apparently driven not by reasonable, if reprehensible desires or goals but by brute instinct or chemical derangement. They now lurk, wander, or simply break down within a spiritual and physical wasteland somewhere outside society's orderly boundaries. And since the structure precludes any knowledge of what might have come before, of who the person is as well as what their social and psychological background might be, the impression of sheer unmotivated madness is driven home. Thus, in place of the orderly plot structure of conflict, crisis, and resolution, we have a series of endless, irrational "disruptions."

In such a format, the traditional construction of violence itself, as we have come to understand it through crime drama, is also radically transformed. For in traditional series, we have a motivated act of violence at the beginning of the hour that then drives the rest of the action: the concerted effort to find the criminal by figuring out his motives, tracking him down, and arresting him. The violence—itself an isolated event that stands out from the rest of the action—is thereby causally connected to a story about the perpetrator in which, by hour's end, a mesh of sociological and psychological circumstances have emerged to explain his act.

This traditional view of even the worst violent crimes as inherently understandable and correctable has its origin, according to Foucault, in the theories developed in the nineteenth century by which crime came to be understood in terms of the discourses of medicine and psychiatry. It was then that the "disease model" of deviance—first applied only to the most pathologically dangerous and demented of killers—gradually came to be extended to criminals of all kinds. "There appear in the field of legal psychiatry new categories such as necrophilia around 1840, kleptomania around 1860, exhibitionism in 1876 and also legal psychiatry's annexation of behavior of pederasty and sadism," Foucault wrote, so that "there now exists, at least in principle, a psychiatric and criminological continuum which permits one to pose questions in medical terms at any level of the penal scale."[10] Thus, one could equate the most horrible criminal act with the most minor and trivial, and establish a systematic, disciplinary process of correction for *all* criminals. For few criminals were (or are today, media hype to the contrary notwithstanding) likely to commit the most serious or repugnant of crimes.

This construction still applies even to the most extremely demonized of criminals—serial killers and child molesters perhaps—as seen on traditional crime dramas. As Ray Surette argues, "The crimes that dominate the public consciousness and policy debates" are not common crimes but the rarest ones, for "the modern mass media have raised the specter of the predator criminal from a minor character to a common, ever-present image." But Surette himself includes among those punitive approaches "intensive individual rehabilitative or educational efforts" of the kind that still adhere to an assumption that criminals are theoretically correctable and reformable.[11]

On *Cops*, however, because of the way in which violence itself is represented, even this vestige of liberal policy assumption seems no longer to apply. For the offenders on *Cops*, while certainly violent or prone to violence, are rarely predators. In fact, on the most obvious level, they are far less threatening than the criminals seen on other crime series or, for that matter, the nightly news. For their acts are not generally directed *toward* anyone or anything. Nor are their worst violent acts generally of the sensational, explosive variety that is most anxiety provoking to the population at large. Rather, they embody a proneness to random, sporadic violence that is represented as a permanent condition of human, or rather subhuman, nature. They are simply violent in ways that make no sense at all. We get no "story" of any kind onto which we might hang a diagnosis or criminal profile. And because of this, treatment or rehabilitation are not options.

Indeed, even when the cops attempt to get at the bottom of things, they rarely get a coherent story. Sometimes this is because witnesses and victims are incoherent, either due to drugs or because they speak another language. More often they simply tell incoherent narratives or contradict each other. And since we see each person only in this isolated moment, when they are most out of control and potentially dangerous, we can't know if there is more to the story than meets the religiously "truthful" eye of the video lens. So powerful is the appeal to "reality" that documentary footage holds, that the missing context—social, emotional, narrative— seems irrelevant or, worse, is never even considered.

Beyond the City: The Postmodern Imaginary of Tabloid TV

The implications of *Cops'* construction of criminal violence must surely strike fear in the hearts of viewers. The creatures portrayed—inscrutable, uncontrollable, and beyond the ken of traditional criminological "expertise"—are after all "somewhere" very near to us, for we see road signs identifying actual U.S. locations. And because of this implied proximity to "normal" society, these creatures are likely, so it is suggested, to seep through our borders and spread their chaos to our own vulnerable communities. But who are these creatures, and where is the landscape they inhabit, which seems to be so near and also a world away? In recent times, there have been two dominant images of the dangerous criminal, both of which have inhabited the city streets. The most common has been the inner-city black male. Indeed, it has been an unfortunate staple of crime drama as well as news reporting to demonize the African American inner-city male as the emblem of what most crime looks like in the United States. But this criminal, while fenced off into a separate area of the city, still inhabits and is free to move within the city's borders. The other dominant image, more recent and menacing perhaps, is Surette's predator criminal. But he too is an urban creature, although particularly fearful because he is less easily identifiable. Often dwelling quietly and unobtrusively on our own streets, and working in our own office buildings, he may seem the epitome of "normality" until his urge for blood sets him off on a crime spree. Here too, however, we have a city dweller, a person we may pass in the streets or sit next to on the subway.

When we enter the world of *Cops,* though, we are somewhere else, in another universe entirely. We may frequently have been to the *kinds* of places pictured here: bars, strip malls, low-rent apartment complexes, convenience stores. Yet somehow they do not look or feel quite the same. For the way things happen—with no before or after, no why or wherefore; the limited nature of the *kinds* of things that happen; and the absence of information about who these people are and how they happened to be where we find them—makes this constructed universe a place we cannot imagine finding ourselves in. For it is a world in which *nothing but* brawls, bars, hookers, mental breakdowns, and outbursts can ever occur.

Of course the footage is real. These are real people encountered in real areas of a real United States. In fact, if we want to attempt a sociological profile of the most common types and neighborhoods encountered, we can fairly safely do so. These are the kinds of people who are habitually in trouble with the police, and the kinds of places in which such people tend to live and hang out. The real segment of the population from which this select group of "police regulars" is drawn—caricatured and distorted as the representation of them may be—is that group of people who are permanently down on their luck for a variety of reasons, momentarily or chronically dysfunctional, inveterate "outsiders" and misfits of various kinds who can't or won't conform to social norms, or at worst, extremely weak of character and prone to the worst kind of judgment. Most, when encountered, are under the influence of drugs or alcohol. Many are petty criminals: hookers, purveyors of illegal gambling games, and scam artists so incompetent that they are always apprehended. Others are immigrants who do not speak English well and have not found a way to integrate themselves into "normal" U.S. life. And still others are homeless because of drug or alcohol problems or because they are mentally ill. Indeed, mental illness seems to be a common problem among those the cops deal with each week. But since this very concept has no place in the universe of *Cops,* those with mental illnesses are simply part of the mix of people who are endlessly out of control and in trouble with the law.

Thus does *Cops* give the impression that there is a world "out there," in "those neighborhoods" in some other part of town where human life as we know it simply ceases to exist. And this world, symbolically and expressionistically contrived out of an infinite amount of videotape from which only a relatively small amount of footage is ever actually put on the air, is filled with people who are aliens, subhuman beasts whose words make no sense and whose actions are bizarre. This is a particularly *postmodern* universe, for it is a world unmoored from the very bases of civilized life and order, in which a potpourri of cultural, ethnic, racial, and sexual "types" are thrown together in a multicultural hodgepodge of generic otherness. Cut loose from community and cultural cohesion, they are set adrift along a metaphoric border territory where so-called normal life disappears.

Within this quintessentially postmodern cultural mix, three types stand out in particular: the drug abuser, the sexual "deviant," and the immigrant. The rhetoric of the Right is, of course, thick with jeremiads about the dangers of sexual promiscuity and deviance, drug abuse and other forms of chemical indulgence, and the economic and sociological threat posed by the hordes of immigrants that we hear are flooding our borders, contaminating our heritage and traditions, and sapping our social services. And it is these very people—representing multiculturalism in all its demonized symbolism—that we see, in their most degraded and chaotic formations, on *Cops.* Here, white characters are as degraded and deranged as black, women are as aggressively violent as men, and there are any number of ethnic characters, mostly immigrants from Middle Eastern and Latin nations, who mix and match with the others indiscriminately. Their households are not stable or permanent, and do not follow any socially "normal" pattern of domestic life. They may contain interracial couples and families, groups of racially and sexually mixed boarders of various ages, immigrant groups for whom English is still a foreign language and whose clothing and furnishings clearly mark them as "foreign," drug and alcohol abusers, flagrantly identifiable gays and transvestites, and so on. Often neighbors and even house members seem not to know each other. And it is implied that virtually every arrangement is temporary and expedient.

To examine specific images and encounters in more detail is to get a clear sense of the qualitative differences etched between those who police and those who are policed, and of how the latter are represented as being inherently different and inferior—and especially violent—in ways that no means of therapy or correction could possibly affect. When called to a domestic disturbance or forced to subdue a driver on the highway, the police invariably find a person so horribly out of control as to respond only to brute force. And in these cases, the producers will allow the tape to roll for longer periods of time than in other instances, often focusing steadily on a person going more and more out of control, in ways which are—finally—painful to watch. Frequently, the person will be wildly rebellious and hysterical. Unkempt, often barely clothed, and surrounded by filth and chaos, they are allowed to gyrate and gesticulate as the cops show saintlike restraint and patience. This stark visual contrast between the hysteria and violence of the offenders and the saintlike calm and patience of the cops is among the most vivid ways in which these criminals are marked as different from "normal" Americans.

On one case, for example, a man stopped for erratic driving refused to give up his knife and surrender. He kept shuffling down the middle of the highway, clearly in a state of derangement. But the cops—five or six of them—simply followed him at a distance, calling over and over again, "Hey Buddy, just drop the knife and we can help you." After several excruciating (to the viewer) moments, the cops were forced to subdue him, and in the process, he was shot and seriously disabled. As he jerked and shook while being cuffed and taken into custody, the cops congratulated themselves on a job well done. "You really showed restraint, man," they kept saying to the shooter. And indeed, under the watchful eye of the video camera, he certainly had, in a way that could only make Rodney King wish he lived in this border territory instead of the one in which he barely escaped with his life on a similar road. But while we learned a lot about the virtues of the police force in this segment, for all its excessive length we knew no more about the man apprehended at the end than at the start. He was simply another madman, unfit to live in civilized society.

This implication is particularly offensive when people of color are involved. On a typical incident, for example, a Middle Eastern couple—he in turban; she in long dress and sandals—were having a physical fight, it seemed. The woman was incoherent, flailing on the ground, wailing, and pointing to her bleeding leg. The man paced outside the house, unintelligibly mumbling as though in a trance. Neighbors were asked to explain, but no cogent story emerged. The issue was domestic violence. Yet the shocking, humiliating imagery, and the couple's incoherent, irrational behavior, shifted the emphasis to something different: the repellent, embarrassing irrationality, hysteria, and violence of "foreigners." Thus, *Cops* so dehumanizes and barbarizes a range of cultural and sexual difference that only the police seem to represent "real" human nature—a superior army patrolling settlements of primitive, barbaric tribes.

And calmly patrol they do, unflappable in the face of the most "freakish" of events and characters. On one segment, a black prostitute was apprehended as she staggered into the road, having narrowly escaped from a violent john who had slashed her face with a knife. As it turned out she was a transvestite, high on something and in high drag, with whom the cop was familiar. Out of control and incoherent, she attempted to flirt with the cop as he worked to subdue her and get her to a hospital. From there, the cop went on to a house call in which a drug-crazed young man wildly waved a gun and staggered about as the woman who had made the call—to whom he referred as "my wife-type"—cringed in terror. This couple was interracial, as were another couple on the scene who looked on in an apparent stupor as a child, a girl of perhaps three, filthy and unkempt, hovered sobbing nearby. All four adults, high and in possession of drugs as well as paraphernalia, were eventually arrested, as backup came to assist the cop, and the child was lovingly calmed, cleaned up, taken into custody, and assured that she would be taken care of as she clung desperately to the heroic cop.

Unlike traditional series, the criminals on reality programming are not seen in terms of deviance from the norms of a coherent community. For there is nothing holding them together that would bind them to a community—even a criminal one. They are not so much deviants as "others," aliens, hovering at our borders, held back only by the thin blue line of police who are our U.S. saviors.

New Paradigms for New Times:
The Criminal as Domestic Terrorist

What is the policy implication of the situation encountered on *Cops?* There is no sense that preventive or corrective measures should be taken. The editing techniques preclude any idea that social conditions, much less racial or economic inequality, play a role here. Even drug treatment programs seem irrelevant since again and again we see junkies stopped who are well-known to the cops, who have been in and out of rehab, and who simply grin sheepishly when caught and arrested yet again. The same is true of the general violence, which is also seen as a choice of lifestyle or, more accurately, a condition of nature. Women in domestic disturbance incidents, for example, are usually presented as "regulars" who—as the cops shake their heads and exchange looks—seem incapable of "learning their lesson" and leaving their violent partners. More often than not, they themselves are accused by the partner or witnesses of being the aggressors. Of course, we get no talking head "expert" testimony to give context and meaning to the plight of battered women and the forces that keep them in place. Prostitutes too are seen as simply perverse by nature, determined to continue in their wayward paths and exhibiting only the most weary annoyance when stopped by the cops.

What is most striking about the image of the various outsiders and misfits pictured on *Cops* is that they are seen as criminals at all. For they are clearly people with a variety of economic, social, psychological, and cultural problems whose violent acts are far less threatening to the public than to themselves. The criminalization of "quality-of-life" issues is certainly not new in U.S. society. But *Cops* extends the implications of this trend to a far broader range of people and behaviors, dragging off virtually everyone encountered who cannot be readily subdued. People of other cultures and languages, the homeless, the mentally imbalanced—anyone who is momentarily out of control for any reason will find themselves apprehended and hauled off to jail by these cops. And more often than not, the means by which this is accomplished is both brutal and free of all reference to civil or indeed human rights. Rarely are Miranda rights read to anyone on *Cops,* at least onscreen, nor does anyone ask for a lawyer. And this, we are led to believe, is appropriate for people so uncontrollably irrational.

If concepts like deviance, delinquency, reform, and rehabilitation are no longer adequate to describe the world of crime and punishment, what discourse might be more appropriate? I would suggest that the criminalized "other" just described bears a striking resemblance to another media icon meant to strike terror in our hearts: the terrorist. For like the terrorist, the criminalized other is an alien, an outsider, who poses a threat because they do not conform to our norms. Terrorists are irrational, inscrutable, and inherently violent. They threaten to infiltrate our porous borders, bringing fear, chaos, and disorder. And they cannot be "reformed" or "rehabilitated" according to traditional correctional methods because they neither recognize nor respect the codes to which such measures apply.

There is a literature of terrorism—both political and cultural—in which just such qualities are depicted in an effort to convince us that new, harsher methods of repression are needed to combat these beings. Terrorists are marked in the media by dramatic signs of difference, physical and psychological, so repellent and horrifying as to justify the use of measures previously unthinkable in the enforcement of so-called normal criminal law. In a fascinating study of the rhetorical image of the international terrorist, legal scholar Ileana Porras uses just such terminology to describe the terrorist as a cultural image. "Terrorism," she writes,

> has come to be the thing against which liberal democracies define themselves; . . . the repository of everything that cannot be allowed to fit inside the self-image of democracy; . . . the terrorist has become the "other" that threatens. . . the annihilation of the democratic "self" and an external force against which democracies therefore must strenuously defend themselves.[12]

"In the expert literature on terrorism," continues Porras, "the terrorist is transformed from an ordinary deviant into a frightening foreign/barbaric/beast," a "border violator" who does not recognize laws or family ties, and who must be subdued and repressed by "extra-normal means." The political and legal implications of this cultural construction are clear: "The rhetorical transformation of terrorists into frightening alien outlaws," observes Porras, "suggests a justification for repression by the state and an excuse for . . . authoritarian regimes." In fact, she writes, "repressive measures short of military dictatorship are virtually recommended by the literature on terrorism . . . because the failure to use all possible means to combat terrorism is to put society at risk of falling into chaos."[13]

This description is close to the image of the border criminal depicted on shows like *Cops*. Out of control, subhuman, incapable of reason or abiding by the law, they are to be repressed by the harshest possible measures. The acts committed by these criminals are, of course, not nearly dangerous enough to be compared with acts of terror. But the idea of inherent otherness—which marks the immigrant, the sexual deviant, and the drug addict—and the grotesque conventions by which they are represented, makes the comparison in kind, if not deed, emotionally resonant. The border dwellers on *Cops* are the dregs of society. Rather than presenting a context that might explain their deplorable state of life or suggest ways to remedy it, however, these shows represent these people as alien, depraved, and inferior, and imply that only the most repressive policies are therefore appropriate. It may seem to viewers of the series that this kind of treatment is more than justified for such subhuman, irrational creatures. But policies set in place to apply to designated, demonized scapegoats—as these aliens, addicts, and misfits of various kinds have become—can all too easily be used against everyone, especially in a postmodern world in which the designation of "otherness" has, in one way or another, come to be a floating signifier that may attach, at any time, to any of us.

NOTES

1. David Kidd-Hewitt and Richard Osborne, eds., *Crime and the Media: The Postmodern Spectacle* (London: Pluto Press, 1995).

2. Martha T. Moore, "Let's Go to the Bloody Videotape," *USA Today,* 12 May 1997, 3A.

3. Stuart Hall, Chas Critcher, Tony Jefferson, John Clarke, and Brian Roberts, *Policing the Crisis: Mugging, the State, and Law and Order* (London: Macmillan, 1978), 145.

4. Richard Osborne, "Crime and the Media: From Media Studies to Postmodernism," in *Crime and the Media: The Postmodern Spectacle,* ed. David Kidd-Hewitt and Richard Osborne (London: Pluto Press, 1995), 42.

5. For a thorough survey of the state of crime and crime control in the late 1990s, see Steven Donziger, ed., *The Real War on Crime: The Report of the National Criminal Justice Commission* (New York: HarperPerennial, 1996).

6. Ibid., 102, 288.

7. Ibid., 146.

8. Hall, Critcher, Jefferson, Clarke, and Roberts, *Policing the Crisis,* 136.

9. Michel Foucault, "The Dangerous Individual," in *Politics, Philosophy, Culture: Interviews and Other Writings of Michel Foucault,* ed. Lawrence Kritzman (London: Routledge, 1988), 134.

10. Ibid., 42.

11. Ray Surette, "Predator Criminals as Media Icons," in *Media, Process, and the Social Construction of Crime,* ed. Gregg Barak (New York: Garland, 1994), 131–32.

12. Ileana Porras, "On Terrorism: Reflections on Violence and the Outlaw," in *After Identity: A Reader in Law and Culture,* ed. Dan Danielsen and Karen Engle (New York: Routledge, 1995), 305.

13. Ibid., 309.

12

"Take Responsibility for Yourself"
Judge Judy *and the Neoliberal Citizen*

Laurie Ouellette

A woman drags her ex-boyfriend to court over an overdue adult movie rental and unpaid loan. A woman is heartbroken when her best friend betrays her and ruins her credit. A smooth-talking ex-boyfriend claims money from his ex was a gift. Welcome to *Judge Judy,* queen of the courtroom program, where judges resolve "real-life" disputes between friends, neighbors, family members, roommates, and lovers on national television. For critics who equate television's role in democracy with serious news and public affairs, altercations over broken engagements, minor fender benders, carpet stains, unpaid personal loans, and the fate of jointly purchased household appliances may seem like crass entertainment or trivial distractions. But such dismissals overlook the "governmental" nature of courtroom programs like *Judge Judy,* which gained cultural presence—and a reputation for "zero tolerance when it comes to nonsense"—alongside the neoliberal policies and discourses of the 1990s.[1]

Judge Judy took the small claims–based court format from the fringes of commercial syndication to an authoritative place on daytime schedules when it debuted in 1996, the same year the U.S. Telecommunications Act was passed.[2] While the legislation has been critiqued for its deregulatory ethos as well as its affinity with the broader neoliberal forces behind welfare reform and the privatization of public institutions from the penal system to the post office, the cultural dimensions of these parallels remain less examined.[3] There is a tendency within policy studies to take the cultural impact of neoliberalism as self-evident—to presume that the laissez-faire principles codified by the Act will erode democracy in predictable ways that typically involve the decline of journalism, documentaries, and other "substantial" information formats found unprofitable by the culture industries. While such concerns have some validity, the metaphor of sub-version needs to be jettisoned, for it reifies untenable cultural hierarchies, and neglects neoliberalism's productive imprint on contemporary televi-sion culture and the "idealized" citizen subjectivities that it circulates.

Reality programming is one site where neoliberal approaches to citi-zenship have in fact materialized on television. From makeover programs (such as *What Not to Wear* and *Trading Spaces*) that enlist friends, neigh-bors, and experts in their quest to teach people how to make "better" dec-orating and fashion choices, to gamedocs (like *Survivor* and *Big Brother*) that construct community relations in terms of individual competition and self-enterprising, neoliberal constructions of "good citizenship" cut across much popular reality television. The courtroom program is a par-ticularly clear example of this broader trend because it draws from the symbolic authority of the state to promote both the outsourcing of its governmental functions and the subjective requirements of the transition to a neoliberal society. *Judge Judy* and programs like it do not subvert elu-sive democratic ideals, then, as much as they *construct* templates for citi-zenship that complement the privatization of public life, the collapse of the welfare state, and most important, the discourse of individual choice and personal responsibility.

This chapter situates *Judge Judy* as a neoliberal technology of everyday citizenship, and shows how it attempts to shape and guide the conduct and choices of lower-income women in particular. As we shall see, *Judge Judy* draws from and diffuses neoliberal currents by fusing an image of democracy (signified in the opening credits by a gently flapping U.S. flag, stately public courthouse, and gavel-wielding judge) with a privatized ap-proach to conflict management and an intensified government of the self. *Judge Judy* and programs like it supplant institutions of the state (for in-stance, social work, law and order, and welfare offices), and using real peo-ple caught in the drama of ordinary life as raw material, train TV viewers to function without state assistance or supervision as self-disciplining, self-sufficient, responsible, and risk-averting individuals. In this way, the courtroom subgenre of reality TV exemplifies what James Hay has called a cultural apparatus for "neoliberal forms of governance."[4]

Neoliberalism and Television Culture

To understand *Judge Judy*'s neoliberal alignments, a brief detour through the concept of neoliberalism is in order. My understanding of neoliberalism begins with political economy and the activism it inspires. From this vantage point, neoliberalism is generally understood as a troubling worldview that promotes the "free" market as the best way to organize every dimension of social life. According to activists Elizabeth Martinez and Arnoldo Garcia, this worldview has generated five trends that have accelerated globally since the 1980s: the "rule" of the market; spending cuts on public services; deregulation (including the deregulation of broadcasting); the privatization of state-owned institutions, "usually in the name of efficiency"; and "eliminating the concept of the public good or community and replacing it with individual responsibility."[5] For critics like Robert McChesney, the upshot of neoliberalism and the reforms it has spawned is that a "handful of private interests are permitted to control as much as possible of social life in order to maximize their personal profit."[6]

While I share these concerns, I have found Foucauldian approaches particularly useful for analyzing the subjective dimensions of neoliberalism that circulate on reality TV. Drawing from Michel Foucault, Nikolas Rose theorizes neoliberalism less as a simple opposition between the market (bad) and welfare state (good) than as a "changing network" of complex power relations. If neoliberal regimes have implemented an "array of measures" aimed at downsizing the welfare state and dismantling the "institutions within which welfare government had isolated and managed their social problems," they still rely on "strategies of government."[7] This manifests as various forms of "cultural training" that govern indirectly in the name of "lifestyle maximization," "free choice," and personal responsibility, says Rose. This diffused approach to the "regulation of conduct" escapes association with a clear or top-down agenda, and is instead presented as the individual's "own desire" to achieve optimum happiness and success. As Rose points out, the "enterprising" individual crafted by this discourse has much in common with the choice-making "customer" valorized by neoliberal economics. Both presume "free will," which means that those individuals who fail to thrive under neoliberal conditions can be readily cast as the "author of their own misfortunes."[8]

Rose makes several additional observations that can help to illuminate neoliberalism's cultural manifestations. First, he contends that the ideal of citizens working together to fulfill mutual and "national obligations" has given way to the "ideal of citizens seeking to fulfill and protect themselves within a variety of micro-moral domains." Second, he observes that the requirements of "good" citizenship have come to include adopting a "prudent" relationship to fate, which includes avoiding "calculable dangers and avertable risks." Finally, Rose cites the media as a cultural technology operating outside "public powers" that works to govern the "capacities, competencies and wills of subjects," and in so doing, translate the goals of "authorities" into the "choices and commitments of individuals."[9]

James Hay has extended this argument to television studies specifically. Because a "neoliberal form of governance assumes that social subjects are not and should not be subject to direct forms of state control, it therefore relies on mechanisms for governing at a distance," through the guiding and shaping of "self-disciplining subjects," Hay explains. Television plays an important role in this governmental process, he contends, one that is not limited to sanctioned forms of news and public affairs. In fact, popular reality TV may be better suited to the indirect, diffuse mode of cultural governmentality that Hay describes. The court program is an acute and therefore symptomatic example of popular reality TV's role in mediating, as Hay puts it, "a kind of state control that values self-sufficiency and a kind of personal freedom that requires self-discipline."[10]

While Hay theorizes television's part in bringing neoliberal techniques of "governmentality" into the home, feminist scholars have shown the extent to which neoliberal policies intersect with an acceleration of self-help discourse aimed at women. From advice books on intimate relationships to self-esteem-building initiatives for welfare mothers, this discourse has been critiqued for presuming to "solve social problems from crime and poverty to gender inequality by waging a social revolution, not against capitalism, racism and inequality, but against the order of the self and the way we govern the self."[11] As Barbara Cruikshank has pointed out, the solution to women's problems is construed as having the right attitude, making smart decisions, and taking responsibility for one's life in the name of personal "empowerment."[12] In this sense, self-help is a cultural manifestation of neoliberalism, a technology of citizenship that encourages women to "evaluate and act" on themselves so that the social workers, medical establishment, and police "do not have to."[13]

Judge Judy fuses television, neoliberalism, and self-help discourse in a governmental address to women living out what feminist philosopher Nancy Fraser has called the "postsocialist" condition.[14] The program presents the privatized space of the TV courtroom as the most "efficient" way to resolve microdisputes steeped in the unacknowledged politics of gender, class, and race, but it also classifies those individuals who "waste the court's time" as risky deviants and self-made victims who create their own misfortunes by making the "wrong" choices and failing to manage their lives properly. The imagined TV viewer is the implied beneficiary of this litany of mistakes, for one's classification as "normal" hinges on both recognizing the pathos of "others" and internalizing the rules of self-government spelled out on the program. The courtroom program has, for precisely this reason, been institutionally positioned as a moral and educational corrective to "permissive" entertainment, suggesting that the discourse of the "public interest" in broadcasting has not been squashed but rather reconfigured by neoliberal reforms. Indeed, it could be that television is increasingly pivotal to neoliberal approaches to government and the citizen subjectivities on which they depend.

"The Cases Are Real, the Rulings Are Final"

Judge Judy is not the first television program to resolve everyday microconflicts in simulated courtroom settings. The genre can be traced to 1950s programs like *People in Conflict* and *The Verdict Is Yours*. In the 1980s, retired California Superior Court judge Joseph Wapner presided over *The People's Court*, while *Divorce Court* used actors to dramatize "real" legal proceedings.[15] *Judge Judy* did, however, rework and revitalize the format, and the program's "no-nonsense" approach to family and small claims disputes generated notoriety and imitators (examples include *Judge Joe Brown, Judge Mathis, Judge Hatchet, Curtis Court,* a revitalized *People's Court,* and *Moral Court*). Well into the new millennium, courtroom programs abound on television, competing with talk shows, game shows, and soap operas for a predominantly female audience.

On *Judge Judy,* real-life litigants are offered travel costs and court fees to present their cases on national television. The price is to drop out of the public judicial process and submit to the private ruling of Judith (Judy) Sheindlin. A former New York family court judge, Sheindlin was recruited for the "tough-love" philosophy she first spelled out in an influential *60 Minutes* profile, and later expanded on in her best-selling book *Don't Pee on My Leg and Tell Me It's Raining,* which faulted the overcrowded court system as a lenient bureaucracy that reflects "how far we have strayed from

personal responsibility and old-fashioned discipline."[16] Spotting ratings
potential, Larry Lyttle, president of Big Ticket Television, a Viacom company, invited Sheindlin to preside over "real cases with real consequences
in a courtroom on television." Called a "swift decision maker with no tolerance for excuses" by the program's publicity, Sheindlin claims to bring to
her TV show the same message she advocated in the courts: "Take responsibility for yourself, your actions and the children you've brought into the
world."[17] In interviews, she situates *Judge Judy* as a public service that can
solve societal problems by instilling the right attitudes and choices in individuals:

> It's a much larger audience. Whatever message I spew—"Take responsibility
> for your life. If you're a victim, it's your fault. Stop being a victim. Get a
> grip! You're the one who's supposed to make a direction in your life." All
> those messages I tried in Family Court to instill in people—primarily
> women. [The TV show] sounded like something that would not only be
> fun, but worthwhile as well.[18]

Like other TV judges, Sheindlin now hears noncriminal disputes that
rarely exceed several hundred dollars or the equivalent in personal property. While these conflicts often speak to broader social tensions and inequalities, the program's governmental logic frames the cases as "petty
squabbles" brought about by the deficiencies of individuals. Sheindlin's
courtroom is filled with feuding relations and typically devoid of people
who wish to sue businesses, bosses, or least of all, big corporations. This
focus makes perfect sense, for the program's impetus as a technology of
citizenship is to scrutinize ordinary people who require state mediation of
everyday affairs, a process that hinges more on the moral radar Sheindlin
claims to have developed in the public court system than on time-con-
suming democratic processes (she has been known to snap, "I don't have
time for beginnings" and "I don't read documents"). While TV viewers are
situated outside Sheindlin's disciplinary address to litigants derided as
losers, cheaters, liars, and "gumbos," their status as "good" citizens presumes the desire to adhere to the neoliberal templates for living she espouses.
    While the opening credits promise "real people" involved in "real cases,"
a male narrator differentiates the program from the public court system
with the reminder: "This is Judy's courtroom," where the "decisions are
final." Onscreen, Sheindlin plays judge, prosecutor, professional expert,

and punctilious moral authority, handling an average of two cases per thirty-minute episode and dispensing justice at "lightning speed," according to the program's publicity. Participants must abide by the program's rules, which include speaking only when spoken to, accepting the authority of the judge ("Just pay attention, I run the show," she tells litigants), and taking humiliating remarks and reprimands without rebuttal or comment ("Are you all nuts" and "I'm smarter than you" are typical examples). More important than the details of any particular case is Sheindlin's swift assessment of the choices and behaviors of the people involved in them. Just as, according to Foucault, the delinquent is characterized not so much by their "acts" as by their life biography, Sheindlin questions litigants about their employment history, marital and parental status, income, drug habits, sexual practices, incarceration record, and past or present "dependency" on public welfare.[19] Such information transcends the evaluation of evidence as the principal means whereby Sheindlin determines who is at fault in the citizenship lesson that accompanies every ruling. Sheindlin is also known to belittle the accents of non-English speakers, accuse litigants of lying and abusing the "system," and order individuals to spit out gum, stand up straight, and "control" bodily functions to her liking. In one episode, a male litigant who denied her accusations of pot smoking was ordered to take a live drug test. *Judge Judy* thus both duplicates and extends the surveillance of the poor and working class carried out by welfare offices, unemployment centers, and other social services.[20]

Judge Judy is part of the current wave of reality TV in that "real" people (not actors) involved in "authentic" disagreements are used as a selling point to differentiate the show from fictional entertainment. While scripts are not used, reality is, as John Fiske reminds us, "encoded" at every level.[21] The program scours small claims dockets for potentially "interesting" cases; would-be litigants must complete a questionnaire, and only those "actual" disputes that can be situated within the program's logic are presented on television. Offscreen narration, graphic titles, video replays, and teasers further frame the meaning of the cases by labeling the litigants, characterizing their purportedly real motivations to viewers and highlighting scenes from the program that reiterate Sheindlin's governmental authority. Due to increased competition for conflicts among the growing cadre of courtroom programs, viewers are now invited to bypass the courts altogether and submit their everyday disputes directly to *Judge Judy*. On-air solicitations like "Are You in a Family Dispute? Call Judy" promise an efficient, private alternative to public mediation of conflicts—and yet, individuals who accept the invitations are ultimately held responsible for their "mistakes" on cases like "The Making of a Family Tragedy."

Judge Judy's focus on everyday domestic conflicts has led some critics to denounce the courtroom program as a new twist on the sensational "low-brow" daytime talk show.[22] Yet Sheindlin insists that her program is a somber alternative to the participatory, carnivalesque atmosphere of the genre it now rivals in the ratings. Indeed, the court setting and overtly disciplinary address of the *Judge Judy* program "code" it in distinct ways that are easily distinguishable to TV viewers. Sheindlin's strict demeanor and authoritative place on the bench are accentuated by camerawork that magnifies her power by filming her from below. The silence of the studio audience, the drab, institutional-like setting of the simulated courtroom, and the presence of a uniformed bailiff also separate the court program from talk shows, a format that feminist scholars have characterized as a tentative space for oppressed groups (women, people of color, and the working classes) to discuss the politics of everyday life. Jane Shattuc, for example, sees talk shows as an offshoot of the social movements of the 1960s to the extent that they draw from (but also commercially exploit) identity politics, consciousness-raising techniques, and an awareness that the "personal is political."[23] For Sonia Livingstone and Peter Lunt, talk shows offer a counterpoint to the white, male, bourgeois-dominated sphere of "serious" news and public affairs; talk shows provide a popular forum that enables women in particular to participate, however haltingly, in democratic processes.[24] Of course, talk shows also operate with their own disciplinary dynamics, as Janice Peck has shown. Relying on psychosocial experts (such as health workers, therapists, or self-help gurus), talk shows present a "televised talking cure" that "manages conflict and crisis" by folding women's personal stories into a "confessional" discourse and "therapeutic" narratives, she contends.[25]

As Mimi White has observed in her analysis of *Divorce Court*, court programs reconfigure the confessional/therapeutic orientation of the talk show in subtle, but important ways: "To the extent that the couple no longer confesses with ease, the injunction to confess must be enforced through the agencies of the . . . legal establishment."[26] On *Judge Judy*, the authority represented by the simulated courtroom setting is often enlisted to "force" such confessions. Sheindlin claims that her past experience as a frustrated state official has enabled her to "see through the bull" ("She can always tell if you're lying. All she has to do is make eye contact," reported *USA Today*). Litigants who refuse to "confess" to suspected actions have

While *Judge Judy* condemns "dependency" on the state, its attempt to govern women indirectly is legitimated by the iconography of the formal courtroom.

been subjected to live background checks, but more often than not Sheindlin simply discounts "false" confessions and replaces the version of events offered by the litigant with an expert interpretation gleaned through biographical information as much as "evidence."

Court programs also magnify the disciplinary logic present on the talk show by disallowing audience participation, controlling the flow of personal revelations, and fusing the therapeutic ethos of the "clinic" with the surveillance of the welfare office and the authoritative signifiers of law and order. This distinction, as much as the absence of the carnivalesque, is what has allowed courtroom programs to be institutionally positioned as a cultural corrective to "tabloid" television. *Judge Judy* is the "antithesis of Jerry Springer," insists Sheindlin. "Jerry Springer encourages people to show off their filthiest laundry, to misbehave. I scrupulously avoid doing that. I cut them off."[27]

The television industry has also been quick to assert that courtroom television "educates" as well as entertains—a claim to public service that is rarely made of most popular reality formats. Big Ticket's Larry Lyttle

maintains that courtroom programs function as a positive moral force because unlike on talk shows, where "conflicts are aired and tossed around,"
a court show like *Judge Judy* "ends with a decision that someone was right
and someone was wrong."[28] WCHS-TV in Charleston, West Virginia, similarly praises the program's "unique ability to act as a true moral compass
for people seeking guidance, insight and resolution."[29] Characterizing the
courtroom genre as a technology of citizenship that can temper the
"effects" of fictional television, one TV judge explained in an interview
that

> America's been looking at soap operas for going on 50 some years, and they
> legitimize the most back-stabbing, low-down, slimeball behavior. That's
> gotten to be acceptable behavior. . . . We find ourselves confronted with a lot
> of soap-opera behavior in our courtrooms. And we resolve them and say,
> no, we know you may have seen this, but it's not right.[30]

Privatizing Justice, Stigmatizing "Dependency"

Judge Judy's claim to facilitate "justice at lightning speed" boldly implies
that commercial television can resolve problems faster and more effi-
ciently than the public sector. In this sense, the program affirms neoliberal
rationales for "outsourcing" state-owned institutions and services. *Judge
Judy* also complements neoliberal policies by conveying the impression
that democracy (exemplified by the justice system) is overrun by individuals embroiled in petty conflicts and troubles of their own making. If the
program feeds off of real-life microdisputes, Sheindlin chastises litigants
for failing to govern their "selves" and their personal affairs. In addition to
lecturing guests about their personal history, she often accuses participants of "wasting the court's time," conveying the idea that "normal" citizens do not depend on the supervision of the judiciary or any public institution for that matter. People who rely on professional judges (including
TV judges) to mediate everyday problems are cast as inadequate individuals who lack the capacity or, worse, desire to function as self-reliant and
personally responsible citizens.

On *Judge Judy*, citizenship lessons are often directed at people who reject marriage, the nuclear family, and traditional values; unmarried couples who live together are of particular concern. While Sheindlin (who is
divorced) does not condemn such behavior as moral disconduct, she does

present rules and procedures for navigating modern relationships, which include getting personal loans in writing, not "living together for more than one year without a wedding band," and not "purchasing homes, cars, boats or animals with romantic partners outside of wedlock."[31] On *Judge Judy*, individuals are told that they must impose these rules on themselves—both for their own protection and because, as Sheindlin explains, there is "no court of people living together. It's up to you to be smart. Plan for the eventualities before you set up housekeeping." When former lovers dispute an unpaid car loan, Sheindlin takes the disagreement as an opportunity to explain the dos and don'ts of cohabitation without marriage. Sheindlin finds the couple incompatible and "irresponsible," and rules that it was an "error of judgment" for them to share an apartment together. This judgment is tied to a broader failure of appropriate citizenship when Sheindlin lectures the pair for then "asking the courts" to resolve a domestic property dispute. "You're not married—there is a different set of rules for people who choose to live together without marriage," she asserts, reiterating that people who stray from state-sanctioned conventions have a particular duty to monitor their own affairs.

If the idealized citizen-subject constructed by *Judge Judy* complements the choice-making neoliberal customer discussed by Rose, that individual is also a self-supporting worker. People who receive any form of public assistance are cast as deviants in particular need of citizenship lessons. The advice they receive evokes Nancy Fraser and Linda Gordon's observation that welfare has become cloaked in a stigmatizing discourse of "dependency" that presumes gender, class, and racial parity. As Fraser and Gordon point out, women (including single mothers) are now held accountable to the white, middle-class, male work ethic, even as they lack the advantages and resources to perform as traditionally male breadwinners. While this marks a shift away from the patronizing assumption that all women are helpless and therefore "naturally" dependent on men or, in their absence, the state, it conceals the structural inequalities that lower-income women in particular continue to face.[32] On *Judge Judy*, all women are presumed to be capable of supporting themselves and their children financially; accepting welfare is construed not as a reflection of gender or economic inequality but as a character flaw. Women are routinely asked to disclose their past or present reliance on government "handouts," and those who admit to receiving benefits are subsequently marked as irresponsible and lazy individuals who "choose" not to work for a living. Welfare recipients are also constructed as morally unsound citizens who cheat taxpayers, as was the case in an episode where Sheindlin demanded to know whether an unmarried woman with three children by the same father had "avoided" marriage merely to qualify for welfare benefits. In another episode, an unemployed twenty-something mother being sued by her baby's would-be adoptive parents was scolded for relying on public assistance to raise the child she had decided not to give up for adoption. While adoption law doesn't allow adoptive parents to reclaim monetary "gifts" to birth mothers, Sheindlin stressed the woman's "moral" obligation to repay them. Presuming that the mother had chosen poverty, Sheindlin also sternly advised her to get a job and "not have more babies she can't take care of." *Judge Judy*'s disdain for so-called welfare dependency extends to charity and other forms of assistance. If individuals are told to take care of themselves and their families, empathy and social responsibility for others are discouraged. "No good deed goes unpunished," Sheindlin advised a family friend who took in a homeless woman who had spent some time in jail. At the societal and community level, the public good is cast in neoliberal terms, as a system of individual responsibilities and rewards.

According to Rose, neoliberal citizens are conceived of as private individuals who must ensure their own well-being through risk management strategies and prudent "acts of choice."[33] *Judge Judy* instills this template for citizenship by discouraging personal contact with deviant and allegedly risky individuals, and by instructing women to make "smart" choices to avoid "victimization." The program functions as a "panoptic" device to the extent that it classifies and surveils individuals deemed unsavory and dangerous.[34] This same point has also been made of reality-based crime shows like *Cops* and *America's Most Wanted*.[35] Sheindlin contends that criminals are largely unreformable, and *Judge Judy* extends this philosophy to people who are not official criminals but are nonetheless judged to possess amoral tendencies, psychological imbalances, drug addictions, and other character flaws. The more pressing message, however, is that all citizens must take personal responsibility for protecting themselves from con artists, "manipulators," abusers, and other risky individuals. In this sense, one of the program's most important governmental roles is to instruct TV viewers how to detect and avoid the risks that certain individuals are shown to represent.

Since the litigants on *Judge Judy* are introduced by name and occupation—this information also appears in onscreen titles—viewers know that individuals cast as risky are often working-class men who drive trucks, wait on tables, enter data, do construction, or perform low-paying forms of customer service. If female welfare recipients are cast as irresponsible nonworkers, men lacking middle-class occupations and salaries are routinely scorned for "choosing" a life of poverty, as was the case when Sheindlin lectured a middle-aged male Wal-Mart cashier for failing to obtain more lucrative employment. In the adoption episode mentioned above, a similar evaluation of male employment was tied to a failure of citizenship. The infant's father, who had worked on and off as a gas station attendant but was currently unemployed, was characterized as a personal failure and societal menace, not just because he refused to admit "personal moral responsibility" to repay the money to the adoptive parents but because he "refused" to enterprise himself in accordance with the middle-class work ethic.

Cases involving men who manipulate women out of money, gifts, rent, or property are a staple on *Judge Judy,* and in these cases, male unemployment and insolvency are closely tied to the detection and avoidance of romantic risk. In a case where a woman met a man on the Internet, loaned him money, and was dumped, Sheindlin fused a harsh judgment of the boyfriend's opportunism and dishonesty in his romantic relationship to an undeveloped work ethic. Demanding to know when he last "held a full-time job," she swiftly identified the man as a freeloader and "con artist," implying that men without economic means are especially dangerous and therefore not to be trusted when it comes to intimate relationships. Female litigants can also be categorized as identifiable romantic risks, as was the case in "Opportunity Knocks," where Sheindlin accused an attractive young woman in court to resolve whether money from her ex-boyfriend was a gift or loan of "using" the man financially with "no intention of marrying him." In most cases, though, it is lower-income men who play this role in a gender reversal of the gold digger stereotype that complements the program's focus on solving the problem of female victimization through better self-management.

Women are typically cast as "self-created" victims in terms that articulate neoliberal currents to female self-help culture. Rejecting what she terms the "disease of victimization" or tendency to blame society for one's hardships, Sheindlin claims, in her books and on her TV program, that all women can achieve happiness and success with a little knowledge along with the right attitude. On *Judge Judy,* women's problems are blamed on their own failure to make good decisions, whether that means pulling one's self up from a life of poverty, "preparing" wisely for financial independence, or avoiding entanglements with unstable, manipulative, or abusive individuals. In her book *Beauty Fades, Dumb Is Forever,* Sheindlin elaborates on the value of personal responsibility, contending that

> victims are self-made. They aren't born. They aren't created by circumstances. There are many, many poor, disadvantaged people who had terrible parents and suffered great hardships who do just fine. Some even rise to the level of greatness. You are responsible for nurturing your roots, for blooming. No one can take that away from you. If you decide to be a victim, the destruction of your life will be by your own hand.[36]

In some cases, female "victims" are lectured for allowing themselves to be mistreated by other women. In "The Kool-Aid Debacle," where a young waitress sued her female ex-roommate over Kool-Aid stains on the carpet and a couch that got smelly, Sheindlin scolded the plaintiff for getting herself into such a situation: "You make a mistake when you let someone into your house who is a slob," she explained. Other times, women are deemed responsible for making their own misfortunes. In a case involving former lovers at odds over an unpaid loan, the program's neoliberal dismissal of female victimization is spelled out. The woman claims that her ex-boyfriend helped cover her hospital bill when she miscarried their baby. The man asserts that she promised to pay him back. As is typical, Sheindlin focuses less on the details of the loan than on the moral and behavioral lessons she discerns from the case. She lectures the young woman (but not the man) for not using birth control, and attributes her "situation" to her own unwise and irresponsible conduct. Refusing to accept this ruling, the young woman insists that the ex-boyfriend should help pay for the cost of the miscarriage since she was uninsured and it "was his baby too." Defying Sheindlin's orders to speak only when addressed, she demands to know what *she* as a woman would do in such circumstances. Rejecting the female litigant's appeal to a sense of female solidarity on the question—and ignoring the broader issue of health care access raised by the episode—Sheindlin tells the litigant that she wouldn't be in her shoes because she's "smarter than that."

Women who claim to have been abused by men appear frequently on *Judge Judy,* where they too are lectured for creating their circumstances. Domestic abuse is never the basis of a legal case, but is typically revealed in the course of Sheindlin's interrogation of the participants involved. In a case involving cousins fighting over a family collection of knickknacks,

Sheindlin determines that the man is a deranged and unstable individual, while the woman he bullied and harassed is an "adult" who has "chosen to let someone do this to her." When Sheindlin learns that an ex-boyfriend in court over a minor car accident has battered his former teenage girlfriend, she maintains that the girl made unwise "choices," sternly advising, "Never let a man put his hands on you." In a case involving former lovers disputing overdue phone and gas bills, the woman reveals that in refusing to pay household expenses, her former boyfriend was addicted to heroin and had spent time in jail for assaulting a minor. She also implies that he physically abused her. Typifying the program's neoliberal solution to the problem of domestic violence as well as the complexities of gender and class, Sheindlin faults the woman for failing to accept responsibility for her own conduct. Taking the troubled relationship as the raw material for a citizenship lesson aimed at women, Sheindlin determines that "being with him doesn't speak well of your judgment." As "young as you are, you allowed someone with a criminal history and no job to live with you . . . and you want the courts to fix that?"

Judge Judy seeks to instill in women a desire to avoid the "disease" of victimization along with the overreliance on state assistance and intervention it is said to have spawned. This message carries traces of liberal feminist discourse to the extent that it promotes female independence and agency. Presuming that barriers to social and gender equality have long been dismantled, the program places the onus to achieve these goals on individuals. Sheindlin, who considers herself a positive female role model, contends that all "women have the power to make decisions, to call it as they see it, to take no gruff."[37] She claims that all women, however positioned by an unequal capitalist society, can reap the benefits of happiness and success so long as they exercise good judgment and cultivate self-esteem. Economic security and "feeling good about yourself" are thus closely bound in Sheindlin's blueprint for successful female citizenship. The responsibility for cultivating self-esteem is placed not on society but on individual women, whose job it is to train themselves and their daughters "to have a profession, have a career . . . so they will never be dependent on anybody."[38] On *Judge Judy*, female litigants are advised to avoid "depending" on boyfriends and husbands for financial assistance in particular. This message has less to do with dismantling dominant ideologies and institutions than it does with ensuring that women "take care of themselves" so that the state doesn't have to. *Judge Judy* conveys the idea that women can no longer "claim" a victim status rooted in bifurcated and hierarchical gender roles; nor, however, can they expect public solutions to the inequalities that structure women's lives.

Sheindlin presents "independence" as a responsibility that all women must strive to achieve, but she also promotes the hegemony of the nuclear family, reconstituted as a two-wage-earning unit. Family troubles underscore many of the cases heard on *Judge Judy*, where mothers suing daughters, children suing their parents, and parents suing each other are the norm. This steady stream of feuding relations paints a portrait of a troubled institution that clearly isn't working, yet Sheindlin uses her authority to promote the sacred importance of family bonds. The contradiction exists in perpetual tension, as illuminated by the treatment of family in two key episodes. In the first, a male cashier is suing his unemployed ex-fiancée for bills paid when they lived together; she is countersuing for "mental distress." After Sheindlin interrogates the woman about why she wasn't working at the time, the woman replies that she quit her job to "build a home together." She also tells Sheindlin that her fiancé stalked her and threatened to come after her with a gun when they broke up. Although this scenario contains the material to cast the male as a deviant individual, Sheindlin rejects the woman's story as an "excuse" smacking of victimization. Comparing her own success as a married working woman who didn't "quit her job to pick out furniture and dishes" to the failure of the "alleged victim of harassment," she orders the woman to pay the back rent. In this episode, the female litigant's embrace of traditional family values is denounced because it includes the desire for "dependency" on a male breadwinner, thereby violating the neoliberal mantra of self-sufficiency that *Judge Judy* espouses. In a dispute involving an estranged mother and daughter, though, the nuclear family is valorized against a woman's quest for independence. The mother, who divorced her husband when she came out as a lesbian, is implicitly cast as selfish and irresponsible for abandoning the heterosexual family unit to pursue her own personal fulfillment. While Sheindlin doesn't condemn the woman's homosexuality, she harshly criticizes her performance and "choices" as a mother, and recommends family counseling to repair the damage. As these examples attest, *Judge Judy*'s advice to women does not seek to expand women's choices, it merely guides them in particular directions. Operating as a technology of citizenship, the program steers women toward neoliberal reforms that are presented as their own responsibilities and in their own "best interests." In this sense, *Judge Judy* seeks to transform what Rose calls the "goals of authorities" into the "choices and commitments of individuals."[39]

Judge Judy *and the Normative Citizen*

Judge Judy constitutes the normative citizen—the TV viewer at home—in opposition to both risky deviants and "self-made" victims. By scrutinizing the dos and don'ts of everyday life as it is presumed to be lived by "troubled" populations, it promotes neoliberal policies for conducting one's self in private. It scapegoats the uneducated and unprivileged as "others" who manufacture their hardships, and thus, require nothing more than personal responsibility and self-discipline in the wake of shrinking public services. Those who reject this logic are deemed abnormal and often unreformable: "I'm not going to get through to her. I have a sense that she's a lost cause at fourteen," Sheindlin once said of a female litigant.[40] TV viewers are encouraged to distance themselves from the "deficient" individuals who seep into Sheindlin's courtroom, therefore avoiding any recognition of the societal basis of women's problems and concerns. While Sheindlin's harshest derision is aimed at the socially "unrespectable," her governmental advice is intended for all women—particularly middle-class viewers—for according to the program's neoliberal logic, their happiness and success hinges on it.

It is untenable to presume that viewers respond to *Judge Judy* in seamless or uniform ways. The program can be read as an authoritarian spectacle that unravels what Foucault has called the "ideology of bourgeois justice." The running parody of *Judge Judy* on *Saturday Night Live,* where Sheindlin is portrayed as an exaggerated version of her insulting, authoritarian television persona, suggests that *Judge Judy* may partly dislodge an image of the courts as inherently objective and fair.[41] Women on the wrong end of unequal class and gender relations may also see in *Judge Judy* a glaring example of class prejudice and professional gumption. Yet these possibilities do not prevent the program from exemplifying a neoliberal form of governing that in various dimensions and forms, cuts across the newest wave of reality TV.

We can see variations of the neoliberal currents examined here in makeover programs, gamedocs, and other reality formats that "govern at a distance" by instilling the importance of self-discipline, the rewards of self-enterprise, and the personal consequences of making the "wrong" choices. *Judge Judy* represents one of the clearest examples of this trend because it articulates neoliberal templates for citizenship to the privatization of public life while self-consciously bringing what Foucault called "the minute disciplines" and "panopticisms of the everyday" into the home.[42] The citizen subjectivities constructed on *Judge Judy* complement a model of government that disdains state authority and intervention, but demands a heightened form of personal responsibility and self-discipline from individuals. Reality TV as exemplified by the courtroom program is not outside democracy, then, but is an active agent in its neoliberal transformation.

NOTES

1. The popular press has emphasized the "no tolerance" ethos of the programs, contributing to the cultural context in which they are received. See, in particular, Melanie McFarland, "Tough Judges Show There's Justice in Watching Television," *Seattle Times*, 30 November 1998, http://archives.seattletimes.

2. See ibid.

3. For a critical analysis of the Telecommunications Act of 1996, see Patricia Aufderheide, *Communications Policy and the Public Interest* (New York: Guilford, 1999); and Robert McChesney, *Rich Media, Poor Democracy: Communication Politics in Dubious Times* (New York: New Press, 2000).

4. James Hay, "Unaided Virtues: The (Neo)-Liberalization of the Domestic Sphere," *Television and New Media* 1, no. 1 (2000): 56.

5. Elizabeth Martinez and Arnoldo Garcia, "What Is Neoliberalism?" *Corpwatch*, 1 January 1997, www.corpwatch.org.

6. Robert McChesney, introduction to *Profit over People: Neoliberalism and Global Order*, by Noam Chomsky (New York: Seven Stories Press, 1999), 7, 11.

7. Nikolas Rose, "Governing 'Advanced' Liberal Democracies," in *Foucault and Political Reason: Liberalism, Neoliberalism, and Rationalities of Government*, ed. Andrew Barry, Thomas Osborne, and Nikolas Rose (Chicago: University of Chicago Press, 1996), 55, 58–59. For a Foucauldian approach to "governmentality," see also Graham Bruchell, Colin Gordon, and Peter Miller, eds., *The Foucault Effect: Studies in Governmentality* (Chicago: University of Chicago Press, 1991). I have also found Toby Miller's analysis of citizenship and subjectivity helpful for thinking through neoliberal modes of government. See his *The Well-Tempered Self: Citizenship, Culture, and the Postmodern Subject* (Baltimore, Md.: Johns Hopkins University Press, 1993).

8. Rose, "Governing 'Advanced' Liberal Democracies," 57–59.

9. Ibid., 57, 58.

10. Hay, "Unaided Virtues," 54.

11. Barbara Cruikshank, "Revolutions Within: Self-Government and Self-Esteem," in *Foucault and Political Reason: Liberalism, Neoliberalism, and Rationalities*

of Government, ed. Andrew Barry, Thomas Osborne, and Nikolas Rose (Chicago: University of Chicago Press, 1996), 231.

12. In addition to Cruikshank, "Revolutions Within," see Heidi Marie Rimke, "Governing Citizens through Self-Help Literature, *Cultural Studies* 14, no. 1 (2000): 61–78.

13. Cruikshank, "Revolutions Within," 234.

14. Nancy Fraser, *Justice Interruptus: Critical Reflections on the "Postsocialist" Condition* (New York: Routledge, 1997).

15. Judge Wapner was brought back to resolve disputes between pet owners on the Animal Channel's *Animal Court.*

16. Luaine Lee, "Judge Judy Has Always Believed in the Motto 'Just Do It,'" *Nando Media,* 28 November 1998, www.nandotimes.com; and Judy Sheindlin, *Don't Pee on My Leg and Tell Me It's Raining* (New York: HarperPerennial, 1997), 3.

17. Cited on www.judgejudy.com.

18. Cited in Lee, "Judge Judy."

19 Michel Foucault, "Complete and Austere Institutions," in *The Foucault Reader,* ed. Paul Rabinow (New York: Pantheon, 1984), 219–20. See also Michel Foucault, *Discipline and Punish* (New York: Random House, 1995).

20. See Frances Fox Piven, *Regulating the Poor: The Functions of Public Welfare* (New York: Random House, 1971); and John Gillion, *Overseers of the Poor* (Chicago: University of Chicago Press, 2001).

21. John Fiske, *Television Culture* (New York: Routledge, 1987).

22. Michael M. Epstein, for example, argues that courtroom programs are an extension of the talk show to the extent that they use law and order to legitimate a sensationalist focus on personal conflict. Epstein also points out that the judge figure is construed as an "ultimate" moral authority less concerned with legal procedures than with the evaluation of personal behaviors. Presuming the "low" status of the genre and concentrating on its misrepresentation of the actual law, however, his critique overlooks the governmental nature and implications of this focus on everyday conduct and behavior. See Michael M. Epstein, "Judging Judy, Mablean, and Mills: How Courtroom Programs Use Law to Parade Private Lives to Mass Audiences," *Television Quarterly* (2001), http://www.emmyonline.org/tvq /articles/32-1-1.asp.

23. Jane Shattuc, *The Talking Cure: TV Talk Shows and Women* (New York: Routledge, 1997).

24. Sonia Livingstone and Peter Lunt, *Talk on Television: Audience Participation and Public Debate* (London: Routledge, 1994).

25. Janice Peck, "The Mediated Talking Cure: Therapeutic Framing of Autobiography in TV Talk Shows," in *Gender, Race, and Class in Media,* ed. Gail Dines and Jean Humez (Thousand Oaks, Calif.: Sage, 2002), 538, 545.

26. Mimi White, *Tele-Advising: Therapeutic Discourse in American Television* (Chapel Hill: University of North Carolina Press, 1992), 69.

27. Cited in Barbara Lippert, "Punchin' Judy," *New York Magazine*, 15 June 2001, www.newyorkmetro.com.

28. Cited in *Judge Judy* publicity, www.wchstv.com/synd_prog/judy.

29. Cited on www.wchstv.com/synd_prog/judy.

30. Cited in McFarland, "Tough Judges Show There's Justice."

31. Judy Sheindlin, *Keep It Simple Stupid* (New York: Cliff Street Books, 2000), 2.

32. Nancy Fraser and Linda Gordon, "A Genealogy of 'Dependency': Tracing a Keyword of the U.S. Welfare State," in Fraser, *Justice Interruptus*.

33. Rose, "Governing 'Advanced' Liberal Democracies," 58.

34. Michel Foucault defines panoptism as surveillance or "systems of marking and classifying" (*Power/Knowledge: Selected Interviews*, ed. Colin Gordon [New York: Pantheon, 1977], 71).

35. See Elayne Rapping's essay in this volume; and Anna Williams, "Domestic Violence and the Aetiology of Crime in America's Most Wanted," *Camera Obscura* 31 (1995): 65–117.

36. Judy Sheindlin, *Beauty Fades, Dumb Is Forever* (New York: Cliff Street Books, 1999), 112–13.

37. Ibid., 105.

38. Sheindlin, cited in Lee, "Judge Judy."

39. Rose, "Governing 'Advanced' Liberal Democracies," 58.

40. The clip was replayed during an interview with Sheindlin on *Larry King Live*, CNN, 12 September 2000.

41. Michel Foucault, "On Popular Justice," in Gordon, *Power/Knowledge*, 27.

42. Michel Foucault, "Panopticism," in *The Foucault Reader*, ed. Paul Rabinow (New York: Pantheon, 1984), 212.

13

See You in Hell, Johnny Bravo!

Jeffrey Sconce

As it turns out, the Partridge family once lived next to a gloomy old mansion. One day a mysterious new boy moved into the old house along with his sister and a stern caretaker. Much to everyone's amazement, the new neighbor looked to be an identical twin of Danny Partridge, the irrepressible carrot-top guitarist in ABC's famous family rock band on *The Partridge Family*. Feeling unappreciated in the daily life of his fellow Partridges, Danny soon becomes fast friends with his British doppelgänger, Robert. When the rest of the Partridges show little interest in Danny's songwriting abilities, he and Robert decide to write a song together.

> Bump on the head
> Bump on the head
> Not as bad as being dead
> But I may get a bump on the head
> Because someone wants me dead

Later, Danny's new friend confesses that he is actually the exiled prince of Carpathia. Later still, as the two boys play a prank at school by exchanging identities, Danny is mistaken for Robert and kidnapped by enemies of the Carpathian monarchy.[1] Things look bad for a while, but Danny finds a way out of the jam just in time to join the family for a big rock concert in Hollywood. "Bump on the head, nobody's dead, we're not looking back, we're looking ahead," he sings triumphantly.[2]

Meanwhile, in a strangely parallel world of suburban enchantment, Greg Brady confronts his own challenge to reconcile music, family, and identity on *The Brady Bunch*. Having organized his siblings into a singing group, Greg finds he has captured the attention of big-shot Hollywood talent agents. The only problem is that they have no interest in Greg's unctuous little brothers and sisters. Instead, they want to turn Greg into "Johnny Bravo," assuring him that he will be the country's next big rock idol. For a while Greg buys into the hype, almost alienating his entire family with his swollen ego. But Greg realizes in the end that the agents aren't really interested in *him*, in his *talent*, just in his looks. Anyone could be made into Johnny Bravo, he realizes, just as long as they can fit into a prefabricated Johnny Bravo suit. Being simply handsome isn't good enough for Greg, though, so he sheepishly reconciles himself with the Brady Kids, who are now more determined than ever to make it as a group.[3]

Sigmund Freud never encountered the Beatles, of course, but if he had, no doubt he would have found these adolescent televisual delusions of interest. While Danny still flirts with a typically nineteenth-century fantasy of mistaken parentage and European grandeur, Greg's story plants this psychic mechanism quite firmly in the late-twentieth-century mythology of pop royalty (Danny is already a pop star, of course, so his fantasy life must come from somewhere else). Each boy meets his fantasy double—rich prince from Europe and groovy girl magnet—just as the target audiences of these tales are encouraged to find their fantasy doubles in Danny and Greg. In the early 1970s, ABC television clearly considered boyish narcissism to be a growth market, and tried its best to tap into a post-Beatle, post-Monkee world where every boy seemingly fantasized about achieving the fame and adulation he so richly deserved and yet never received from his miserly family. Most little boys eventually give up this delusion of sudden fame as a fortuitous rescue from familial injustice (if not, they are destined to become Rupert Pupnick or a virtuoso on "air guitar"). And yet, as Freud would no doubt also remind us, no childhood memory or dream ever really goes away. Some critics complain that baby boomers and Gen-Xers are incapable of ever growing up, but it might be more accurate to say they are doggedly pursued by a culture industry that refuses to ever let them close a highly profitable toy chest. Thus, against any clear rationale or insurgent populist demand, audiences have been forced to remain intimately acquainted with the Brady and Partridge families for over thirty years. *The Brady Bunch*, in particular, simply will not die—it lives on in variety hours, TV sequels, TV movies, theatrical films, books, ad parodies, and even a theater group that for a time re-created favorite episodes onstage.[4] As kids born in the 1960s grew up and went about their more mundane lives, these eternally anachronistic families moved from cool to kitsch to confusion. Is today's continuing interest in the Bradys and Partridges born from warm nostalgia or mocking contempt? Can anything be done about either family, or must they simply be endured even as they one day sell today's thirty-somethings dentures, adult diapers, and caskets?

What a pleasure, then, that Fox television allowed the nation to watch on 13 March 2002 as Danny Partridge beat the shit out of Greg Brady. It provided a kind of catharsis and symbolic resolution rarely allowed in popular culture. As a sporting event between two former teen idols, the fight was of limited interest. As a tragic farce, on the other hand, a dramatic showdown between fame and failure, Fox's *Celebrity Boxing* was a masterpiece of celebrity schadenfreude. Much to the twisted pleasure of aging boomers and bitter Gen-Xers everywhere—those who perhaps once dreamed of fame, adulation, and a perfect family with its own psychedelic bus—time has not been kind to Danny and Greg in the years since the networks canceled their fantasy lives. Though he once succeeded weekly in out-cooling his older brother (the prissy Keith Partridge), Danny's post-Partridge life included an embarrassing "solo career" as well as a few brushes with the law before finally ending up as a belligerent drive-time "radio personality" in Los Angeles and one of three chattering host-dudes on *The Other Half.*[5] Greg, meanwhile, became the self-appointed spokesperson and historian for the fictitious Brady family, even writing a tell-all about his experience "growing up Brady" (which included a vaguely disturbing, semi-incestuous account of his attempts to bed his TV mom, Florence Henderson).[6] Once professionally crafted to market "coolness" into the elementary school system, Danny and Greg ultimately didn't amount to much in the end. Their "fame" eroded from teen idols to rank-and-file Hollywood hangers-on, child stars who don't know when their protracted birthday parties are over and it's time to go home.

Amazingly, Fox's generosity in staging this cautionary tale—an important moment of generational restitution—was met with almost universal condemnation. Numerous critics cited the show as a new low in the ongoing reality TV craze, with NBC Sports chair Dick Ebersol calling it "pretty sick stuff."[7] Meanwhile, *TV Guide* ranked *Celebrity Boxing* as the sixth-worst program in the history of television (between *Hogan's Heroes* and *AfterMASH*).[8] Judging the then three-month-old *Celebrity Boxing* as a worse show than such timeless clinkers as *Pink Lady and Jeff* or *Manimal* testifies to the general climate of panic around reality TV, the latest in television's seemingly endless string of cultural contagions. *Time* critic James Poniewozik was perhaps the most charitable in writing, "It should have been a guilty pleasure, but there just wasn't enough pleasure to cut the guilt." Realizing that someone, somewhere must have liked the program (judging by its high ratings), Poniewozik tried to play along as best he could. "TV critics are probably worst qualified to review spectacles like *Celebrity Boxing*," he conceded, "because they sit in a quiet room, alone, watching entertainments that are probably best enjoyed loudly with other people, preferably drunk."[9] Score that erudite TV critic one, and beer-soaked proles zero.

Unfortunately, such a reflexive dismissal of reality TV has become all too predictable. In a world where television has gradually accumulated some limited cachet as an artful medium (at least on HBO), reality shows have become a dependable yardstick by which to measure one's own good taste. As in most of television's previously reviled genres, reality TV requires tasteful critics to imagine an audience of cruel and gullible louts (preferably drunk) gathering to exalt in the misfortune of others. A critic may possess some slight populist sympathies, but in the end, the demands of superior taste require a line to be drawn in the sand. "From where I was sitting," writes Poniewozik, "*Celebrity Boxing* was not nearly as pleasurable in practice as in concept."[10] In the climate of contemporary television, however, arguing a difference between practice and concept becomes as futile as previous attempts to disentangle form and content. The brilliance, joy, and success of a program like *Celebrity Boxing* stems from its very existence, regardless of what actually transpires on the screen. No one tuned into the show hoping to see a stunning display of the sweet science. It is doubtful also that anyone had any real stake in who won or lost the evening's three matches. But who could resist the spectacle (or even the *concept* of the spectacle) of six infamous has-beens and lowlifes actually agreeing to fight one another on national television? The program was an unqualified success the moment Partridge and Brady soiled themselves by stepping into the ring. Such conceptual pleasure is key to many reality broadcasts. Who wants to marry a millionaire? The more pertinent question for many viewers was, "Who would show up to be on *Who Wants to Be a Millionaire?*"

In the early days of his act, culture-jamming "comedian" Andy Kaufmann featured a segment called "Has-Been Corner." The bit consisted of Kaufmann bringing a former minor celebrity onstage—one often still hoping to make it big. After a thoroughly uncomfortable interrogation from Kaufmann, the once marginally known celebrity would be allowed to share their mediocre talents with the audience. On his PBS *Soundstage* special Kaufmann targeted Jim Brandy, a singer whose brief moment in the limelight was cut short by Elvis Presley's return from the army.[11] "How does it feel now," asks Kaufmann, "when you look back and you think about all the success you at one time had and were supposedly going to have, and never had? When you think about it now, how does it feel?" Brandy laughs nervously. "Lousy," he says. In another installment, Kaufmann ridicules a former child star in the Broadway production of *The Sound of Music,* a woman now hoping to return to the stage after a brief stint in medical school. "Good luck with your comeback," he says, "but I doubt it's going to work out." As she plods through "The Lonely Goatherder," Kaufmann smirks rudely, laughing at her (and our) desperation to be famous in a world where anonymity is a curse. "Most nonfamous people," writes Cintra Wilson, "are in a frequent state of dull torture from lack of . . . boundless international adoration in their lives, as if they lived with a constant low-grade toothache, which makes us all grouchy and unkind."[12] Much of Kaufmann's schtick—the second job at Jerry's Deli, the taunting of Memphis yahoos for failing to acknowledge his Hollywood stature, the phoenix-like Latka to Elvis transformation—pounded on this perpetual U.S. toothache, satirizing the capricious caste lines that separate the fabulous from their adoring wage slaves.

In its day, Kaufmann's routine played as profoundly rude and "outthere," violating the until then sacrosanct U.S. value of polite tolerance for everyone's "dream," no matter how insipid, destructive, or narcissistic. One can only hope that *Celebrity Boxing* demonstrates that the humiliation of debased, frustrated, and faded celebrity has now found a mass audience. What other explanation could there be, after all, for the nation's interest in the Winona Ryder shoplifting trial? Certainly, many sympathized with the actress (as evidenced by the flurry of "Free Winona" T-shirts), but how many more were stunned at her sense of entitlement in arguing she was simply researching a movie role (as if that should exempt her from the property laws of mere mortals)? In a culture that chooses to repress the politics of class division, celebrity baiting—from the Kaufmann fringe to huge numbers on Fox—may well be the last simmering refuge of populist hatred for the spoiled rich. In this schizophrenic universe, audiences nod approvingly as Fox News condemns a "class warfare" strategy in debating tax policy, and then change channels to Fox Broadcasting in the hope of seeing Milli Vanilli cry like little schoolgirls on *Celebrity Bootcamp.*

Rather than complain about such programs, then, I think we should do more to encourage their proliferation and success. We have in *Celebrity*

Boxing, Celebrity Bootcamp, and *Celebrity Justice* an emerging genre pos-
sessing almost unlimited potential and positive social utility, a return of
the repressed to counter the bottomless promo-pits of *Access Hollywood*
and *Entertainment Tonight.* In a society that closely monitors the length of
Brad Pitt's beard and allows Tom Cruise venues to opine on war with Iraq,
any attempt to humiliate the celebrity class should be embraced and celebrated. If nothing else, these programs might serve as cautionary tales for
aspiring fame-mongers across the country. Sure, one day you might have a
hit song or sitcom, but you're always just one paycheck away from bobbing
for earthworms on *Celebrity Fear Factor.* The same nation of taste that
made you is now, thankfully, ever ready to laugh at your avarice, narcissism, and stupidity. In this new post-Warholian future, ten minutes of
fame will cost you five more of public mockery and loathing. And that, to
quote another beloved target of U.S. hatred, "is a good thing."[13]

For those who didn't get the wicked joke about fame and psychosis in
Celebrity Boxing's first round, Fox followed a few months later with the
even more inflammatory series, *American Idol.* Here, the burnout trajectory of celebrity was condensed into a twelve-week competition among
young hopefuls vying for the opportunity to become obscenely famous,
ostensibly as pop stars. To the delight of jaded Adorno enthusiasts everywhere, thousands of teens lined up—not just happy but begging to wear
the Johnny Bravo suit. Interestingly, in the days of Partridge and Brady, the
teen fantasy industry recognized that "authenticity" was a significant component in crafting adolescent delusions of talent and fame. Danny, after
all, wants to write his own material, the Dylanesque "Bump on the Head,"
while Greg refuses to become merely a pawn of greedy record executives.
Adolescent consumers of these texts assumedly had a similar interest in
the fantasy of unique personal creativity. Refreshingly or disturbingly, depending on one's perspective, teens of today have no such hang-ups over
romantic illusions of creative freedom and authenticity. Nowhere was this
more apparent than on the face of Justin Guarini, the ever hopeful, totally
positive pawn of greedy television executives who finished second (behind
Kelly Somebody) in *American Idol* voting. His entire persona seemed to
scream, "I have no soul," not just in a James Brown or Satan Lord of Darkness way but as a can-do guy willing to wear anything and sing anything
in the hope of sharing his haircut with the world. A month after the final
broadcast, Justin and the entire *American Idol* cast were on the road showcasing their unexamined desires and impoverished muses in sports arenas

across the country. Who went to see them? Idolaters, presumably those hoping to be the next generation of disposable celebrities; or perhaps parents taking their kids to a cautionary freak show. Study harder, or one day you'll be forced to sing "Without You" in spandex and dry ice at the Tallahassee Cultural Arts Center. Someone should give Rupert Murdoch a medal.

Round Two

Eighty years ago, when broadcasting was still an unforeseen side effect of more sober forms of wireless commerce, well-intentioned do-gooders felt they could "regulate" this upstart medium by imposing a few agencies, guidelines, and penalties. Some presciently recognized that broadcasting would one day present immense possibilities for centralized profit, that the emerging networks would scheme to dominate their lowly affiliates by transforming them into mere distribution points for advertisers. And so it was that early reformers attempted to mandate the idea of "public service," a philosophy that would hopefully balance the avarice of the networks with the public's right to democratic debate and enlightenment via the airwaves. If media flow could just be guided, went this logic, if it could be channeled through a series of tributaries, locks, and reservoirs, then "the people" would still be able to communicate and debate actively rather than merely consume passively.

One would think Jean Baudrillard's "Requiem for the Media" would have put a stop to such utopian canal-building many years ago. As Baudrillard notes (in his critique of Hans Magnus Enzensberger):

> All vague impulses to democratize content, subvert it, restore the "transparency of the code," control the information process, contrive a reversibility of circuits, or take power over media are hopeless—unless the monopoly of speech is broken; and one cannot break the monopoly of speech if one's goal is simply to distribute it equally to everyone.[14]

All unilateral mass communication, in other words, no matter how variegated or targeted, is inherently imperialist. Giving communists, Mormons, or the left-handed their own special content solves nothing. Such publics can never be served through an ever more fragmented media; at best, such programming only further solidifies each group's isolation and reification. Despite the best intentions, content, meaning, and power cannot be channeled through a system of benevolent irrigation. Flow, channels, streams; if one wants to cling to aquatic metaphors of media distribution, perhaps it is best to think of television as a fog—dense, shifting, obscuring, and depthless. Such a metaphor serves several theoretical models—from poststructural riffs on indeterminacy to good old-fashioned marxist false consciousness. And who *can* say with any precision exactly what is going on "out there"? What is the significance, personal and/or cultural, of Partridge fighting Brady? How can we ever really know the pleasures and politics involved in such a contest, playing as it does on the complex textual and neural networks of three generations of viewers?

One thing is for sure: *Celebrity Boxing* proves yet again that television is, in general, smarter than the people paid to write about it as well as those who earnestly want to regulate it. Such critics often judge TV according to obsolete standards of taste, decency, and value, while the medium itself—in its crassness, vulgarity, and cutthroat competitiveness—has usually left old aesthetic forms and criteria choking in the dust (or lost in the fog). Every so often a throwback to the past will arrive, like *The Sopranos,* that seems to offer hope by looking backward (in this case, to the second Golden Age of the hour-long serial drama). After four seasons of the mob drama, however, the *New York Times*'s early claim that *The Sopranos* is "the greatest work of American popular culture of the last quarter century" looks appropriately goofy, the product of perhaps too much brie and Merlot.[15] It may well be the most important show ever for those who don't watch television, but the real energy in the medium is elsewhere. What critics miss in their bread-and-circus reviews of *Celebrity Boxing* and its ilk is the dense semiotic complexity of what actually takes place onscreen (and to a lesser extent in society). Reality TV may look no better than the spectacle of Christians being thrown to the lions, but in point of fact, the genre takes great care in pairing specific Christians and handpicked lions. *Celebrity Boxing*'s matchups, after all, were not purely random pairings of generic has-beens. There were no dadaist Gary Burghoff–Gavin MacLeod bouts on the bill that evening. Rather, each fight demanded contestants with meaningful pop-cult résumés, icons that could be pitted in fights that were as much symbolic as pugilistic.

At first glance, for instance, the fight between Todd "*Diff'rent Strokes*" Bridges and Vanilla Ice might seem little more than a repetition of the first round's joke: the hilarity of has-beens still clinging to any and all possible national exposure. For those with a more subtle knowledge and morbid interest in the misfortunes of celebrities, however, it would be difficult to find a more meaningful and poignant matchup. While *Diff'rent Strokes* remains a less-than-memorable show—part of a brief sitcom cycle of white liberals adopting cute black dwarves in feel-good stories of timeless Caucasian paternalism—the series has achieved some notoriety for its supposed and perhaps well-deserved "curse." Each of the three children on the show have had troubled lives following the series' cancellation, from Gary Coleman's public scuffles and ongoing infantilization to Dana Plato's shoplifting busts and eventual death by overdose. Bridges himself has had a number of run-ins with the law, including some jail time for drug possession and attempted murder. Vanilla Ice, on the other hand, rose to the height of billboard celebrity in 1991 with his mega-smash hit, "Ice, Ice, Baby." Throughout his rise to the top, Vanilla claimed to be "from the streets," hoping to quell critics fond of dubbing him the Pat Boone of rap. It turns out, though, that the Iceman was actually a suburban kid from Dallas—the Johnny Bravo of rap—cashing in on the latest growth field in Negro music. His apocalyptic loss of street cred plus his appearance in the abysmal *Cool as Ice* quickly made him a pop pariah. Even a return to his birth name and a stab at speed metal could not save a flat-lined career.[16]

When Todd and Vanilla squared off in the ring, then, they brought much more with them than simply two rather undistinguished celebrity pedigrees. Bridges's trouncing of Vanilla provided another strange chapter in the story of a middle-class black kid cast to play a ghetto refugee who then descended into an actual life of street crime. On the other side stood the middle-class white kid who played at life in the hood, blew his own cover, and then spent the rest of his days claiming others had "forced" him into "selling out." The mind reels in considering the implications of race, representation, and "reality" at work here—a testament to the pop-cult savvy of the fight's "promoters." This was truly a fight where nothing and *everything* was at stake at the same time. The contest itself was rather one-sided (as many pointed out, those who had actually done time in prison made short work of their civilian opponents), but it resonated with untold extratextual complexity. For a brief moment, the two pugilists were not simply faded stars but emblems of a much longer history of violence, entertainment, and exploitation. Just as the O. J. Simpson case crystallized decades-long struggles over race, class, and gender, the Bridges-Ice fight (in much less dramatic fashion, of course) provided a brief moment of symbolic reparations. A ten-part Ken Burns documentary on the history of race and music might have been more informative, but who is to say Bridges whaling on the Iceman in front of millions was not more therapeutic? In this respect, one might argue that *Celebrity Boxing* is the true public service broadcasting of our time. Rather than flatter liberal elites with what they already know (à la PBS) or craft a radical politics for televisual oblivion (à la public access), *Celebrity Boxing* activated an entire history of racism, both profound and absurd, in a three-minute pummeling witnessed by a nation that was, for the most part, extremely grateful.

Round Three

The Partridge-Brady undercard on *Celebrity Boxing* demonstrated how famous TV characters leave hollow human shells in their wake for our therapeutic amusement. The second fight allowed audiences to work through crucial political issues in a theater of the cruelly absurd. As befits a title match, the top card that night showed just how horrifying and/or hilarious the stakes of hyperreality have become, not just on reality TV proper but in our demented mediascape as a whole. In one corner stood Tonya Harding, the crazed white-trash wolverine who almost ten years after entering the public arena for her insanely inspired yet wholly moronic plot to smash the kneecaps of rival skater Nancy Kerrigan, still retained enough TV-Q to rate top billing. Fox's dream match, of course, would have been to pit Harding against Kerrigan, but alas, that was not to happen. Their second choice was almost as inspired, however—pairing Harding against Amy "the Long Island Lolita" Fisher, a young woman famous for sleeping with the loathsome Joey Buttafuoco and then shooting his wife in the face at point-blank range. The Harding-Fisher matchup, announced weeks before the actual broadcast, accomplished all the promotional buzz the network could have hoped for—disgust, outrage, and intense interest. Would Fox, already seen as the lowest of the low, actually be so tasteless as to mix tragedy and fluff so heartlessly? No one cared about Kerrigan's feelings or kneecaps since no one really cared about ice skating until Harding's goons bungled their "hit." But would Fox exploit Mrs. Buttafuoco's very real pain and permanent disfigurement for such incredibly insipid entertainment?

Whether Fox really planned to book Fisher is unclear, as is the final explanation as to why Fisher did not actually participate in the fight. Nevertheless, her exit, whether "real" or orchestrated, left Fox looking for another female combatant that matched Harding's basic profile as a low-rent sleazeball involved in some form of diverting illegality. This opened the door for Paula Jones, whose tortured memories of Bill Clinton's elegant pants-dropping seduction technique eventually and rather circuitously led to only the second impeachment ever of a U.S. president. Perhaps by accident, then, Fox had stumbled on a true fight of the century—two corn pones whose media careers spanned the full spectrum of historical stupidity, from the felling (almost) of the president of the most powerful country in the world to the felling (almost) of an Olympic hopeful, who incredibly, became almost as unlikable as her attacker. The fact that both fighters have become "celebrities" is a testament to the media's democratic and/or deranged inability to maintain perspective or proportion on anything.

As in the earlier fights, Jones's appearance in the ring that night held both manifest and latent pleasures. On the one hand, there was the explicit spectacle of her pathetic attempts to deflect Harding's punishing blows, and on the other, the displaced struggle over the Republicans' attempt at a coup d'état as punishment for blow jobs. Which fight was "real" and which was purely meaningless theater? The impeachment of a president, as we all learned in junior high civics class, is supposed to be the most supremely solemn and important event enabled by the Constitution. Richard Nixon quit, jumped on a helicopter, and went into exile just to avoid even a vote on impeachment. Everyone of an age no doubt remembers the day Nixon resigned and fled to San Clemente. Who remembers (or will remember) anything about the Clinton impeachment? Having made up their minds months earlier, most Americans simply could have cared less about this elaborate, yet ultimately boring theatrical charade. No one believed Clinton was innocent, whatever that might mean, and no one believed any Republican was genuinely outraged, either by Clinton's abuse of his intern or our sacred Constitution. Even though this "monumentally" significant public event was televised gavel to gavel, no doubt the Food Network enjoyed higher ratings throughout the proceedings.

No one saw the impeachment proper, but everyone followed the characters in the opening act: Ken Starr, Donna Tripp, and of course, Paula Jones. And here is where Fox, despite its well-known Republican leanings, performed a wonderful public service for the vestiges of the political Left. For Clintonites, seeing Harding mercilessly decimate a flabby Jones (and endanger her Republican-financed nose job) was a dream come true. Harding always read as a trailer-trash Democrat, perhaps because Kerrigan read so easily (and perhaps unfairly) as a preppy Republican. No one could ever condone smashing Kerrigan's kneecaps, of course, but in the aftermath of this heinous (but let's face it, absurdly hilarious) event, many no doubt felt a little sympathy for the perpetually outclassed, outspent, and outperformed Harding. Her lead-pipe gambit seemed little more than an affirmative action program for jilted prom hopefuls the world over. What made the fight especially delicious for left-leaning political junkies was the transformation in Jones's attitude during the course of her "fight." She entered the ring joking and giggling, as if this was just another personal merry moment in the ongoing eight-year hallucination she had forced on the nation. Once the fight began, though, the *reality* of reality TV started to intrude. Harding absolutely pasted Jones, chasing her around the ring in terror, giving her a solid lesson that even in a world marked by the play of postmodern signification, history is what hurts, to quote Fredric Jameson.[17] Even more delicious for Jones haters was her crybaby response afterward. It was all so unfair that Harding had actually decided to box on *Celebrity Boxing*. Turning off the TV or pondering the pummeling in the days after the broadcast, audiences had the opportunity to work out this syllogism on their own. Only an idiot would agree to fight a trained Olympian on national TV and think she wouldn't get hurt. Similarly, only an idiot would accept a private invitation to the hotel room of a notoriously womanizing governor and not expect to get equally "hit on." Conclusion: Jones is an idiot.

In the early days of reality TV, conscientious television critics delighted in warning viewers that the programs were not actually all that *real*, that what the networks presented as documentary fact was actually a highly manipulated product. The only people to look stupider in such revelations were the rejected housemates of *Big Brother*, who on exiting the house complained that the editing made them look bad or "didn't tell the whole story." Such a critique, professional or otherwise, fails to recognize that "reality" in reality TV is merely one of many fluid plot conventions and not an inviolable foundation. More accurately, the promise of the real on these programs (or in these people)—however distant, strained, and artificial—enables forms of textual play like those unique to any genre. For example, many argue that the current reality cycle began with MTV's *The Real World*, a soap opera for media-savvy teens somehow remotely anchored in the real. Even without magnanimous critical intervention, most viewers understood from square one that a redneck country and western singer and a black lesbian activist would probably not choose to live in the same house for six months. The entire affair is wholly staged for maximum (potential) conflict. But at the same time, viewers invest in the idea that said redneck and lesbian are not actors (or at least are *performing* the role of *not* being actors, at least not yet), and that they do claim (or are assigned) membership in the conventionally real social categories of redneck and lesbian. Fake redneck and lesbian in a haunted house, in the Wild West, behind enemy lines, would activate one set of generic expectations. *Real* redneck and lesbian in a wholly fabricated Gen-Y urban dreamscape creates another. Producers, participants, and viewers of reality TV have thus taken the Documentary 101 lesson of "the camera changes everything" to be an enabling condition for textual play, not a limitation of objective reality. When the "news" broke that producers of *Survivor* had staged certain events more than once in order to pick up long shots and standard coverage for editing, the public could have cared less. There was no *Survivor* backlash, no diminution of audience pleasure. Viewers already considered the program to be *Gilligan's Island* with "real" castaways. Who could be upset if the director needed a better shot of Gilligan covered in coconut pie or, for that matter, Richard Hatch strolling along the beach in the nude?

Some dismiss reality TV as merely a savvy economic move by increasingly cash-strapped networks no longer able to bankroll "dramatic" programming seven nights a week. Perhaps that explains the "genre's" formative moments, but it does little to address the ongoing popularity of these programs. After all, if audiences really wanted more half-hour sitcoms, there remains an army of hacks and wanna-bes eager to provide them, no doubt at criminally low wages. More likely, the form thrives, like all "realist" aesthetics, in its ability to distort our lived social world in a manner that many find pleasurable. Here we might gain theoretical insight not in writings on "nonfiction" forms but in the analysis of those genres that have a more explicitly playful and/or tenuous relationship to so-called reality. In his work on the literary "fantastic," for example, Tzvetan Todorov argues that the power of horror fiction lies in its ability to suspend readers between two competing systems of explanation: the natural and supernatural. The pleasure of the fantastic is in this hesitation, the reader's thrill in entertaining the rational and irrational, the known and unknown. As Todorov writes:

> In a world which is indeed our world, the one we know, a world without devils, sylphides, or vampires, there occurs an event which cannot be explained by the laws of this familiar world. The person who experiences the

event must opt for one of two possible solutions: either he is the victim of an illusion of the senses, of a product of the imagination—and the laws of the world remain what they are; or else an event has indeed taken place, it is an integral part of reality—but then this reality is controlled by laws unknown to us."[18]

Reality TV, one could contend, is our new genre of hesitation, thrilling us with its confusion of once distinct realms. After all, who can explain with certainty these otherworldly demons we have come to call the "Darva Conger" and "Rick Rockwell"? After witnessing the deliciously embarrassing spectacle of their shotgun video wedding, the tales of an aborted honeymoon, Conger's sudden conversion to morality and good taste, Rockwell's desperate attempts to pretend the entire affair didn't bother him, and Conger's ridiculous pleas to respect her privacy even as she posed for *Playboy*, we also had to consider ourselves "victims of illusion," or worse, part of a world where "reality" is "controlled by laws unknown to us." We have to assume that both are (or were once) "real people," but like Michael or Jason of 1980s horror film fame, they too simply will not go away, they too cannot be defeated, repressed, or ignored. Currently they are both lying low, but we all know one or both of them might spring forward at any moment from some hidden media recess to scare the bejesus out of us once again. (If only Fox could have signed them to fight.) We spend a great deal of time complaining about the "feeding frenzies" in the media that burn such supernatural icons into our brains; indeed, even the media will critique itself for its "unhealthy" fascination with Conger, Rockwell, Harding, Jones, Condit, O. J., and the like. But truth be told, these vampires of the media age migrate between two states of being—fact and fiction, event and elaboration, real and hyperreal—in a manner audiences obviously find endlessly fascinating. The pleasure of hesitation here is in wanting to know the putative "truth" about such characters, and yet enjoying the escalating insanity and perverse dream state that issues from their unending media wake. If Fox sneaked a hidden camera and microphone into a golf bag to follow O. J. for eighteen holes, would we watch? Absolutely. Should we feel guilty about it? Only if we think we would have the strength of will to turn down a similar invitation to watch Frankenstein's monster run amok at a day care center.

Todorov sought to describe a hesitation based on a simple binary. Is that really a ghost or just a crazy nun running around in a sheet? As the new and appropriately postmodern genre of hesitation, however, reality

TV creates fascination by submerging us in the fundamentally indecipherable quality of all media. Michel Foucault noted that prisons exist to distract us from the fact that all of society is carceral.[19] Baudrillard followed suit with his infamous assertion that Disneyland's fakery exists to distract us from the more profound unreality of Los Angeles.[20] In this tradition, one might derivatively argue that the panic over the "reality" in reality TV distracts us from the unsettling/liberating realization that all of television is now equally real and/or unreal—or in true hyperreal fashion, that it is no longer possible to make this distinction. "Illusion is no longer possible," asserts Baudrillard, "because the real is no longer possible."[21]

No one is surprised that the yokels on *Jerry Springer* are performing. The interest, as with much reality/tabloid TV, is in seeing how "real" people will perform their "Jerry Springer" roles. At this point in the history of television and the South, what would an authentic cracker appearance on television look like anyway?[22] In this respect, the "hesitation" in reality TV is not between real and unreal, natural or supernatural; rather, reality TV celebrates the exhilaration of occupying a world where true and untrue, reality and artifice, event and gesture, premediated and postmediated have lost their meaning. What really happened in the Florida recount of the 2000 presidential election? What really happened between Conger and Rockwell on their ill-fated "honeymoon"? What is the motivation behind the sequel to the Gulf War? Gore's lawyers blew it. Conger is clinically insane. Cheney owes favors in the oil industry. Katherine Harris and Jeb Bush were having an affair. Rockwell raped Conger on the airplane. George always was Barbara's favorite. The media allows us to pursue whatever story and theory we find most compelling, and there's little difference in believing well-executed literary tropes are leading us to the truth or the truth is leading us into a strange literary adventure. Todorov's nun eventually pulls off the sheet and the novel is over. *Celebrity Boxing*'s ability to generate compelling entertainment out of Jurassic pop stars, ex-con sitcom players, rap's favorite punch line, the world's meanest figure skater, and the face that sunk a thousand political ships, suggests that our current state of hesitation is a world without end.

NOTES

1. For a more extended discussion of this recurring device in adolescent sitcoms, see Moya Luckett, "Girl Watchers: Patty Duke and Teen TV," in *The*

Revolution Wasn't Televised: Sixties Television and Social Conflict, ed. Lynn Spigel and Michael Curtin (New York: Routledge, 1997), 95–118.

2. Vic Crume, *The Partridge Family #10: Marked for Terror* (New York: Curtis Books, 1972).

3. "Adios, Johnny Bravo," 14 September 1973.

4. Campy stage presentations of the original *Brady Bunch* scripts began in Chicago in 1990.

5. Those interested in Danny's solo work are referred to "Dreamland" (MGM single 145, 1973).

6. Barry Williams, *Growing Up Brady: I Was a Teenage Greg* (New York: Good Guy Entertainment, 2000).

7. Cited in Bob Wolfley, "Ebersol No Fan of *Celebrity Boxing*," *Milwaukee Journal Sentinel,* 19 May 2002, www.jsonline.com.

8. "50 Worst Programs Ever," *TV Guide,* 29 July 2002, www.tvguide.com.

9. James Poniewozik, "*Celebrity Boxing* Is a Stiff," *Time,* 14 March 2002, www.time.com.

10. Ibid.

11. Enthusiasm over the return of Elvis (and new Presley products) knocked Brandy's top-twenty hit "Wild, Wild Lovin'" off the charts.

12. Cintra Wilson, *A Massive Swelling: Celebrity Re-Examined as a Grotesque Crippling Disease* (New York: Viking, 2000), xv.

13. This beloved target is, of course, Martha Stewart. Long a divisive figure in U.S. pop culture, Stewart came under increased satiric attack after allegations of insider trading on Wall Street.

14. Jean Baudrillard, "Requiem for the Media," in *For a Critique of the Political Economy of the Sign* (St. Louis, Mo.: Telos Press, 1981).

15. Stephen Holden, "Sympathetic Brutes in a Pop Masterpiece," *New York Times,* 6 June 1999, 2.23.

16. Fans live on at the website *Vanilla Ice at His Prime* (http://www.dopey-web.com/vanillaice/). As one fan writes with mock incredulity, "There are the people that claim that they have seen Vanilla as a busboy, taking orders at Taco Bell and pumping gas for a living. How could we believe that the Master of Rap would be working at Mickee D's???? It is not possible."

17. This comment, of course, concludes Fredric Jameson's famous *The Political Unconscious* (Ithaca, N.Y.: Cornell University Press, 1982), 102.

18. Tzvetan Todorov, *The Fantastic: A Structural Approach to a Literary Genre* (Ithaca, N.Y.: Cornell University Press, 1975), 25.

19. See Michel Foucault, *Discipline and Punish: The Birth of the Prison* (New York: Vintage Books, 1979).

20. Jean Baudrillard, *Simulations* (New York: Semiotext(e), 1983), 24–25.

21. Ibid., 38.

22. Discussing outrage over "fake" guests appearing on daytime talk shows,

Kevin Glynn observes, "It seems . . . senseless to distinguish categorically between 'real' guests and 'fakes' . . . for like other 'reality-based' television forms, talk shows depend on a certain media role playing that is demanded of everybody involved in their production" (*Tabloid Culture: Trash Taste, Popular Power, and the Transformation of American Television* [Durham, N.C.: Duke University Press, 2000], 222).

Part IV

Reception

Got to Be Real
Mediating Gayness on Survivor

Kathleen LeBesco

During its tenure on U.S. television, reality TV has had a hand in changing images and perceptions of transgressive sexuality for better and worse. Both its texts and audiences reveal understandings of gay lives patterned on, but often departing from the conventions established by generations of television thought to be purely fictional.[1] Given the political ugliness of those old conventions for gay viewers and their allies, reality TV has been applauded for ushering in a new era of inclusive, "real," and diverse representations of queer sexuality. Efforts to validate these claims must examine not only the politics of the texts themselves but also the ways in which fans integrate ideologies about sexuality into their own worldviews. This chapter is an attempt, through case studies of the first three seasons of *Survivor,* to analyze the limits and possibilities of the genre and fan readings in order to gauge how reality shows impact public discourses about gay, lesbian, bisexual, and transgendered lives.

Gay characters, at least men, are no longer facing the issues of outright media invisibility that used to plague them. Most network reality shows regularly feature at least one gay character—a representational habit made ratings-safe by *The Real World.* Because these characters are framed as honest-to-goodness people and not merely the figments of wild Hollywood imagination, their representation and reception carry significant weight in terms of reaffirming or altering ideas about sexual difference. At stake in the rush of acclaim for increased visibility, however, are issues of the quality and complexity of the ways in which gay characters are now being represented. It is necessary to unpack issues of representational framing and audience reception before celebrating the jump in quantity of representations. In terms of quantity, representations of gay men on *Survivor* can hardly be faulted. Nevertheless, these divergent representations warrant analysis for quality, which can be accomplished by turning to the text of the show itself and the responses generated by viewers.

The *Survivor* series has featured two out gay characters: Richard Hatch, the cunning winner of the first season, and Brandon Quinton, an effusive member of the Africa cast. While no other cast members have publicly announced anything other than normative heterosexuality, fans have quickly stepped in to assign sexually transgressive identities to a host of other cast members, most notably Jeff Varner and Mitchell Olson from *Survivor 2: Australian Outback*.[2] Textual and audience analyses are necessary to understand the most influential forces in shaping audience perceptions of characters like these, whatever their publicly divulged proclivities. An obvious choice with which to begin this analysis is Hatch, an out gay man whose prominence on the show's first season garnered much attention.

Fan responses discussed hereafter are drawn from one of two on-line communities: MightyBigTV.com (MBTV) or SurvivorFire.com (SF). MBTV is a website dedicated to the critical dissection of popular culture, in which its users tend to be well versed. The tone adopted by both recappers (site members who are paid to author lengthy, detailed summaries of each episode) and discussion board participants (regular users who post their opinions about various topics) is hip, hypercritical, and ironic, as reflected in the website's new subtitle, "Spare the Snark, Spoil the Networks." In a clear departure from on-line conventions of linguistic informality, grammatical and mechanical errors in writing are rare in recaps and on discussion boards. Philosophical and literary references abound, as demonstrated in a *Survivor 1* recap that invokes Friedrich Nietzsche's thoughts about the relationship of the individual to the group and another that compares Hatch to Satan-as-hero in John Milton's *Paradise Lost*. As excerpts will later show, members of this community are well equipped to reflect on how manipulation by editors produces certain impressions about characters that may or may not be accurate. Demographically speaking, of the roughly 500,000 site visitors per month, around 75 percent are female, most are eighteen to thirty-four years old, most are American or Canadian, and all speak English.[3]

My other source of fan impressions, SF, bills itself as the biggest and best website for *Survivor* fans. According to figures offered by SF's youthful Canadian proprietors, the site receives around 25,000 weekly visitors and

Richard Hatch was the first openly gay character on *Survivor,* one of the many popular reality programs that viewers have come to see such a character on.

boasts 45,000 message board posts.[4] Unlike MBTV, SF focuses exclusively on one series, covering it in great depth. Users tend to be extremely knowledgeable about *Survivor* history and lore; they are also far more earnest and considerably less sophisticated in their abilities to produce oppositional readings than their MBTV counterparts. Site users have an array of options, from participating on discussion boards and voting on likely ejectees to viewing daily original comics and reading articles by SF columnists. Discussion board participants follow the conventions of online chat: their posts tend to be brief, overpunctuated, grammatically and syntactically problematic, and rife with emoticons.[5] For the purposes of fan research, SF fan perspectives balance nicely with those provided by MBTV users in order to offer a well-rounded picture of audience discourse about sexuality and *Survivor.*

Fat and Evil, Oh No! Gay, Who Cares? Survivor 1

Hatch was defined neither in the public imagination nor in press accounts by his sexuality; former Gay and Lesbian Alliance Against Defamation (GLAAD) National Research Advisory Board member Peter Nardi points out that "the talk about Richard has been about his personality—not the fact that he is gay. People referred to him as the 'obnoxious one' or the 'conniving one' or the 'smart one.' But 'gay one' was way down on the list."[6] While this facet of his existence was not kept secret, neither was it played up to the extent that would later be true of Quinton on *Survivor 3*.

Other stories presented in the popular press lend to Hatch's framing as a villain in the minds of *Survivor* fans. In April 2000, Hatch was arrested for allegedly overpunishing his adopted son by forcing him to exercise, though the charges were later dropped. Then, in August 2001, Hatch was charged with domestic assault after shoving a former boyfriend who was trying to enter Hatch's house.[7] Mentions of these events (especially the former) made their way into press accounts and fan discourse as in the MBTV recap of episode one. This recap featured unrepentant acts of villain framing, such that readers had a hard time deciding whether it was Hatch's alleged abuse of his son, his heavy, flabby body, or his peculiar brand of corporate arrogance that was his worst crime against humanity. True to the end, in the MBTV recap of the final episode, the author refers to *Survivor* as the show where "a magnificent, corpulent bastard takes center stage." That Hatch is evil and fat defines him for posterity. Perhaps there is something threatening to the stability of heteronormativity in the representation of Hatch. A *Washington Post* critic cheekily called Hatch an "Evil Queen," noting that "the straight world is conditioned to think of homosexuality as a handicap, a weakness, a fey stereotype. The gay rights movement tries to present a warm, united front and yet somehow amplifies the notion that gay men and lesbians are marginal, lacking in power. This is exactly where the Evil Queen strikes."[8] Hatch's portrayal and victory are powerful precisely because they position the gay man as unstoppable. But is this "menace to society" imagery socially and politically productive for advancing an agenda in favor of sexual diversity? It is likely that general audiences, conditioned by homophobia, will read such representations as threatening to the established social order; thus, some mechanism is required to defang the menace. The lack of attention to Hatch's gayness in popular discourse may have functioned as one way to diminish his subversive representational power.

A popular way to diminish the power of gay men, television characters or not, has been to taint them by association with femininity. Yet unlike on the discussion board response to *Survivor 3* character Quinton, who was frequently referred to as "she" and "Brandi," neither MBTV nor SF fans ever overtly feminized Hatch. Instead, he was demonized for his megalomaniac attitude and "unkempt" body. The implications of this strand of fan response are important; Hatch's representational power for the gay world was not diluted by fan reactions dismissing him on the basis of his sexuality. Rather, other features of Hatch's existence were the target of potshots. While many of these attacks were equally unfair, they were very much in line with fan attacks on other, straight *Survivor 1* cast members. According to fans, Hatch was fat and evil, Sean Kenniff was shallow and dumb, Rudy Boesch was cranky and malevolent, and so on, but none of the descriptions were generated as the result of sexual preference. Perhaps it was Hatch's corporeal departure from the visual stereotypes of gayness that discouraged readings of him as feminine.

Where one might expect a nonspecifically gay audience to deride out gayness, in fact Hatch receives little notice on MBTV recaps or discussion boards for his sexuality at all.[9] It is possible that Hatch's performance of his sexuality fails to square with prevalent stereotypes about gay men, and thus detractors must look elsewhere for ammunition with which to malign him. This theory, however, presumes the presence of homophobic attitudes among fans—a presumption undermined by their retaliatory responses to homophobic comments on both the show and discussion boards.

Time after time in fan response to *Survivor 1,* it is *homophobia* that provides the impetus for fan mockery. On SF discussion boards, though homophobic comments are made with some regularity, vitriolic posts spawn a significant amount of negative response. For example, when one fan derides Hatch as "an asshole fag," nineteen different respondents chide the fan for such an ignorant attitude—an event that signals the multiple readings at work on the boards and suggests the stakes viewers have in representational politics. And on MBTV, fan recappers work scathing critiques of homophobic attitudes into their episode summaries. Recappers have, for instance, declared open season on intolerance in highlighting the misguidedness of other *Survivor* cast members: cranky Rudy's disdain for

Richard being "a queer," Sean's ill-at-ease embrace of the term "fat naked fag" to describe Hatch, and Dirk Been's religious aversion to the "sinfulness" of homosexuality.

In one recap, readers encounter a summary and interpretation of Hatch's relationship with Dirk, his young Christian tribe mate. A conflict between the two is cited wherein Dirk displays annoyance at Hatch's refusal to stop talking about his homosexuality, and the fan writer infers that "Dirk pretends like it would be better if Richard would stop talking about sex; but we know he really means it would be better if Richard stopped being gay." The slant is avowedly antiproselytizing and in favor of sexual diversity. How do these examples of fan reaction to expressions of homophobia on *Survivor* serve as counterpoints to the claim that, for instance, Boesch's (*Survivor 1*) and Tom Buchanan's (*Survivor 3*) frequent use of the slur "queer" to describe their gay cast mates has made TV safe for gay bashing? Admittedly, one need only watch the post–*Survivor 1* town meeting special and listen to the audience cheers when Rudy uses the term "queer" for evidence that some audience members see *Survivor* as a vehicle for the denigration of sexual difference.[10] But MBTV and SF fan reactions demonstrate that the picture is more complicated than this, much like controversies over the audience function of Archie Bunker's racist rants on Norman Lear's groundbreaking sitcom *All in the Family* in the early 1970s proved that TV shows are polysemic. Nonetheless, it is possible that when the audience laughs after Rudy's use of the slur, plenty are laughing *at* his bigotry, not *with* it. And in a different vein, sitcom writer Terry Maloney Haley notes that while Rudy used the word "queer" in a derogatory sense to portray Hatch on *Survivor 1*, "eventually, he ended up rubbing lotion on Richard's shoulders and voting for him, so maybe spending time with a gay person made a difference."[11] Perhaps the embrace of a homophobic slur was merely Navy SEAL (Boesch's former occupation) effrontery for an attitude streaked with acceptance—an attitude likely to cause trouble in Rudy's conservative military community.

Tellingly, MBTV fans *do* choose to complain when they perceive attitudes and behaviors on the show that are more homosexual than homosocial and that are not owned up to or are outright denied by *Survivor* characters. In an MBTV recap of the final *Survivor 1* episode, readers are exposed to a biting critique of what its author understands as repressed homosexual desire between two women tribe mates, Susan Hawk and Kelly Wiglesworth.

Sue gets the next bit of spotlight as she prattles on about sleeping next to your enemy, eating next to your enemy and just having to treat them civilly. Sue is of course required by the laws of the show to sleep next to Kelly every night, sit down and eat next to Kelly, pop Kelly's pimples, rub mud off Kelly's glistening, wet body and, oh I don't know, think lustily about Kelly and then cry about how Kelly reminds Sue of her long-lost best friend that died, right? Those are the rules, correct? How terrible that must be, Sue, to be forced into doing all that by CBS. You've got my vote, if only in sympathy, dear, tortured woman.

This passage represents one of the few instances on MBTV when a fan frames homoerotic desire negatively. It seems that the catalyst for the author's negativity, however, is the character's *denial* of said desire, rather than her embrace of it. The implication is that MBTV fans seem to be supportive of a variety of sexual and relational practices, but deeply suspicious of attempts to closet transgressive sexuality for the purpose of saving face on national television.

Come Out, Come Out, Wherever You Are: Survivor 2

No discussion of thwarted desire or repressed sexual identity on *Survivor* is complete without examining its second season. On *Survivor 2*, while there were no out gay or lesbian characters, there was much speculation and tittering among fans as to the potential sexual transgressiveness of a variety of cast members. The first survivor ejected from the Outback was Debb Eaton, a New Hampshire corrections officer whose marriage to her stepson made headlines. While Eaton's romance cannot easily be described as breaking cross-generational taboos given that her stepson was not significantly younger than she, it struck enough fans as morally inappropriate to cause Eaton to break down in tears on the postshow town meeting episode from the scorn that had been directed at her by the viewing public.[12] On a lighter note, on-line fans had great fun with runner-up Colby Donaldson's enthusiastically confused proclamation that he couldn't wait to have a conjugal visit with his own mother, who visited the set late in the series. Most fans recognized Donaldson's expression as a vocabulary error, but some speculated about an erotic mother-love complex on his part, replicated in his on-show alliance with *Survivor 2* winner (and older woman) Tina Wesson. Kel Gleason, the second tribe member ejected from the game, was shown in the context of the show to have been booted over questions about whether he had indulged in secretive beef jerky eating. Many fans, though, have speculated (on an unclear basis) that public masturbation was really what earned Gleason his ticket to ride.

Perhaps more interesting, however, than these moments of audience attention to perceived sexual transgressiveness is fan discourse about two *Survivor 2* characters who were presented as heteronormative on the show, but were understood quite differently by a number of fans. Varner and, to a lesser extent, Olson were cast by a number of fans as "the gay guys" on *Survivor 2,* despite the absence of any public claim to that identity on the show. Some fans speculated that Varner, a former college cheerleader with a snarky attitude and winning smile, was indeed out on the set, but that editing practices closeted him. This makes sense if one believes that network executives were worried about the show becoming "too gay" after the win of Hatch on *Survivor 1.* Other fans took both Varner's and Olson's primary friendships with women cast members (Varner with Alicia Calaway; Olson with Jerri Manthey) as indicative of their homosexuality, in essence saying that "straight guys bond with other guys, not women, unless they're looking for romance." Because there was no apparent sexual tension in any of Varner's or Olson's pair-bonds, some viewers concluded that the men must be gay. Whether or not these conclusions are accurate, their preponderance among on-line fans frames reality TV as a habitual space for the representation of sexual difference.

Still other viewers underscored particular personal attributes of both Varner and Olson that link with stereotypically gay characteristics. Varner was presented as catty; in his confessionals and conversations with gal pal Calaway, he eagerly swiped at tribe mates for superficial reasons, and generally seemed inclined to gossip about those around him. This behavior, combined with his status as a former cheerleader, culminated in an impression of him as "the gay one." (On an MBTV forum, he was referred to as a "bitchy queen.") Olson's sensitivity and creativity as a musician, paired with his subservience to Manthey, led many viewers to a similar conclusion about him. One post by "Queen of the Harpies" just after the beginning of *Survivor 3* compares Quinton to Varner, Olson, and Hatch: "I'll give [Brandon] a few episodes to improve his standing, but as of now he doesn't strike me as a funny swish like Jeff (LOVED HIM!). He seems like an annoying, whiny one like Mitchell and Rich."

These impressions were developed because of audience interpretation of the show itself, but in the case of Varner and Olson, fans also look for clues outside the text of the program how to learn about the sexuality of the cast members. For instance, in an MBTV forum post just weeks before the premiere of *Survivor 3*, "Diane114" mentions having seen an article on another website (zap2it.com), the language of which leads her to believe that someone from the *Survivor 2* cast is gay. "I cracked up at this quote in the article: 'Also, like previous casts, there is the requisite gay player.' Note the plural, hee!" Diane114 picks up on an easy-to-miss pluralization in order to infer that Hatch was not the only prior player who is gay.

Fans seem so trained by the traditions of the reality genre that they now expect to encounter at least one gay character in any cast—a precedent set by MTV's *The Real World*. In a review of competing reality shows like *Big Brother* and *Fear Factor*, *New York Times* critic Julie Salamon wrote, "In just one year, the reality genre has developed its own set of clichés. The group of contestants must be attractive, they usually include a gay person and a countervailing homophobe."[13] Absent any declaration of outness, viewers are in effect telling producers through the speculations I have discussed that they will find a gay character anyhow.

Gay Man? Check. Raging Stereotype? Check. Survivor 3

Audience members desperately seeking gayness found eye candy in the form of *Survivor 3* cast member Quinton, who was out from the start. In the *Survivor 3* preview edition of *TV Guide,* Quinton is described as "single, gay. Former makeup artist for major department store. Handy skill: Could give immunity idol a makeover. Luxury item: ChapStick."[14] While Quinton provided the raw material for this depiction in his application to the show, selective presentation on the part of *TV Guide* emphasizes his most easily feminizable attributes, leading the audience to certain presumptions even before they have viewed the first episode.

Fan response to the persona of Quinton has been varied and voluminous. From the first week *Survivor 3* aired, there were twice as many MBTV posts on the topic of Quinton than on any other tribe member. Midway through the thirteen weeks of the third season, the topic of Brandon had accumulated 1,560 SF messages from fans, as opposed to 795 for Ethan, who would go on to win, and far fewer for other tribe mates.

A week before the show's October 2001 premiere, MBTV commentary began to crop up: Quinton was hailed as the "irritating" "drama queen" whose "overdramatic arm-flailing irritated [the viewer] as much as his squealy voice." Other comments pitted him as the "Love Child of Jeff Varner and Mitchell Olson," a not-so-subtle reference to fan assumptions about the homosexuality of two *Survivor 2* cast members. One poster quoted *Entertainment Weekly*'s reference to Quinton as "a confused, model type, Richard Hatch," again targeting his homosexuality as one of the defining features of his existence. It is noteworthy, though, that Hatch was received by MBTV audiences as a gay man in a much more favorable manner than Quinton. With some regularity, Quinton was disparaged for being a gay stereotype by both gay and straight fans alike.

Denigration of Quinton on the basis of his expressiveness, however, was met with resistance by some fans. Even in defending him, viewers continued to keep his sexuality in the foreground. Immediately after chastising other fans for rushing to judge Quinton on the basis of a few seconds of footage, MBTV's "SpoilerKing" added, "I hope he's like Jack from *Will and Grace*." In other words, don't mock him for his mannerisms, but keep in mind that they're *undeniably* gay. "Sher," also of MBTV, urged Brandon to flame on and declared her hope that he would be bitchy. Another poster to the same discussion, "Highwaygirl," countered Quinton's detractors, suggesting that although "the only way Brandon could be more of a queen would be if he started wearing a tiara around camp," it didn't matter because "he's camp, funny and entertaining." Quinton is lauded for his love-me-or-leave-me attitude and sense of humor in this post, but his "swishiness" is presented as a potential liability; Highwaygirl utilizes a "but" to reassure her readers that despite his effeminacy, Quinton is still a good time for the straight people. This makes a fascinating contrast to the audience response to Hatch, whose "evil" demeanor seemed to threaten straight fans.

Some armchair critics have pointed out that Hatch was positioned as a rapacious villain, much in the tradition of older TV and film representations of gay characters as bad guys. Interesting, then, is Quinton's framing on *Survivor 3* as neither a pure "black hat" nor a purely angelic overachiever. Yet the complexity of his in-between status has not received universal acclaim among gay fans, who cannot see past the degree to which his stereotypical mannerisms help to reinforce a limited and shopworn notion of gay masculinity as nonexistent. In other words, despite the benefits of Quinton's portrayal as neither wholly good nor wholly evil, his success as an icon for progress in gay representation is compromised because he is exceedingly feminine.

When *Survivor 3* ended, Quinton admitted that part of his desire to appear on the series was to remedy a problem with representation of gays on television as overly promiscuous and partying excessively. (Of course, it is nearly impossible to appear promiscuous when one is stuck in a remote location with no available sex partners.) Instead, Quinton said that he wanted to convey flamboyance and fun, but that perhaps he had failed and was just viewed as bitchy.

Fan response to Quinton on MBTV forums ranged from warmly embracing to sympathetically pitying to outright disdaining his character. From the sympathetic corner comes a post from "Furbgrrl," who frets over Quinton's potential bashing at the hands of "alpha male" tribe mate Silas Gaither: "Since Brandon is close to [Silas's] age (and gay) (and not too athletic looking) I think he makes an obvious target for frat boy Silas." A more critical read of Quinton comes from "Donut," who says, "His 'the-whole-world-owes-me' attitude coz he's gay will draw the boot to his face," and predicts that Quinton's physical weakness will lead to early banishment. On-line fans who support Quinton tend to play up his devastating good looks, sardonic wit, and potential as a poster boy for pride and acceptance of one's sexuality.

Whatever the specific concerns they sought to articulate, the vast majority of fans integrated some consideration of Quinton's gayness into their on-line posts. "Bean," an MBTV participant, predicted in early October 2001 that Brandon would win *Survivor 3* "because everyone's going to hate him in a Richard Hatch kind of way." This is a curious comment, given that Quinton had not evidenced any cunning behavior at this point in the season. The only obvious connection between Hatch and Quinton is their shared homosexual identity, so the "Richard Hatch" kind of hate is presumably homophobia. It is unclear how being the object of homophobia might propel one to the top of a challenging, political game like *Survivor*. Instead, it seems that the function of this post is to remind us once again that Quinton is gay, and as such, his very existence threatens to disturb heterosexual stability. The power of his threat is diluted again and again, however, through fan emasculation of Quinton.

If preshow fan posts like Bean's failed in cementing Quinton's gayness, the visual symbolism of the first episode succeeded. In what can best be described as a semiotics of sexual submissiveness, the viewer is treated to shots of Quinton in sexually receptive poses wherein he thirstily sucks down water from a canteen, and bends over in a rather prone and vulnerable position. Tellingly, the only time that shots of Quinton are de-emphasized on the first episode is during the first Immunity Challenge; perhaps this is the case because Quinton's competent performance in a challenge requiring athleticism allowed editors no visual way to produce a reductive image of him as a weakling.

Beyond the bevy of framing shots on episode one, the rest of *Survivor 3* is edited to frame Quinton as flamboyant, weak, and stereotypically gay. Any mention of weakness is typically accompanied by a shot of Quinton flailing about in a nonverbally expressive and not traditionally masculine manner. At Tribal Councils, host Jeff Probst singles Quinton out to ask if he feels vulnerable, when Brandon has done no more than anyone else that would make him so. The camera lingers on Quinton crying, curled up nearly in a fetal position, after an unusually emotional Tribal Council in episode six. Beyond his camera-manufactured weakness and vulnerability, Quinton comes off as manipulative, too, when in a confessional he criticizes his best friends on the show, Kim Powers and Lindsey Richter, as "bitching, complaining girls." While pride might be taken in his outness, alliances with women fans were knocked asunder when Quinton complained, "It's such a great thing that I'm gay because I could not stand to put up with a crying woman right now."

Discussion of Quinton on MBTV forums just after *Survivor 3* ended shows an overwhelmingly negative reading of him, though whether or not this negativity is the result of homophobia is debatable. "Julieyousuck" argues that "Brandi's one of those snots that [sic] thinks he's way more clever then [sic] he is and is just SO much better than anyone else," and gripes that Quinton was too quick to take center stage in promoting himself via the AIDS charity event that the cast was to be involved in. "Yolliebear" agrees that "Brandi . . . is neither charming, witty or insightful. He's like one of those bubble-headed gossipmongers that are under the illusion that every quip makes them look somewhat intelligent." It is possible to attribute the distaste of these fans for Brandon to their attitudes that his confidence was far more inflated than it should be for someone so likely to be a target of homophobic disparagement. In other words, I do not believe that these MBTV fans disliked Quinton simply for being gay. Trained by reality show conventions to expect more humility from stigmatized characters, these fans were instead put off by his far-from-humble attitude.

Indeed, Quinton's confident attitude may have been surprising and offputting for fans who had come to anticipate a gay cast member (like *Big Brother 2*'s Bunky Miller) who is devastated by the homophobia of a tribe mate. (On *Big Brother 2*, Miller wept in confessionals and agonized over letting an extremely homophobic housemate know of his homosexuality.) Prior to the premiere of *Survivor 3*, entertainment news sources did their part to ratchet up interest in its forthcoming homophobic displays. The *San Francisco Chronicle*, when promoting *Survivor 3*, stated, "Looking for a new variation on Richard Hatch and Rudy Boesch? Watch Brandon and Frank, Probst says. 'Brandon and Frank are definitely on opposite ends of the world.'"[15] While it might be tempting to assume that the Richard/Rudy dynamic replicated by polar opposites Brandon and Frank Garrison is one marked by general competitive tension and dislike, in fact Richard and Rudy got along quite well on *Survivor 1*, remaining loyal to a long-held alliance to one another. On *Survivor 1*, their only disagreement revolved around Rudy's disapproval of Richard's homosexuality. Thus, in playing up the Richard/Rudy–Brandon/Frank similarities, what the *Chronicle* is really doing, in the guise of marketing dramatic conflict, is flagging controversy over the moral appropriateness of homosexuality as a selling point of the new series.

Sure enough, fans picked up on this troubled relationship between Quinton and Garrison and were discussing it on the MBTV forum even before *Survivor 3* premiered. Sher argued that Samburu (one of the two tribes) would be in disarray largely because of this conflict: "The only one who might INSIST on order—Frank—will be locked in battle with Brandon." In popular discourse, there is little correlation between gayness and a lack of tidiness; if anything, fastidiousness is overassociated with male homosexuality. What this excerpt really seems to get at, then, is the connection between homosexuality and deviance, a break from order. It is interesting to see how this post ends up asserting Quinton as the very antithesis of order—an unmakable claim unless one considers his sexual orientation, one of the few preshow tidbits divulged about him. Fan comments of this ilk solidify a reading of Quinton as nonnormative in a troubling way. This interpretation is supported in winner Ethan Zohn's final episode commentary that his competitor, Kim Johnson, would win the votes from women jurors, and that he himself would garner the "guy" vote, and that Quinton had the swing vote. Such a remark places Quinton outside of gender entirely. Such de-gendering of Brandon happened at the hands of fans as well, as in the case of MBTV poster "Model88man," who mused, "How perfect were the pairings for the reward challenge. Hmmmm, boy, girl, boy, girl, boy, girl, boy, . . . Brendon [*sic*]."

On *Survivor 3* itself, through the early episodes, the notion that Frank and Brandon dislike one another is confirmed, though no clear explanation is provided as to why this is the case. Other cast members suggest that Frank would vote Brandon off "on general principle alone," but whether the general principle concerns Brandon's sexuality or something else is never clarified until after the show, when we learn that Frank disapproved of his "lifestyle." The relationship between Frank and Brandon reaches its zenith on episode ten, Brandon's last appearance. After they are forced together as teammates for a Reward Challenge and win, Brandon announces that he's "got a date with Frank" to enjoy dinner and a movie in Africa. To Frank's likely chagrin, this starts a joke fest among other tribe members, who play on the sexual tensions inherent in a typical dinner-and-a-movie situation. Back at camp, Tom Buchanan and Lex Van Den Berghe kid about Brandon's burst of taskmaster energy during the challenge, laying the innuendo thick with lines like "He assumed his position well" and "They found their rhythm together." This can be read as a general expression of heterosexual anxiety, or as a knock on either Frank (whose perspective is "old-fashioned" and thus he would be disturbed by the date with Brandon) or on Brandon (whose disgust for Frank's "redneck" ways looms large).

After Quinton was ousted from *Survivor 3*, his appearances were mostly limited to silent sashays to the jury box. On one episode, he appeared wearing a sarong, and the director quickly cut to other cast members for giggly reaction shots, which were later replicated by fans on-line who took the opportunity to sneer at what they deemed Quinton's gayness-motivated fashion faux pas. Yet fan response to overt displays of homophobia by other fans as well as cast members tolerating homophobia is surprisingly, though not uniformly negative.[16] SF fan "TheTruth" pointed out that "reality shows have [not] showed me how to look at the gay population . . . but instead to look at the other people on the show who are NOT gay, and how they treat them." That TheTruth focuses on the opportunities provided by gay cast mates to make straight characters appear kind and open-minded is troubling; however, TheTruth seems wise in not expecting reality TV to be a standard-bearer for real-life gay folk.

A series of MBTV posts made after the second episode of *Survivor 3* negotiated issues of gay representation on reality shows. "BooHooBaby" kicked off the discussion by asking, "Why oh why can we not have a decent homo on this show???" and categorizing Richard as "a smug bonehead," and Brandon and Mitchell as "closeted jerks." Beyond the reference to fan-perceived homosexuality of Varner and Olson on *Survivor 2,* this post is intriguing in its demand for a "decent homo." Clearly, for BooHooBaby and other viewers, closeting is not an honorable option but being out and "smug," or out, lazy, and unfunny is undesirable as well. Hatch did plenty of work on *Survivor 1*—he caught almost all the fish—but apparently he was not adequately humble. It seems that what fans are asking for in this case is a gay hero/angel—someone who is out, works hard, and is funny and affable. Even for straight reality show cast members whose identities are relatively uncontroversial, this representational ideal is hard to come by, especially given that their TV personas lie in the hands of crafty, conflict-hungry editors. Despite the ideals, almost any reality TV fan will admit that perfectly well-behaved cast members are much less interesting to watch than the seriously flawed types. In response to BooHooBaby, MBTV poster "Gaboriau" maintains that the gay hero ideal is an inappropriate one: "Since most people on these reality shows are not decent human beings to begin with, why should the gay ones be better? That's the result of real acceptance: being portrayed as being as capable of being a jerk as anybody else."

The history of the *Survivor* series shows us that gay male characters have indeed had as much opportunity as anyone else to seem like jerks, and thus have scored a victory for acceptance. From a critical media perspective, where *Survivor* clearly falls short is in its representation of lesbians and bisexuals. But as much attention as gay men garnered in fan discussions, there was relatively little discourse about the absence of out lesbians. One of the few MBTV posts to address the issue came from "Retail Queen," who questioned what people would think about having a real butch lesbian on the show: "A lot of people, including myself, got some gay vibes from Kelly, Sue, and Maralyn, and I wonder how people would perceive a lesbian's talk, walk, demeanor, and body language in the context of the game like they do Brandon and the aforementioned players?"

With few exceptions, fans ignored these types of questions, instead focusing on the easily perceptible affectations of "flamingness" and "swishiness" on the part of male cast members; this speaks to the tradition of lesbian invisibility in media. As I write, *Survivor 5* is two weeks from premiering, and fans are beginning to speculate about the possible lesbianism of a number of the new batch of women characters, none of whom have been identified as such in promotional material. Time will tell if *Survivor* can match the complicated portrayal of gay male sexual identity developed over the first three series with an equally intricate portrayal of other varieties of sexual transgressiveness.

The dialectic between representation of gay men on *Survivor* and fan discourse is suggestive for understanding the mediation of sexual difference by reality TV. In the tradition of youth-oriented reality shows like *The Real World*, *Survivor* remedies gay invisibility problems, though in a limited and not terribly risky manner. Still, even when television images of sexual transgression are conservative and stereotypical, many fans are willing to talk back, to produce contrary readings that value sexual diversity and tolerance of difference.

NOTES

The author acknowledges the Gay and Lesbian Alliance Against Defamation (GLAAD) and the GLAAD Center for the Study of Media and Society for providing grant funding for this study. Special thanks to the director of research at the GLAAD center, Van Cagle, as well as the editors of this volume for comments on the chapter.

1. For scholarship on "fictional" gay media representations, see Larry Gross, *Up from Invisibility* (New York: Columbia University Press, 2002).

2. A possible exception to this presentation of normative heterosexuality might be Greg Buis, the "Ivy League graduate" of the original cast, who explained during episode eight that his sexual experience with men was limited to experimentation. It is unclear whether Greg's admission was a strategic lie or instead an honest revelation of nonnormative sexual practices.

3. "Uber Interactive Publications: Mighty Big TV Information Kit," 2001, http://www.uber.com/publications/mighty_big_tv_information_kit.shtml; viewed 27 August 2001.

4. "Media and Hype," 2001, www.survivorfire.com/faq/php; viewed 6 March 2002.

5. Chris Mann and Fiona Stewart define emoticons as "a form of electronic paralanguage which are used to show affect and to establish relational tone" (*Internet Communication and Qualitative Research: A Handbook for Researching Online* [Thousand Oaks, Calif.: Sage, 2000], 15). Some examples include :-(to indicate sadness, 8-) to indicate a happy spectacle-wearer, and so on.

6. Cited in David Colker, "He Won, He's Gay . . . Now Get over It," *Los Angeles Times*, 28 August 2000, 2.

7. See Amy Forliti, "Ex-'Survivor' Charged with Assault," *Salon.com*, 22 August

2001, http://salon.com/people/wire/2001/08/22/hatch/print.html; viewed 27 August 2001.

8. Hank Stuever, "Hard to Beat, Impossible to Avoid: In Richard, *Survivor* Shows Us an Archetype," *Washington Post,* 23 August 2000, C1.

9. Homophobic comments are made with greater regularity on SF than on MBTV, perhaps as a result of the different communities that congregate on each website. Participants on the former tend to offer less sophisticated, more reactionary responses to show happenings, while at the latter, literate and hip commentary is the norm.

10. See John Carman, "Rudy Survives His Politically Incorrect Act," *San Francisco Chronicle,* 28 August 2000, D1.

11. Cited in Colker, "He Won, He's Gay," 2.

12. An MBTV recap of the "Back from the Outback" episode refers to her as "Debb 'Don't hate me because I have sex with my son-in-law [*sic*]' Eaton," then tells of Eaton's expressed remorse over the "witch-hunt" started by the *National Enquirer.*

13. Julie Salamon, "Evolving Reality TV Tests the Audience's Endurance," *New York Times,* 7 July 2001, B7.

14. "Now Voyagers," *TV Guide* 49, no. 40, 6–12 October 2001, 22. Other entertainment news sources are less leading in their descriptions; for instance, the *San Francisco Chronicle* refers to Quinton as "a gay Dallas bartender who calls himself 'affectionate, smart and manipulative'" (John Carman, "*Survivor* on Safari: Reality Show Treks to Africa with Most Diverse Contestants," *San Francisco Chronicle,* 11 October 2001, B1.

15. Carman, "*Survivor* on Safari."

16. For more on reality show fan frustration with both homophobia and a lack of intervention in homophobic attitudes, see Robert Bianco, "New Rules Won't Buff Up *Big Brother*: It's Promising More Sex, But Nobody Cares," *USA Today,* 10 July 2001, D4. Bianco nominates to the "reality hall of shame" "Kent, the bigoted dolt who proudly proclaims his homophobia, and Bunky, the weepy gay man who puts up with Kent's rants. Kent, get a clue; Bunky, get a spine."

15

The Meaning of Real Life

Justin Lewis

The growth of reality TV or "factual entertainment" has created a hybrid in which the codes of reality and appearance are blurred. We now live in what John Corner refers to as a postdocumentary culture, one in which the traditional codes of documentary realism intermingle with genres based on celebrity and artifice.[1] Perhaps the most conspicuous exercise in genre blending is the gamedoc, which remorselessly blends ideas of authenticity and contrivance to produce a smattering of vox pop celebrities. If we place such developments in the elusive postmodernist narrative, we might argue that the conceptual divisions that distinguish fact from fiction appear to be on the point of collapse.

And yet the very notion of reality TV or factual entertainment suggests a *refusal* to relinquish basic epistemological distinctions. Whether it is makeover shows on which style counselors transform people's living rooms, gardens, personalities, or love lives, or the more fanciful world of gamedoc captivity, the idea that we are watching *real people* in all their unscripted vulnerability is central to the premise of reality TV. As Jon Dovey writes: "The widespread success of programs with this appeal to authenticity occurs at the same time as the widely acknowledged triumph of simulation and spectacle."[2] Television has become postmodern in form while remaining steadfastly modernist in its assumptions.

This chapter considers the drift toward a formal televisual postmodernity in the context of what might be called the *popular epistemology* of TV viewing. How do audiences make sense not only of reality TV but of the relationship between reality and television? Drawing from qualitative research on television audiences, I will suggest that the distinction between authenticity and pretense, between reality and artifice, remains vital to the pleasure and politics of contemporary TV viewing. These distinctions are not simply a reading of formal realist codes but a set of judgments based on specific cultural contexts. Indeed, the contradictions of the popular epistemology of TV viewing precede the genre blending of reality TV. Reality TV, in this sense, has not precipitated any profound shifts in popular consciousness; rather, it expresses the epistemological contradictions already involved in watching television.

Reality TV and Realism

In the academy, it has been some time since realism was considered to be anything other than a construction—an elaboration of codes rather than a form of transparency. Despite this, evocations of "reality" are still a constant presence in public discourse. Our everyday conversations are full of references to reality and real life, and these conversations are filled with distinctions between what is real and what is not. We may not always refer to the same reality, yet the conceptual roots of reality in popular epistemology are deep, and we persist in alluding to it.

If we read through the last twenty years or so of qualitative TV audience research, we might well be struck by how often the words "real" and "unreal" are used in people's discussions about television. In David Morley's book on *Family Television*, Andrea Press's study of *Women Watching Television*, Sut Jhally and Justin Lewis's study of the *Cosby Show*, Lyn Thomas's analysis of fans of "quality" British fiction, and Annette Hill's study of audience responses to factual entertainment, respondents not only invoke the concept of reality persistently, they also use it as a key indicator in their critical evaluation of television and radio programming.[3]

In most audience studies, the ability to signify reality on television is generally seen as positive, while pure fantasy is sometimes dismissed as a pleasant indulgence. This association between realism and value can spill over into other discourses—most notably, as part of a gendered discourse whereby women-oriented television like soap opera is ridiculed for its departures from traditional realism, while the more "masculine" world of news and current affairs is regarded as more serious. In this case, however, the distinction is less between reality and fantasy, and more between the traditional ideas of domestic and public space. Indeed, the popular notion of realism, I would argue, has surprisingly little to do with genre conventions. Even in the postmodern era, perhaps the most common criticism or apologia of television, almost regardless of genre, is that it is unrealistic or that it lacks authenticity. It has to be real.

The only genre that remains free from such criticism, ironically, is the one in which the failure to represent reality might be seen as most germane. News and current affairs programs are still so ideologically loaded with codes of transparency that while their partiality is often questioned, their claim to signify real life is not. So, for example, we might reasonably assert that soap operas give a more accurate representation of the everyday experience of crime than news programs do. Yet news programs remain sacrosanct in terms of popular criticism. This does *not* mean that news programs necessarily play a more pivotal role in popular constructions of reality. As I argue shortly, the kinds of reality evoked by the news have their own distinct conditions of existence, which frequently have less to do with everyday life than with other significations of reality in the mediascape.

Reality TV operates in a more fragile epistemological space, but it is nonetheless part of the continuum between reality and fantasy that remains part of the ritual common sense of TV viewing. Hill's 2002 study of British audience responses to reality TV is full of discussions and assessments of the authenticity or realism of shows like *Big Brother*. Just as with fiction, the notion of the authentic or real is an evaluative and interpretative tool in making sense of factual entertainment. Hill's study suggests that many viewers retain a high degree of skepticism about the reality or authenticity of factual entertainment programs: over half the sample in her survey felt that "the stories in entertainment programs about real people" were sometimes (or in a few cases, always) "made up," and 70 percent felt that members of the public generally overacted for the cameras. Nevertheless, transcripts from discussion groups in the study indicate it is precisely *Big Brother*'s perceived authenticity that constitutes an important part of the show's pleasure. As Hill puts it, viewers "looked for moments of truth which could be glimpsed through the improvised performance of *Big Brother* contestants."[4]

But what does this really mean? A careful reading of the audience research literature generally indicates that the codes most of us actually use to demarcate between fiction and reality are fraught with contradiction and ambiguity. This is so much so that while viewers might, in the abstract sense, adhere to fairly traditional theoretical criteria for evaluating television's attempts at realism, what happens in practice is often quite different.

Television uses various codes to evoke real life (realism in both documentary and fiction are, of course, well documented and contested traditions).[5] One would imagine that it might be helpful to list these codes, thereby constructing an analytic framework to assess where a particular show might fit on a spectrum between reality and fantasy, or authenticity and pretense. The problem with such an exercise is that a program's realism is not perceived as the sum of its parts. Thus, a cartoon loaded with impossibilities—like *The Simpsons*—might be seen as closer to real life than a more conventionally realist form of television. Indeed, the realism of *The Simpsons* can be seen as an offshoot of a popular critique of how families are represented on the conventional U.S. situation comedy. So, for example, unlike more conventional sitcom families, the Simpsons, like their audience, are not especially gifted or attractive and spend much of their time in front of the TV set. What makes this funny and even rather poignant is the contrast with the routine fakery of most other forms of more formally "realist" U.S. television. *The Simpsons* achieves realism, in this sense, through hyperbole, parody, and satire.

In *Family Television*, Morley describes how a number of his respondents compare two television portrayals of working class Londoners: the sitcom *Only Fools and Horses* and the soap opera *Eastenders*. One after another, respondents in Morley's study judge the former to be more "real" (and therefore better) than the latter. At first glance, these evaluations seem to be straightforward. What makes them more complicated is their unpredictability: the program generally criticized by these respondents for its failure to mimic reality, *Eastenders*, is in the tradition of British working-class community dramas based solidly on the conventions of television realism. Like *Eastenders*, the sitcom *Only Fools and Horses* also deals with the vicissitudes of everyday working-class life, and yet its characters are self-consciously more stereotypical and its plotlines considerably less plausible. Realism is, at the very least, *not* the most obvious critical tool with which to simultaneously flaw *Eastenders* and applaud *Only Fools and Horses*.[6]

Both cases imply that the use of everyday words like "real," "realistic," or "authentic" does not coalesce into a coherent system of references. In other words, it is neither clear what is meant by real life or how it is signified televisually. Thus, we cannot assume that reality TV—or even news and current affairs—is, despite its privileged status, any more or less successful in the signification of real life than television fantasy.

It is at this point that postmodernist cultural theory is useful—if only up to a point. The traditional distinctions between everyday experience (or what is commonly understood as real life) and the artificial products of the cultural industries may be part of our culture's common sense, but they preserve a distinction that has become cognitively impractical. John Berger's well-known example of the contradiction between knowledge and experience provides an appropriate metaphor for television viewing: we *know* the earth is revolving around the sun, but our *experience* of a sunset is of the sun revolving around the earth.[7] We know television is a series of simulations, and yet television is so much a part of everyday life that it is difficult to put these simulations into a discrete epistemological category. The world of television does not simply merge with our own; it is as much a part of it as the furniture arranged around it. It is, for most people, part of a daily routine: we arrange our rooms around it and spend a large part of our leisure time watching it.

Television is not a social abstraction—we cannot systematically pluck those hours of the day we spend watching it and disregard them as nothing more than a vicarious, secondhand class of experience. When we turn off the TV we do not suddenly return to a more vivid, less ephemeral space. Watching television is, nonetheless, a different kind of experience, and our partial ability to hold it at a critical distance distinguishes it from most of our other encounters. But unlike the washing up, its epistemological status is continually ambiguous.

Television's capacity to slip in and out of reality's domain makes it acceptable to a culture that might feel uncomfortable with attributing too much importance to something often regarded as essentially frivolous. Our language is full of references to TV's triviality: "it's only television," "it's nothing more than entertainment," and the ultimate dismissal, "it's not real." When, in the early 1990s, U.S. vice president Dan Quayle attacked the popular television character Murphy Brown for choosing to become a single parent (and thereby setting what he felt was a bad example), comedians used the idea of gullibility to ridicule him—pointing out, as one would to a stupid child, that Brown was not a real person. The same kind of gibe was made when TV evangelist Jerry Falwell expressed concern about the gay iconography surrounding Tinky Winky of the *Teletubbies*.[8] The joke works because it appeals to an epistemological common sense. The majority of respondents in Hill's study who expressed doubts about the veracity of factual entertainment like *Big Brother* are therefore making a well-rehearsed gesture. It's TV; of course it's not real. And our ability to be skeptical becomes a form of self-flattery, a measure of our own sophistication.

It is worth noting that this allows the other side of television's ambiguity—those moments, for example, where we do accept Murphy Brown as a realist discourse—to go uninterrogated. At a distance, the audience knew that Brown was not real, but most viewers did not then simply disregard her or the world she inhabits. There may, for instance, be aspects of Brown's world of pinkish, worthy journalism that feed a powerful, ideologically loaded discourse in the United States about the "liberal media." For all our self-professed savvy about the "unreal" nature of the TV world, fictional television provides semiotic resources to draw on for describing the category of real life.

In our culture, television's influence is contingent on this ambiguity. During audience research on the meaning of *The Cosby Show* in the United States, this ambiguity manifested itself with remarkable clarity.[9] *The Cosby Show* was understood by most of the respondents as both very real and patently unreal. A typical pattern emerged from analysis of the transcripts. Respondents would often begin a discussion of *The Cosby Show* with favorable comments about (for want of a better word) its "realness." The show was repeatedly contrasted with less convincing sitcoms for its persuasive representation of family life, of a familiar everyday world. It was, to paraphrase many respondents, "just like real life," an assessment that encouraged a high degree of identification from black and white viewers alike. As one discussion group member put it: "I think Cosby is much more true to life [than other sitcoms]. You can put yourself right into the picture. Just about everything they do has happened to you, or you've seen it happen."[10] Later during the same interview, this respondent—like many others—would frequently adopt a more critical posture, and in so doing, chastise the show for its distance from the real world, for its candy-floss portrayal of genial familial affluence.

Thomas's study of fans of the long-running British BBC radio soap opera (something of a misnomer—over fifty years old, the radio show has never been used as a vehicle to sell soap powder) *The Archers* suggests very much the same back-and-forth: a "tendency to slip from the critical commentary mode, often expressing awareness of the text as a construction and of the agents of its production, to talk about the characters, or stories, as if they were real."[11] And as other audience studies reveal, the moments when the fiction does not "ring true" (as one *Archers* fan puts it) are generally troubling.

These contradictions are neither conscious nor overt; at one moment in the conversation it is appropriate to talk about the show's realism, and at another it becomes necessary to take a philosophical step backward and expose the shallow nature of that realism. This points to a culture with the ability to move almost seamlessly in and out of different perceptual planes, to think of a fictional program as both real and unreal.

Faced with neatly typed interview transcripts, the contrast between such contradictory declarations about *The Cosby Show* or *The Archers* is, with the luxury of hindsight, fairly noticeable. At first, the contrast appears like an aberrant moment in an otherwise consistent discourse, but a closer reading of the transcripts indicates quite the opposite. The conversations shifted continually and effortlessly between two distinct and different epistemological frameworks. Once we begin to appreciate the way the two frameworks operate, these shifts start to make sense. Put simply, at one moment the shows are discussed as a piece of fiction, at another as if they are a piece of real life. Reality TV, with its mix of vox pop authenticity, fakery, and contrivance, expresses these contradictions more overtly, but in doing so, it merely triggers an epistemological paradox that precedes it.

Reality TV is thus merely a reflection of television's own ambiguity: as an object, it is both external and internal to our world. Its characters live in two dimensions, they enter our lives from another place, beamed from distant worlds to take a routine and everyday part in the ordinariness of our own. While others have made a similar point about television as an interface, the ideological consequences of this ambiguity require exploration.[12] In the case of *The Cosby Show,* the ability to see television as both an expression of reality and an inconsequential fantasy is not just an innocent curiosity. This ambiguity is associated with specific beliefs about what the real world is and how it works. There are, moreover, pervasive racial attitudes that are contingent on it.

For most white respondents, television shows like *Cosby* fed into a discourse that, as one man put it, "there really is room in the United States for minority people to get ahead, without affirmative action."[13] This belief sits side by side with the grimmer reality of widespread black poverty, a world *also* signified by TV on news programs, alongside countless fragments of other everyday experiences. Caught in the glare of this racial contrast, television's host of black professionals seem tangential. For a moment they become irrelevant, like intruders from a happier world—at least until they insinuate themselves back into a routine punctuated by the grammar of television's realist narratives. In a rather different context, both Press and Thomas suggest that viewers and listeners make judgments based on ideological suppositions about social class, and these judgments are in turn reinforced by fictional constructions of class behavior.

This ideological framework is not entirely a product of television, but the complex epistemology of TV viewing has helped shape its form and given it substance. It is in this sense that television plays a significant part in the construction of real life. Just as there are moments of critical detachment, when the distinction between the television world and real life are at the surface of our culture's consciousness, there are also times when we draw on television to define the parameters as well as properties of what we understand as reality.

The Two Epistemes

One of the features of public life in the mediascape is that for most of us, most of the time, it is beyond our tactile experience—it is something that goes on elsewhere. We can accept the veracity of two distinct realities: the one we live in and the mediascape. The first is generally signified by the people and things that surround us, and the second within the broad parameters of the cultural industries. I have suggested that in contemporary culture, these two worlds are juxtaposed so routinely that they seem to be two aspects of a single epistemological category. We eat dinner, watch TV, talk about TV, do the dishes. The other world overlaps with our own: it is part of us, and we feel that we are part of it.

On the surface, this appears to match the strain in postmodernist theory that suggests we have reached a point where the two worlds have become indistinguishable. Jean Baudrillard's version of an organic metropolis—where television viewers are merely an animate extension of television itself, fully ingesting television's exterior world—is a compelling piece of hyperbole.[14] Research on cultural reception indicates the presence of a more intricate, complex process. It is not just that television viewing is more existentially active.[15] There is evidence that even though we may only consciously refer to one reality, we can identify *two adjacent realities,* each with its own conditions of existence. One is the world of everyday experience, and the other is the world of, say, asylum seekers, experts, the victims of "collateral damage" in some foreign land, celebrity culture, politicians, and whoever else occupies the mediascape. The two worlds may intermingle and overlap, but they have their own identifiable norms and values. The gamedoc epitomizes these two epistemes: it places people from the everyday world and thrusts them into an adjacent tele-reality—whether it be the virtual verité of the *Big Brother* house, the studio wilderness of *Survivor,* or the tabloid wonderland of *Temptation Island.*

In an elegant twist, George Orwell's metaphor has turned in on itself, as people compete with one another to live in a house under constant surveillance—watched not by shadowy government officials but by people in search of entertainment. The connotations of the phrase "Big Brother" are no longer sinister but benign, a chance for people defined as ordinary to reach the modest heights of C-list celebrity stardom (and in case we miss the point, it is the TV series that has attempted to fix this connotation through the sinister apparatus of trademark law). This creates something of an epistemological tension as the "ordinary folk" in the *Big Brother* house drift into the other reality of the mediascape.

In these ambiguous moments, how do we decide which epistemological rationale to use to interpret what we see? On one level, this depends partly on our distance from the world represented in the mediascape. In short, the closer television gets to the circumstances of our own lives, the closer our scrutiny. Morley's respondents were able to cast doubt on the realism of *Eastenders* because they were, in a geographic, cultural, and demographic sense, close to the world being represented. In much the same way, the middle-class white women in Press's study were (superficially at least) apt to question the truth of television's portrayals of middle-class white women.[16] Working-class women, on the other hand, were more inclined to accept the realism of these representations. In Thomas's *Archers* study, the nuances of social class become more acute, with middle-class fans using their own cultural milieu to comment on the perceived implausibility of cross-class relationships. In their cross-cultural study of *Dallas,* Elihu Katz and Taimar Liebes indicated that those least familiar with U.S. culture seemed to accept the program as a realist discourse. The closer respondents came to a familiarity with life in the United States, the more *Dallas* faded into the realm of a pleasant but inconsequential fantasy.[17]

Similarly, as Hill's study suggests, if we apply high levels of epistemological scrutiny (at least at certain moments) to reality TV, it is because we "know" enough about the kinds of people thrust into its spotlight to judge whether or not they might be faking it. Watching *Celebrity Big Brother,* on the other hand, would appear to be a quite different epistemological experience, one in which we watch *other* people in another world.

The pattern indicated here is not quite as simple as it might initially appear. It is not explained by the notion that familiarity breeds a contempt for television realism. Press describes moments in her study, for example, when her middle-class respondents appear to forget their critical distance and accept the "realness" of their televisual counterparts. Respondents in the *Cosby* study reveal a similarly ambiguous relationship to realist television. Rather, what these studies suggest is the presence of two discrete sets of criteria for evaluating what (on television) is real and what is not: the more tactile reality of our immediate environment and the more symbolic reality of the world beyond it.

These two realities may be interspersed, but they are analytically dichotomous. Some of the judgments we make about public life spring from our own direct experience of the world—an experience that may allow us to evaluate attempts at television realism. Others are made in terms of our cultural environment—an environment in which we produce meanings but not messages. It is an environment inhabited by other people (some like us, others not), and its features are constantly signified by television and the other cultural industries. Even though we only partially accept the truth of the television world, the sum total of everything we do accept (consciously or unconsciously) blends with countless more semiotic fragments from magazines, books, advertisements, and other representations to constitute the vast, pulsating mass of the reality beyond our own. If we are unable to make judgments in terms of our immediate experience, we make them in terms of our experience of this parallel world.

Some of the most profound moments of this process occur when we make political decisions. The idea that we, the public, vote with our wallets or pocketbooks is one of the more misleading political clichés of our age. The use of the cold, hard measure of economic self-interest—with all its implications of an integrated, rational system of representation-is rarely what governs our occasional metamorphosis into "voters." For most people, the political world has little domestic relevance. It is much more identifiably part of an opaque reality that is familiar yet remote. It therefore makes sense to evaluate politicians—who appear on our screens or in newsprint as the characters from a sometimes impenetrable and often rather tedious soap opera—in terms of the more distant realities constructed by, for example, television news. Put bluntly, if these characters appear to perform well *within the specific ideological confines of the mediascape,* then we are more inclined to vote for them.

In this context, we are encouraged to assess political debates or campaigns in the journalistic terms of the mediascape rather than immediately rational terms. What matters is not the specific effects of policy proposals on our own lives but who "won" and who is, by inference, the "best candidate." Thus, with a curious concoction of alienated altruism, we are deciding what is best in terms of a more distant reality. We think in terms of grand ideological entities such as "the nation" or "the economy"— places where the contradictions and oppositions that are the stuff of politics melt into mythical commonalities, and where we, as a mere audience, are reduced to a single identity united by archaic metaphors. It is a place where we are, like passengers on the ark, "all in the same boat."

Even the political science literature supporting notions of a functioning democracy based on a rational public avoids interrogating the notion of rational self-interest too closely. The body of scholarship in support of a "rational public" suggests little more than that when we vote or give responses to public opinion pollsters, we do so for a reason (rather than arbitrarily) based on the available information.[18] What remains relatively unexplored are the different rationalities that apply both to the mediascape and our own more immediate realities outside that media world.[19]

It is in these terms that the commonly made declaration that "I'm not interested in politics" makes sense. Politics, in this instance, is not what happens to me or my immediate environment; it is removed and neatly compartmentalized. Politics is not understood as a practice but as *genre*. To find politics dull is, in this sense, a form of disinterest that we might equally apply to sitcoms or cookery programs.

Like other genres, politics has its own codes without being entirely autonomous. Although we understand sport on television in terms of its own distinct conventions, the meaning of TV sport may be connected to our experience of other genres, such as TV drama or advertising. Politics may be substantively constructed by political programs (like news and current affairs), but it is elaborated by all the other realist discourses on television, by the conglomeration of signs whose final signification is the real world as we know it.

In *Women Watching Television,* Press describes how a number of the working-class respondents in her study "do not trust their experience of the middle-class world . . . seeming more inclined instead to accept television's representations of that world."[20] She cites a conversation with one of her interviewees about the reality of women in the law. They are discussing female lawyers, and her respondent is asked to say who is more "typical," the one female attorney she happens to have met or Clair Huxtable, the fictional lawyer from *The Cosby Show*. She is, indirectly, being asked to choose between the veracity of her immediate reality and the more distant reality of television. Her response is unequivocal:

> *Interviewer:* You know one woman attorney. Did she remind you of Clair?
> No. Not even closely. Because she wasn't as feminine as Clair Huxtable.
> *Interviewer:* Who do you think is more typical of female attorneys?
> Clair Huxtable.
> *Interviewer:* Why?
> Well, because I've seen other ones on television like on the news and other things like that, and they are all more feminine than the one I knew.[21]

If we see the world as two adjacent realities, her answer makes a great deal of sense. The world inhabited by attorneys is something she is much more likely to experience on television than in her everyday life. The female lawyer she knows is an anomalous intrusion into her immediate environment, the kind of person who fits more naturally into a quite different, though vividly familiar version of real life. In this instance, she is bound to trust her experience of television more than her own fairly fleeting encounter. This is, for her, television's territory, and so she prefers the logic of the mediascape to make judgments about authenticity.

Her response also reveals the epistemological conventions behind the intertextual construction of television reality. When asked to make statements about what we know, to self-consciously give evidence about the nature of real life, we still privilege the genres of reality TV (like the news). It is less convincing—even gullible—to be heard to cite television fictions as a form of knowledge about the real world. And yet, in this case, given the paucity of female attorneys on the news and their comparative abundance in fictional genres, she must inevitably be drawing on images established in the latter rather than the former. The merging of realism with reality TV is a condition of our experience of the world, even if it is at odds with the common epistemological framework that generally keeps them apart.

Making Sense of TV Realities

It is difficult to consciously draw a line between the logic of the mediascape and the way we make sense of the unmediated world. This is not only because we are taught to acknowledge one reality, not two, but because for much of the time, most of us do not need to. The two epistemological logics survive in modern democracies partly because they only rarely encroach on one another. When obvious contradictions arise, one episteme tends to be dominant enough to impose a framework with which to refute the other. The immediate experience of working-class East London was, in Morley's study, coherent enough for respondents to question the realism of *Eastenders.* Conversely, for one of Press's interviewees, the television experience of members of the legal profession was more extensive and authoritative than her own personal encounters.

Part of the pleasure of reality TV is the way it allows us to apply our expertise about so-called ordinary people to the less tangible logic of the mediascape. Unlike politicians or characters on a soap opera, whose realities follow their own particular scripted narrative, the actions of ordinary people are more intimately knowable. For all the artifice of the mediascape surrounding them, they appear to be "people like us." We know (or like to think we know) when they are authentic or when they are faking it. As a respondent in Hill's study explains, "It's like I watch it and see if I was on *Big Brother,* I'd want everyone to like me. . . . I'd be acting different . . . maybe that's why I think they're acting up."[22] This "acting up" is not the carefully scripted kind of a public figure or TV actor but from our closer, more amateur world.

It is, in many ways, astonishing how smoothly our culture negotiates the tension between these realities. If the notion of real life that emerges is postmodern—in its elevation of appearance—its foundation is a very modernist denial of the different epistemologies that constitute it. It is a framework that regardless of its instability, stays remarkably intact.

After all, we have passed the stage where our cultural industries merely litter the landscape. The metropolitan environment is a confusion of things and representations of things: layers of images—from television screens, storefronts, billboards, magazines, and T-shirts—merge into the bricks and mortar, the furniture and functionalism, of everyday objects. Some of the objects themselves are so remorselessly commodified that they are both literal and metaphoric entities: in a jumble of connotations, the car parked on the streetscape signifies within the system of slick advertising images and the more mundane system of objects that surround it. This is not new: but whether we regard it as an excess of modernism or the onset of postmodernism, it is now pervasive. And while there is a commentary on this process within the academy, the culture itself is cognitively and philosophically ill equipped to deal with it.

If the epistemological conditions of culture have been transformed by the twentieth century, epistemologies themselves are, like continents, far less mutable. It is not that a sturdy, modernist epistemology is no longer appropriate (without wishing to be coy, it is as appropriate as it ever was). It is, however, hard to sustain. The culture teaches us to accept commonplace remarks about the realism of images—that they are true to life, realistic, unreal, or unbelievable—at face value.

Consequently, and without acknowledgment, our culture's notion of reality works within two parallel, but quite distinct frames of reference. It infers two discrete notions of truth: so, for example, a representation may be unreal because it is incompatible with our own immediate reality, or it may be out of kilter with a more distant notion of realism.

The two meanings have their own inflections. They are based on different epistemes with their own distinct conditions of existence. The first depends on the more interactive, concrete semiotic structure of our immediate environment, and the second relies on the complex signifying systems used by the cultural industries to invoke a less local reality. In one vital ideological sweep, both are unified under the heading of "real life."

Most of us inhabit a space in the gray area between these two epistemes. We flit back and forth so often and so habitually that we lose our grip on where we are. If we are in theory sure of our ground, the practicalities of living almost simultaneously under two sets of epistemological conditions engulf us. Shows like *Big Brother* or *Survivor* express these two sets of conditions perfectly—it is here, perhaps more than anywhere else, that the ordinary world invades the mediascape. But the consequent intermingling does not change the epistemology of TV viewing; it merely juxtaposes two epistemes rather more vividly.

NOTES

1. John Corner, "Performing the Real: Documentary Diversions," *Television and New Media* 3, no. 3 (August 2002): 255–70.

2. Jon Dovey, "Reality TV," in *The Television Genre Book,* ed. Glen Creeber (London: British Film Institute, 2001), 137.

3. See David Morley, *Family Television* (London: Comedia, 1986); Andrea Press, *Women Watching Television* (Philadelphia: University of Pennsylvania Press,

1991); Sut Jhally and Justin Lewis, *Enlightened Racism: The Cosby Show, Audiences, and the Myth of the American Dream,* (Boulder, Colo.: Westview, 1992); Lyn Thomas, *Fans, Feminisms, and "Quality" Media* (London: Routledge, 2002); and Annette Hill, *"Big Brother*: The Real Audience," *Television and New Media* 3, no. 3 (2002): 323–39.

4. Hill, *"Big Brother,"* 324.

5. See, for example, John Corner, *The Art of Record* (Manchester: Manchester University Press, 1996); John Fiske, *Television Culture* (London: Methuen, 1987); and Brian Winston, *Lies, Damn Lies, and Documentary* (London: British Film Institute, 1995).

6. See Morley, *Family Television.*

7. John Berger, *Ways of Seeing* (Harmondsworth, U.K.: Penguin, 1972).

8. See Heather Hendershot, "Teletubby Trouble," *Television Quarterly* 31, no. 1 (2000): 19–25.

9. See Jhally and Lewis, *Enlightened Racism.*

10. Ibid., 28.

11. Thomas, *Fans, Feminisms, and "Quality" Media,* 124, 110.

12. On TV as an interface, see, for example, Roger Silverstone, *The Message of Television* (London: Heineman, 1981).

13. Jhally and Lewis, *Enlightened Racism,* 88.

14. Jean Baudrillard, *America* (London: Verso, 1988).

15. See John Docker, *Postmodernism and Popular Culture: A Cultural History* (Cambridge: Cambridge University Press, 1994).

16. Press, *Women Watching Television.*

17. Elihu Katz and Tamar Liebes, "Mutual Aid in the Decoding of *Dallas,*" in *Television in Transition,* ed. Philip Drummond and Richard Paterson (London: British Film Institute, 1985), 187–98.

18. See, in particular, Benjamin Page and Robert Shapiro, *The Rational Public* (Chicago: University of Chicago Press, 1992); Samuel Popkin, *The Reasoning Voter: Communication and Persuasion in Presidential Campaigns* (Chicago: University of Chicago Press, 1991); and Paul Sniderman, Richard Brody, and Philip Tetlock, *Reasoning and Choice: Explorations in Political Psychology* (New York: Cambridge University Press, 1991).

19. See Justin Lewis, *Constructing Public Opinion: How Elites Do What They Like and Why We Seem to Go Along with It* (New York: Columbia University Press, 2001).

20. Press, *Women Watching Television,* 111.

21. Ibid., 110.

22. Cited in Hill, *"Big Brother,"* 334.

16

"Kiss Me Kat"

Shakespeare, Big Brother, *and the Taming of the Self*

John Hartley

This chapter is about the democratization of playing. The performance of the self is now done by citizens for themselves and for each other, not by representative actors. The source of meaning is now located in the consumer, not the producer. The creation of meaning is now an editorial or "redactional" act, not an authorial one. *Big Brother* is a latter-day version of William Shakespeare's "the taming of the self."

Reality Shakespeare

> The *Value*, or WORTH of a man is . . . not absolute; but a thing dependent on the need and judgment of another. . . . And as in other things, so in men, not the seller, but the buyer determines the Price. For let a man (as most men do) rate themselves as the highest Value they can; yet their true Value is no more than it is esteemed by others.   Thomas Hobbes, 1651[1]

Like Endemol's *Big Brother,* Shakespeare's *The Taming of the Shrew* was a modern, interactive, commercial entertainment, produced by an entrepreneurial joint stock company and performed for profit to a secular, anonymous, popular audience of mixed class, age, and gender. Similarly, Endemol, cofounded by theatrical impresario Joop van den Ende and TV producer John de Mol, combined theater and live events with TV entertainment.[2] Like TV audiences, spectators in the Elizabethan playhouses were encouraged to reconsume formats (for instance, comedy bearbaiting), but to watch a given production only once.[3] Such shows like *Big Brother* and *The Taming of the Shrew* were full of "mirth and merriment," as one of them put it, but they also touched on important contemporary issues of identity formation, including citizenship, domestic comportment, and self-management.

The Taming of the Shrew included various stock characters, as carefully chosen as the housemates on *Big Brother*, to portray familiar types within the target demographic of the popular audience—for instance, a drunk (Sly), a braggart (Petruchio), a "shrew" or scold (Katharina), and the Elizabethan equivalent of a young cutie (Bianca). It was full of stagy artifice— disguises, inversions, cross-dressing—and was not above some bawdy humor. Like *Big Brother*, *The Taming of the Shrew* put these formulaic elements into an unfolding series of tests, observing how the characters dealt with situations and relationships about which the audience knew more than they did, and the game eventually produced a winner—Petruchio (5.2.187–88).

All this theatrical artifice was in the service of a greater transparency. Like a contemporary television audience schooled in recombinant formats, reversioning, and remediation, Shakespeare's audience was "literate" as to the format and characters of comedies like *The Taming of the Shrew*. Spectators could see the "pleasing stuff" of the play and enjoy that; but they could also see *through* it to the conduct of human relationships within.

Scott Olson has claimed this kind of transparency for Hollywood narrative: "*Transparency* is defined as any textual apparatus that allows audiences to project indigenous values, beliefs, rites, and rituals into imported media."[4] He suggests that an audience's *readings* of "transplanted" dramatic narratives such as those from Hollywood (which conform to an identifiable typology) are "indigenous" to the culture where the audience is located. For Olson, therefore, transparent formats are the reverse of media imperialism (luckily for Hollywood): "The indigenous culture actively reaches out, haggles, and does not merely absorb . . . some set of injected cultural values."[5]

Olson is at one with Shakespearean scholar Terence Hawkes. For him, the whole point of Shakespeare, like Hollywood and television for later ages, was to draw disparate populations together, to address humanity in scale. Hawkes argues that the Elizabethan theater was part of a "communal experience":

Its audience, and its plays, were genuinely "popular"; the result of an amalgam of the elements of the culture, and an artistically honest "projection" of it. When that amalgam disintegrated, the "universality" which can be felt in the plays vanished. . . . [Elizabethan] theatre can never be reproduced, but its true heir in our culture can only be television. Television constitutes the only really "national" theatre our society is likely to have.[6]

The "universality" for its own time that Hawkes felt in both Shakespearean theater and television is nothing other than the "transparency" Olson discovered in Hollywood narratives.[7] Olson's assertion is couched in the language of national cultural competitiveness amid fears of media effects at the international as well as individual level. Hawkes's language is that of the humanist interpreter of drama who sees television *as* Shakespearean theater, not least in its relationship with a popular audience who is by no means passive in either case:

[Television] does encourage . . . participation, vocal and positive. . . . And this kind of participation . . . is of the same order as that which formed a distinctive part of the traditional theatrical experience in Shakespeare's theatre. The interjected comments of the audience on a play, and their "participation" in it became common enough practice for this to be included as part of plays themselves; e.g. *The Taming of the Shrew.*[8]

For its part, *Big Brother* is taken as both indigenous (local housemates) and universal (human qualities, dilemmas, and ruses) in each of its national territories—Argentina, Australia, Belgium, Brazil, Denmark, France, Germany, Greece, Hungary, Italy, Mexico, Netherlands, Norway, Poland, Portugal, South Africa, Spain, Sweden, Switzerland, the United Kingdom, and the United States.[9] It features multinational transmission and interactive reception. It betrays nothing of its Dutch origins in any version outside the Netherlands. It is popular in the United States, but it did not originate there. *Big Brother* engages audiences in much more activity than just narrative reception, using phone, modem and screen, extensive media coverage and tie-ins in the press, radio and live events, and the independent yet linked efforts of advertisers, fans, and critics. It gathers international populations while recognizing national differences, and encourages cross-demographic and multiplatform talk about human character, interaction, and plot.

For Shakespeare's own early modern audience, caught imperfectly between cultures (for instance, medieval role and rank versus modern job and identity), plays such as *The Taming of the Shrew* could be regarded as transparent narratives in Olson's terms, universal in Hawkes's, and interactive in *Big Brother*'s. Here was a textual apparatus about rich Italians (the Renaissance equivalent of North Americans) for which hard up English subjects were prepared to pay. Shakespeare's entertainments evidently spoke directly to the conditions in which the audience lived, drawing people in the thousands to the unregulated south bank of the Thames, where they merrily projected their human "values, beliefs, rites, and rituals," both individual and socialized, into *The Taming of the* Shrew, even though it was set in Padua and performed by celebrity actors—one of whom was Shakespeare.

Like television, Shakespeare's theater was dedicated to cross-demographic communication. This was also its business plan since the production costs of the plays and capital costs of the theaters required audience maximization. As in any modern commercial entertainment, the customers were in a pecuniary relationship with a capitalist corporation, but at the level of meaning, the cash nexus did not prevent something worthwhile passing between producer and consumer. Posterity is clear on this point.

Because of the semiotic intensity of the English vernacular in the Elizabethan period, Shakespeare was part of a culture that transmitted through time as well as across demographic and national borders. His plays could be received by later audiences as applicable to, indeed part of, their own cultural and personal identity, and therefore as "indigenous," "universal," and "participatory" all at once. Since the 1590s, *The Taming of the Shrew* itself has been reversioned into various new media formats, including the 1807 prose narrative of Charles Lamb's *Tales from Shakespeare*, Cole Porter's 1948 musical *Kiss Me Kate*, a 1957 Bolshoi opera, and a 1967 Franco Zeffirelli blockbuster starring Richard Burton and Elizabeth Taylor. It was rescripted into the 1999 teen movie *Ten Things I Hate about You*, set at Padua High School, and starring Kat Stratford (Julia Stiles), Patrick Verona (Heath Ledger), and Kat's cute sister Bianca (Larisa Oleynik).[10]

The Taming of the Shrew was indigenized in places culturally even more remote from Elizabethan London than a Tacoma, Washington, high school. For instance, it was successfully produced in Moscow in 1937–1938 by Alexei Popov, known as the people's artist of the Soviet Union, as a play for the Red Army; "Shakespeare's humanism is understandable and congenial to our men and to our officers," Popov maintained.[11] And it was also performed by the Kazakh Theatre of Drama in Alma-Ata in 1943—a testing year for the USSR. Its spirit lived on. Popov justified putting on a play that some thought "ideologically doubtful":

> Shakespeare the humanist makes it clear that the union of man and woman is only possible on a basis of mutual love and respect. And this makes Shakespeare a great ally in our struggle for a happy, self-respecting and strong humanity. . . . The popular eternal wisdom of Shakespeare leads him to resolve this question [how to achieve a happy marriage] *in the spirit in which it is resolved by all progressive minds.*[12]

This was narrative transparency incarnate, as was Hollywood and TV during the American Century; as is *Big Brother*.[13] In each case—Shakespeare, Hollywood, television, reality—highly artificial and commercial forms work because despite demographic differences, audiences are able to "read" them as "we" rather than "they" for the purposes of exploring the vicissitudes of human relations as entertainment. Their transparency arises from their universalizing human interest within a popular dramatic tradition.

This requires of audiences something that the critic S. L. Bethell has called "multiconsciousness."[14] It is necessary for playgoers to attend to the unfolding immediacy of the diegetic world imagined in a play, while remaining delightedly aware of both its artifice and their own active presence within it. In Shakespeare's day, shows were put on during daylight hours, in the all-too-visible round of the "wooden O," and many plays featured direct address to individuals in the audience.[15] *The Taming of the Shrew* capitalized on the fuzzy line between audience and show by opening with characters (Sly and his supposed wife) who settled down, in character, amid good-humored banter that was nevertheless scripted, to enjoy the show with the paying customers. In this multiconscious context audiences attended, with the lively and interactive pleasure of "communal experience," to the narrative, action, and characters, and to the spoken dialogue that both contributed to and resolved the uncertainty of outcome over a fairly substantial period of time.

How would the actors, especially various couples of marriageable age, deal with each other, with the trials and tribulations of the plot and with the artifice itself, using modern personal resources (such as native wit and mental stratagems) rather than medieval social position (say, paternal authority), as they strove—and this was the entertainment at the time—to achieve personal goals and manage interpersonal relations to maximum individual benefit within generic expectations and social norms? That was the question. How can men and women live, together, at home? *Big Brother* uses the resources of multiplatform broadcast and interactive media to pose it again.

Like *The Taming of the Shrew, Big Brother* draws attention to its audience in a big way. In the Australian version (with which I am most familiar) the *Big Brother* house is located in a theme park called Dreamworld in Queensland, where a live audience of up to one thousand regularly gather on the set—about as drunk and randy as Shakespeare's Christophero Sly by the look of some of them—and the show constantly invokes, exhorts, and includes them as well as the viewers at home, interactively through votes and polls, and in their dealings with commercial partners such as purveyors of pizza and soft drinks.

Indeed, the triumph of the audience over the players is what has made *Big Brother* an interesting phenomenon, but not by any means a one-off. It is the latest in a long line of successive developments that has made each new medium seem both more transparent and more interactive in its dealings with audiences, at least to observers. Like Shakespeare, *Big Brother*'s appeal is that it comes across as unmediated (that is, as reality) in relation to people's character, while remaining intransigently artificial in its form of presentation. Technique delivers transparency; artifice enables human interaction—live, now.

Broadcast television itself was welcomed thus by its own pioneers. Writing at the end of the 1940s, Maurice Gorham (a top BBC executive) mused on what it was that made television into a distinctive medium in its own right:

> The ability to transmit images of things that are actually happening, whether or not they are enacted specially, is the hallmark of television as compared with films. . . . The appeal is simplest and most unmistakable when it is a question of real events in which people are interested, and not events created by the effort of writers, actors, and producers.[16]

In other words, reality TV came in with the medium. The demand was for an immediacy of contact with events that were as unmediated as possible. Television promised a *more* transparent access to allegedly real events than was possible with cinema or radio, and this was taken to be its sign of real value. In historical terms, the promise of the new medium was not to supplant its predecessors but to increase audience access to unmediated actuality.

From the audience's point of view, television was not only "now," but also "here." From the outset, the domestic location of broadcasting as an audience experience was welcomed. In 1952, film documentarian Michael Clarke hailed television because it could draw modern society's otherwise atomized and selfish individualists together. TV would lessen the "isolation of the individual. . . . For the television set in hundreds of thousands of homes ought to be a tremendous influence to make us better informed about the fascinating detail of the complex, modern world." This influence occurred "in our homes, where we are least vulnerable to the illusions to which, in the group, we might succumb. . . . We all need the easy, informal education that television can provide."[17]

Gorham thought "real events" meant public staged happenings that were independent of their transmission on television—that is, sport and spectacle from horse racing to coronations. Clarke thought the "easy education" provided by TV would be about science and politics. But the "fascinating detail of the complex, modern world" that really interested families at home was domestic life itself—their own relationships and self-formation within that context. Those "real events in which people are interested" turned out to be pitched at an anthropological as well as a social level, like meeting a potential romantic date (*Perfect Match, Blind Date*) or—and this is *Big Brother*'s appeal—getting along with people who might turn out, as in real life, to be both friend and competitor, neighbor and enemy/lover, a sleaze or a shrew. It took TV a while to perfect the techniques whereby such real events could be artificially produced, live and now, for prime-time entertainment. With *Big Brother,* audiences have found a highly artificial, but trustworthily transparent vehicle to observe and participate in human emotions, stratagems, characters, and relationships as they unfold in a domestic setting, and as they are tested, sometimes to destruction. And *Big Brother* shares the authorial function with the audience, making the progress and outcome of the onscreen drama a collective "act."

Both *The Taming of the Shrew* and *Big Brother* begin with a reflexive episode that draws attention to their status as shows. In the case of *Big Brother* in Australia, it is the scene-setting opening episode of the second series, April–June 2002. Would audiences "get in character" and follow the show, or would they heave a collective shrug of "been there, done that," and leave the new housemates to their fate? *Big Brother* rose to the challenge with a season opener that according to one ratings expert at the time, "brained everything across the market."[18] It was the number two show nationally that week. Ostensibly it was to "meet the housemates," but the preview was also a revealing exposé of *Big Brother* itself: a show about the show. It tutored viewers in what happened on the set and how it was done, including footage showing how potential housemates were auditioned and chosen on dramatic criteria as characters in a cast. Simultaneously, it relied on the audience's existing knowledge to increase their fun and involvement. It was about the "literacy" of viewers in the format; allusive, knowing, upgrading the skills and insights that viewers would need to get the most out of the series. It shared the gag with them while asking them to enjoy the show, displaying the artifice to expose the art.

The Taming of the Shrew also opens with an episode that is about the play to come. The "Induction" is a comic scene in which a lowlife character called Christophero Sly is sleeping it off after having been thrown out of a pub. He is found by a passing lord, who decides to "practice on this drunken man" by concocting a "flattering dream or worthless fancy" that will make Sly "forget himself." His attendants will take the still sleeping drunkard to the Lord's own "fairest chamber." On awakening, Sly is to be treated like a lord, and convinced by everyone in the household—including the Lord's page boy, who will pose as the man's wife—that he is in fact a lord and not a beggar. As one of them says, "We will play our part, as he shall think . . . he is no less than what we say he is" (Induction.1.36–71).

The Lord has a lascivious fantasy about his pageboy as a woman:

> Such duty to the drunkard let him do
> With soft low tongue and lowly courtesy,
> And say "What is't your honor will command,
> Wherein your lady and your humble wife
> May show her duty and make known her love?"
> (Induction.1.113–17)

The prospect of a compliant wife asking, with "kind embracements, tempting kisses," how she might show her love would certainly have attracted some participatory and lewd suggestions from the audience. The page duly meets the drunkard, who doesn't even know his supposed wife's name. Informed that lords call their wives "madam" he asks if she's "Alice madam, or Joan madam?" Without pausing for an answer, he invites her to "undress you and come now to bed." She entreats delay, at least until sunset, for the sake of his health. "I hope this reason stands for my excuse." Sly's bawdy reply puns on the word "stands"—"Ay, it stands so, that I may hardly tarry so long" (Induction.2.102–67). Sexual excitement is urgent and, it seems, all too physically manifest. Here, the entertainment for spectators is to enjoy a scene where someone is so aroused by his proximity to a previously unknown, yet apparently up-for-it housemate that he gets an erection, with the added delight of knowing that the object of desire is not at all what "she" seems but (as all female roles were) a cross-dressed adolescent boy.

At this very moment, the players arrive onstage to perform *The Taming of the Shrew*, being the entertainment Sly must watch while tarrying before bed. An ordinary bloke, who both *represents* the audience and *performs* it onstage, is put in an unfamiliar domestic setting, in a house belonging to an organization of vastly greater economic resource than his own, so that his behavior might be observed for the entertainment of the onlookers. He is surrounded by paid professionals whose scripted interactions come across to him as convincingly personal, while entertaining those in the know. Welcome to *Big Brother*, 1590s style.

Today's housemates don't need to be duped like Sly: they choose willingly to go into that unfamiliar house, to take on a lifestyle totally at odds with their own, in order to provide onlookers with an entertainment based on inversions of status, experiments with identity, and the comedy of errors as people play with personalities they don't get to express in the outside world. But like Sly, some of them are all too immediately smitten with desire, and that pleases the audience as it did in Elizabethan London. The bottom line for both *The Taming of the Shrew* and *Big Brother* is marriageability, and the role or performance of the self in that context.

Kiss Me Katrina

> Why, there's a wench! Come on, and kiss me, Kate.
>
> *The Taming of the Shrew*, 5.2.181

The second series of *Big Brother* in Australia (2002) introduced a new character to the world, by the name of Katrina. Unlike Shakespeare's Katharina, Katrina Miani is a real person. But her self-image appeared to be very different from what the other housemates saw—along with the *Big*

Brother editors, commentators, and audiences. In one profile she likened herself to Audrey Hepburn, in another she thought she was "a bit of a mother figure." Others seemed to agree that here was a "Katharina" worthy of Shakespeare's shrew:

> Katrina comes across as highly opinionated. . . . She seems to speak without thinking about the consequences of her comments. Some of these comments can be quite brutal and this appears to have rubbed some of the others in the group the wrong way.[19]

Kat was discussed in fan postings, which focused on her shrewishness:

> From Hot Chicky [27 June 2002, 5:02 P.M.]. Katrina—do you know that lots of people hate u, including me. I think u were a winger and a pain in the ass!!![20]

Or this from a young blogger called Emma:

> [Katrina] has narcissistic personality disorder. She uses people, has no regard for their feelings, thinks she always deserves praise, thinks she's above other people, refuses to accept that not everyone agrees with her, and does things solely so that she can feel more important than others and have them admire her for that.[21]

Katrina received the most nominations for eviction from her housemates in the first week, and was all too visibly upset, angry, and incredulous. She didn't handle the situation well. But she wasn't evicted—in fact, she received the lowest vote of the three nominees from the viewing public. They chose instead to evict a plausible, but sly young man who'd been trying his luck with several of the girls (like a "Bianca" subplot). Katrina was nominated again in the second week, however. In the days before the vote was announced, she was noticeably more in control and performed several helpful tasks for the house. But this time Katrina was evicted with 57 percent of the popular vote.

The contrast between her "hissy fits" on the show and her composure afterward led to further comment as well as discussion of the extent to which editing was used to control viewers' reactions: "The people behind the scenes are responsible for making fools or stars out of the contestants.

I bet tearful Katrina from *Big Brother 2* had little idea that she had become one of Australia's most annoying young women."[22] Big Brother himself (alias producer Peter Abbott) replied to this criticism:

> As for the conspiracy theory that Big Brother chooses who's going to be a hero, and who's going to be a villain, BB finds the whole idea amusing. "We're neither clever enough to achieve it, nor stupid enough to try it," he said. . . . "Kat's crying, Damo's lines and Aaron's outbursts all happened—we all saw it. How the audience then choose to perceive those moments in their overall judgment of that housemate is up to them, not us," he said. So what does determine which footage makes it to air? Character development, and basic entertainment values, according to [supervising producer] Chris Blackburn.[23]

Big Brother's live studio audience got in on the act and into the national news. It commiserated with Kat about her pet goldfish Bubalah, whose death had been reported to her by Big Brother while she was in the house, provoking one of her famous crying episodes. On her eviction, Katrina was greeted by fans sporting "RIP Bubalah" signs:

> When Katrina Miani emerged from the Big Brother house to see strangers mourning her dead pet goldfish, she gained a sudden appreciation for the reach of the reality phenomenon. . . . "When I saw all these people with 'rest in peace' [signs] on their heads, I (thought) 'Oh my God—the nation knows that my goldfish died,'" the 22-year-old . . . said.[24]

The evening of Katrina's eviction on Channel 10 was also the night of the Logies, Australian TV's industry awards. Miani appeared on a live cross to that event, which was broadcast on rival Channel 9. *Big Brother* won the best reality program award. And "RIP Bubalah" went on sale as an icon for mobile phones.

Katrina unwittingly became an international political story.

> *Big Brother* has become Australia's newest political battleground as Young Liberal and Young Labor supporters attempt to influence the reality TV show. The revelation that one of last week's eviction nominees, Katrina Miani, was a Victorian Young Liberal, sparked an email campaign by Young Liberals in her home state and New South Wales to keep her in the house.[25]

Not to be outdone, Young Labor supporters claimed her eviction as a political triumph:

> Katrina became the target of the campaign when news website crikey.com.au revealed that the perky Brighton dweller was—shock, horror—a Young Liberal. . . . NSW [New South Wales] Young Labor president Chris Minns started the anti-Katrina campaign with an email to members. "It is time for a good old-fashioned 'Kick the Young lib off *Big Brother*' grassroots campaign," it read.[26]

Although she was later convinced that this, together with certain photographs, explained her eviction, Katrina apparently took it in good spirit:

> "I am so not like anyone else in the Young Liberals," she laughed, adding that she was now contemplating canceling her membership. "I did have political aspirations but to make it in politics you have to be a particular type of person and I don't think I have the nastiness in me," Miani said.[27]

But it was too late to abandon politics. This was already an international story, duly reported on news sites around the world; for instance, in Brazil a headline read, "'Big Brother' australiano vira guerra política."[28]

Katrina's appearance two years earlier in *Picture* magazine, where she had posed nude, was prominent in accounts of her career on *Big Brother*. Soon, the pictures were made public again, both on the Internet and reprinted in *100% Home Girls*.[29] But when Katrina was evicted, it was the content of her character that was reckoned memorable, not (as one commentator put it) her "wobbly bits":

> Love her, or hate her, there's no doubting Kat has been the most talked about housemate on Big Brother, thus far. Trials and tribulations, tantrums and talking to herself . . . Kat's antics on BB have made for must-see TV. . . . One thing's for sure. For good or bad, she will be remembered.[30]

Once out of the house, Katrina could speak for herself:

> How do you feel about yourself? Did you feel better after time went on? There's been less crying episodes and I've been feeling a lot better about myself just this week. . . . I think having the task to throw myself into, and show that I am worthwhile and have a place in the group, was good.[31]

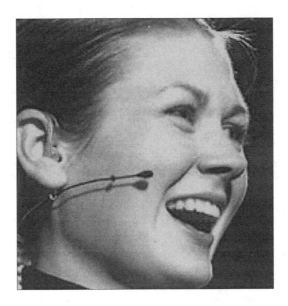

Katrina Miani on her eviction show, *Big Brother 2*,
Australia, 28 April 2002 (http://www.geocities
.com/sacchi_80/Kat_Eviction2.jpg).

When asked, "Who do you think will win?" she replied, "I'm thinking Pete.
He's just an all round good Aussie bloke." (Peter—a latter-day Petruchio—
did win.)

Katrina appeared on numerous media including *Rove Live* on Channel
10 and Radio National's *Media Report*,[32] where presenter Mick O'Regan
quizzed her about the reality of the show: "It's a very abbreviated version,
but what was shown is definitely part of me," responded Katrina. O'Regan
then asked her,

> Do you feel as though you've been sort of marketed as a media product?
> *Miani*: No, actually. Like I came out, and you just get thrown in the deep
> end, and I thought, Boy, I wish I'd had some training. But now I've kind of
> realized that there are so many reality TV shows, and so many personalities
> have come out from that sort of stuff, that you basically get thrown in, and
> it's sink or swim, because there's just too many of us. So if you can handle it,
> you survive, and if you can't you go by the wayside. And it's just the battle of
> the fittest. The game is not in the house. The real game is out here.
> *O'Regan*: Too right it is.[33]

Her media appearances tapered off after that, and Miani went back to work, although she continued to join post sessions on the Web, and make appearances at clubs and events.

Like Katharina in *The Taming of the Shrew,* Katrina was perceived as shrewish to begin with, and later redeemed herself, both on the show as she took on household tasks and saw them through, and afterward by her articulate and "tamed" comportment. But there remained a difference: Katrina was not tamed by a suitor and husband. In these Foucauldian times, she had to learn to "govern" herself while playing a part. If she was tested by anything, it was by a television program rather than a suitor. Indeed, she listed self-exploration as one of her motivations for going on the show:

> BB: *What did you personally get out of the BB experience?*
> K: I think that BB helped my self-confidence. I know a lot of people have
> called me arrogant and stuck-up but I actually often feel intimidated more
> than anything else. Being in such a challenging environment made me see
> that if I put my mind to it I can achieve the things that I dream of if I just
> put in the effort.[34]

Her other motivation was to take part in a "social experiment," having read George Orwell's *1984.* This *social* experiment of *self*-exploration might be called "the taming of the self."

The Source of Meaning

> What if Big Brother was already here, as the (imagined) Gaze for whom I
> was doing things, whom I tried to impress, to seduce, even when I was
> alone? What if the *Big Brother* show only renders palpable this universal
> structure? In other words, what if, in our "real lives," we already play a cer-
> tain role—we are not what we are, we play ourselves? The welcome achieve-
> ment of "Big Brother" is to remind us of this uncanny fact.
>
> Slavoj Žižek[35]

Big Brother was a worthy successor to Shakespeare, as Katrina was to Katharina. But despite the interesting family resemblances between Renaissance theater and reality TV, the two are not the same. In the intervening period, something had happened to meaning. Its supposed source has drifted down the "value chain."

In the realm of manufacturing, the value chain links origination/production, via commodity/distribution, to use/consumption. Businesses like to add value at all points in the chain. Recently, the most intense value-adding initiatives have been focused on consumers. For instance, customers of furniture stores like Ikea supply their own labor to assemble the goods they buy. Users of interactive computer games like *The Sims* contribute to the development of the game itself. It's not just "user pays"; it's also "user makes."

If *meaning* has a value chain, then it links the author (producer) via the text (commodity, distribution) to the reader (consumer). Over the years, value has been added to meaning by progressively extending its supposed source along the chain. The extension of meaning to the next link in the value chain can be seen to correlate with successive periods:

- In *premodern* (medieval) times, the source of meaning was understood to be divine, fixed in texts such as the Bible by God. Authorial *intention* was therefore unarguable: a text meant what its (divine) *producer* said it did. All that remained for readers was to work out what the author "meant." Priests were on hand to provide that service. Shakespeare himself stood on the cusp of medieval and modern times, and part of his fate is to enjoy the status of a kind of secularized authorial deity.

- In *modern* times, meaning was sourced to the *text*. Locating meaning in the "thing itself" was also the basis of empiricism and realism, the scientific observation of actually existing objects, documents, or "sources" to determine the truth. Texts meant exactly what they said. Readers must get at meaning themselves, without the help of authorities, by using techniques such as "practical criticism," a close critical reading without reference to contextual features, including knowing who wrote it and when, or what other critics had said about it. For better or worse, most academics, intellectuals, and critics are still "modernist"—that is, trained to source meaning to its commodity form.

- In *contemporary* times, the source of meaning has drifted to the other end of the value chain. It has been taken to reside in the consumer—the *audience* or *reader*. Given the anonymous popular sovereignty of mass democracy, this is an egalitarian approach to meaning. It requires large-scale sampling and ethnographic methods to get at what a text means because it means what several million people say it does. The way to find that out is by poll, survey, and sample—by *plebiscite*. One of its imaginative or ritualized forms is *Big Brother*.

Katrina Miani had no more control over her meaning than she did over her tear ducts. What she meant depended not on her own authorial intentions, nor those of *Big Brother*'s producers, nor even on its textual content. Katrina very clearly meant what her viewers—including journalists, political activists, bloggers, and the voting viewers—said she did.

While the fact that she was a real person experiencing real emotions guaranteed the transparency of *Big Brother*, her own sense of her reality had almost no bearing on how she was presented and received. Gossip media and bystanders concentrated on judging her character. Quality newspapers enjoyed all that too, but filed it under "political news." Some commentators used her image to discuss the artifice of the reality format itself. Others were interested in gazing at a desirable young woman or, conversely, judging her adversely for the "pictures from the past." In each case, Katrina meant what *they* said. But her dependence on the audience went further. As a contestant on *Big Brother*, Katrina was also a character in an unfolding story in which the mass audience had an active part to play. They played it by making judgments about her character and actions in comparison with the other players, and voting accordingly. The meaning not only of Katrina but also of the entire show and format was determined by plebiscite, which was itself the high point of the entertainment, drawing much higher ratings to evictions than to the routine daily shows. Endemol itself claims that

for the first time, ordinary people and the mass media have been given the opportunity to really interact. . . . If one thing has been proven, it's the eagerness of modern consumers to be involved in as many ways as possible. Spearheaded by massive TV coverage, the community has found its way to interactive media, with cross media links to all platforms. TV, website, email, SMS, WAP, and interactive TV refer to each other and keep the fans updated. More importantly, these media keep the community involved by means of voting, chatting, playing and other options.[36]

In such a context, *Big Brother* represents one example, and reality TV one form, of an anthropological extension of "performance" to the whole population. Not only does everyone "perform the self" but everyone knows that they are doing it (and *how* to do it), so that the form taken by "self-exploration" is "playing a part." Some—like Katrina—are even driven to check the ratings and reviews to learn about themselves:

> BB: *Any low moments?*
> K: Well, there have been some. Probably the lowest was after reading the web forums about a week after I left the house. But even in my darkest moments when I thought "is it still worth it?" the answer is still a resounding yes! I think that the darker moments just make the good times feel even better.[37]

This is a democratization of playing; the mass audience is participating in their own fifteen minutes of fame. That this is not always a comfortable quarter of an hour is itself a hard-learned part:

> From Spearbear. My question is: "What was your perception of fame before going into the House? And how has the experience changed your perception of fame?" Thanks.

> From miani69@yahoo.com [13 July 2002, 7:15 P.M.]. . . . My answer for spearbear's question is yes, my perception of fame has changed. I grew up thinking that famous people were glamorous and rich and didn't have any worries. I was very wrong. I feel just the same—except people now know who I am. That's the only difference fame makes.[38]

The intimate "I" has become a public property to be judged by strangers.

Because there is too much readily accessible meaning out there among the millions of people, media, sites, and sources, the *creation* of meaning is no longer an authorial act; it's now an editorial one, resulting from a textual practice that I've called *redaction*.[39] Redaction—the creative editorial function of bringing existing materials together to make new texts and meanings—is the art form of the age (and also the "method" of this chapter), a product and promoter of the long-term drift of meaning to the consumer. Redaction adds value to the end of meaning's value chain.

Once again, *Big Brother* makes the point, being itself a redactional text. Each episode of the show requires heroic acts of creative editing to take the multicamera, twenty-four/seven footage of transparent, live, unmediated reality and turn it into something like TV serial drama, or a very long frat movie, with three story lines per episode. At the macrolevel, *Big Brother* also symbolizes a redactional society—its overall meaning and appeal is the amalgam of elements drawn from the house and housemates, the audience and commentators, surrounding media and business partners, adding up to a coherence that could only be achieved by editing those existing materials into something legible.

Such developments were accompanied by, and required, changes in literacy, of which they are also a symptom.

- In the medieval era, audiences were just that—they "audited" what authors had created. Literacy needed to be *hear only,* whether in church or theater. Audiences only had to hear the spoken word, be it the divine variety in the liturgy and sermon or merely divinely inspired in Shakespeare's plays.
- Modern audiences were true readers, but their literacy was largely *read only.* In order to partake of public life in democratic societies, for instance, the modern citizen had to be able to read the newspapers, but not write for them.
- The contemporary period is witnessing a further change in literacy—the popular audience is achieving a *read and write* capacity in publicly distributed media, not least via their participation in shows like *Big Brother.*

For Katrina to mean what consumers said she did, the viewing public has to be able to contribute in scale to the process of meaning creation. Those plebiscitary contributions need to be re-presented by redactional means so that both actors and audience could learn how their very identity is an outcome of consumer choices beyond their control. That's how they can both perform the self and submit that performance to the judgment of the entire community, and how an "imagined community" uses TV's highest-rating entertainment show to explore questions of personality and relationship, and therefore also of marriageability and citizenship. That's how shrewishness is tamed. That's what *Big Brother* has done, and it is an achievement of no less significance than Shakespeare's. As Katrina herself has said, "The game is not in the house. The real game is out here."

NOTES

1. Thomas Hobbes, *Leviathan* (1651; reprint, Harmondsworth, U.K.: Penguin, 1968), 151–52.

2. See http://www.endemol.com/corporate/history.jsp; Albert Moran, *Copycat TV: Globalisation, Program Formats, and Cultural Identity* (Luton, U.K.: University of Luton Press, 1998), 33–37.

3. See Terence Hawkes, *Shakespeare in the Present* (London: Routledge, 2002), 83–87.

4. Scott Robert Olson, *Hollywood Planet: Global Media and the Competitive Advantage of Narrative Transparency* (Mahwah, N.J.: Lawrence Erlbaum Associates, 1999), 5–6.

5. Ibid., 6.

6. Terence Hawkes, *Shakespeare's Talking Animals* (London: Edward Arnold, 1973), 231. See also Alfred Harbage, *Shakespeare's Audience* (Chicago: University Press of Chicago, 1941).

7. But see Hawkes's own critique of de-contextualized universalism (*Shakespeare in the Present*, 117, 122).

8. Hawkes, *Shakespeare's Talking Animals*, 230–31.

9. See www.bigbrotherworld.tv.

10. See http://movieweb.com/movie/10things/10things.txt.

11. Alexei Popov, "Shakespeare and the Theatre" [extract from *"The Taming of the Shrew"* in the Central Theatre of the Red Army, 1940], in *Shakespeare in the Soviet Union*, ed. Roman Samarin and Alexander Nikolyukin (Moscow: Progress Publishers, 1966), 165.

12. Ibid., 166–68.

13. See Hawkes, *Shakespeare's Talking Animals*; Harbage, *Shakespeare's Audience*; and S. L. Bethell, *Shakespeare and the Popular Dramatic Tradition* (London: Staples, 1944). See also Richard Butsch, *The Making of American Audiences: From Stage to Television, 1750–1990* (Cambridge: Cambridge University Press, 2000).

14. Bethell, *Shakespeare*, 28–29.

15. For an analysis of a challenging direct address in *The Winter's Tale*, spoken to "many a man" in the audience who "even at this present, Now, while I speak this, holds his wife by th'arm, That little thinks she has been sluiced in his absence" by "Sir Smile, his neighbor" (1.2.189–96), see Hawkes, *Shakespeare in the Present*, 97.

16. Maurice Gorham, "Television: A Medium in Its Own Right?" in *The Cinema, 1951*, ed. Roger Manvell and R. K. Neilson Baxter (Harmondsworth, U.K.: Penguin, 1951), 137.

17. Michael Clarke, "Television Prospect: Some Reflexions of a Documentary Filmmaker," *The Cinema, 1952*, ed. Roger Manvell and R. K. Neilson Baxter (Harmondsworth, U.K.: Penguin, 1952), 184–86.

18. Alan Robertson of Initiative Media, cited in *Age*, 8 April 2002.

19. Katrina was introduced thus at the beginning of the series on the *Big Brother* website, http://www.bigbrother.iprimus.com.au/news.

20. Http://www.geocities.com/sacchi_80/art_kat_forums.html; see also http://www.gusworld.com.au/tv/bigbro/bb2002.htm.

21. Http://tarnish.net/written/mundane/20020430.html.

22. Http://members.hn.ozemail.com.au/~voyager/letsgetreal/letsgetreal.html

23. Http://www.bigbrother.iprimus.com.au/news, 25 May 2002.

24. Kathryn Torpy, "Katrina Out in Landslide," *Courier Mail,* 29 April 2002.

25. Dale Paget, "Big Brother Goes Political," *Age,* 24 April 2002.

26. Olivia Hill-Douglas, "No Room for a Party-Girl, Big Brother's Watching," *Age,* 30 April 2002.

27. "ALP Claims Big Brother Scalp," *Age,* 29 April 2002.

28. See http://www.mundifm.com.br/news/index24042002.htm.

29. *Picture* 564, 2000; and *100% Home Girls* 1, 2000. The pictures were republished on the Internet (for example, http://watchersweb.com/30754.htm), and in *100% Home Girls* 17, 2002.

30. "Katrina's Out of the House," 28 April 2002, http://bigbrother.channel4 .com. For the "wobbly bits," see Luisa Browett, "The Dirt," http://www.ourbrisbane .com/entertainment/tv_guide/newsandgossip/2002_05_01.htm.

31. "Katrina's Out of the House," 28 April 2002, http://bigbrother.channel4 .com.

32. 30 April 2002 and 23 May 2002, respectively.

33. Http://www.abc.net.au/rn/talks/8.30/mediarpt/stories/s562394.htm.

34. Http://www.geocities.com/sacchi_80/katrina.html, 10 July 2002.

35. Slavoj Žižek, "Big Brother, or, the Triumph of the Gaze over the Eye," in *Ctrl [Space]: Rhetorics of Surveillance from Bentham to Big Brother,* ed. Thomas Y. Levin, Ursula Frohne, and Peter Weibel (Cambridge: MIT Press, 2002), 226.

36. Endemol Interactive International, http://www.endemol.com/interactive /formats_big_brother.jsp.

37. Http://www.geocities.com/sacchi_80/katrina.html, 10 July 2002.

38. Http://www.geocities.com/sacchi_80/art_kat_forums.html.

39. John Hartley, "Communicational Democracy in a Redactional Society," *Journalism: Theory, Practice, Criticism* 1, no. 1 (1998): 39–47, and *A Short History of Cultural Studies* (London: Sage Publications, 2003), 82–87.

17

Jamming *Big Brother*

Webcasting, Audience Intervention,
and Narrative Activism

Pamela Wilson

This is the story of the first season of the U.S. version of *Big Brother* and how its "reality" narrative was almost hijacked by a motley assortment of activist on-line fans and media/culture jammers. The setting is a spectacularly conjunctural moment in media history, right at the cusp of the new millennium. A window of opportunity emerged for only a brief period of time, allowing for the invasion of a slickly produced corporate television game show by amateur narrative terrorists whose weapons were clever words rather than bombs. The intervention could perhaps only have happened once, during a period of technological and programmatic flux, when the format was new, the formula was flexible, the unscripted narrative was emerging from the psyches of the not-yet-jaded improvisational players, the events were being closely followed around the clock by avid on-line viewers, and the Hollywood set was relatively unprotected. Prior to this time, no one at CBS or Endemol Productions suspected that chaos could or would come from the skies. After it, contestants were selected more for their ratings-drawing glamour than their down-home naïveté, the formula became more fixed, and chances for narrative disruption became increasingly curtailed.

The introduction of *Big Brother*—a hybrid concept inspired by George Orwell's classic treatise on political oppression in a futuristic police state that held control over the minds of its subjects—spawned a form of media activism rooted in the intersections of a countercultural and anticapitalist social movement ("culture jamming") with the shifting technological sands of the show's dual webcasting/broadcasting. *Big Brother*'s narrative was multilayered: it emerged minute by minute on the streaming Web feeds, but was controlled, produced, and structured through the selective editing of the producers for the nightly television recap. The "characters" were real people living in a fishbowl, surrounded by cameras and creating an emerging narrative shaped partially by the producers' constraints, but open enough to allow for improvisation. Enter the culture jammers, seeking to disrupt and subvert the intentions of the corporate producers as well as to influence the outcome of the "story." A new type of intervention into television was born: *narrative activism.*

The narrative activism triggered by *Big Brother* can be seen as a form of media/culture jamming, a purposefully playful and subversive activity that reflects both the postmodern condition as well as anticorporate and anti-globalization sentiments. Culture jamming might be defined as the appropriation of new media technologies and information systems to invade, intercept, and disrupt corporate systems and their products. The earliest conception of culture jamming is attributed to William S. Burroughs, who in a seminal 1969 piece stated, "Our aim is total chaos."[1] The theory and practice of culture jamming have been elaborated most fully by Mark Dery in his 1993 essay "Culture Jamming: Hacking, Slashing, and Sniping in the Empire of Signs." According to Dery, "'Culture jamming' . . . might best be defined as media hacking, information warfare, terror-art, and guerrilla semiotics, all in one. Billboard bandits, pirate TV and radio broadcasters, media hoaxers, and other vernacular media wrenchers who intrude on the intruders, investing ads, newscasts, and other media artifacts with subversive meanings are all culture jammers."[2] Similarly, Naomi Klein calls culture jamming "semiotic Robin Hoodism" or "counter-messages that hack into a corporation's own method of communication to send a message starkly at odds with the one that was intended."[3]

There are many forms of culture jamming, but those that focus on media consider it to be semiological guerrilla information warfare, using words as weapons (a concept attributed to Umberto Eco), turning the tools of mass media against the corporate forces themselves. This has been a movement especially enabled by the rise and rapid growth of on-line media culture and the radical possibilities of the Internet; it is part of what Kevin Michael DeLuca and Jennifer Peeples describe as the transformation of the public sphere into the "public screen."[4] For critics like Dery, culture jamming is also an intensely political act, even as it grows out of a postmodern impulse:

I'm deeply committed to a progressive politics whose calls for social justice, economic equality, and environmental action are founded on an economic critique of the catastrophic effects of multinational capitalism. At the same time, I'm profoundly influenced by the postmodern emphasis on cultural politics (as opposed to the old New Left emphasis on political economy). The intertwined histories of feminism, the civil rights movement, multiculturalism, and gay and transgender activism remind us that hacking the philosophical code that runs the hardware of political and economic power is crucially important, too. In that light, I'm naive enough to believe that ideas matter and that intellectual activism can, in its own small way, be an engine of social change.[5]

Whether social change—or at least public cultural critique—might be produced by attempts to affect, subvert, and disrupt the well-oiled mechanisms of commercial television is a question that begs to be asked in light of the narrative activism that surrounded the multimedia corporate production *Big Brother.*

Big Brother *and an Innovative System of Program Delivery*

The premise was simple: "Ten people. No privacy. Three months. No outside contact." In summer 2000, the Dutch company Endemol Productions, working with CBS television, selected ten contestants to participate in the first U.S. version of *Big Brother*: part game show, part documentary, and part soap opera. This group would live together for more than twelve weeks, isolated in a house on a Hollywood studio lot, surrounded by corridors of surveillance cameras. Every two weeks, one contestant would be voted off the show, with the last remaining contestant winning the $500,000 grand prize.

The CBS television version of *Big Brother,* with concurrent live-streaming on-line feeds in partnership with America Online (AOL), received public regard as a moderately successful, but mediocre television event. It gained even more acclaim as an unprecedented, momentous hit on the Internet, with a remarkable crossover on-line presence along with a strong and loyal on-line audience. In fact, this became the most noteworthy aspect of the venture: journalist David Kronke reported that *Big Brother* "has changed the way television and new media can interact."[6] AOL's publicity articles touted the "unprecedented convergence between television and the

Internet" achieved by the CBS-AOL *Big Brother* alliance as the "largest on-going webcast in history," and claimed a "tenfold increase in participants [of] the streaming webcast during peak usage time in the first week."[7] The official AOL website, however, was only the tip of the iceberg in terms of on-line audience involvement in *Big Brother*. On-line fans created and contributed to dozens of private websites and portals devoted to *Big Brother*, and AOL itself sponsored more than fourteen thousand unofficial fan pages about the *Big Brother* program.[8]

While the "action" that took place in the *Big Brother* house was supposed to be naturally occurring, producers structured the daily activities of the houseguests around a series of programmed "challenges." A high degree of self-consciousness also curtailed the spontaneity of the contestants' behavior. As Endemol producer John Kalish later remarked of the U.S. contestants, "They were always talking about how they were being edited, story lines, looking into cameras, being aware of it. They never let go of what the other House Guests in other countries did, which was finally to let go of the idea of being observed. These guys never did. They always referred to themselves as 'characters' as opposed to people."[9] The only site in the house from which events were not transmitted over the live Web feeds was the Red Room, a room to which the houseguests could go as individuals for private interviews with the producers (who often used these interviews as a way to elicit plot information or otherwise manipulate the developing narrative) and where they revealed their choices for banishment.

Although the premise of *Big Brother* only required audience participation in limited and ritualized ways (the call-in votes every two weeks to oust the one member of the household), audience involvement—to the point of intervention and disruption—proved to be a hallmark of the U.S. version of the *Big Brother* phenomenon. Neither the producers nor the network anticipated the level of public involvement that the *Big Brother* TV/on-line programming innovation would incite. The opportunity to contribute to the narrative of a live television series appealed both to fans and critics of the show, and intersected with a number of personal and organizational agendas unknown to the producers.

The dramatic highlight of the first season was the escalating narrative tension in the tenth week. Increasing interventions from the outside world coupled with a "groupthink" mentality among the six remaining sequestered houseguests culminated with the houseguests planning a mass walkout from the show, ostensibly to embrace an idealistic collective solidarity. Seeking their "chance to make history" and to make a profoundly anticapitalist statement as they chose friendship over prize money, they gravely threatened the very premise of the show's competitive commercialism and the network's ability to continue its run. The planned walkout was ultimately defused and contained by the producers, and the show ended successfully by commercial standards, but the producers' hold over the narrative outcome was tenuous for a few days as chaos from outside intervention and internal rebellion threatened to radically alter the program's planned plotline.

Big Brother broke new ground in establishing a multiplicity of ways that a television program could reach its audience. In fact, one might argue that *Big Brother* consisted of several different programs, several distinct audiences, and multiple versions of its narrative. In addition to television, press accounts, and the Web feeds, the other official mode of disseminating the narrative of the program was the CBS/AOL *Big Brother* website, which posted daily summaries of narrative highlights and contained the official commentary from the producers.[10] Other, unofficial versions of the narrative were posted by on-line audience members as updates on message boards, chat rooms, and portals with links to a variety of connected sites.[11] Based on these distinctions, we might theorize that the perception of the narrative events (that is, the actions and happenings in the lives of the *Big Brother* houseguests/contestants) would be complex, and that these perceptions would vary depending on exposure to selected media forms (the TV show, on-line feeds, message boards, official *Big Brother* website, and press commentary). Endemol producer Douglas Ross noted the privileging of the on-line viewer in particular: "I think that the Internet viewer really does understand the show better than the average TV viewer. People who aren't involved in the Web, and just watching it on TV—except for the dedicated viewer who just watches it as a soap opera—I don't think the average viewer really gets it."[12]

Big Brother was highly unusual in that the circumstances of its production provided for a shared role in shaping such meanings. How did amateur culture jammers "invade" the narrative world and irreparably affect the "plot" of the series? Who, in the end, produced *Big Brother*?

Invasions from the Skies and Other Interventions

The first outside invasion of *Big Brother* occurred when someone tossed several tennis balls containing fake newspaper articles over the fence into the *Big Brother* compound. In spite of the producers' efforts to try to prevent the contestants from seeing the balls' contents, the contestants managed to read two of these "articles" containing negative comments about the show and its participants. These pieces had an immediate effect on the contestants' morale. This, the first incursion of the outside world into the seemingly secured diegetic one of the houseguests, created enough alarm both inside the house and among the producers that the CBS/AOL website ran the following disclaimer, titled "A Statement from the Executive Producer":

> The minute we saw what was going on, we told the House Guests over the PA system to bring the tennis balls and the papers into the Red Room. We quickly discovered that the photocopied newspaper articles were fake. We then told all the houseguests that this was a hoax and that the articles were bogus. We acted quickly to set the record straight because our number one concern, of course, is for the houseguests' safety and psychological well-being.[13]

Shortly thereafter, a Web page (ZAP Design) claimed responsibility for the intrusive tennis balls.[14]

The producers' reaction was strong. Concerned that one particular contestant might request a voluntary exit in response to this prank, Endemol broke its own rules about no outside contact and provided him with a packet of reassuring letters they had hastily requested from his family. The contestant, George, a roofer from Rockford, Illinois, had quickly become popular based on his sympathetic embodiment of a U.S. archetype of the simple, beleaguered working man. As an added bonus, the reading of the letters from his young daughters to the other houseguests supplied Endemol with some tear-filled, poignant moments for the television viewers.[15] Thus, Endemol appropriated the events and used them to their own advantage.

Day fifty marked the beginning of the intensified external campaign to shape the narrative events. That afternoon, the contestants were in their enclosed outdoor courtyard. The producers, having apparently received a

Culture jammers ignored the corporate rules of *Big Brother* by initiating contact with the confined houseguests and encouraging them to walk off the set.

phone tip about a low-flying plane with a banner, came over the loud-speaker and asked the houseguests to sequester themselves immediately in the men's bedroom. A few hours later, the banner-bearing plane returned. According to the CBS/AOL website, "The airborne prankster returned and passed the house at low altitude, proudly and clearly displaying the streaming message, 'BIG BROTHER IS WORSE THAN YOU THINK—GET OUT NOW.'"

The on-line activist group Media Jammers later claimed responsibility for this first banner. The "media jamming" plans were hatched via an on-line *Big Brother* forum on the website Salon.com. According to Media Jammers founder Jeff Oswald, "We were just goofing around trying to think of ways to get messages in. We talked about catapults, compressed air cannons like the ones they use to shoot T-shirts into the crowd at sports events, etc. We had a guy scout out the location and tell us how difficult it would be to get in range. So . . . I figured our best shot was the banners."[16] There would be more to come from Media Jammers.

A campaign by George's fans to "Save George" soon emerged as well. The website OurBigBrotherGeorge.com was set up by corporate supporters to raise money for George's family in his absence. It was rumored on the message boards that the site was either illegal or unethical, and it was eventually shut down. Nevertheless, George's hometown rallied behind its local television hero with spaghetti dinners and other fund-raising campaigns. Some fan groups used their websites to sell T-shirts to benefit George, while others mobilized massive phone campaigns to get viewers to cast their telephone votes for another contestant so that George could maintain his chances of winning the $500,000. Most of the on-line fan community scorned this attempt by supporters, especially corporate interests, to help a particular contestant win an unethical and unfair intervention.[17]

While message boards heated up with irate fans protesting the Save George campaign, tensions grew inside the house. The houseguests were bonding with each other and feeling a growing distrust against "Big Brother" (the producers), perceived as their captors and programmers. A collective ethos had developed among the houseguests; the conditions of the shared lived experience had become antithetical to the competitive spirit of the game show mentality. The tension between competitive individualism and collaborative collectivism informed the group dynamics for several weeks, and ultimately, it led to their most dramatic moments.

In the wake of the airplane banner chartered by Media Jammers, the activist on-line organization began to receive a great deal of attention. On 27 August 2000, Media Jammers' Oswald posted an update on the group's website describing its philosophy and intent for future involvement in the *Big Brother* operation:

> As our belief is that this is a universal, grass roots operation, we fully advocate and encourage anybody with a desire to engage in interloping on *Big Brother* to do so of their own accord on their own terms the best way they see fit. . . . Our ultimate goal is to make actions stick, that will generate ongoing dialogue about the destructive force of this CBS debacle. . . . A unanimous [contestant] walk-out, although it would be a thing of poetic beauty, is highly unlikely right now. However, if we maintain our efforts, we're confident they will eventually see that we . . . were honest about our motives, and sincere in our belief that losers talk, heroes walk. We maintain that the message is, has been and always will be that by walking out together, they will be respected for it, salvage their dignity, and have more of a chance to accomplish their individual goals. If they stay and participate to the end, they will only be ridiculed and forgotten: *Nine losers, one wealthy loser.* . . .

More planes will fly, more banners will be seen. Count on it. Have fun with it. Keep watching the skies.[18]

On 30 August, three more banners flew simultaneously, also reportedly commissioned by Media Jammers: "9 LOSERS AND 1 WEALTHY LOSER? OR 10 WINNERS?" accompanied by "LOSERS TALK—HEROES WALK—TOGETHER" and "THERE IS DIGNITY IN LEAVING." That day, Media Jammers reiterated their goal to tell the contestants to "walk out on this turkey of a production. . . . We state clearly that our ONLY target is CBS/Endemol Entertainment and the production *Big Brother*."[19] That evening, the audience voted contestant Brittany off the show. The on-line fans—especially those who did not like George—attributed Brittany's loss to the "Save George" campaigns and vowed to get retribution. The houseguests, though, were unaware of the attempt by George's supporters to vote Brittany out of the house. The dramatic tension now hinged on the irony of what viewers knew that the houseguests on the inside did not know. Would "Big Brother" tell them? Would the Media Jammers banners tell them? Would they find out? And what would they do if they found out?

The Megaphone Lady, Brittany's Secret, and More Banners

On 2 September, a new character known as the Megaphone Lady unofficially entered the world of *Big Brother*. Kaye Mallory, a Los Angeles–area schoolteacher and an active member of the on-line "Big Brother Watchers" fan group, had been participating as usual in the discussions and updates on the fan e-mail list when she announced that she was "getting a bullhorn and going down there to yell messages to them!" Early that evening, Mallory drove as close to the *Big Brother* house as she could get and began shouting through a megaphone: "Fight Big Brother—the editing sucks! We love you guys!"[20] Mallory's cohorts on the Big Brother Watchers fan list were ecstatic. A half hour later, Mallory went back to the *Big Brother* house and shouted, "You're worth more as a group against Big Brother. If you walk out together, you will be famous!" The *Big Brother* producers promptly called all the contestants into the house. When Mallory returned home to her computer, she rejoined the discussion on the fan e-mail list about her actions. Although some fans criticized Mallory for interfering where she did not belong, others gave her suggestions for future drive-by shoutings, and many applauded Mallory's initiative in allowing the voice of the fans to penetrate the *Big Brother* house.

Two days later, Mallory returned to the house to reveal CBS's plan to revive the flagging audience interest in the show by bribing one of the boring houseguests to leave and replacing that person with a provocative alternate. "On Wednesday, Big Brother will offer you money to leave. Don't take the money! It's a trick! Don't take the money! We hate Big Brother! We love you guys! Don't take the money! Fight Big Brother!" Mallory yelled. On her website, Mallory reports on what followed:

> As a delightful surprise, Ms. Megaphone was featured as the opening of the Monday night BB show on TV. They even had subtitles so everyone would know what was said. Subsequently, on the live Wednesday show, BB offered them the money, but they'd upped the initial offer to $20,000 and when that was refused, they upped it to $50,000. Nobody took the offer. We're very proud of them for not selling out! . . . I'm glad the HGs had two days to think about their options.[21]

That Wednesday night brought a producer-sponsored intervention. Endemol decided to bring banished Brittany to the studio and allow her to speak to one of the remaining contestants by phone for two minutes. Josh, her erstwhile love interest on the show, was sent to the Red Room for a private conversation. In the days that she had been out of the *Big Brother* house, Brittany had gained a better understanding of the dynamics of the household and the motives of the players. She revealed cryptic pieces of information about the orchestrated campaign to save George and told Josh which contestants he should trust. When later questioned by the other houseguests, Josh refused to divulge what he had learned, but he seemed troubled.

The next day, Mallory returned with her megaphone to find security guards patrolling the *Big Brother* lot. When she got the chance, she shouted more information to the houseguests. The following description on the CBS website of her visit reflects a growing corporate attempt to discredit the narrative intrusions by the fans: "At 9pm PDT, 'Crazy Megaphone Girl' began screaming muddled messages to the House Guests. Each guest listened intently, with the hope of garnering some information from the outside world. Big Brother swiftly sequestered the group."[22] When Mallory returned once more to the *Big Brother* house, she was harassed by the security guards, who engaged her in a car chase to try to intimidate her to leave the area and not return.[23]

In the meantime, new banners had been trying to discredit George. The information from the outside was making the houseguests uncomfortable, especially George, who felt attacked, and Josh, who had secret knowledge he was afraid to reveal. While tensions rose, the houseguests tried to decipher the fragmented messages from the Megaphone Lady and the banners.

The Climax: The Aborted Walkout

Our first project "Jamming Big Brother" is almost complete. We have interfered with the creative direction of this CBS "reality" show to the point of altering the outcome and raising awareness of the abuses the producers have committed against the contestants, their families and the viewers of the show. We have done so by introducing outside messages to the contestants who are supposedly cut off from any contact from the outside world. Our most successful tactic has been to fly aerial banners over the "house" on the CBS studio lot in Los Angeles, with messages encouraging the contestants to walk out or otherwise rebel against the manipulative producers. We have also worked with other groups who have tried to communicate with the contestants through various means including bullhorns and delivery of written messages into the "compound."

—Media Jammers[24]

On Saturday morning, Josh revealed Brittany's "secret" to George, and George then called a meeting. When the houseguests gathered in the kitchen to hear George's plan, the streaming Web feeds blacked out for about ten minutes. CBS/Endemol censored this crucial discussion from the on-line audience.[25] When the Web feeds returned, it was apparent that an impassioned George was trying to convince the others that they should walk out and split the money between them. Influenced by Media Jammers and Mallory, George explained that, "That thing with the Megaphone Lady, I put it together. Think back to the beginning, and it's obvious. . . . I'm positive, we all could have been winners long before this. The thing was there all along. We are bigger than the show and they need us. . . . We are all winners." Despite some skepticism among the houseguests, many saw the opportunity to make "television history" by undermining the rules of the game and proving that, as one stated, "*We* are more than money."

Within forty minutes, all the players agreed that they would walk out together on the following Wednesday, realizing that their action would sabotage the show. They also correctly anticipated that the producers would try to talk them out of it. Having made a pact, however, they were proud and self-congratulatory: "We have decided to make all decisions as a group. . . . It's about sticking together," said one player. According to George, the information from the Megaphone Lady and the banners helped make the outcome clear.

Endemol producer John Kalish later remarked that he and the other executive producers, Douglas Ross and Paul Römer, had gathered to watch the "riveting" actions of George and the other houseguests: "It was startling. It was engaging, but looking at the reactions of the rest of them is what alerted me to the fact that this was something completely different. This was something that needed to be dealt with. Ultimately, it was a combination of fascination, excitement, and a little bit of concern. . . . This was the greatest thing that could happen to the show, and yet potentially the most devastating. [We were] living at the edge here."[26]

After their decision, the houseguests were riding high on their ebullience. They felt defiant and independent of the control of the producers. They also realized that the world knew their plans through the program's Web viewers. As they headed outside to toast their decision, Big Brother commanded them to go inside because the Megaphone Lady was back. Defying Big Brother, they stayed in the yard, and Mallory told them to walk *that* night. The producers blasted loud music over the intercom to drown out her words, making it difficult to hear the houseguests as they discussed their walkout. At the same time, all Web feeds switched to empty rooms inside the house, so the on-line audience could not hear or see what was happening in the courtyard. Once again, the producers implemented an information blackout strategy during a moment of high narrative tension.

After the walkout decision had been made, another batch of airplane banners arrived. Some supported the rebellion, while others told the contestants to stay in the house. The houseguests began to realize the magnitude of their decision to leave, and some exhibited misgivings. In the Red Room, the producers explained to individual contestants that if everyone voluntarily walked, they would forfeit the grand prize as well as their weekly stipends. The ensuing dialogue between the contestants revealed a clash of value systems, between the "noble" act of defying Big Brother in favor of group solidarity and the competitive, materialistic desire to stay, play the game, and win the grand prize. When discussing leaving, one contestant commented, "They will ask us why we came in the first place," to which others replied, "I think the money is why we all came in the first place, but the game taught us . . . that you should not give up control of your integrity or image to someone else." One added, "It's an amazing sign of America that the six of us are so different and so cohesive. . . . If I'm gonna walk, we're showing our integrity, that even though we all need money very bad we are gonna make something bigger than that. To put a message like this to society is worth much more than money."

On Saturday evening, when the houseguests prepared to enter the Red Room as a group to confront the producers, Big Brother made them wait. About ten minutes later, they were told to come to the living room. The Web feeds were switched to the chicken coops at this point, effecting another blackout of information. Apparently, a group meeting took place during this period when the cameras were not on the houseguests. Soon thereafter, in the Red Room, contestant Jamie had a long but unrecorded discussion with producer Kalish. When she emerged, she told the others that he said they had "made a commitment to the people outside who are watching this show to be in the house, and that they are breaking that commitment if they leave."

About this pivotal conversation, Kalish later observed, "I thought, 'This is the moment of truth.' . . . We couldn't let them think they were going to undermine the show or undo us by making this decision. We had to be very strategic in how we were going to respond to it." So the producer "called their bluff" and told the houseguests that the producers were making preparations for them to leave the house. Just as a parent might react to a young child who packs a suitcase and threatens to run away from home, Kalish reportedly told the most gullible contestant, Jamie, "I'm not going to try and change your mind," just as he planted many doubts in her mind about the wisdom of the decision.[27]

After the Red Room meeting, contestants Jamie's and Eddie's support for the walkout began to waver. Fellow contestant Curtis encouraged them to stay, astutely explaining that "I can see John's point of view . . . [but] John, however, DOES work for *Big Brother*." Similarly, houseguest Cassandra suggested that the "guy in the Red Room" might not have everyone's best interests at heart.

The following morning, negotiations continued and Kalish returned to the control room to again target Jamie. Interestingly, many fans at this time believed that Endemol and CBS had engineered the walkout scenario as a publicity ploy, to trick the contestants, or to play "mind games" with the viewers. Fans were also divided as to whether the group should stay or leave.

The houseguests gathered early that afternoon for a final decision. After some negotiation, they realized that they were no longer unified. A fan post on the Updates Board summed up the situation exquisitely:

> Eddie says he came to his senses.
> The rest now have changed their minds.
> Back to routine.

The "revolution" was effectively squelched. Big Brother had maintained control.

Narrative Activism and the
Exposure of "Reality's" Constructedness

The thwarted rebellion by the *Big Brother* contestants was the most dramatically compelling aspect of the series in its first U.S. incarnation. The moment-by-moment suspense of the walkout weekend was especially riveting to the on-line viewers, who watched the webcast and heard the houseguests wax lyrical about leaving en masse, even as they waffled about trading in the chance to win the game (and prize money) for a moment in television history. The audience who watched only the television program and not the Internet feeds missed this dramatic arc. Internet viewers were shocked to find that CBS did not feature the planning of the walkout on its Saturday show at all. Only on Monday, when the *Big Brother* household was safely "back to routine," did CBS air a half-hour recap of the plans for the walkout and its demise.[28]

Big Brother spawned a remarkable level of narrative activism in spite of the producers' attempts to limit contact between participants and the outside world. The emergence of disruptive and subversive elements, both within and beyond the confines of the *Big Brother* house, provides a new model for conceptualizing the interactive potential of the new hybrid television/Internet documentary–game show genre. *Narrative involvement* by an audience might be considered to be the contribution of audience members to reshaping the narrative in complicity with the program's producers. This might range from suggestions about plot developments to more activist campaigns to save a program or protest a particular story line. In the case of *Big Brother*, narrative involvement would include the invitation for viewers to call in to vote on which contestant should be banished from the show. In contrast, *narrative activism* involves audience interventions that contradict the plans or desires of the corporate producers and change the narrative outcome of a program. In the case of contrived documentary game shows such as *Big Brother*, both types of narrative intervention are potentially subversive since producers shape the so-called naturally occurring actions that produce the narratives even if the programs are seemingly unscripted. Yet it is the documentary aspect of the narrative intervention into *Big Brother* that is the most notable.

There is a well-documented history of audience activism around dramatic and comedy television series. Letter-writing campaigns and campaigns to boycott advertisers have been used in attempts to save programs with low ratings but loyal audiences, attack programs with values contradicting those of the viewers, and show other types of support for the "quality" or nature of certain types of programming. No doubt such responses have affected the way that producers and writers subsequently shaped characters and story arcs to cater to viewer likes and dislikes.[29] *Big Brother*, however, is perhaps the first time that viewer activism has focused on documentary programming. The impetus of most reality TV has been to air episodes of edited documentary action (and I use the term "documentary" in the loosest sense here) into a completed narrative that had taken place in a more distant past than that of the edited *Big Brother* footage, which was at most two to three days old when it aired, often on the same day. Most important, Web viewers could watch and hear the events as they were unfolding in the daily lives of the houseguests; viewers could also compare and contrast what they had observed via the Web feed to the edited narrative that Endemol/CBS constructed for the nightly broadcasts.

The discrepancies between these two versions of narrative reality created a major source of disgruntlement and discontent for the on-line fans and other viewers since they exposed the constructedness of this (as any) documentary narrative in a way never before revealed on a U.S. reality TV show. Rarely, if ever does a documentarian provide an audience with a parallel version with the full, unedited footage, allowing them to see what has been selected and what has been omitted to create the final "documentary." We are socialized to believe that documentary and other nonfictional (reality) forms are "truth"; however, the dual modes of sharing the *Big Brother* happenings created a disjunctive and troubling awareness for many viewers that the two audiences were receiving two different versions of the "reality" of the lives of the houseguests. The ability of fans to use the Internet not only to follow the moment-by-moment action but also to organize and mobilize as activists as well as interventionists supplied a crack in the surface of the network or producer's total control over the television product. In so doing, it inadvertently offered a space through which viewer-fans could actively participate in the production of the program and affect its narrative outcome, even (especially) having the opportunity to work toward goals at odds with those of the official network and program producers. In effect, the audience and fans caught the network and its production company off guard as they appropriated an opportunity to become, to a significant extent, coproducers of the program's narrative. Ultimately, though, Big Brother (the corporate producers) regained control of the wheel and steered the show back onto its original course.

Narrative activism and media/culture jamming take the much discussed concept of interactivity to a new level. Following Mark Dery's theory of culture jamming, we might consider narrative activism to be an act of social protest in its potential desire not only to subvert the narrative outcome of a television program but also to make larger statements about the media and capitalist globalization at a larger level.

> Media Jammers exemplifies this broader intervention in its belief that Media Jammers is a grass roots "culture jamming" organization created to raise awareness of irresponsibility in the news and entertainment media through high profile stunts, hoaxes and general media mayhem. . . . We practice and advocate safe, legal means of interfering with media events, taking control of the message and exposing the incompetence, lack of integrity, distortions and abuses of the media, holding them accountable for the consequences.[30]

As Oswald remarked in retrospect, "Our 15 minutes of fame was a lot of fun, and I did enjoy the notoriety. I really liked knowing that we were making network executives sweat. I never thought it would be seen as such an impact on future 'audience interactivity.' I was amazed at how people were inspired to influence the show after we did our thing. We had control of the direction of the show for a few days, and then others stole our thunder and inspired complete anarchy." When asked about how the idea for "jamming" *Big Brother* originated, he explained that "the *Big Brother* project happened because it was just too easy. CBS provided us with all the tools we used to mock them. The live video feeds were crucial to our success. And every time we forced the producers to make a choice, they accommodated us by making the wrong one. It all played to our favor."[31]

The culture jamming of *Big Brother* came from various sources with diverse agendas—political activists, fans, pranksters. The long-term effectiveness of their interventions may arguably have been minimal due to the appropriation of the interceptions by the producers and their subsequent integration into the program's structure. Still, the short-term effects of media/culture jamming presented a jolt to corporate producers, and influenced the behaviors and beliefs of the *Big Brother* participants. In their decentralized efforts to disrupt and subvert the corporate control of the outcome of reality TV, even for a short time, the culture jammers provided new insights into the more radical possibilities of challenging the hegemonic control of the media giants by throwing small rocks with their slingshots.

NOTES

1. William S. Burroughs, "My Mother and I Would Like to Know," *Evergreen* 67 (June 1969); see also "The Electronic Revolution," 1970, http://www.syntac.net/dl/elerev2.html.

2. Mark Dery, "Culture Jamming: Hacking, Slashing, and Sniping in the Empire of Signs," Open Magazine pamphlet series, 1993, http://www.levity.com/markdery/culturjam.html. See also Stephen Downes, "Hacking Memes," http://www.firstmonday.dk/issues/issue4_10/downes/index.html; and David Cox, "Notes on Culture Jamming: Spectres of the Spectrum; A Culture Jammer's Cinematic Call to Action," http://www.sniggle.net/Manifesti/notes.php.

3. Naomi Klein, *No Logo* (New York: Picador, 1999), 280–81.

4. Kevin Michael DeLuca and Jennifer Peeples, "From Public Sphere to Public Screen: Democracy, Activism, and the 'Violence' of Seattle," *Critical Studies in Media Communication* 19, no. 2 (June 2002): 125–51.

5. Http://www.levity.com/markdery/inform.html.

6. David Kronke, "Web Interaction on *Big Brother* Could Alter Reality TV," *Miami Herald,* 5 October 2000, http://www.herald.com/content/tue/entertainment/tv/digdocs/077750.htm. See also Anick Jesdaunun, "*Big Brother* Finds Fans

Online," Associated Press/Internet, 28 September 2000, http://dailynews.yahoo
.com/h/ap/200000928/en/big_brother_Internet_1.html; and Mindy Charski, "TV
Companion Site Creates Buzz," Inter@ctive Week 7, no. 28 (17 July 2000): 48. News
reports indicated that the AOL-sponsored site was the most highly visited new Internet site during July 2000, the month the program premiered, with more than
4.2 million visitors. Some of the most notable of the reviews and cultural com-
mentaries on the reality TV game show trend in the popular and academic press
included Bill Carter, "Television's New Voyeurism Pictures Real-Life Intimacy,"
New York Times, 30 January 2000, 1; Robert Sheppard, "Peeping Tom Television,"
Maclean's, 10 April 2000, 58–62; Mark Boal, "Summer of Surveillance," Brill's Content 3, no. 5 (June 2000): 66–71, 122–25; James Poniewozik et al., "We Like to
Watch," Time, 26 June 2000, 56–63; Steven Rosenbaum, "Peeping Tom TV: The Beginning of the End or the Birth of Meaningful Media?" Television Quarterly 31, no.
2–3 (summer 2000): 53–56; Edward D. Miller, "Fantasies of Reality: Surviving Reality-Based Programming," Social Policy 312, no. 1 (fall 2000): 6–16; Edward Roth-
stein, "TV Shows in Which the Real Is Fake and the Fake Is Real," New York Times,
5 August 2000, B11; James Wolcott, "Now, Voyeur," Vanity Fair, September 2000,
128–32; Rob Sheffield, "Reality," Rolling Stone, 14 September 2000, 138; Ziauddin
Sardar, "The Rise of the Voyeur," New Statesman, 6 November 2000, 25–28; John
Podhoretz, "Survivor and the End of Television," Commentary (November 2000):
50–52; Brian D. Johnson, "We Like to Watch," Maclean's, 29 January 2001, 56–58;
and Brooke A. Knight, "Watch Me! Webcams and the Public Exposure of Private
Lives," Art Journal 59, no. 4 (winter 2000): 21–26. An issue of Variety on 25 September 2000 had a number of articles devoted to the spread of reality TV programming in various countries, including the United Kingdom, Hungary, Switzerland,
South Africa, Argentina, Brazil, the Philippines, Australia, Korea, and the United
States. Also, there was an interesting BBC News–sponsored opinion forum titled
"Are We Turning into Peeping Toms" on 23 July 2000, just after the premiere of
both the U.S. and U.K. versions of Big Brother, to which viewers on both sides of
the Atlantic (as well as some from Asia) posted their insights; see
http://news.bbc.co.uk/hi/english/talking_point/newsid_834000/834731.stm.

7. See "AOL's Big Brother Web Site Setting Records in Unprecedented Convergence between Television and the Internet: Ambitious Alliance between Popular
CBS Television Series and World's Largest Interactive Services Company Sets Webcasting Records as Largest Ongoing Webcast in History," Hollywood Reporter, 18
July 2000, http://news.excite.com/news/bw/000718/va-america-online.

8. Many fan sites were internationally based and served as sites for fans of the
Big Brother series in various countries, such as the U.K.-based Orwell Project
(http://www.orwellproject.com) or the Netherlands-based Big Brother Central
(http://www.BigBrother2000.org). Others were specifically devoted to serving the
audience of the U.S. show.

9. *Big Brother* 2000 official website (http://bigbrother2000.com).

10. See http://bigbrother2000.com or http://webcenter.bigbrother2000.aol .com.

11. For the best literary commentary on the *Big Brother* phenomenon, in a tone alternately fond, fascinated, and scathing, see the series of *Salon* articles at http://www.salon.com/ent/tv/bb/index.html.

12. Cited on *Big Brother* 2000 official website.

13. Ibid.

14. Graphic designer at ZAP Design, Los Angeles, http://www.zapdesign.net /articles/.

15. See *Big Brother* 2000 official website.

16. Jeff Oswald, personal correspondence; and *Big Brother* 2000 official website. For information on the grassroots activist Media Jammers organization, see http://www.mediajammers.org.

17. See letter titled "CBS/BB Improprieties," 1 September 2000, from "D I N Only" and posted on an AOL message board, then reposted 3 September 2000 on Joker's Commentary Board by "Kerry." The letter writer urged fans to take action against the perceived ethical improprieties.

18. Media Jammers website statement, 27 August 2000.

19. Statement made about philosophy behind banners, Media Jammers website, 30 August 2000.

20. "An Interview with Ms. Megaphone," Kaye Mallory's Ms. Megaphone website, http://bennyhills.fortunecity.com/billmurray/532/bb/meg-run1.html. The remarks from the Big Brother Watchers fan group can be found in the archives of the Big Brother Watcher e-group, http://groups.yahoo.com/group/ bigbrotherwatchers.

21. Kaye Mallory's website.

22. *Big Brother* 2000 official website, CBS/AOL, article 389.

23. Kaye Mallory's website.

24. Information page (FAQ), Media Jammers website, http://www .mediajammers.org/faq.htm.

25. There was a running joke among the on-line fans that CBS/Endemol would place one or more cameras on the chicken coop in the courtyard, with close-ups on the chickens, whenever the producers did not want the on-line audience to see or hear some action happening in the house. This move was affectionately dubbed the "chicken cams" by the fans and recognized as a strategy by the producers to engineer an information blackout. In an interview on the official website, longtime Endemol producer Paul Römer discussed his use of the "panic button" by which the producers could blackout the on-line feed. In his earlier European shows, he remarked, he had tried to keep the breaking news off the Internet to "save" it for the TV program. After a while, however, he realized

the advantage of showing most of the action on the Web feeds: "People saw things happening live and they wanted to see what we did with it on television. The moment I would show it on television the Internet side went sky-high because people wanted to see what happens now. I learned there was a mutual benefit. We are not competitors. We were really helping each other—but that's a big change of mindset for a television producer."

26. Cited on *Big Brother 2000* official website.

27. Ibid. Apparently on Endemol's Spanish version of the show, *Gran Hermano*, the producers also encountered resistance by the contestants to "Gran Hermano's" authority.

28. For some popular press accounts of the aborted walkout, see Lynn Elber, "*Big Brother* Members Mull Walkout," Associated Press, 9 September 2000, http://news.excite.com/news/000909/19/big-brother; Greg Braxton, "*Big Brother* Guests Threaten Walkout," *Los Angeles Times*, 11 September 2000, http://www.calendarlive.com/calendarlive/calendar/20000911/t000085524.html; Frazier Moore, "*Big Brother* Walkout Flops," Associated Press, 13 September 2000, http://news.excite.com/news/ap/000913/22/ent-big-brother; Mark Armstrong, "Squashing Another *Big Brother* Revolt," *E! Online*, 11 September 2000, http://www.eonline.com/News/Items/0,1,7074,00.html?ibd; and Robert Bianco, "*Brother* Walkout?" *USA Today Online*, 13 September 2000, http://www.usatoday.com. Some postmortems of the U.S. *Big Brother* phenomenon included Bill Wyman, "Who Screwed Up *Big Brother*? Everyone," *Salon*, 29 September 2000, http://www.salon.com/ent/tv/feature/2000/09/29/bb_final/print.html; Gail Shister, "Lack of Sexual Chemistry Hurt *Big Brother*, Producer Says," *Kansas City Star Online*, 28 September 2000, http://www.kcstar.com/item/pages/fyi.pat?file=fyi/3774cb5a.928; Mike McDaniel, "O, Brother; At Last, the End Is Near," *Houston Chronicle*, 27 September 2000, http://www.chron.com/cs/CDA/story.hts/headline/entertainment/683555; and Antonia Zerbisias, "Big Brother Made Reality TV Real," *Toronto Star*, 29 September 2000, http://www.thestar.com/editorial/entertainment/20000929ENT11b_EN-ZERBTV.html. During the run of the program, the CBS/AOL website published extensive interviews with several of the *Big Brother* executive producers, including Paul Römer (24 August 2000), Douglas Ross (21 September 2000), and John Kalish (13 October 2000) (see http://webcenter.bigbrother2000.aol.com/entertainment/NON/).

29. See Sue Brower, "Fans as Tastemakers: Viewers for Quality Television," in *The Adoring Audience: Fan Culture and Popular Media*, ed. Lisa Lewis (London: Routledge, 1992), 163–84; Julie D'Acci, *Defining Women: Television and the Case of Cagney and Lacey* (Chapel Hill: University of North Carolina Press, 1994); Henry Jenkins, *Textual Poachers: Television Fans and Participatory Culture* (New York: Routledge, 1992); Kathryn C. Montgomery, *Target: Prime Time: Advocacy Groups and the Struggle over Entertainment Television* (New York: Oxford University Press, 1989); Charlotte Ryan, *Prime Time Activism: Media Strategies for Grassroots Orga-*

nizing (Boston: South End Press, 1991); Ellen Seiter, Hans Borchers, Gabriele Kreutzner, and Eva-Maria Warth, eds., *Remote Control: Television, Audiences, and Cultural Power* (London: Routledge, 1989); Dorothy Collins Swanson, *The Story of Viewers for Quality Television: From Grassroots to Prime Time* (Syracuse, N.Y.: Syracuse University Press, 2000); and Heather Hendershot, *Saturday Morning Censors* (Durham, N.C.: Duke University Press, 1999).

30. Information page (FAQ), Media Jammers website.

31. Jeff Oswald, personal correspondence, 28 February 2001.

About the Contributors

Nick Couldry is Lecturer in Media and Communications at the London School of Economics and Political Science, where he is also the director of the master's program in Media and Communications Regulation. He is the author of *The Place of Media Power: Pilgrims and Witnesses of the Media Age, Inside Culture,* and *Media Rituals: A Critical Approach* as well as numerous articles on media and cultural studies.

Mary Beth Haralovich teaches film and television studies in Media Arts at the University of Arizona in Tucson. She is the coeditor, with Lauren Rabinovitz, of *Television, History, and American Culture: Feminist Critical Essays.* She is a founder and board member of the International Conference on Television, Video, New Media, and Feminism: Console-ing Passions. Haralovich's research on film advertising has appeared in *Screen, Wide Angle, Current Research in Film,* the *Rebecca* electronic library, *Screen Histories,* and in Polish translation.

John Hartley is Dean of the Creative Industries Faculty at Queensland University of Technology in Australia. Previously, he was head of the School of Journalism, Media, and Cultural Studies at Cardiff University in Wales. He is the author of many books and articles on television, media, journalism, and popular culture, most recently *A Short History of Cultural Studies, The Indigenous Public Sphere, Uses of Television,* and *Popular Reality.* He is the coeditor of *American Cultural Studies: A Reader,* and the editor of the *International Journal of Cultural Studies.*

Chuck Kleinhans is the coeditor of *Jump Cut: A Review of Contemporary Media.* He teaches in the Department of Radio/Television/Film at Northwestern University.

Derek Kompare is Assistant Professor in the Department of Radio-Television-Film at Texas Christian University. He is preparing a book on the cultural and industrial history of broadcasting on U.S. television.

Jon Kraszewski is a Ph.D. candidate and associate instructor in the Department of Communication and Culture at Indiana University in Bloomington. He has an article on blaxploitation film advertisements in the fall 2002 issue of *The Velvet Light Trap,* and is currently writing his dissertation on Rod Serling and television authorship.

Kathleen LeBesco is Assistant Professor of Communication Arts at Marymount Manhattan College, where she teaches communication theory and media studies. She is the author of *Revolting Bodies: The Struggle to Redefine Fat Identity,* and the coeditor of *Bodies out of Bound: Fatness and Transgression* as well as the *Drag King Anthology.*

Justin Lewis is Professor of Communication and Cultural Industries at Cardiff University. He has written several books about media and culture, including *Constructing Public Opinion: How Elites Do What They Like and Why We Seem to Go Along with It.*

Ted Magder is Chair of the Culture and Communication Department at New York University. He is the author of two books, *Canada's Hollywood: Feature Films and the Canadian State* and *Franchising the Candy Store: Split-Run Magazines and a New International Regime for Trade in Culture* as well as numerous articles on the political economy of the cultural industries and international trade in media products. He is also the director of the Project on Media Ownership at New York University.

Jennifer Maher is a freelance writer and Adjunct Assistant Professor of Women's Studies and Media Studies at the University of Wisconsin in Milwaukee. She has published on the topic of gender and representation in both academic and popular presses. She is currently working on a fictional autobiography, *My Orthodontist Was a Porn Star: Memoirs of a Southern California Girlhood.*

Anna McCarthy teaches in the Department of Cinema Studies at New York University. She is the author of *Ambient Television: Visual Culture and Public Space.*

Rick Morris, J.D., LL.M., is Assistant Dean in the School of Communication at Northwestern University and teaches in the Department of Radio/Television/Film.

Susan Murray is Assistant Professor of Culture and Communication at New York University. Her work has appeared in *Television and New Media* and *Cinema Journal* as well as numerous anthologies.

Laurie Ouellette is Assistant Professor of Media Studies at Queens College, City University of New York. She is the author of *Viewers like You? How Public TV Failed the People.* She has written about television and media culture for a variety of journals and anthologies, including *Cultural Studies; Television and New Media; Media, Culture & Society;* and *Gender, Race, and Class in Media.*

Chad Raphael is Assistant Professor of Communication at Santa Clara University. His articles have appeared in journals such as *Jump Cut* and *Quarterly Review of Film and Video,* and the University of Minnesota Press anthology *Culture Works: Essays on the Political Economy of Culture* (ed. Richard Maxwell).

Elayne Rapping is Professor of Women's Studies and Media Studies at the State University of New York at Buffalo. She has written extensively on issues of media and society for both mainstream and academic publications. Among her books are *The Culture of Recovery: Women, Addiction, and the Self-Help Movement, Media-tions: Forays into the Culture and Gender Wars,* and the forthcoming *Law and Justice as Seen on TV.*

Jeffrey Sconce is Associate Professor in the School of Communications at Northwestern University and the author of *Haunted Media: Electronic Presence from Telegraphy to Television.* His current research centers on the politics of irony in recent U.S. film and television.

Michael W. Trosset is Associate Professor of Mathematics at the College of William and Mary. A former programmer for the Arizona Media Arts Center (AZMAC) in Tucson, Trosset curated for the Arizona International Film Festival and the Screening Room, AZMAC's exhibition venue. He has written numerous articles, and is currently an associate editor for the *Journal of Computational and Graphical Statistics.*

Pamela Wilson teaches communication and cultural studies at Reinhardt College in Georgia. Wilson's writing has been published in journals such as *South Atlantic Quarterly, Camera Obscura, Quarterly Review of Film and Video, Historical Journal of Film, Radio, and Television,* and numerous anthologies.

Index